Education and Learning

An Evidence-Based Approach

Jane Mellanby
Katy Theobald

Library of Congress Cataloging-in-Publication data is available for this book.
ISBN 9781118454107 (hardback); ISBN 9781118483619 (paperback)

A catalogue record for this book is available from the British Library.

Cover image: Molecule illustration © Milos Dizajn / Shutterstock; Tablet computer © L_amica / iStockphoto; Geometrical set © ntstudio / iStockphoto
Cover design by Simon Levy Associates

Set in 11/13.5 pt SabonLTStd-Roman by Toppan Best-set Premedia Limited
Printed in Malaysia by Ho Printing (M) Sdn Bhd

1   2014

To Harriet

JM

Contents

Acknowledgements

I had the excellent idea of asking Katy to join me in writing this book when I realized that both I and the book needed energizing – I had become too distracted with minutiae. I am most grateful to her, and we have had great fun doing it together – even if it has put rather a strain on our families. I am particularly grateful to my daughter Harriet Impey for her many helpful criticisms and ideas throughout the process and for reading and correcting the entire final version. The educational histories of my grandchildren and the children of my friends have all provided the stimulus for writing this book. I am grateful also to all the schools and school children with whom I have worked for giving me some insight into what goes on in schools today. I am delighted that Sarah McElwee, who worked with me on our verbal reasoning test (VESPARCH) for five years, agreed to write the chapter on Metacognition since she knows so much more about this than we do. Thanks are also due to Susanna Blackshaw and Michael Humphreys for going to New Lanark and photographing the timelines in the schoolroom. I owe a great debt to Professor Larry Weiskrantz for encouraging me over the years on my journey from neurochemistry to psychology (and also for providing the photograph of the all-male Delegates of the Oxford University Press). Finally, I would like to thank my son Lawrence Impey for his example concerning the writing of books and for his help with choosing the title.

JM

Whilst writing this book I have lived and worked in many cities and even different countries, often collecting inspiration and material along the way. The enthusiasm of the people I have met and their genuine interest in the topics in this volume acted as invaluable motivation to keep writing, so I am grateful to them all. Particular thanks are owed to my family and friends who have been ever patient as my writing has taken up weekends and holidays. I hope they will enjoy taking the odd weekend or holiday to read the book now it is finished. Most of all, I would like to thank Jane for giving me the opportunity to work as a co-author with her. Needless to say, I could not have done this without her, and it has been a pleasure.

KT

Preface

Educators, politicians, students and parents have diverse ideas about the ways in which individuals learn and can be taught, but these ideas are not always backed up by empirical research. Educational psychology has its roots in educational theory rather than experimental psychology, and is one area of expertise that can provide evidence to inform educational practice. In this book we consider some of the psychological functions that are particularly important for education – language acquisition, learning and memory, ability, sex differences and creativity. In each case, we present an account of the basic psychology (and where necessary, neurology[1]) related to this area, alongside seminal studies and cutting-edge research that link the psychological knowledge back to education. In later chapters, we look at particular applied areas in the field of educational research: reading, the role of metacognition (thinking about learning), the effects of academic selection, the changes in cognition that occur with ageing, and the role of technology in the classroom. We consider how these areas are treated in different countries across the world and how they impact on social policy in England.[2]

We have, of course, been highly selective in choosing which studies to report, only including those which we feel best illustrate the points we

---

[1] Sarah-Jayne Blakemore and Uta Frith's book, *The Learning Brain* (2005), Blackwell, UK contains a particularly readable account of the background neurophysiology and a glossary of terms.

[2] Since education policy is devolved in the UK, we focus largely on English education policy and explicitly note where we are referring to Scotland or Wales.

are making. In some cases considerable detail is provided, in order to give the reader a chance to evaluate the evidence presented and form an independent opinion on its implications. References to the relevant scholarly research papers are also included in order to make it easier for academic readers to follow up on our conclusions. A summary at the end of each chapter addresses the question so often asked when new research findings are presented: 'So what?' We review the ways in which we believe the psychology we have described could support, and in some cases possibly change, the practice of teaching.

This book is intended not only for teachers and those studying education as an academic subject, but also for parents, grandparents and others who are interested in the education of the children and young people of today.

What Do We Mean by 'Evidence'?

This section is intended for any of our readers who are not familiar with reading articles in scientific journals.

Throughout this book we have emphasized the importance of evidence for the effect of interventions and for demonstrating the detection of differences in education. We do, however, need to make clear what we are looking for when we present the findings of a scientific paper. We have sought to present empirical evidence which relates to contemporary methods of teaching and to the organization of our education system. However, it is essential to view such evidence critically, because at times researchers are just as likely as politicians to present data in a way that serves their own interests rather than giving a balanced view. So what sort of things do you need to look out for when you read about studies in this book and elsewhere?

Firstly, there are some basic aspects of research design of which you ought to be aware. Unless they use census data, all studies involve a sample of people and it is important to consider the nature of this sample if we want to know whether the results apply to the general population. How were participants recruited? By advertising, for example, or by buttonholing people in a supermarket, by using all the available children in a school year, or by following up particular birth cohorts? Actually, quite a lot of psychological research is done using university students. A second question to ask is what selection criteria were used and what proportion of the original sample was discarded as a result of applying these criteria. For example, in the study of ageing, were elderly people with organic disease or dementia included or not? Different methods of obtaining and selecting participants will introduce different possible biases.

Research can range from the highly qualitative to highly quantitative, with every mixture imaginable in between. Such studies can tell you different things. Qualitative studies, for example case studies or a small number of in-depth interviews, are very helpful for exploring people's motivations, why they do things, but are not so good for identifying general rules. We cannot necessarily assume that one set of people will behave like another. In contrast, large quantitative surveys can be good for capturing representative views and for identifying patterns of behaviour but they rarely tell us why these patterns occur. Large sample sizes are good because then small individual differences or errors will have less of an impact on the results. However, they also present a risk because with large samples many differences can be statistically significant without necessarily being that important.

When doing quantitative research most researchers will run statistical tests such as t-tests or ANOVAs (which tell us whether differences between average group results are significant) and correlations or regressions (which tell us if two factors vary together). These typically produce a 'p' value between 0 and 1. A p value of 0.05 indicates there is a 1 in 20 probability that the result occurred by chance and is a common criterion for statistical significance. It is worth noting, therefore, that if a researcher simply runs endless statistical tests then eventually they are likely to get a significant result by chance. In other words, don't assume that a significant result proves something, instead try to think about what it means and whether it actually makes sense.

Another caution is in the temptation to over-state findings, particularly when talking about causality. The key mantra is that correlation does not equal causation. In other words, although two things might vary together, it does not prove that one causes the other. You might think this is obvious, but it is easy to be convinced by an argument that intuitively sounds correct. For example, it is easy to note that socioeconomic status correlates with many educational outcomes such as attainment and the likelihood of going to university. However, being of low socioeconomic status does not in itself cause a pupil to have lower attainment. It is the various associated factors, for example the likelihood of parents reading to their children or the likelihood that a parent can pay for extra tuition, which actually have a direct impact on attainment.

Studies can either be cross-sectional – a snapshot in time – or longitudinal, with measures taken before and after a time interval. If we want to demonstrate causation then either we can use qualitative interviews to ask why people do things (and rely on the accuracy of introspection) or we have to conduct a formal, longitudinal experiment where we try to hold as many things constant as possible and then vary the factor of interest. If we start with two similar groups and find that after an intervention with one of them they differ significantly, there is a good chance this can be attributed to the intervention. However, it is important to be sure that the two groups were matched on relevant factors. In education such factors that are likely to affect outcome are: measured 'ability'; socioeconomic background; parents' educational level; age; and sex. Of course, whilst this approach is ideal when working with levers, cells or chemicals, it is impossible in practice to find two identical classes and teachers, so these experiments are always open to critique. One should also check whether any control group undertook a comparable activity to the intervention activity, but one not targeted at the outcome of interest. This accounts for 'tender loving care' effects – that people can change their behaviour just because they know they are being studied. Longitudinal studies make the strongest case for proving causation but they are never perfect. This is one reason why it is so important to conduct multiple studies and replicate findings.

Unfortunately, it is very difficult for academics to get studies published if all they do is replicate the work of someone else. For this reason, we tend to get a lot of research that is similar but not identical. If we still want to pick out patterns across the papers, then one technique available is meta-analysis. Here, a researcher will collect together multiple papers addressing a single topic and try to aggregate the findings to see whether overall they are positive, negative or lack a clear pattern. This method has a lot of potential, but it relies on the researcher collecting a comprehensive sample of literature, filtering out poor quality studies and weighting the remainder to account for factors like sample size. It is also susceptible to problems of publication bias, because it is much less likely that a study will get published, and therefore included in the meta-analysis, if it includes no significant findings (after all, would you be more interested in reading about a food that boosts attention span or one that has absolutely no impact on it?). A good meta-analysis provides a helpful aggregation of literature, but you should not take the findings as fact.

This, actually, is the core message when reading empirical research: just because a researcher writes a very convincing paper highlighting the importance and relevance of their findings, you should not assume they have proved anything. You must always think through the logic of the study and consider every possible alternative explanation before coming to your own conclusion about what it means.

Chapter 1

Introduction
What Can We Learn from the History of Education?

> *It is therefore the interest of all, that everyone, from birth, should be well educated, physically and mentally, that society may be improved in character, – that everyone should be beneficially employed, physically and mentally, that the greatest amount of wealth should be created, and knowledge attained.*
>
> Robert Owen (1771–1858), industrialist, promoter of the Co-operative movement, educator and philanthropist[1])

Do you agree? If you ever have the chance, visit New Lanark, a World Heritage Site on the River Clyde near Glasgow. This was Robert Owen's mill town where he implemented his educational ideas. Visitors can still see the lofty schoolroom, which was intended not only for the instruction of reading, writing and arithmetic but for the introduction of pupils to much wider knowledge. For example, the walls are still hung with charts of timelines of historical events in different countries all over the world (Figures 1.1 and 1.2). Owen's holistic approach included the workers' and their children's health and well-being: the children had a daily dance class before lessons (Figure 1.3) and he rebuilt family living quarters as relatively comfortable small apartments. Today we would regard his attitude as paternalistic, but I think we would also agree that his vision contains much to which contemporary education should aspire.

Education and Learning: An Evidence-Based Approach, First Edition. Jane Mellanby and Katy Theobald.

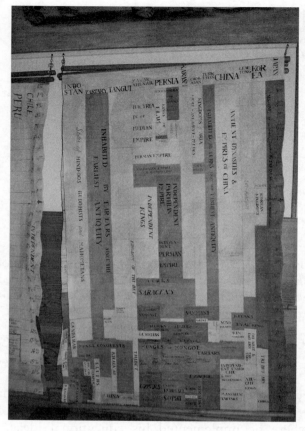

Figure 1.1   Hanging scrolls of timelines in the New Lanark schoolroom. Photograph by Susanna Blackshaw

In modern Britain, an array of educational practices can be found in schools and universities, based on diverse and sometimes conflicting educational theories.

It is well worth taking an interest in the content and process of education, both in Britain and beyond, because the working of the education system affects everyone, whether as a learner, employer, teacher, parent or politician. It is evident that there are many views on the purpose of education and what a good education ought to entail. Some traditional views can seem old-fashioned, but in fact many apparently modern innovations only repeat what has been tried before, albeit under another name. After all, questions about the role, practice and purpose of educa-

The streams of Time

Seven large maps laid out on the principle of the streams of time, and which were originally purchased from Miss Whitwell, a lady who formerly conducted a respectable seminary in London – are hung around a spacious room. These, being made of canvas, may be rolled up at pleasure.

On the streams, each of which is differently coloured, and represents a nation, are painted the principal events which occur in the history of those nations. Each century is closed by a horizontal line drawn across the map.

By means of these maps, the children are taught the outlines of ancient and modern history, with ease to themselves and without being liable to confound different events or different nations.

Figure 1.2   Purpose of the timelines at New Lanark. *Source*: Extract from Robert Dale Owen's '*Outline of the system of education at New Lanark*', 1824.

tion have been actively considered in advanced societies for more than 2,000 years.

A traditional view is that education is the reproduction and perpetuation of the culture of a society – as Jaeger,[2] in his book *Paideia: The Ideals of Greek Culture*, has put it, how a community 'preserves and transmits its physical and intellectual character'. A second perspective on the purpose of education emphasizes the need for the transmission of skills between the generations – reading, writing, arithmetic, playing musical instruments, painting and sculpture and more recently the use of IT (information technology). The literacy and numeracy hours in primary schools and training in PowerPoint or Access in secondary schools exemplify this trend. A rather different view of education is a political one – that it should provide a suitably qualified workforce. This was a view held in fourth-century BC Sparta where education was aimed at providing a well-trained army. Nor is such a view limited to the ancients. Thomas Sheridan (1756) wrote, 'in every state it should be the fundamental maxim that the education of youth should be particularly formed and adapted to the nature and end of its government'. It was also a part of, but only a part of, Robert Owen's vision. Thatcher's government and those that followed have undoubtedly taken a similar stance. Indeed, today, when academics write applications for money to support their research they have to show that their work will not only add to existing knowledge or understanding, but will have 'impact' on society. It is important to be alert to, and even question, the views that policymakers and educators have regarding the nature and the role of education, because this has a great

Figure 1.3   Children at New Lanark dancing before morning lessons.
G. Hunt, 1825. Reproduced with permission from the New Lanark Trust;
www.newlanark.org.

and often unacknowledged effect on what is taught, how it is taught and
to whom.

Education for the reproduction of a culture

Why should a society wish to reproduce its own culture? And what role
does education take in this? Culture encompasses a society's history, its
social structure, its values and its creative achievements. Understanding
our own culture is an important part of developing our own individual
identity; seeing how we as an individual fit into a wider society. Once
we have come to understand our culture, if we are comfortable with it
and have chosen to embrace it, then it is human nature to seek to per-
petuate it.

If we are looking at education as the reproduction of our culture, then
a statement in a lecture[3] by Nick Tate, a former Director of QCA (the
Qualifications and Curriculum Authority), is particularly apposite: 'education should give all children access to all those things that as a society we
have decided we value and wish to pass on to our successors'. Such a view

supports that of Thomas Arnold, the nineteenth-century educationalist: education should contain 'the best that has been known and thought'. However, the problems here lie in the decision as to what is worth passing on to the next generations: who decides on the content of education? The National Curriculum (implemented in 1988, revised in 1995 and reviewed in 2007) was intended to encompass the corpus of knowledge that every educated person should be expected to possess, along with the basic skills of reading, writing and mathematics. Over the years, the curriculum became overloaded, as the proponents of many different subject areas fought to have their knowledge included. The 2007 review of the National Curriculum favoured reducing the factual content and proposed a radical change in the organization of knowledge – that is, the removal of subject boundaries. These boundaries have often been seen as supporting an elitist approach to learning, somehow following from the twentieth-century practice of subjects such as Latin being taught only in independent schools and grammar schools. However, in 2011 Michael Young[4] forcefully argued against this: 'Knowledge is not powerful just because it is defined by those who are powerful; it is powerful because it offers understanding to those who have access to it.' The curriculum for all 'should stipulate concepts associated with different subjects' and enable pupils to 'gain access to knowledge which takes them beyond their experience and their own preconceptions'.

A continual updating of curriculum content was supported in the 2007 review on the basis that this would ensure that pupils would see the curriculum as 'relevant' to them and to the society in which they lived. There has always been tension between views on the relative importance of 'pure' knowledge as opposed to applied knowledge in the classroom. The emphasis on 'relevance' can be traced to the work of John Dewey (1859–1952). He was an immensely wide thinker and a highly influential force in education. He believed that it was essential for education to be embedded in the ordinary life experience of the child at home and in the community – an emphasis on the applied aspects of knowledge. But the continual updating that is needed to maintain 'relevance' to contemporary life has caused considerable extra work and stress for the teaching profession. Tim Oates, who has chaired the most recent review determining the nature and content of the National Curriculum in primary schools, has taken a different point of view.[5] He has pointed out that if the curriculum consists of core knowledge, such as the basic laws of physics and chemistry, then these will not change unless knowledge itself changes. Furthermore, he favours the division of knowledge into subjects since it can then be readily made coherent, so that one layer of knowledge follows another depending on the level of understanding of the developing child. Subjects rather than grandiose 'themes' are frameworks into which knowledge can be fitted – an essential aspect of the learning process. Oates has concluded that the curriculum should list the core knowledge, and that it should be left to the expertise of teachers to make the content relevant and motivating for the individual pupils. He has underlined the importance of looking to other countries that have successful education systems to try to learn from them, particularly in relation to the organization of the knowledge to be taught.

Treating education as a way to transmit our culture to a new generation makes sense in an insulated society where older and younger generations are broadly alike. But what about a multicultural society with much immigration of people from other cultures? The production of 'community cohesion' in a successful multicultural society requires many people to acquire two (or more) such individual identities – that of the adopted culture and that of the culture of origin. Where these conflict, for example in the role of women in society, this can lead to problems. Education then goes beyond reproduction of culture. Instead it takes on an important role in encouraging both coexistence and assimilation through the acquisition of knowledge and understanding of different cultures.

Lessons from History

At a time when education is so much in the public eye, it is worth considering what we might learn from education systems of the past. We can try to understand the value (and constraints) of the methods of teaching employed: how to teach reading, for example; the role of rote-learning; or the importance of memory versus documentation. It is interesting to recognize how the content and structure of past systems map onto the contemporary National Curriculum. And, most importantly, we can seek out common factors in different 'successful' systems that might be applied today.

Education in Ancient Greece

The origins of our traditional attitudes to education lie in the work of philosophers in fifth- and fourth-century BC Greece. The Greek philosophers conceived the conscious idea of culture and created a self-consciousness about the educational process in which they gave consideration to what the nature and intention of education should be. They devoted much thought to the idea of a standard, an ideal person and an ideal community. We must remember that we are not really any different from the inhabitants of Ancient Greece: they were at least as intelligent as we are and their brains at birth would have been similar to the brains of our babies, following the same developmental trajectories, although also being moulded by specific experiences which would have had similarities to, and differences from, our own. So, if we can understand what worked for the Greeks, then that might well work for us too.

Even in ancient Athens, the tension we see today existed between the belief that education should involve teaching facts and the belief that it should prepare the mind for future action. The *trivium* (three parts), grammar, rhetoric and dialectic, formed the central part of education. Grammar involved the full understanding of the structure of the language. Nowadays, the explicit teaching of English grammar is not often undertaken in English schools, but it was an integral part of the grammar school curriculum 50 years ago and the teaching of native grammar is still given time in the curriculum of many modern European systems, including those of France, the Netherlands and Germany. We do not know how much explicit teaching of grammar helps us to express ourselves, but the correct use of complex grammar does allow one to communicate subtleties that tend to be lost when language is simplified.

Rhetoric involved the processes leading up to the presentation of a reasoned argument. Firstly, the student would need to accumulate the relevant knowledge; then this knowledge would need to be organized; then, since rhetoric involved oral presentation, the style of delivery needed to be considered; then the speech would need to be committed to memory; and finally it would have to be delivered to the relevant audience. Rhetoric involved a combination, therefore, of acquiring knowledge and of the 'transferable skill' of presentation.

Dialectic involved the search for truth through a dialogue between teacher and student. Even today, in a classroom with many pupils, we see teachers using a similar approach in asking questions and steering discussion.

By the middle of the first century BC, the intellectual gymnastics of rhetoric and dialectic had been afforced by the more fact-based *quadrivium* (four parts), arithmetic, geometry, music and astronomy, to form the seven liberal arts curriculum. It is clear that there is much in common between the current National Curriculum and the seven liberal arts: the importance of language, the importance of the transferable skill of oral delivery, the importance of mathematics and science (although admittedly astronomy, being largely astrology at that time, would not now be considered a science). Indeed, Michael Gove's proposed 'English Baccalaureate' is even closer to the seven liberal arts formula.

One obvious difference between the National Curriculum and education in fourth-century Athens is the integral part played by music and physical exercise in the past compared with the peripheral role that it now has in British schools. Music, poetry, dance and gymnastics were all deemed to be very important, and indeed even used to teach moral values. It is interesting that there is now scientific evidence that physical exercise both improves intellectual function and helps to preserve that function during ageing, and that this is supported by evidence concerning the underlying physiological mechanisms (Chapter 2). This valuing of physical movement, therefore, which at the time was based on little more than intuition, is now empirically supported.

Another difference between education in ancient Athens and ours was that it was offered only to an elite part of the population – those from amongst whom leaders were to be chosen, and only boys and men. That does not, however, mean that there are no lessons to be learnt from the Greeks.

Education in Ancient China

A thousand years after fourth-century BC Athens, the Chinese started an educational system that seems at first to be the very antithesis of what the Greeks believed should constitute education: rote-learning of literature took centre stage. The intention of the system, which started in the Sui Dynasty (AD 589–618) and lasted until 1905, was to select a highly educated elite to run the administration[6] – a meritocracy to replace the established aristocratic rule. In this it might be compared with the selection method used until recently for the British Civil Service. The Chinese education started in the home from 3 to 7 years of age, when children learnt their first 25 Chinese characters (Box 1.1).

Apparently, the initial teaching involved giving the child the outlines of each character, to be coloured in with ink on a brush; a rather similar method is often used in early schooling nowadays to familiarize a child with the shapes of letters and numbers.

The next 10 years of education required a vast amount of rote-learning, as the four books derived from the teachings of the philoso-

Box 1.1 The first 25 characters

Translation:

Let us present our work to father,
Confucius himself taught three thousand,
Seventy were capable gentlemen.
You young scholars, eight or nine.
Work well to attain virtue,
And you will understand propriety.

可佳八尔七化孔上
知作九小十三乙大
礼仁子生土千己人
也

pher Confucius (551–479 BC) had to be committed to memory, about 450,000 characters in all. The children learnt these first by reciting the words 50 times whilst reading them, then reciting them 50 times from memory. Today this amount of rote-learning would be considered ridiculously excessive in Western education, but it was necessary since written texts were not widely available. Whereas we can refer to books and the Internet, these Chinese scholars had to rely on their memories. However, even if stores of knowledge are more readily accessible nowadays, there may still be advantages to having a large amount of knowledge actually 'in one's head'. We shall consider this point later in Chapters 2 and 13.

The Chinese did not, of course, just learn by rote. They read literature, they wrote poems in the style of the great poets, they considered philosophical and political problems and they used their accumulated knowledge to enlighten these activities. The initial rote-learning of information, as a basis for subsequent creative thought and production, is a recurrent theme in early educational practice and is still prevalent in many East Asian classrooms, not least because their orthographies require the acquisition of a vast number of different characters. Additionally, in stark contrast to the Ancient Greek method, the inculcation of respect for teachers and for established knowledge means that questioning and argument are often discouraged in the classroom. Although one might think that a combination of rote-learning and suppression of argument would result in poor understanding (see Chapter 7), recent research has actually shown that, as in Ancient China, modern East Asian students are able to use their rote-learnt knowledge base to think deeply about the subjects they study and make connections between different areas (see Chapter 11).

Teaching in medieval Europe

In medieval times, education took place within monasteries. John of Salisbury, a distinguished diplomat and philosopher (1115–1180), wrote about the phonological approach to reading in monastic schools. He promoted a method that is not very different from the synthetic phonics approach used in the modern primary school Literacy Hour. The pupil learnt to read not in his native (vernacular) language but in Latin. Latin was the language in which science, and religion and business, were conducted in medieval Europe and therefore educated people needed to learn it. Interestingly, Latin has a regular orthography (system of spelling), like modern Italian or Finnish but unlike either old or modern English. Although, of course, we do not actually know precisely how it would have been pronounced, it is likely that the words could be readily decoded phonologically. So perhaps serendipitously, it was particularly suitable for the phonological approach to learning to read. One of the controversies facing British educators over the past 50 years has been the question of whether English, as an irregular language, is really suited to this phonological approach (see Chapter 4). The medieval education would have put emphasis on reading the Bible (in the Latin translation) as well as Roman texts (such as Horace). Pupils learnt large amounts of text by rote, building up what might be called a 'library in the mind'. Suzanne Reynolds[7] has termed this approach a 'memorial culture' in her book on medieval education, to contrast with modern text- (and Internet-) based culture. The pupils were taught to 'mine the text for meaning' in order to acquire vocabulary. This reflects the main way that both children and adults naturally acquire new vocabulary – from hearing or reading a new word in context.

In order to be able to understand Latin texts, it was necessary for the pupil to acquire a comprehensive knowledge of Latin grammar. This entailed a great deal of rote-learning. Through the acquisition of this knowledge, the pupil would gain insight into the structure of language as well as becoming proficient in reading, writing and speaking Latin.

Pedagogical Methods

In Ancient Greece, the dialectical method involved teacher and pupil discussing propositions in order to determine the truth through dialogue (OED – dialectic: 'the art of critically investigating the truth'). Such a process is still the basis of tutorial teaching, at least in arts subjects, at Oxford and Cambridge universities.

The method and content of teaching in medieval Europe was challenged in the seventeenth century by the German philosopher John Amos Comenius. He strongly opposed the notion that there was intrinsic value in 'memorizing unintelligible grammatical rules' of Latin, but at the same time did agree that the language had to be learnt so that the pupil could attain knowledge. Comenius was well ahead of his time in insisting that education should be available to the poor as well as the rich and to girls as well as boys. His proposal of the 'Right Order for Learning' (Box 1.2) has much in common with current views of what should be taught at what age, with the exception of the time allotted to foreign (particularly ancient) language learning.

When we consider different methods of teaching in schools, both in the past and the present, we again have several schools of thought. If you walk into a classroom in one school you may find pupils arranged in rows where the teacher instructs from the front – the so-called traditional 'talk and chalk' approach. In another school you may find pupils sitting around tables collaborating whilst the teacher roams the classroom and discusses the work with small groups. The small-group method can be used to encourage learning by discovery and discussion rather than by direct instruction (but does lend itself also to irrelevant discussion of football or TV).

Box 1.2   John Amos Comenius (1592–1670)

The Right Order for Learning

- **Up to 6 years old**
  Exercise the external senses.
- **6–12 years**
  Develop the internal senses: imagination and memory.
  Reading, writing, arithmetic, measuring, singing, history, geography, principles of mechanical arts, morality and religion.
- **12–17 years**
  Develop understanding and judgement: four languages (Greek, Latin, Hebrew, a European language), science, arts.
  Gymnastics every day.
- **18 years upwards**
  Acquire 'the principles, causes and purposes of all the main facts about the world' (his *Pansophic* ideal).

A belief in the importance of applied knowledge is one thing that underpins the current emphasis on 'transferable skills'. It has led to the change, for example, in history courses, which have become less focused on memorization of key dates and more dependent on learning how to assess the reliability and importance of sources concerning (say) the Second World War. On the downside, this leaves less time for pupils to acquire knowledge of the seminal events that occurred before or during the war. However, the pupil will at least learn to view evidence critically and their mind will be prepared for the 'search for the truth', which must also be an important goal of education.

Rote-learning has come into disrepute in the British educational system. Emphasis on understanding before learning something such as the multiplication tables has directly led to the situation where many young people cannot multiply even simple numbers. In support of the old-fashioned way, there is research that shows that for learning the multiplication tables, rote-learning provides a faster route to multiplication becoming automatic than does learning through understanding. And indeed it is still the case in Japan that young children learn their multiplication tables by singing them. Understanding can then follow.

The Organization of This Book

The chapters in this book take us on a journey from the building blocks of learning through to a consideration of the structure and social impact of education. Naturally, the first area of psychology that we consider (Chapter 2) is learning and memory. We look briefly at the rules governing simple learning that have been demonstrated in non-human animals and ask whether and where these might be relevant to learning in the classroom. We discuss short-term and working memory, which are needed for following instructions and for problem-solving. Working memory also interacts with our long-term store, which comprises memory for facts (semantic) and memory for events (episodic) as well as procedural memory, which we use automatically. From learning to read to the establishment of enduring and well-organized memory, we need frameworks (schemata) into which to put the information. Knowing about the characteristics of memory helps teachers and students to decide how it may be best to teach and to learn different sorts of information. However, there is not much research on this subject outside the laboratory and in the context of real classrooms – it is badly needed but raises difficult organizational and ethical problems.

Language skills (Chapter 3) are, of course, fundamental to educational success, because almost all teaching is delivered through speech and writing, even mathematics. It is therefore not surprising that measures of vocabulary and syntactical understanding and production predict educational achievement. This is a key area where socioeconomic differences impact heavily on outcomes. Children from low-SES (socioeconomic status) backgrounds on average enter school with lower levels of vocabulary and complexity of language and this influences their future success at school. Teachers, parents, school governors and government alike believe that it is desperately important to raise the educational achievement of children from disadvantaged backgrounds, both to promote equality of opportunity and to have a productive economy. We discuss the causes of poor language development and ways in which intervention may improve it.

Whilst the acquisition of our first language is essential for us to function in society, acquiring a second language has many advantages, particularly in terms of giving us full access to other cultures. In recent years, the British educational system has seen a reduced emphasis on second-language learning, with dramatic reductions in the numbers of pupils carrying this on beyond the age of 14. However, recent work on the new National Curriculum is emphasizing the importance of introducing modern language teaching into primary schools. Chapter 3 also considers what research does and could tell us about the most efficacious age at which to start classroom teaching of a foreign language.

Language development has a clear role in learning to read, both with respect to word recognition and to understanding what is read (Chapter 4). Following the Rose Review (2005), guidelines have been implemented in English and Welsh schools for the teaching of reading by synthetic phonics. We present the evidence that has supported this change, and discuss the controversies surrounding it. In fact, our understanding of how we learn to read is far from complete, as is our understanding of the causes of specific reading disability (dyslexia). Dyslexia is a heterogeneous condition and probably has multiple causes.

One factor that is often cited as explaining educational achievement is 'ability' or 'intelligence'. The trouble is that neither of these terms has a simple definition and there is wide disagreement about the unitary or multiple nature of ability. There is also disagreement about the relative contribution of hereditary and environmental factors, of nature versus nurture, to the development of intelligence and abilities, and hence to their stability throughout life. We consider (in Chapter 5) the evidence relating to these differing points of view and the implications for the structure of the education system. For example, if we believe that children are all born with the same potential then there is good reason to invest in early intervention and intensive support with the expectation that every primary school pupil ought to reach the same level of attainment. In contrast, if we think intelligence is mainly heritable, then we may as well teach pupils in ability groups from a very young age so that those who are more able are not held back by slower peers. As with most topics about which there are extreme views, it is likely that the truth lies somewhere in between. However, in Britain a common response to variation in pupil attainment, evident even when children start primary school, has been academic selection and setting (see Chapter 6). It is then necessary to consider the consequences of such selection and how to make such differentiation as fair as possible. How do we prevent socioeconomic factors influencing our assessment of academic potential? And how do we protect pupils from the adverse consequences of selection? We may find lower-attaining pupils 'coasting' if they only compare their progress to that of similarly attaining peers, or see higher-attaining pupils suffer from the 'Big Fish Little Pond effect', where able pupils selected for entry into elite schools and universities may lose academic self-confidence when they are suddenly surrounded by people of equal or greater 'ability'.

Of course, there are many factors beyond 'ability' that influence academic success. We know that the approach to learning that pupils adopt, their attitudes and the way they structure their working, can also affect the level of knowledge and understanding they acquire. This is why researchers are interested in metacognitive strategies that can be used to optimize pupils' learning (Chapter 7). Another extraneous influence on attainment is the perception that 'people like me' are not expected to do well. Indeed, psychologists have a name for this phenomenon: stereotype threat. In certain contexts, ethnic minority students or those of a certain sex can be seen to underachieve solely because of a dominant perception that their group is not good at that subject or task. However, there are other reasons that we see sex differences in attainment (addressed in Chapter 8). There may be inborn differences between the sexes that explain variations in behaviour and educational performance, but culture can also place great constraints on the environment that children experience and hence cause further sex differences to emerge. There are many preconceptions among the general public about sex differences in behaviour: for example, that women and girls can't navigate effectively, or that women are better at reading and writing whilst men are better at mathematics and physics. There is scientific evidence for some differences, but others are the result of poorly designed research, such as poor matching of comparison groups. However, the media love the subject of sex differences and so these differences have become part of the general consciousness.

Creativity is also of interest to the general public because it is relevant to so many aspects of life: both at work and during leisure time. Most educators also regard it as an important trait among pupils, worth fostering in the classroom. However, some aspects of creativity are not easy to manage in the classroom; indeed creative personality traits have been linked with increased rates of school dropout and with learning difficulties such as ADHD (attention deficit hyperactivity disorder). This is why it is so important to have strong research into the traits and behaviours associated with creativity and the most effective ways to support it in schools (see Chapter 9).

We know that at present the British education system is still not effectively serving the needs of all young people. Over half of young people from the lowest-income families do not achieve five GCSEs including English and mathematics at a C grade or above. This means they have not acquired the basic literacy and numeracy skills needed for further study or for a wide range of employment. Such social inequalities are present throughout the education system, as are some very subtle ethnic inequalities that mean, for example, that more ethnic minority pupils attend university but fewer attend the most selective institutions. Research can give us reasons for these inequalities, but there is an ongoing search for evidence-based interventions to address them (Chapter 10).

One way to identify new interventions or educational methods is to look at other countries. The increasing globalization of education and employment means that educators are now more than ever interested in the factors that make certain education systems particularly successful. We can learn a lot from research conducted in other cultures, not least the extent to which cultural assumptions rather than empirical evidence underpin the structure and pedagogy of our own education system (Chapter 10). For example, we see big differences in attitudes to children's potential in Eastern and Western countries: these feed into beliefs about the extent to which academic performance depends on innate ability rather than effort, and consequently about the appropriateness of ability grouping and individualized teaching. We focus on comparisons with a select group of countries including Japan, China, Finland and Singapore, which have gained international reputations for their pupils' high attainment.

A rather neglected area for more research concerns the educational needs of older learners. With the rapidly increasing number of people over 65 and the ever-increasing need for a technically qualified workforce, it is important to find ways of training people to be able to continue to work effectively into old age (Chapter 12). We know that memory starts to fail as people enter middle age and so methods of teaching that will allow long-term retention of what is learnt may need to be adapted for the old. However, we don't yet know much about how this would be achieved.

Of course, the increasing technological content of our lives is creating a challenge for educators working with all ages. As innovative ways of teaching using new technologies are being developed at an increasing pace, research is badly needed to find out where this aids and where it might impede learning (Chapter 13). For example, in some schools digital devices such as mobile phones are completely banned, whilst in others they are being embraced as a new way to engage learners. Similarly, we have some educators arguing that the Internet is a worrying source of unreliable information and others suggesting that it makes the learning of facts completely redundant. As Baroness Susan Greenfield pointed out in her book *Tomorrow's People* (2005), the use of the many technological devices such as tablets and laptops, particularly by young people, may actually change our brains and hence the way we think and learn. We need evidence of these changes if we are to understand how best to teach new generations.

References

1 Donnachie I. *Robert Owen. Owen of New Lanark and New Harmony*. Edinburgh: Tuckwell Press; 2000.

2 Jaeger W, Highet G. *Paideia: The Ideals of Greek Culture*. Oxford: Oxford University Press; 1986.

3 Tate N. What Is Education For? The Fifth Annual Education Lecture. London: King's College London; 1998.

4 Young M. The return to subjects: A sociological perspective on the UK coalition government's approach to the 14–19 curriculum. *Curriculum Journal*. 2011;22(2):265–278.

5 Oates T. *Could Do Better: Using International Comparisons to Reform the National Curriculum in England*. Cambridge: Cambridge Assessment, University of Cambridge; 2010.

6 Miyazaki I, Schirokauer C. *China's Examination Hell: The Civil Service Examinations of Imperial China*. Yale, CT: Yale University Press; 1981.

7 Reynolds S. *Medieval Reading, Grammar and the Classical Text*. Cambridge: Cambridge University Press; 1996.

Chapter 2

Memory
How Do We Remember What We Learn?

Where were you when you heard about the horrific event of 9/11? Can you visualize your environment at that point? Or, if you are old enough, can you visualize where you were when you heard of the assassination of President Kennedy? It is likely that you have a rather clear memory of your situation at the time. These are extreme examples of episodic memory where an explicit memory has been acquired consciously. Can you remember from your early childhood learning the rules of the grammar for your mother tongue? No, because you acquired that memory implicitly; you were unaware of acquiring it. These examples allow us to contrast two sorts of memory: declarative and non-declarative memory (also called explicit and implicit memory).

Whether we consider education to involve the transfer of information or the development of skills, or most likely, both of these, the process would be useless to the learner unless s/he remembered what had been taught. In this chapter we describe the different sorts of learning and memory that have been identified and consider how we should capitalize on their use in different ways for different purposes.

Historically, different aspects of learning and memory tended to be investigated by different groups of psychologists and in different animals: learning was studied in non-human animals such as rats and pigeons, and even in invertebrates such as sea slugs and cockroaches. Short-term

Education and Learning: An Evidence-Based Approach, First Edition. Jane Mellanby and Katy Theobald.

memory was studied in humans. Long-term memory, particularly its chemistry, was studied in non-human animals, including rats and cockroaches. We shall first give a very simple description of some of the rules governing animal learning and then discuss the types of memory which psychologists work on in humans. We shall be considering the ways in which different sorts of learning and memory are relevant to how we teach and how we learn. We shall also examine the evidence concerning factors that affect memory and discuss ways in which it may be possible to improve aspects of memory.

Stages of memory processing

Memory processes involve firstly encoding. This then leads to storage. Storage may be labile and short term (like the telephone number you have just looked up which will last whilst you dial it but will have decayed by the time the person answers the telephone) or long term, lasting from hours to years. The process(es) that convert a short-term labile store into a long-term stable store is termed consolidation. Later, when you require the stored information, it has to be retrieved. The neural processes involved in encoding, short- and long-term storage and retrieval are all different and all important in understanding how we learn and remember.

Learning

Non-associative learning

A very general definition of learning is 'a change in behaviour as the result of experience'. By this definition some very simple types of behavioural change would be considered 'learning'. Two of these are habituation and sensitization. Habituation and sensitization are described as non-associative forms of learning because they do not require the organism to learn a specific association between one stimulus and something else; they only require a changed response to the stimulus. These simple types of learning can readily be demonstrated in simple animals such as sea slugs as well as in humans. Habituation describes the decreased response to a stimulus that occurs after a number of repetitions. Indeed it is widely used in work on human babies to ascertain whether they can discriminate between two objects: they are shown one object several times and then a new object is introduced. If the baby now looks more at the new object than at the familiar one, it must have habituated to the first one. I used to demonstrate habituation to classes of undergraduates by standing behind the desk and dropping a large stick on the floor in such a way that they could not see what I was doing. This made a loud noise and the students would jump. The loud noise would not have any consequence, either positive or negative, for the students. I would then repeat the action several times (again not letting them see what I was doing) and their response would rapidly decrease on successive exposures.

Sensitization is in a sense the opposite of habituation: the difference is that now the loud noise, or other neutral stimulus (that is, a stimulus that does not signal anything, positive or negative), is coupled with an aversive stimulus, such as an electric shock. This can lead to exaggerated responses not only to the loud noise but also to other 'neutral' stimuli. In the context of teaching, it can be argued that habituation is one example of a source of boredom – as all teachers know, too much repetitive content or activity in the classroom will reduce the amount of attention that the learners pay to the lesson. It is possible that sensitization occurs after a teacher shouts at pupils, or that in the past corporal punishment may have resulted in long-term sensitization to the context of lessons.

Classical and operant conditioning

Classical and operant conditioning are forms of simple learning that require learning that two things are associated (e.g. a light predicts food or pressing a bar delivers food).

Ivan Pavlov (1849–1936), the Russian physiologist, discovered classical conditioning in dogs. His well-known finding occurred serendipitously in the course of physiological experiments on the production of saliva in the dogs' mouths and digestive juices in their stomachs in response to food. What was interesting was that secretions also came to be produced in response to the arrival of the technician who fed the dogs, even in the absence of food. Pavlov later showed that a similar effect could be produced if a bell was rung before food was presented – the dogs learnt to associate the bell (a neutral stimulus) with food and the digestive system automatically became prepared for digesting it. In schools where there is a bell rung to signify dinner time, children can experience the same salivatory response as Pavlov's dogs and also report feeling hungry.

Operant conditioning was discovered by Thorndike, a psychologist working in America. Here, the association that the organism learns is between what it does itself and what the result is. Thus it may learn that making a particular motor action leads to its obtaining food – positive reinforcement; or that stepping down from a platform onto a grid leads to its receiving a small electric shock – negative reinforcement. Thorndike promulgated his 'law of effect' (1911) – that the strength of the association would depend on the number of such pairings.

Learning theory is the scientific description of the laws governing classical and operant conditioning.

How is conditioning relevant to human behaviour?

Operant conditioning probably does play a role in the way in which young children acquire certain patterns of behaviour. This may be particularly true with respect to negative reinforcement: for example, if a child approaches something dangerous such as a hot fire or tries to run across a busy road, an adult is likely to grab the child rapidly and stop it carrying out the risky behaviour, accompanying this with angry words of reprimand. A few repetitions of this will usually suffice to stop the child from trying to engage in these behaviours in the future; indeed just one exposure (one-trial learning) may be enough. Work on animal learning has shown that for maximum effectiveness the negative reinforcement needs to be administered close in time to the behaviour – delay reduces its effectiveness. Jeffrey Gray, in his book *The Psychology of Fear and Stress*,[1] also points out from work on animals that 'swift certain punishment can be as effective as a more intense punishment applied in a dilatory or inconsistent manner'. Even though this is stated in the context of animal learning, many parents and teachers could find resonance in this. In the past, the fear of corporal punishment may have produced a form of operant conditioning – this negative reinforcement reducing the likelihood of further performance of the bad behaviour. In today's schools, many of the punishments, such as detention, do not produce much fear or anxiety. Probably, a 'telling off' from a respected and scary teacher is more effective as a negative reinforcer. Also, where detention is only carried out at the end of the day or even deferred until the next day, this will make the punishment seem detached from the bad behaviour.

A number of general factors that make learning more effective in animals are likely to be relevant to human learning: these include surprise and salience (how important the to-be-learned association is to the animal). Whilst these have been investigated in the context of conditioning, they are also important in all sorts of learning. Another aspect of animal learning that may be relevant to the classroom is latent learning: if a rat is allowed to explore a maze without receiving any positive or negative stimulation, when it is then trained to find food at a point in the maze it is quicker to learn than a rat not previously so exposed. The rat has learnt something about the environment of the maze even though it has not been rewarded or punished there. This sort of learning is perhaps occurring when pupils are exposed to the general context of a subject, for example by having relevant posters on the classroom walls, before they are taught about it directly.

Behaviourists such as Skinner considered the study of interesting things, such as the kinds of memory that make up our record of everyday experience, to be beyond the scope of proper science, but these are just the sorts of memory that are studied today. The growth of cognitive psychology, the study of understanding and conscious awareness, has overshadowed simple learning procedures studied by learning theorists.[2] But of course both sorts of learning are actually taking place during our lifetimes, all the time.

Memory

Short-term and working memory/executive function

William James (1842–1910), the distinguished American philosopher, elder brother of the novelist Henry James, thought and wrote extensively about the nature of the human mind. It was he who first made a clear distinction between short- and long-term memory. We still think about learning and memory in these terms, though the meaning that we attach to them, and the ways in which we define different subcategories of them, are complex and not always agreed upon.

We have already mentioned that if we want to remember some experience or fact then this memory needs to be encoded. Short-term memory encompasses encoding and short-term storage and manipulation. Verbal memory and visuospatial short-term memory appear to require separate cognitive space. Verbal memory involves auditory input of words or numbers; visuospatial memory involves information presented visually. It appears that there is a specific short-term store for verbal material, the phonological loop,[3] which is what we use for example to remember a telephone number while we dial it. A particularly important feature of short-term/working memory is that it has a limited capacity. It is overseen by processes in the prefrontal cortex which have been named by Baddeley[3] and colleagues the central executive. This involves the control of attention to what is being studied, which itself will involve not just registration of information (the process for which some researchers such as Tracy Alloway[4] reserve the term short-term memory) but also its manipulation

Figure 2.1   Photograph of the Tower of London. © chrisdorney/Shutterstock

in working memory (a type of memory that other researchers have included under the umbrella term of short-term memory). Working memory then involves manipulation of the information held in short-term memory. The easiest way of testing for the distinction between this sort of verbal short-term memory (STM) and working memory (WM) is digit recall for STM and backwards digit recall for WM. The tests are simple: for STM, repeating a series of digits in the same order as they have been said aloud by the experimenter; for WM, repeating such a list in reverse order. In the classroom, STM is used to store information such as instructions about which page of the textbook to open and where on the page to look. Meanwhile, working memory is used in all kinds of problem-solving and in the classroom will be involved in mathematics and literacy, and indeed in virtually all of the work that the child carries out (if this is not rote-learning). When we are learning something, we allow the new information to interact in our working memory with relevant information that we already have stored in long-term memory. This allows us to store the new information in the 'right place' and makes it retrievable from a variety of possible relevant stimuli. For example, when we learn that the building of the White Tower at the Tower of London (Figure 2.1) was started in

1068, we might activate information about the Tower being on the Thames, we might activate pictures/facts about other castles in England, we might activate information about William the Conqueror, and so on. And each of those pieces of information will itself be able to activate the date at which the White Tower was built.

The role of working memory in education   In view of its role in learning, it is not surprising that measures of working memory are found to be related to measures of intelligence. It is thought of as a component of fluid intelligence (since in factor analysis it is found to load strongly on *g*; see Chapter 5 on Ability). However, it is not the same thing as intelligence (although there have been proposals that it is identical).[5] Working memory measured at age 5 has been shown to be a more important predictor of academic success in children than are components of IQ tests such as vocabulary, which depend to some extent on experience.[6]

Can we improve working memory?   Since working memory is so important in learning and hence in education, we need to consider factors that may affect it. Working memory requires attention to be paid to the information being processed, and anything that disrupts attention will interfere with learning. Working memory (unlike procedural memory, see later) is something that has a developmental trajectory – it increases throughout childhood and it decreases in ageing (see Goswami[7(p292)]). It has long been assumed that working memory is a trait that cannot be changed by experience – its trajectory in a given individual is fixed. However, some recent research suggests that with extensive training it can actually be improved, and this of course also opens the way to suggesting that working memory development may be affected by early experience.

There is nowadays a general belief that the concept of 'use it or lose it' applies to mental as well as physical abilities. Thus we are aware that jogging or going to the gym is likely to improve our physical fitness and we think that likewise using our brains, for example by doing crosswords or sudoku, will maintain our intelligence. So it is not unreasonable to try to improve working memory by practising tasks that put a load on working memory. Klingberg and colleagues have devised a programme involving computerized training of working memory, which is available commercially (Cogmed Systems Inc.). Klingberg[8] showed in children with ADHD that this programme would not only improve working memory but produce transference to more general behaviour including leading to a reduction in hyperactivity and distractability. In typically developing pre-school children they also obtained significant transfer effects with

Cogmed training. Holmes et al.[9] have shown that training with *Cogmed* in children aged 8 to 11 years, selected on the basis of having poor working memory, improved not only working memory itself but also, 6 months later, had produced an improvement in mathematical reasoning. An important feature of the *Cogmed* programme is that it is adaptive – that is, the difficulty of the training is adjusted throughout to the partici-pant's level of performance. The *Cogmed* training is very time-consuming – 30 min per day, 5 days a week for 6 weeks – which makes it difficult to get schools or parents to adopt it. An educationally important transfer-ence effect of working memory training has recently been reported[10] comparing 20 university students who received training with 20 controls. Training of both verbal and visuospatial WM was carried out for 5 days per week for 4 weeks and each session took between 30 and 45 minutes. Both types of memory improved by about 20% – a typical practice effect – but there was also a transfer effect to reading comprehension. Perhaps counter-intuitively, it was the improvement in spatial working memory that correlated significantly with improved reading comprehension. The authors interpret this effect of the training as 'expanding the mind's work-space'. It is important to find out whether this finding can be replicated.

Can working memory training improve intelligence?

The idea that the WM training might boost intelligence has inspired an array of commercially successful computer programs and games. However, most of these do not involve the intensity of training that the experimen-tally successful programs use. A recent experiment was conducted at Cambridge University in collaboration with the BBC, to test whether commercially available 'brain training' did produce transfer to non-trained tasks (see BBC lab UK web site to try out the training).[11] They recruited more than 11,000 participants, covering the age range 18 to 60 years, and divided them into 3 groups: one group who carried out a control task (looking up obscure facts on the Internet), and two training groups: one doing six tasks including reasoning, planning and problem-solving – that is, working memory/executive function tasks – the other doing non-reasoning tasks consisting of six tasks for memory, attention, visuospatial processing and mathematical calculating. The participants were all tested before and then after the 6 weeks of training, on a series of established 'benchmarking' tests of grammatical reasoning (a test closely related to fluid intelligence), digit span, spatial working memory and learning the place of specific objects. The findings were clear-cut: there was virtually no transfer of the learning from either of the types of training utilized.

This finding contrasted with the quite substantial gains in scores on the actual training programme as a consequence of practice. An important finding was that there was no relation between change in benchmarking scores and the number of sessions of training that each participant actually reported having undertaken (which ranged from one to 180). This supported the interpretation that the training was not effective in producing a transferable improvement. Whilst these results must be disappointing for commercial producers of brain-training software, it is possible that more intensive training or different training could have been effective. For the present, however, it would seem unwise to encourage people to use this as a way of improving intellectual ability until new programmes have been validated experimentally in large studies. Obviously, if the training programmes do not lead to gains in behaviours that are important in education and/or in life in general then they are a waste of time (and money). It must be emphasized again that the training regimes that successfully improved working memory and generalized to other behaviours involved very intensive, adaptive training over an extended time period.

Stress and working memory

Working memory, as we have mentioned, is crucial for academic activities. It has been shown to be adversely affected by ongoing stress and this effect is particularly important in examinations where a degree of problem-solving is required. Eysenck's attentional control theory considers that such 'state anxiety' is made up of two components: worry and emotionality. It is worry that interferes with performance because it acts on the central executive to reduce goal-directed attention (that is, attention to the question under consideration) and diverts attention to the irrelevant stimulus, in this case that which is causing the worry: the threat.[12] This of course means that reduction of stress should be important in education and particularly important with respect to exams. Methods of reducing stress in school have included the introduction of meditation sessions (see Wellington School website). However, it is also important to remember that there is an inverted-U-shaped curve relating most psychological functions to levels of alertness/arousal: we don't learn if we are worrying excessively but we don't learn if we are half asleep either. A certain amount of anxiety causes increased vigilance – it increases attention and makes a given stimulus more salient. This naturally increases learning. So there is some optimal level of arousal for learning that in theory we should be trying to find. It is interesting that probably the main motivation for rote-learning in many past systems was fear of physical punishment. Since such learning was apparently highly effective, this could be taken to support the view that rote-learning occurs independently of working memory.

Long-term memory

We mentioned at the start of this chapter that we have both non-declarative (implicit) and declarative (explicit) memories. Traditionally, these are considered as separate processes involving different brain circuitry. However, recent research suggests that they may in some instances overlap and even use the same brain circuitry.[13]

Implicit memory

Implicit memories can be acquired either consciously or without conscious awareness. Procedural skills such as learning to drive, play the violin or read are acquired consciously, but these skills become automatic through practice and once they are automatic, thinking about them consciously does not necessarily improve them and may impair them. The acquisition of the grammar of our first language occurs implicitly (see Chapter 3).

The distinction between explicit and implicit memory originated in the study of amnesic patients. The original observation here was on the patient H.M. who had undergone brain surgery for the treatment of uncontrollable epilepsy. The surgery had involved bilateral removal of a large part of the medial temporal lobe, including the hippocampus. H.M. was involved in a vast amount of research which led to the conclusion that the hippocampus had a central role in the formation of explicit memories. H.M. and other patients with temporal lobe damage suffer from serious anterograde amnesia – an inability to form new conscious memories. It was, however, found that whilst H.M. and other amnesic patients could not even remember having met the doctors looking after them on many previous occasions, they could demonstrate forms of implicit memory. Thus, if for example they were instructed on how to do mirror drawing, which requires tracing a simple diagram whilst looking at one's hand only as a reflection in a mirror, they could learn how to do it. When tested later, they could still perform the task, but they had no conscious memory of having done the task before. The distinction has led to the rather circular definition that implicit memories are those that are preserved in amnesic patients.

In this case, the initial learning of mirror-drawing skills involved conscious awareness. There is, however, as mentioned above, learning that transfers to implicit memory that does not involve conscious awareness during learning. Examples of this in the laboratory involve, for example, being exposed repetitively to a series of letters that appear to be random but which actually constitute a repeated pattern. Eventually people exposed to this pattern will be able to pre-empt the letter that is going to come next, demonstrating learning, even though they will deny any explicit knowledge acquisition.

Another example of implicit learning is 'priming', defined as 'an improvement in the ability to process, detect or identify words or objects after recent experience with them'.[14] The initial experience does not need to be conscious and there may be no acknowledgement of having seen the stimuli, yet priming is detected.

We also have implicitly acquired category knowledge: living versus non-living, for example, which can be demonstrated even in very young children. In a nice experiment on this, infants were shown pictures of animals drinking from a cup and then shown pictures of an aeroplane doing the same. They rejected the second set of pictures whilst happily approving the first. Thus they had demonstrated the category 'living' versus non-living even though they had never been explicitly told that aeroplanes don't drink out of cups.

Rote-learning and practice

Hermann Ebbinghaus, a German psychologist (1850–1609), published a monograph in 1885 describing his self-administered tests of human learning and memory. He studied the acquisition of lists of novel nonsense syllables (a technique he invented, the stimuli consisting of three letters: two consonants separated by a vowel). He used these meaningless 'words' so that he could study learning and memory processes without having to consider the relationship that real words would have had with already established knowledge in his mind. He learnt these lists by simple repetition and showed that there appeared to be two sorts of memory formed – a short-term form in response to a single exposure, which decayed if not rehearsed within less than a minute, and a long-term form produced by many repetitions. The permanence of this long-term store depended on the number of repetitions. He was able to fit a mathematical function to the decay of memory (forgetting). The most important outcome of this research was the recognition that human learning and memory was something that could be investigated in a scientific research laboratory and that a function of the human mind was subject to laws as were other natural phenomena.

The rules that Ebbinghaus discovered from studying himself are applicable to rote-learning in the classroom. For example, whilst much repetition is necessary, groups of repetitions followed by a rest period are more effective than massed trials (the same number of repetitions in a single session). Ebbinghaus also introduced a useful way of measuring residual memory for apparently forgotten tasks – savings on re-training. Here it is found that it is easier to learn something to which a person has previously been exposed but has forgotten than to learn it the first time. There must be an unconscious memory remaining that we can tap into on re-learning. The concept of savings has been extensively used in the study of non-human animal learning.

A vast amount of teaching and learning in past educational systems involved rote-learning (see Chapter 1) comparable with the regimes with which Ebbinghaus taught himself. The Chinese system involved learning thousands of characters by rote. Latin grammar was memorized by rote in grammar schools in Britain from their inception (mainly in the fifteenth century) up to modern times. In the twentieth century, O-levels (the school exams at 16+ which GCSEs have replaced) in physics, maths and chemistry required memorization of formulae and most pupils simply did this by rote-learning.

It is often argued that since we have access to information on the Internet and we have readily available calculators (e.g. on our mobile phones), there is little need today to rote learn things such as our multiplication tables. However, if one needs to know whether one has enough money in one's pocket to buy eight tins of tomatoes at 60p, it is much quicker 'just to know' they will cost £4.80 than either to use a calculator or laboriously 'count on'. Under these circumstances it is undoubtedly advantageous just to know the multiplication tables. And the same argument can be applied to formulae etc. Thus there probably still is a role for some rote-learning in school education (and probably also in university education) but there is a serious need for research on when and for what it would be most valuable.

Amongst educationalists in Britain, rote-learning is generally frowned upon as being a method of 'surface learning' (see Chapter 7) which is usually considered inferior to the 'deep learning' that involves looking for meaning and relating information to what is already known. However, as we note in Chapter 11, research into East Asian education systems suggests that pupils can acquire information by repetition and still carry out processes associated with a deep learning approach.

Information that is acquired by rote-learning eventually becomes accessible automatically. In this it resembles the acquisition of a skill such as playing a musical instrument, driving a car, serving a tennis ball or reading rapidly. All of these are acquired by practice, at first consciously but later becoming automatic and even difficult to access consciously – a skilled tennis player's performance is impaired by thinking about how to serve the ball, and the concert pianist playing a sonata is likewise impaired by wondering which finger goes where. The advantage of automatic retrieval is that it works without putting a load on the limited capacity of working memory (see above) and therefore can increase the efficiency of performance in many spheres. However, the acquired skill does not generalize to other areas – pianists are not particularly likely to be better tennis players.

Implicit memory does not appear to have a steep developmental trajectory, unlike working memory (see above), and so is well developed in young children. This suggests that we should perhaps capitalize on this in the teaching of young children and it reflects the success in the past of teaching them by rote. Such early learning becomes very firmly established and we can argue that perhaps it is more 'hard-wired' into the nervous system than later-acquired learning. It is probably easier to motivate younger than older children for this sort of learning – a class of nursery children singing their multiplication tables doesn't seem as weird as the same with 13-year-olds would be. Indeed, a class of nursery children can easily be persuaded to sing their tables, but the same might not be said for a class of teenagers.

A form of rote-learning that has been employed in efforts to remediate failing memory in people with degenerative diseases or brain damage has been errorless learning (EL). The idea is that rather than allowing the learner to make mistakes and so learn by trial and error, the training will be designed so that all responses are correct – in a way comparable to rote-learning (see Chapter 12). In this way, exposure to incorrect answers, which will enter memory, is avoided. However, not all the research supports the belief that the errorless learning is implicit; it may at least in part be supported by some intact explicit memory function.[15]

Explicit/declarative memory

Long-term declarative memory can be further subdivided into semantic and episodic memory. This distinction was first promoted by Endel Tulving in the early 1970s. Baddeley[16] has clearly defined these two processes: semantic memory, 'our knowledge of the world: the meaning of a word, how many yards in a mile, or what is the colour of ripe bananas'; in contrast to episodic memory, 'the capacity to represent a specific event and locate it in time and space'.

You might think we are mainly concerned with semantic memory in education. However, it is likely that the formation of episodic and semantic memories actually occur in parallel and the distinction between the two is nowhere nearly as clear-cut as first envisaged. From the point of view of teaching, it is important that episodic memory encodes context. Since episodic memories are often vivid and emotionally charged, making information personally relevant at the time of learning should make it more memorable. This means that students may remember things better if the learning process involves him/her incorporating the context of learning into the memory. Activities such as field trips in biology or museum visits in history should allow a personal memory to be formed into which it may be easier to insert new knowledge – the personal memory has become part of the framework. Such personal memory could, however, have disadvantages if the context is one where the student was humiliated or otherwise made anxious; then we may have the source of, for example, maths anxiety.

Depth of learning increases memorability

It is universally accepted that increasing the 'depth' of learning something increases its memorability. An experiment published more than 50 years ago[17] showed that this could occur even without explicit instruction to use a context to aid memory. The experiment involved allowing students to study a list of 100 words in 3 different ways: they either had to cross out all the letter 'o's in the words, to copy them out in their own handwriting or to assess on a scale of 1 to 7 whether the words were related to the concept 'economic' (in each case they had been given a spurious reason for what they had been instructed to do). Immediately after this they were tested on their recall of the words in the list. It was found that those instructed to rate the words with respect to their relevance to 'economic' remembered four times more words than those instructed to cross out the 'o's – the effect of processing the words had greatly increased their memorability. A further interesting finding was that this processing had apparently sensitized the students to the 'economic' concept: the most commonly remembered words for these students were more likely to be 'economic' related. Furthermore, unlike the students in the control groups, their incorrect responses included words that are indeed related to economics but were not in the learnt list, such as investment, stock, money. A final interesting point in the study was that the memory for economics-relevant words was relatively stronger 48 hours after learning than at immediate recall, suggesting that the memory, over time, gets more specific to the sensitizing concept, 'economic'. This experiment provides good evidence for the importance of increasing the depth of processing to improve retention of information.

The paper contains a completely different but rather interesting observation, though one on which the authors did not comment – the students who copied the words in their own handwriting remembered twice as many words as those who crossed out the 'o's. Nowadays, many students take notes on what they are studying by copying and pasting information from online sources into their own documents. It can be argued that even copying information verbatim but by hand requires more effort and would be more likely to involve deeper processing. More processing is undoubtedly involved where information is re-phrased before it is transferred to notes (whether by hand-writing or by typing). There are many intriguing questions to ask about the presentation and transference of information to students. In the past 30 years, classroom teaching has moved from presenting information written on a blackboard (or whiteboard) or via cylostyled handouts (an old-fashioned rather messy method of reproducing), via overhead projection or slides, to complex PowerPoint presentations including videos. In Chapter 13 we discuss the use of new interactive media in the classroom and the urgent need for more research on the most memorable ways of presenting information.

To acquire new facts, it is useful to have a context or framework in which to put them. Whatever the overall pattern of teaching, 'talk and chalk' or more interactive methods, probably the most important factor influencing the students' acquisition of information is the presence in their knowledge base of a schema or framework into which they can insert new knowledge. This was demonstrated many years ago by David Ausubel (1960)[18] who proposed that 'new meaningful material becomes incorporated into cognitive structure in so far as it is subsumable under relevant existing concepts'. This then allows deep rather than surface learning (see Chapter 7). Ausubel carried out a carefully controlled experiment where students had to memorize a 2,500-word passage concerning the metallurgical properties of plain carbon steel – an area of knowledge with which the students were not familiar. Beforehand, one group of students was presented with a passage containing material that would help to organize their thoughts on this topic, whilst the control group was given a passage about the history of the topic. The students studied the 2,500-word passage for 35 minutes and then 3 days later took a multiple choice test on its content. Those who had first studied the relevant introductory passage (which did not contain any specific clues to the information tested on the multiple choice questions) performed about 20% better than the controls (who had only had the historical information).

Thus one of the first tasks for teachers is to help children to construct these frameworks. Examples of such frameworks would be: the periodic table of the elements for learning the chemical properties of elements; the classification of living things for learning about the characteristics of different species; the timeline of historical changes such as the mechanization of industrial processes to learn about the factors that influenced their development. We have argued in the Introduction (Chapter 1) that the new National Curriculum for primary schools should provide the structure of such frameworks. These should then be able to provide the basis for knowledge acquired at secondary school and beyond.

Physical Changes in the Brain

Where in the brain?

The formation of memories has been extensively studied in non-human animals and we have accumulated a large body of information about the sorts of biochemical and physiological processes that underlie it. We can consider physical changes both at the systems level, that is, concerning the connectivity between different areas of the nervous system, or at the cellular and molecular level. At the systems level, conditioning, habituation and sensitization involve reflex-like activity and do not require an intact brain since they can occur at the level of the spinal cord or in very simple organisms such as cockroaches and sea slugs. Other forms of memory have been related to specific brain areas: procedural memory involves the prefrontal cortex but also the cerebellum; explicit memory involves the hippocampus and related areas early on but also requires a dialogue with the prefrontal cortex. A hippocampus-independent memory will eventually be stored in the cortex. A major portion of research on the physical basis of memory has been carried out with respect to hippocampal function.

Box 2.1   Long-term potentiation and the storage of memories

Long-term potentiation (LTP) was discovered[20] in rabbit hippocampi as a long-lasting increase in synaptic efficacy as the result of repetitive stimulation. It can also be demonstrated in other parts of the brain. There is more than one molecular mechanism involved but the one that is most researched, particularly in the hippocampus, has been shown to involve potentiated responses to the excitatory neurotransmitter glutamate. Induction of LTP requires that the postsynaptic membrane already be partially depolarized. This means that two inputs to the same cell can interact and can form the basis of associative learning (association of two different inputs). A specific type of glutamate receptor (NMDA receptor) in the membrane is then able to be activated by an incoming signal – it acts as a molecular coincidence detector. Its activation leads to entry of calcium ions and these are then involved in a cascade of biochemical changes which lead to an increase in the number of another kind of glutamate receptor (AMPA receptor) which is the one used all the time in excitatory transmission. This then constitutes relatively short-term LTP. Long-term persistence of LTP requires further stimulation and needs transcription of genes, the synthesis of proteins and changes in the position, structure and efficacy of synapses in order to be established. Long-term depression, where the strength of connection between synapses is weakened, also involves the NMDA receptor, and occurs in response to low-frequency stimulation of relevant synapses.

What sort of physical changes underlie memory?

At the cellular/molecular level, it is generally assumed that the relevant changes involve a change in synaptic efficacy – either an increase in the ability of a particular input to excite a neuron, or a decrease. Processes, respectively termed long-term potentiation (LTP) and long-term depression (LTD), whose biochemical mechanisms are quite well understood[19] are considered to be good candidates for the cellular and molecular changes underlying memory (see Box 2.1).

So how do we think that the change in synaptic strength can represent memory in the brain? If we subscribe to a connectionist theory, then this is the way in which the relative weights of different nodes (synapses) are altered. Whilst information on LTP and LTD is interesting, we cannot even begin to relate it to what education does to the brain until we have more knowledge about where the changes in synaptic weighting and connections are occurring.

The total number of neurons in the brain does not change much in humans after birth, but the number of synapses does change dramatically. In early infancy the numbers increase and then after about the age of 2 there is a large amount of synaptic pruning (that is, reduction in the number of inputs per neuron), which is well known to be part of a predetermined developmental programme. This programme continues throughout childhood and adolescence and occurs independently of experience unless that experience is grossly abnormal (e.g. light or sound deprivation). However, the brain is also re-modelled by experience and this can continue throughout the lifespan. There are now many well-established examples of the effects of experience on the *volume* of relevant parts of the brain. Well-known examples include the increased volume of the hippocampus in experienced London taxi drivers associated with their exceptionally extensive knowledge of the streets and landmarks of London (see Chapter 5),[21] and the increased volume of specific parts of the motor cortex (the part of the brain involved in governing voluntary movement) representing finger movements in violinists. Such changes could be due to a number of different possible anatomical adaptations. These include an increase in the number of synapses (connections between neurons), or to there being more glial cells (the 'supporting' cells of the brain, which constitute about three-quarters of the cells found in the brain), or to more vascularization (that is, an increase in the number of blood vessels). It has also been shown that the acquisition of some skills can be associated with changes in the amount of white matter, that is, the myelinated nerve fibres. Myelinated fibres are nerve axons ensheathed in a fatty layer, myelin, which increases the speed at which they can conduct information (action potentials). An increase in white matter could involve there being more myelinated nerve tracts or, more likely, an increase in the thickness of myelin sheaths. The latter effect would increase conduction velocity and thus could have profound effects on behaviour (see Chapter 5).

During their development, children's experiences interact with and refine their behaviour. Jean Piaget (the Swiss philosopher and psychologist who can be considered the 'father of developmental psychology') termed this process constructivism. More recently, the term neuroconstructivism[22] has been coined to describe the process whereby the experience of the child models the structure and function of the brain, allowing specialization of different areas to occur (see also Chapter 5). For example, whilst sounds activate a wide area of the cerebral cortex in babies, the naturally occurring exposure to visual and other stimuli means that the greatest activation to an input of a particular modality will occur in the area with an inbuilt bias to processing stimuli of that modality. Through this, in the typically developing brain, the area destined to become visual cortex will become specialized for visual input and the area destined for auditory input likewise. Evidence for this comes from children who are born deaf or blind – in which cases the representation of the intact input spreads to include the area originally destined for the deficient input. If the concept of neuroconstructivism applies to later development, and even into adulthood (and evidence quoted above suggests that it does), then the effect of education on the brain is obviously an important area of study. Unfortunately, enthusiasm in the media and with the general public for the idea that we can improve children's academic development by all sorts of extra experiences, including 'brain gym', has gone far ahead of academic research and we are still in the position advanced by Bruer in 2001[23] that relating education to brain structure is 'a bridge too far'.

However, there is some recent evidence for education's effect on brain structure. An interesting study was carried out on medical students by Draganski and colleagues.[24] They investigated changes in the brains of students doing the intensive study required for the German preclinical medical exams, which take place after the first two years of university training. The students are examined, both orally and in written papers, in biology, chemistry, biochemistry, physics, human anatomy and physiology. Before the exams, they undertake three months of intensive revision. The study involved MRI imaging of their brains (which shows up the volume of different parts) before and after this three-month period and in addition some of the students were scanned again three months after that. They were compared with matched students who were not involved in a pre-exam study period. There were substantial changes in the structure of posterior hippocampus (which we have already mentioned has a pivotal role in the formation of explicit memories) and parietal cortex. In the hippocampus, the grey-matter volume had increased relative to baseline when measured immediately after the exams and had further increased three months later, whereas there was no change among the control group. In the parietal cortex there was a bilateral increase in grey matter evident immediately after the exams. This study supports the belief that learning itself involves changes in the gross structure of the brain.

The mechanism for neuroconstructive specialization of particular areas of the brain presumably involves the strengthening of the effective inputs by frequent activation. This strengthening could involve all or some of: changes in efficacy of existing synapses; changes in the number of synapses; and changes in the efficacy or number of nerve fibres in transmitting information. It could also possibly involve changes in the number of functional neurons through the inward migration of new neurons – neurogenesis.

The possible role of newly born neurons – neurogenesis

Neurogenesis and its possible relevance to learning and memory is a subject that has received a lot of attention in recent years. During the 1990s scientists became aware that the long-standing belief that the nerve cells in the adult brain had all been formed before or soon after birth was incorrect. Nottebohm[25] had actually already shown that new neurons were formed each spring in the 'song centres' of some songbirds, but this observation had been overlooked or not thought to have any relevance to mammals. It is now well established that new neurons are formed in the brains of mammals throughout life. Of particular possible relevance to memory is their formation within the dentate gyrus of the hippocampus – an area that can be regarded as the 'gateway' into the explicit memory-forming area. They may play an important role in humans even though their rate of formation is much slower in 'higher' mammals than in rodents, which is where their role has been extensively studied. Many of the new neurons die but some become incorporated into neuronal circuits. They are particularly good candidates for being involved in LTP since they are more excitable than older neurons (partly because they are excited rather than inhibited by the inhibitory transmitter, GABA). It has been found that blocking neurogenesis impairs learning of hippocampal-dependent tasks and that factors that impair memory such as stress, sleep deprivation, poor diet and ageing all reduce neurogenesis. Furthermore, learning itself and factors that appear to improve memory, such as exercise, actually promote either survival or birth of new neurons through the action of brain-derived neurotrophic factor (BDNF).[26]

Retrieval of Information

We introduced early on in this chapter the notion that memory involves first encoding, then storage and then retrieval. We have an enormous amount of information stored in long-term memory, but how do we gain access to it? Alan Baddeley proposed that retrieval takes place independently from episodic, semantic and perceptual memory. We will all be familiar with the tip of the tongue phenomenon – we know the name of something, yes we know we know, but we cannot produce it. Later, when we have stopped thinking about it, the word comes to mind. Computational models provide explanations both of how we retrieve and also of how we fail to retrieve memorized information. The more elaborated the schemas in which we embed information, the easier they are to recall because there are more cues that will activate the schema. The fact that it is names that we have particular difficulty in remembering is just because these are 'one-off' words that very often have no particular connection with anything else. A doctor I knew well used to find names particularly difficult: when a patient entered her consulting room she would recognize them and be able to say 'ah yes, you live at 2 Laburnum Road, your 2-year-old daughter had measles last year, your husband works at British Leyland – but please remind me of your name'. All that information was stored related to the patient's face, skin, gait etc., but the name was somehow not related to those and so could not be retrieved. So when we need to remember a name it is important that we embed it in a more complex schema.

Factors that Affect Memory

Sleep

Most of us are well aware that when we are short of sleep we tend to be bad-tempered or even depressed and find it hard to concentrate. This is of course true of children too. So it is obviously important that school children and university students should get adequate sleep if they are to maximize the profitability of their education. Additionally, a regular life pattern (including going to bed and getting up at roughly the same time each day) is important since an irregular pattern disturbs the basic circadian (about 24 hours) rhythm of the body. This rhythm includes sleep stages and hormone levels in the blood as well as other physiological functions that wax and wane regularly. There is a large amount of evidence implicating the importance of sleep for the consolidation of memories – both explicit and procedural memory (for a review see Diekelmann and Born[27]). One factor that has been explored is whether different sleep stages might be relevant for the different sorts of memory.

During the night, sleep consists of several cycles lasting around 90 minutes, containing a sequence of different stages of sleep. These different stages are characterized by different patterns of electrical activity, as recorded from electrodes applied to the scalp in the electroencephalogram (EEG). In each cycle, there are stages 1, 2, 3 and 4 which involve the change from light sleep at the start of a cycle (stage 1) through stages of increasingly deep 'slow wave sleep' (SWS). SWS is characterized by large slow waves which pass across the brain, starting in the neocortex, occurring less than once per second (hence the name). This is followed by a period of rapid eye movement sleep (REM sleep) which seems to be particularly associated with dreaming, as more dreams are reported when people are awoken from REM than from SWS. REM sleep is often called paradoxical sleep because the EEG recorded looks like the EEG in an awake person even though it is a very deep sleep and the main part of the body is particularly relaxed. As the night progresses, there is less SWS and more REM sleep. Diekelmann and Born propose that SWS is particularly important for the consolidation of explicit memory and maybe REM sleep is more important for procedural memory. However, it also appears that SWS may be important for consolidating procedural memories that have been acquired explicitly. It has also been suggested that it is actually the cyclical production of SWS followed by REM sleep that is relevant to the consolidation of memories.

The experiments on consolidation of memories have involved teaching people things and then testing memory at various times afterwards with or without intervening sleep. A very different experiment that supports a role for SWS, which hit the headlines when it was published, involved seeing whether artificially inducing slow waves like those in SWS could boost the retention-promoting effects of SWS.[28] This was done by applying transcranial electrical stimulation at the same frequency (one every 45 seconds) as naturally occurring slow waves for 5×5 minute applications (separated by one minute) during the time when the person was in SWS. Transcranial stimulation is a simple non-invasive procedure that involves delivering weak electrical pulses through electrodes applied to the scalp. This did indeed boost the effect of sleep for memory of word pairs in 13 students – a declarative task.

It does, however, appear that neither SWS nor REM sleep is essential in order to aid consolidation. In the daytime, even a nap of 6 minutes (much too short for the person to enter SWS) or, better, a nap of about half an hour, can improve memory of information (word lists) learnt just before sleep and tested one hour after learning.[29] In this experiment, although some of the students who were allowed to sleep for the longer period did show just a few minutes of SWS, there was no relation between whether this occurred or not and the memory effect. The effect of the naps was quite small but highly statistically significant – seven words remembered without the nap, eight for a 6-minute nap and nine for a 35-minute nap.

Another interesting possibility is that sleep is involved in acquiring insight. Many people can remember personal instances of when they went to bed thinking about a problem and woke up in the morning with a partial or complete solution. Furthermore, sleep may have a role to play in creativity. Some artists have used the content of dreams to inspire their creativity (e.g. Alfred Kubin, see Chapter 9). The role of sleep in insight has been investigated in a well-controlled study by Wagner and colleagues,[30] described in the enticingly named paper 'Sleep inspires insight'. This was an experiment on the effect of sleep on the emergence of an implicit memory. They presented participants with a sequence of numbers which had to be transformed according to simple rules. Hidden within the sequences presented was another rule which allowed the solution to be attained more efficiently and hence faster. Sixty-six participants carried out the experiment. Of these, 22 slept afterwards from 23.00 to 07.00 and were then re-tested; 22 were kept awake during that period and then re-tested; 22 were trained and tested during the daytime without intervening sleep. They found that 13 out of 22 (59%) of those who slept after learning had gained insight into the hidden rule eight hours later whilst only 5 out of the 44 in the control groups (11%) had gained insight. The controls showed that the effects were not just due to circadian effects, i.e. performance being generally better at certain times of day. This work has been followed up by Wagner's group and it appears that the restructuring involved in gaining insight for that task occurs during SWS rather than during REM sleep.

The importance of SWS is again emphasized when we consider the sequence of events in the formation of long-term memories. Firstly, synaptic changes (facilitation and depression as appropriate; LTP and LTD) might be facilitated by the slow waves making neurons more excitable. System changes, involving the interaction between different parts of the brain, are at a later stage involved in the 'dialogue' between hippocampus and neocortex, whereby memories originally relying on the hippocampus are transferred to the neocortex and become hippocampus independent. This feature of consolidation apparently takes place during SWS.

There is some evidence that the effects of sleep may be linked to the actions of hormones whose release is linked to the sleep stages. During the first SWS episode there is a surge of growth hormone release from the anterior pituitary gland. In the later part of sleep there is a rise in plasma cortisol (caused by the action on the adrenal cortex of ACTH released by the pituitary). There is recent evidence that growth hormone plays a role in the consolidation of declarative memory during sleep.[31] Work on rats[32] demonstrated a possible mechanism for the effect of growth hormone via a strengthening of LTP in the hippocampus. Interestingly, raising cortisol levels during SWS (which is not what happens normally) impaired consolidation of hippocampus-dependent declarative memories, suggesting a possible mechanism whereby experiencing stressful events could impair memory.

So, in summary, there is ample evidence for the importance of slow wave sleep in consolidation of memories. The fact that SWS occurs predominantly in the early part of the night (the usual time for diurnal animals such as humans to sleep) emphasizes the importance that a sensible bed-time is likely to have for maximizing the learning potential of children and adults. Recent research[33] has shown that children who have a television in their bedroom obtain lower grades at school than those who do not have one. It is a reasonable assumption that as well as being distracted from homework, children with a television in the bedroom will keep themselves awake by watching it. The resulting sleep deprivation could be a contributory factor to their poorer performance.

The work suggesting that memory can be improved by even a short nap during the day might have relevance to the organization of the school day. Some primary schools do include a rest period after lunch and if this could improve the children's memory for what they had learnt before lunch, this would have obvious benefit.

Exercise

There is much evidence from human and animal work that exercise has a beneficial effect on cognitive function and general brain health. Most of the work in humans has been done on ageing populations and particularly those with neurodegenerative diseases (see Chapter 12). However, two recent papers have reported significantly higher memory scores in children (aged 9–10) who had higher fitness levels (measured as respiratory efficiency). The studies involve rather small numbers of children (around 50) but the groups were matched on relevant factors such as intelligence and socioeconomic status. In the first of these studies,[34] the authors measured aerobic fitness and the volume of the hippocampi and nucleus accumbens (an area used as a control since it is not thought to play a direct role in memory) with MRI. They compared recognition memory for items either encoded in a way that is known to activate the hippocampus (relational) or in a way that does not activate this area (item). The memory was for pictures which were either presented in groups of three or individually. The child was then presented with groups of three items and asked whether all three had occurred together before (relational memory) or whether any of the items had not been seen before (item memory). They found that the fitter children had larger hippocampi but similar sized nucleus accumbens and that they were more accurate at the relational memory task. There was no difference between the groups on the 'item' memory task. A second paper[35] also looked at relational and non-relational memory, using a different visual task, and again found a difference between fit and unfit children for the relational task only. These findings are interesting and suggest that the time is ripe for further research, particularly involving longitudinal studies, on the effect of exercise on cognition in children. The authors propose that public policy should move towards providing more fitness training in schools.

Historically, in Ancient Greece and indeed in grammar schools and public schools in Britain, exercise has formed an important part of the daily curriculum. In the school of the philanthropist and mill owner, Robert Owen, at New Lanark in Scotland, early morning dancing by all the children preceded instruction. A recent experiment by Pontifex et al.[36] on young adults showed that a bout of aerobic and resistance exercise produced improvement in working-memory tasks both immediately and after a 30-minute interval. This suggests that perhaps modern school children could benefit from exercise interspersed with lessons throughout the day. We know that British state-school children have less time scheduled for exercise than those in many other countries (see Chapter 11). If exercise for the young does improve cognitive processes this would argue strongly for the inclusion of more rather than less physical exercise in the curriculum. It is encouraging to hear British governments promoting more time for physical exercise in schools; however, the removal of minimum requirements for hours of physical education per week and the selling off of school playing fields are unlikely to help this worthy cause.

Exercise improves brain health in a number of ways: it increases neurogenesis (see above) via stimulating the levels of BDNF (brain-derived neurotrophic factor[26]), which increases new synapse formation. BDNF also stimulates vascularization of the brain, which will improve the survival of neurons. Exercise has a good indirect effect on the brain by reducing obesity and generally improving circulatory fitness, and improving the immune system.

We will discuss the experimentally demonstrated effects of exercise on older adults in Chapter 12 on ageing.

Diet

A few years ago there was excitement in the media about a report that dietary supplementation with fish oils, specifically because they contain omega-3 fatty acids, could improve children's behaviour and their reading and spelling.[37] We will discuss this briefly here because although the research did not look specifically at any effects on memory in humans, work on rodents has shown that deficiency of omega-3 fatty acids in the diet is associated with deficits in learning and memory. Furthermore, supplementation has been shown to increase hippocampal BDNF – and BDNF seems to be a common factor for the effects of learning and memory-promoting factors (see above).

It has long been known that at least some fat in the diet is essential for normal development and health. It was shown in rats in the 1930s that this was because some particular fatty acids were essential: those containing double bonds at particular positions. Synthesis of these cannot be carried out in the mammalian body and yet fats containing these double bonds are important components of the fats in cell membranes. In mammalian brain, DHA (docosahexaenoic acid) is the main omega-3 fatty acid in the membranes of cells and it is particularly concentrated in the brain in grey matter. The amount of grey matter in the brain increases during development and decreases during ageing. So it was a reasonable suggestion that diets deficient in the precursors to DHA (omega-3 fatty acids, particularly linolenic acid) might cause impaired brain function.

Omega-6 fatty acids, whilst also incorporated into cell membranes, compete in the synthetic pathway for DHA with omega-3s; therefore a balance between the two is important if optimal levels of DHA are to be produced. Omega-6 fatty acids are present in large amounts in vegetable fats and hence the high fat content of foods fried in such fats, which most fried fast foods are, leads to disproportionally high levels of omega-6 fatty acids which will depress the synthesis of DHA. Furthermore, since fats in maternal blood cross the placenta in pregnant women, and also enter breast milk during lactation, the diet of the mother has a marked influence on foetal and infant omega-3 fatty acid level.[38] The prediction is therefore that a maternal diet high in omega-6 fatty acids and low in DHA is likely to be detrimental to foetal and neonatal development. Work in humans has shown that supplementation of the milk given to bottle-fed babies, which usually contains medium to high levels of omega-6s, with DHA overcomes the detrimental effect of excessive omega-6 fatty acids in the milk. Helland et al.[39] showed (in a small sample) that this supplementation was associated with better visual acuity and higher IQ at 4 years of age.

The belief then is that the omega-3 fatty acids may be important for nervous system development and that their omission from the diet might lead to cognitive problems. The best source of omega-3s is seafood, particularly salmon. Hibbeln and colleagues[40] showed (in 11,875 pregnancies) that children whose mothers reported that they had consumed little or no seafood during pregnancy (less than 340g per week as recommended in the United States because of the risk of neurotoxicity from mercury contamination) had lower IQs and had lower scores on a number of measures of general behaviour at age 8 than those whose mothers had consumed more. This was an interesting finding and was based on over five thousand mothers' responses.

Of course, much more research is needed on the effects of these fatty acids on cognitive function, but routine supplementation with omega-3s via, for example, cod liver oil, as happened for children in Britain during and after the Second World War, might well be of considerable advantage.

There are two other types of dietary compounds that have been implicated in memory and other cognitive functions: choline, the precursor of the neurotransmitter, acetylcholine and also a constituent of cell membrane lipids (as phosphatidylcholine); and the flavonoids, which are present in tea, cocoa and many fruits, particularly berries. The flavonoids have been shown in rodents to have widespread stimulatory effects on pathways which are involved in increasing neuronal survival and maintaining brain plasticity. Studies in humans have mainly been directed to effects on the ageing process (see Chapter 12).

Summary

Classification of learning and memory

Non-associative learning:	Habituation
	Sensitization
Associative learning:	Classical conditioning: Learning that an originally neutral stimulus (e.g. a bell ringing) predicts an unconditioned stimulus (e.g. food).

	Operant conditioning: Learning that carrying out a particular action leads to reinforcement. Can be positive (e.g. food) leading to increased occurrence of the action or negative (something unpleasant) leading to reduction in the action.
Short-term memory (STM):	Short-term store lasting seconds (e.g. holding a telephone number whilst you dial it).
Working memory (WM):	Executive control, encompasses central executive which operates on briefly stored information, integrates it with long-term memory and directs attention.
Non-declarative/ implicit memory:	Memory revealed when it 'facilitates performance on a task that does not does not require conscious or intentional recollection of what was learnt'. **Priming:** Unconscious increase in attention to an apparently new stimulus if it, or a related stimulus, has recently been presented. **Procedural LTM:** Acquired slowly through much repetition. Can be learnt without conscious awareness of what is being learnt. Habits and skills are acquired first consciously but later performed without conscious attention e.g. serving a tennis ball.
Declarative/ explicit memory:	Learnt consciously; can be acquired in a single exposure. **Semantic:** Long-term memory for factual information. **Episodic/Autobiographical:** Long-term memory for personal experiences and events and their contexts.

- Factors that affect associative learning include the temporal contiguity of factors to be associated, stress (negative), surprise and salience (positive).
- Working memory can possibly be improved by extensive, adaptive training (e.g. *Cogmed*).
- The consolidation of memories is impaired by lack of sleep. It appears that slow wave sleep, occurring mostly in the early part of the night, is particularly involved in the consolidation of explicit memories.
- Exercise and physical fitness are associated with increased volume of the hippocampus, an area of the brain known to be actively involved in the formation of memories, and are related to better retention of contextual explicit memory.

- Diets containing enhanced levels of omega-3 fatty acids may improve general cognitive function which will include memory. Raised levels of omega-6 fatty acids, as present in most fried fast foods, impair the formation of DHA (the relevant compound in the brain) from ingested omega-3 fatty acids and may therefore impair cognitive function.

Educational applications

- Non-associative learning (habituation and sensitization) may have relevance to avoiding boredom and raising anxiety in the classroom.
- Short-term memory/working memory have limited capacity and develop throughout childhood. It is therefore important not to overload pupils, especially young children, with instructions in the classroom.
- Working memory is more predictive of later academic success than measurements of IQ. Thus any input that would improve working memory could have major implications in education. The commercially available *Cogmed* programme, which is 'adaptive' and very intensive, can apparently improve working memory and may have long-term advantageous effects on educational performance. It could be helpful for children identified as having poor short-term/working memory.
- It is emphasized that efficient knowledge storage and retrieval requires frameworks (schemata) into which to insert new knowledge.
- Frequently used information, such as multiplication tables, may be best learnt by rote – and stored in implicit procedural memory. Since procedural memory is relatively well developed even in young children, rote-learning, when introduced in an interesting way, can have a role in the primary school classroom. Procedural memory is separable from working memory and need not be disrupted by stress. This probably explains why, in the past, rote-learning was successful where failure was discouraged (negatively reinforced) by corporal punishment.
- Encouraging parents to get children to bed at a reasonable hour is likely to be important for consolidation of what they have learnt at school. The introduction of rest periods during the school day might also be beneficial.
- Research suggests that in children (as well as in the old, where there is more research evidence) physical fitness may be an important factor in maximizing explicit memory and maintaining hippocampal volume.

- Encouraging the adoption of a diet high in omega-3 fatty acids and low in omega-6 fatty acids may raise cognitive function and would be expected to aid memory – hence support for Jamie Oliver food.

References

1 Gray JA. *The Psychology of Fear and Stress*. 2nd ed. Cambridge, UK: Cambridge University Press; 1987.

2 Mackintosh NJ. *Conditioning and Associative Learning*. Oxford, UK: Oxford University Press; 1983.

3 Baddeley A. Working memory: Looking back and looking forward. *Nature Reviews: Neuroscience*. 2003;4(10):829–839.

4 Alloway TP, Gathercole SE, Pickering SJ. Verbal and visuospatial short-term and working memory in children: Are they separable? *Child Development*. 2006;77(6):1698–1716.

5 Kyllonen PC, Christal RE. Reasoning ability is (little more than) working-memory capacity? *Intelligence*. 1990;14(4):389–433.

6 Alloway TP, Alloway RG. Investigating the predictive roles of working memory and IQ in academic attainment. *Journal of Experimental Child Psychology*. 2010;106(1):20–29.

7 Goswami U. *Cognitive Development: The Learning Brain*. Hove, East Sussex, UK: Psychology Press; 2008.

8 Klingberg T. Training and plasticity of working memory. *Trends in Cognitive Neurosciences*. 2010;14:317–324.

9 Holmes J, Gathercole SE, Dunning DL. Adaptive training leads to sustained enhancement of poor working memory in children. *Developmental Science*. 2009;12(4):F9–F15.

10 Chein JM, Morrison AB. Expanding the mind's workspace: Training and transfer effects with a complex working memory span task. *Psychonomic Bulletin and Review*. 2010;17(2):193–199.

11 Owen AM, Hampshire A, Grahn JA, *et al*. Putting brain training to the test. *Nature*. 2010;465(7299):775–778.

12 Eysenck MW, Derakshan N, Santos R, Calco MG. Anxiety and cognitive performance: Attentional control theory. *Emotion*. 2007;7(2): 336–353.

13 Dew ITZ, Cabeza R. The porous boundaries between explicit and implicit memory: Behavioral and neural evidence. *Annals of the New York Academy of Sciences*. 2011;1224:174–190.

14 Squire LR, Kandel ER. *Memory: From Mind to Molecules*. New York: Scientific American Library; 2000.

15 Clare L, Jones RSP. Errorless learning in the rehabilitation of memory impairment: A critical review. *Neuropsychology Review*. 2008; 18:1–23.

16   Baddeley A. The concept of episodic memory. *Philosophical Transactions of the Royal Society, London, B.* 2001;356:1345–1350.

17   Tresselt ME, Mayzner MS. A study of incidental learning. *Journal of Psychology.* 1960;49:339–348.

18   Ausubel, DP. The use of advance organizers in the learning and retention of meaningful verbal material. *Journal of Educational Psychology.* 1960;31(5): 267–272.

19   Collingridge G. 1. Synaptic plasticity. The role of NMDA receptors in learning and memory. *Nature.* 1987;330(6149):604–605.

20   Bliss TV, Lomo T. Long-lasting potentiation of synaptic transmission in the dentate area of the anaesthetized rabbit following stimulation of the perforant path. *Journal of Physiology.* 1973;232(2):331–356.

21   Maguire EA, Gadian DG, Johnsrude IS, *et al.* Navigation-related structural change in the hippocampi of taxi drivers. *Proceedings of the National Academy of Sciences of the United States of America.* 2000;97(8): 4398–4403.

22   Sirois S, Spratling M, Thomas MSC, Westermann G, Mareschal D, *et al.* Precis of neuroconstructivism: How the brain constructs cognition. *Behavioral and Brain Sciences.* 2008;31:321–356.

23   Bruer JT. Critical and sensitive period primer. In: *Critical Thinking about Critical Periods.* London: Paul Brookes Publishing Company; 2001:3–26.

24   Draganski B, Gaser C, Busch V, Schuierer G, Bogdahn U, May A. Neuroplasticity: Changes in grey matter induced by training. *Nature.* 2004; 427(6972):311–312.

25   Goldman SA, Nottebohm F. Neuronal production, migration, and differentiation in a vocal control nucleus of the adult female canary brain. *Proceedings of the National Academy of Sciences of the United States of America.* 1983;80(8):2390–2394.

26   Cotman CW, Berchtold NC. Exercise: A behavioral intervention to enhance brain health and plasticity. *Trends in Neurosciences.* 2002;25:295–303.

27   Diekelmann S, Born J. The memory function of sleep. *Nature Reviews: Neuroscience.* 2010;11(2):114–126.

28   Marshall L, Born J. The contribution of sleep to hippocampus-dependent memory consolidation. *Trends in Cognitive Neurosciences.* 2007;11(10): 442–450.

29   Lahl O, Wispel C, Willigens B, Pietrowsky R. An ultra short episode of sleep is sufficient to promote declarative memory performance. *Journal of Sleep Research.* 2008;17(1):3–10.

30   Wagner U, Gais S, Haider H, Verleger R, Born J. Sleep inspires insight. *Nature.* 2004;427(6972):352–355.

31   Born J, Wagner U. Sleep, hormones and memory. *Obstetrics and Gynecology.* 2009;36(4):809–829.

32   Kim E, Grover LM, Betolotti D, Green TL. Growth hormone rescues hippocampal synaptic function after sleep deprivation. *American Journal of Physiology.* 2010;298(6):R1588–1596.

33 Borzekowski, LG, Thomas, N. Robinson, MD. The remote, the mouse and the No. 2 pencil. The Household media environment and academic achievement. *Archives of pediatric and adolescent medicine.* 2005;159(7): 607–613.

34 Chaddock L, Hillman CH, Buck SM, Cohen NJ. Aerobic fitness and executive control of relational memory in preadolescent children. *Medicine and Science in Sports and Exercise.* 2011;43(2):344–349.

35 Chaddock L, Erickson KI, Prakash R, *et al.* A neuroimaging investigation of the association between aerobic fitness, hippocampal volume, and memory performance in preadolescent children. *Brain Research.* 2010;1358: 172–183.

36 Pontifex MB, Hillman CH, Fernhall B, Thompson KM, Valentini TA. The effect of acute aerobic and resistance exercise on working memory. *Medicine and Science in Sports and Exercise.* 2009;41(4):927–934.

37 Richardson AJ, Montgomery P. The Oxford–Durham Study: A randomized, controlled trial of dietary supplementation with fatty acids in children with developmental coordination disorder. *Pediatrics.* 2005;115:1360–1366.

38 Innis SM. Dietary omega-3 fatty acids and the developing brain. *Brain Research.* 2008;1237:35–43.

39 Helland JB, Smith L, Saarem K, Saugstad OD, Drevon CA. Maternal supplementation with very-long-chain n-3 fatty acids during pregnancy and lactation augments children's IQ at 4 years of age. *Pediatrics.* 2003; 111(1):e39–44.

40 Hibbeln JR, Davis JM, Steer C, *et al.* Maternal seafood consumption in pregnancy and neurodevelopmental outcomes in childhood (ALSPAC study): An observational cohort study. *Lancet.* 2007;369(9561):578–585.

Chapter 3

Language
What Determines Our Acquisition of First and Second Languages?

> *Where have you putted my keys?*
> *Will you like eat cake?*
> *I am clever you*
> *He went to park and he saw beautiful flower*

Do these sentences 'feel right' to you? I am sure they don't, and I am sure that you did not reach that conclusion so quickly by explicitly considering the grammatical rules that have been violated. Your instant response that there is something wrong with the English structure shows that our use of the grammar of our first language relies on automatic, implicit memory[1] (see Chapter 2). If we have never been explicitly taught the grammatical rules that we use automatically, we will find it quite difficult to explain precisely what is wrong with those sentences.

In this chapter, we shall briefly consider the current theories of how the brain acquires language. We shall then present evidence concerning the environmental factors that affect this process. The level of language proficiency that a person reaches has important effects on how much that person can gain from education; conversely, the level of education a person has experienced will affect the sophistication of the language they can produce and understand. One of the major reasons for the educational disadvantage of children from deprived backgrounds is that they are likely to have been exposed to less talk and less complex language at home and

Education and Learning: An Evidence-Based Approach, First Edition. Jane Mellanby and Katy Theobald.

this has meant that their language comprehension and production is not as advanced as that of their more fortunate peers. This can impact not only on their oral communication but also on their acquisition of reading skills. We shall discuss whether it is important to acquire a first language early in life – that is, whether there is a critical or sensitive period after which implicit acquisition becomes more difficult or perhaps impossible.

The use of an implicit language-learning process for our first language assumes immersion of the child in the language, as will occur naturally in the home, at school and in society at large. An important question is to what extent this implicit process is or should be used in the acquisition of a second language. Obviously where a child is brought up from birth in a bilingual environment (usually with each parent speaking a different language), the process of acquiring the two languages will be similar. Where a child moves to a new country and attends a school in which their mother tongue is not spoken, s/he will be exposed to many hours of the new language each day and this can constitute immersion and hence presumably allow implicit acquisition of the new language. We shall consider whether there may be a sensitive period for this second-language acquisition.

Learning by immersion contrasts with learning through explicit teaching of the grammar and vocabulary of a second language in the classroom. We shall discuss empirical research on the question of whether it is advantageous to try to mimic immersion in classroom teaching and what the role of explicit grammar teaching should be. There is surprisingly little research concerning at what age it is most effective to start explicit teaching of a second language.

Acquisition of Our First Language

So, how do we acquire our first language? There are three differing views on the nature of this process: nativist, connectionist and neuroconstructivist. The nativist approach to first-language acquisition proposes that the motivation and facility to construct language is innate. Noam Chomsky[2] proposed his theory of universal grammar in 1965 – to a largely baffled audience, since the complexity of his oral and written delivery made the content indigestible. However, his theory has been made clearer and has been to some extent modified by Stephen Pinker in his book *The Language Instinct*.[3] According to Chomsky, the functionality of the human brain naturally includes a universal language acquisition device, or grammar module, which permits the implicit acquisition of the grammar of whatever language it is in which a child is immersed. This nativist theory proposes that the grammar module contains unlimited possible grammar rules and that exposure to specific language(s) leads to the suppression of those not encountered and the strengthening of those that form part of the language being acquired. There is evidence for a critical or sensitive period for first-language acquisition from a variety of situations. For example, if congenitally deaf children who are born to hearing parents are not exposed to sign language, they will invent a kind of language, 'home sign'. This does not have the complexity of a mature language but does quite well for communication and does contain its own consistent grammatical rules such as word order. We know from the study of well-documented and widely used sign languages (such as ASL, American Sign Language) that despite using a spatial rather than an auditory medium for communication, sign languages share all the general grammatical properties of spoken languages. In terms of specific areas of the brain activated by the languages, if they are acquired from birth they activate the same left-sided areas as spoken languages (whilst also recruiting a right-sided, presumably spatially related area as well).

An important 'natural experiment' is often referred to as evidence for the Chomskyan view of language acquisition: an isolated community of deaf people in Nicaragua produced a grammatically quite complex sign language amongst themselves without external instruction. It could be described as a form of 'pidgin' language. It was not anywhere nearly as grammatically complex as the 'creole' language which the young children of these people produced spontaneously from being exposed to this pidgin. Thus these children were able to generate a new, complex language without previous exposure to such a complex language.

Proponents of the Chomskyan view consider that the 'language acquisition device' may only be optimally active during early childhood; thus the language exposure must occur during this 'critical' or more likely 'sensitive' period for it to be switched on effectively. The connectionist view need not have this requirement.

The connectionist view of language acquisition was a direct challenge to the theory of an innate grammar module.[4] Connectionist models try to replicate the way that neural networks in the brain form from experience of naturalistic inputs. Connectionist language models are specifically designed to replicate patterns of human language learning and production. The idea here is that language acquisition occurs in a distributed network of neurons which are interconnected at 'nodes' whose weights (i.e. effectiveness) are determined by previous experience. The network 'learns' by extracting the most likely combinations from exposure to a large number of examples in ordinary speech. It is said to be able to represent the 'statistical structure' of the inputs it receives. Scientists have constructed computer models of connectionist networks and have 'fed' them an enormous amount of normal speech derived from immense databases of recorded language. The model has been shown to be able to reproduce over time some of the properties of the emergence of language in children – for example, the regularization of the past tense (e.g. 'went', then 'goed', then 'went').[5] It must of course be admitted that even when the properties of the units in the model are chosen to be similar to some of the properties of real neurons, the fact that the model can exhibit some of the properties of the acquisition of natural human language does not prove that human language acquisition actually works like that – it just shows that it could.

The more recent neuroconstructivist view of development (summarized in Sirois et al.[6]) views the adult brain organization as resulting from an interaction between innate biases in regional receptivity (e.g. the area that becomes auditory cortex is particularly suited to auditory input) and environmental input. According to this view, in early development most inputs will activate very widely distributed networks but, since certain brain areas are more receptive to certain inputs, over time the brain becomes modularized and thus a language 'module' emerges.

The main interest for us in the tension between the different accounts of how children acquire their first language lies in the relative importance that the theories give to the input to which the child is exposed: the connectionist and neuroconstructivist accounts give external inputs a more extended role during development.

Stages of language acquisition

Studies of first-language acquisition have mainly concentrated on the early stages, both of phonetics and of vocabulary and grammar acquisition. There are very detailed studies (usually of small numbers of children) that identify the order in which various aspects of language emerge, starting with the burbling and babbling, followed at around 2 years of age with the vocabulary spurt, then two-word 'sentences' (obeying the word order of the language to which the child is exposed, e.g. 'daddy chair', 'have milk'), then longer 'telegraphic' sentences lacking the function words (e.g. the, a etc., e.g. 'Johnny go park', 'Mummy make cake'). The natural development of children's language is evident from the way in which they unconsciously impose new morphological rules as they acquire them. For example, children will initially, and correctly, use individual examples of the past tense such as 'I went to bed'. As they acquire implicit knowledge of the past tense, they will then regularize this to 'I goed to bed', similar to that of the past tense of the majority of verbs in English. Later, the child will give up this process and rely on the stored memory for 'went'. The child is not of course aware of this imposition of rules – it is an implicit process that occurs automatically, interacting with stored memory. This sequence of events in the acquisition of the past tense is one of the features of language acquisition that emerges in connectionist computer models.

By the age of 4–5 years, it is generally considered that most children will have acquired fluent speech with correct grammar in the language to which they have been exposed. Nevertheless, there are big differences in the width of vocabulary and the complexity of grammar employed by children when they enter Nursery or Reception class at primary school (see later and Chapter 10).

Environmental factors affecting acquisition of first language

An individual's linguistic ability will impact almost every area of their life. When growing up, a child needs to be able to understand their teacher and the written materials provided at school. Many adults also interpret the complexity of a child's language as an indicator of their intelligence. Later on in life, linguistic skill can affect an individual's chances of passing university or job interviews and even making effective presentations at work. It is therefore important to understand how we can support children to develop their language skills as effectively as possible.

It is widely acknowledged today, not least by government, that, on average, children from lower socioeconomic status (SES) backgrounds start school with less developed language skills than their contemporaries from more advantaged backgrounds. The children from relatively deprived backgrounds use shorter sentences, have a more restricted vocabulary and their grammar is less complex. There is a wealth of evidence that children's early language development, in terms of both syntax and vocabulary, depends in part on the nature of the language input from their carers. Successive British governments have been concerned with the reasons for the educational disadvantage experienced by children from lower-SES homes and have tried to implement interventions, such as Sure Start, to overcome this (see Chapter 10).

The 'difference in language between those from high- and low-SES backgrounds was investigated by Basil Bernstein in the 1960s and 1970s[7] and led to his contrasting the 'elaborated code' used by the former compared with the 'restricted code' of the latter. At that time, this distinction was part of the teaching in teachers' training colleges. Nowadays we would probably regard such a distinction as 'politically incorrect'. He tested two groups of 16-year-olds: Post Office messenger boys from unskilled and semi-skilled backgrounds who had left school at 15 and a group from British Public Schools (that is, independent fee-paying schools). Bernstein was a sociologist, not a psychologist. His aim was not so much to study the structure of language used as to determine its different uses as a mode of communication and in the development of individuality. He concluded that the messenger boys were 'limited to a form of language which although allowing for a wide range of possibilities provides a speech form which discourages the speaker from verbally elaborating the subjective and progressively orientates the user to descriptive, rather than abstract, concepts'. He found that the messenger boys had a narrower vocabulary and that their syntax contained less complexity. One of the reasons that his work has been 'lost' or ignored is probably because of the realization that whilst the language of more deprived groups (such as many African Americans) differs from that of more advantaged groups (e.g. educated white Americans), their 'dialect' is not impoverished grammatically – it has grammatical rules, they are just different. The same is likely to be true of the language employed by the 'working-class' boys whom Bernstein studied. However, since the language of textbooks, literature, newspapers, scientific papers etc., and the language employed by most teachers, is the language of the more advantaged (i.e. standard English or American English), there is a need for all children to acquire this too. A most striking finding was that for messenger boys who scored in the upper ranges on non-verbal intelligence (IQ >115) there was a marked discrepancy between this score and their vocabulary score – the latter being much lower. In the boys educated at public school the scores were similar on the two tests. Amongst a total of 309 messenger boys tested he found that 20.7% would have qualified for grammar school on the basis of their non-verbal intelligence. That only a few of them actually went to grammar school would be because the 11 plus examination for grammar schools contained a large vocabulary section.

Children mainly acquire their language from interaction with their carers – most usually the mother (Figure 3.1) – at least before widespread use of day nurseries.

The relationship between mothers' speech in the home and children's speech in infancy and the relation of these to SES was investigated by Hart and Risley[8] and by Hoff/Hoff-Ginsberg and by Huttenlocher and colleagues (for a review see Hoff[9]). Hart and Risley made an intensive longitudinal study of 40 families chosen to represent the spread of

Figure 3.1   Interaction between mother and child. Photograph by Angela Luchianiuc/Shutterstock

American society: including some white, some black (matched for SES), distributed across upper, middle and lower SES. They used unstructured observation in the children's homes of one hour every month for two and a half years, starting when the children were 7 to 12 months old. They recorded a wide range of parental input, including the proportion of time that the parent was with the child, instances of the parent joining in with the child's activity, taking turns with the child, the number of words and the number of different words used, the mean length of each parental utterance (MLU) and the difference between this and the child's MLU, the number of responses to the child's initiatives, the number of repetitions and expansions of what the child said, the number of questions and the number of prohibitions (see Box 3.1).

They reported very large variations in language production by the parent and hence in language exposure of the child – a fivefold range in the number of different words (from 100 to 500 in an hour) and in the amount of 'active listening' by the parent (e.g. repetitions and expansions). They found that the relative measures of parental style – that is, when parents were ranked according to each measure in the study – were stable over the two and a half years of the study. They looked at correlations between SES of the parents and the parenting measures. Whilst the overall amount of interaction and the difference between parental and child MLU did not correlate, all the other measures did correlate significantly with SES. They found that SES was particularly strongly correlated with the number of words and the number of different words used (Pearson's $r = 0.57$ and 0.63) and strongly negatively correlated with prohibitions

---

Box 3.1   Examples of parental responses

Repetitions
Charlie.   *This is Charlie's box.*
Parent.   *Yes, that is your box.*

Expansions
Charlie.   *I want go playground.*
Parent.   *I would like to take you to the playground.*

Prohibitions
Don't touch that.
Shut up.

($r = -0.61$). Interestingly, whilst prohibitions were rare in the middle- and upper-SES groups, they constituted 20% of the parental utterances in the lowest-SES group. In other words, lower-SES parents were more likely to tell their children not to do something. Hart and Risley's findings of the importance of parental repetition and expansion of child language fitted well with some work carried out 20 years earlier by Nelson et al.[10] They used an intervention in which they introduced the process of re-casting and expanding a child's utterances and found that this was effective in improving children's syntactic development. In contrast, just introducing new sentences with different content but the same grammar did not improve the children's grammar. A further point in Hart and Risley's paper is that the children's IQ, measured with the Stanford–Binet test at age 3, correlated similarly with these measures. In view of the fact that this test contains verbal measures, this suggests that the amount of vocabulary input that the children had received from parents will have affected their IQ scores.

Hoff-Ginsberg[11] (1986) looked in detail at the relation between the language used by the mother (as principal carer) and children's syntactical development (see Box 3.2). The study used 22 children aged between 2 years and 2½ years at the start and recorded four 20–30-minute samples of mother–child conversation at two-month intervals over a six-month period. She found that both functional (that is, the purpose of the mother's utterance) and structural characteristics of the maternal language influenced children's language.

Box 3.2   The function of maternal speech

Hoff-Ginsberg showed that using 'real' questions (i.e. questions to which the mother did not already know the answer) and verbal reflective questions (e.g. if the child says 'Mummy breakfast', the mother replies 'yes, Mummy is eating her breakfast, isn't she?') was correlated with the growth of auxiliaries (modifying verbs such as the verb 'to be') per verb phrase in the child's speech. In contrast, acknowledgement of the child's declarative statements had a negative effect (e.g. 'I like teddy' 'Yes'). There were also correlations between the grammatical structure of maternal speech and the structure of the child's production. For example, noun phrases per utterance from the mother correlated with the same measure in the child, and Wh- questions (Why, Where When) from the mother correlated with auxiliaries per verb phrase (and nearly significantly with auxiliaries per noun phrase) in the child.

Hoff-Ginsberg[12] followed this up by looking at the role of language input in causing the social class differences in children's language attainment. In this study, she compared two groups of children (30 from a working-class background, but not impoverished) and 33 from a middle-class background. The children were selected to be at the stage when they were just beginning to combine words. They recorded conversation between mother and child in four different settings (mealtime, dressing, story reading and toy play) and found social class differences in all contexts. The main difference was seen in topic-continuing replies from the mother to child-initiated speech – that is, once again the finding that the incidence of the mother's extending the child's utterances was social class dependent and relevant to child language development (see Hart and Risley, above). Interestingly, even though there were these differences in mother/child language interaction, Hoff-Ginsberg did not find any class difference in mothers' attitudes to talking to children. Some years later, the author[13] further analysed these data to look specifically at vocabulary development. She was able to show, statistically, that the social class difference in vocabulary could be explained by the maternal language input as assessed by mean length of utterance and the number of word types and word tokens.

Huttenlocher et al.[14] also looked at the influence of mother's language on child language development. In this study they concentrated on the growth in vocabulary development in children aged 14 to 26 months and showed that it was related to the amount of maternal speech directed to them and to the number of different types and tokens of words spoken by the mother. They used the data to support a view of the importance of input for vocabulary development, which contrasted with a widely held view at the time that the wealth of a child's vocabulary was primarily a reflection of its 'ability to learn' – that it was an aspect of innate intelligence and would therefore not be susceptible to the influence of language experience. Indeed, even today, a vocabulary measure is often used as a surrogate for a full-scale IQ measure.

Huttenlocher and colleagues also studied the relationship between maternal and child language syntax. In 48 parent–child pairs with children aged around 54 months, they used video recording for two hours on a single occasion in the child's home and analysed transcripts of the tapes. From this they calculated language complexity of both parents and children as the proportion of sentences that had multiple clauses and as the proportion of noun phrases per utterance. They also measured children's sentence comprehension using a task with sets of three pictures from which the child had to choose, which corresponded to a sentence presented orally. A strong relationship was found between the mother's language complexity and that of both the child's language production and comprehension (14% of variance). An educationally important further study[15] showed the effect of the complexity of teachers' language on the development of language complexity in the children in their classrooms. For this study, they worked with 305 children in 40 different classrooms in 17 schools. They found, as expected, that children from lower-SES backgrounds used less complex language at the start of the study but they then found that growth in children's use and comprehension of complex language correlated with their teacher's input (r = 0.51, p < 0.01, having controlled for the children's initial language complexity). The authors concluded that 'This means that children from low-SES families, whose syntactic level is quite low at the beginning of the year, may grow as much or more than children from higher-SES families, if their teachers provide input comparable to or greater than the input in the higher-SES preschools'.

Huttenlocher and colleagues[16] have more recently carried out a very detailed longitudinal study of factors that affect language development in 47 children from 14 months of age up to 46 months. By statistically modelling the growth curves for lexical diversity, they supported Hoff's

2003 finding that the language input effect was responsible for the SES difference found.

To sum up so far: caregiver (usually mother's) language input is a strong determinant of child vocabulary and complexity of language. Lower-SES mothers speak less and use fewer types of words and less complex syntax in conversation with their young children. Consequently, children from lower-SES backgrounds tend to start school with a lower language level than higher-SES children. This can put them at a disadvantage as their textbooks and teachers' instructions may be in a more complex language that they find hard to understand. However, this difference can be overcome by experience of more complex language input from teachers. But this raises the question of whether this disadvantage could be overcome at any age by making sure that the teachers' input contains the more complex forms of language. Or is there perhaps a critical period for the acquisition of complex language?

Is there a 'critical period' for first-language acquisition?

The concept of critical periods in development was first proposed by H Spemann in the 1930s with respect to the embryonic development of the Amphibia. A critical period meant that if a particular factor was not present during a specific time window then development would not take place normally and the deficit would be irreversible – that is, presentation of the specific factor at a later time would not 'undo' the abnormality. A further aspect of critical period involved the effect of toxic substances – particular developmental stages were sensitive to factors which would not have detrimental effects outside the relevant time window. An example would be the effect of rubella in causing foetal abnormalities in human pregnancy if the mother contracted the illness during the first trimester; later on in pregnancy the foetus would be unaffected.

Critical periods have been shown to occur in a number of physiological and behavioural phenomena. Probably the best known are in the development of binocular vision in cats and monkeys and in imprinting behaviour in birds such as hens and geese: newly hatched chicks and goslings will follow the first moving object that they see. Normally this would be their mother but they can become imprinted on humans or even inanimate objects that move.

Konrad Lorenz was the first to study critical periods in the development of behaviour. He observed the process of imprinting in geese: goslings would follow the first moving thing that they saw after hatching, even if this was a human being (i.e. Lorenz himself: Figure 3.2). This behaviour

Figure 3.2 The zoologist Konrad Lorenz, followed by goslings imprinted on him. Photograph by Thomas D. Mcavoy/Time Life Pictures/Getty Images

was firmly entrenched and they would not transfer allegiance to a goose if they were introduced to her later – demonstrating that this behaviour had a critical period.

In the typical adult brain, different cortical areas are activated in response to sensory inputs of different modalities; for example, the auditory cortex is activated in response to a new noise but not in response to a new texture. However, in a newborn child the responses of cortical areas are not modality-specific and, for example, visual or auditory stimuli will cause activation across a wide area of cortex. During normal development of the sensory systems, experience with a wide range of sensory stimuli leads the sensory cortices of the brain to become specialized for their relevant input. However, if such stimuli are not experienced then the normal specialization does not take place; for example, if one eye is light-deprived, then it becomes functionally blind because the cortex of the brain has not developed normally. In kittens, this critical period lasts about six weeks. If the eyes have both been exposed to light up to this time then depriving one of light no longer affects the development. These external stimuli affect the development of the nervous system because the nerves from the uncovered eye, which are activated in response to the visual stimuli, compete to maintain functional connections on target cells with those nerves which are not being activated. Thus with repeated activation and successful competition the connections from non-stimulated nerves (e.g. those from an eye kept in darkness) cease to function. Under normal circumstances, the presence of light would simply have a permissive effect for the normal development of the visual system, whilst in congenitally blind or deaf individuals the existing sensory input will continue to activate both its own sensory cortex and that normally occupied by the other input.

It was these seminal experiments that paved the way for the belief that there were likely to be critical periods for the acquisition of many sorts of skills in humans and hence that this could be relevant with respect to when we should teach what to children. However, whilst such 'critical periods' may exist for basic biological functions, the periods when humans can most easily acquire higher-level skills are likely not to be rigidly determined – and it is probably better to think of them as sensitive periods[17] or as times with differing sensitivity to different inputs. It is interesting to note that the original embryological meaning of 'critical period' has been thoroughly hijacked by the human behaviour story – if you look it up in Google, you will be directed to masses of information about human behavioural, particularly language, development.

Almost all children are exposed to language from birth by their caregivers. It would not of course be ethical to carry out experiments on the effect of language deprivation in infancy in order to see whether there is a critical period for first-language acquisition. The tragic stories of the rare children, such as Genie,[18] who were deprived of language in childhood supports the belief that grammatical development requires input during the early years. One group of children that may be deprived of language input during infancy are those who are born deaf and whose hearing parents do not use sign language. Often because deafness is not recognized early, such children may not encounter sign language until they are 5 or 6 years old. Studies of such children have shown that when they do come to learn sign language, whilst they have little problem in acquiring vocabulary, early language deprivation means that the acquisition of grammar is less good. This has led to the conclusion that the acquisition of vocabulary is not time-limited in childhood but that there probably is a sensitive period for the acquisition of grammar by implicit learning. The evidence comes from fairly small studies, since congenital deafness is rare and many such children will be exposed to sign language in infancy. Those who are not tend to come from societies who disapprove of sign language; (indeed there are several local authorities in Britain who strongly discourage its use in deaf babies for fear of causing confusion with later language learning either through the aural route with cochlear implants or through lip reading). The proposed sensitive period for grammatical acquisition probably closes sometime around puberty. This could therefore mean that it will be particularly difficult to get children to develop full grammatical understanding and production if they are not exposed to it early enough. For language exposure to be effective, it of course requires the child to attend to it; a good way to ensure this is for the child to be interacting with an adult who may elaborate the child's utterances. The work on young children has shown that a child expands its grammatical repertoire when the parent expands the child's own utterances or rephrases them with the same content (see earlier). Thus passively watching/listening to television probably does not achieve the same goal as interacting linguistically with a carer or teacher. And if a child with poor language comprehension sits in a classroom and hears constructions that s/he does not understand s/he is likely not to listen, just to switch off. So active intervention will be needed to improve the child's language development. And it is of the utmost importance that a child's language has reached a level where s/he can understand textbooks and what senior teachers are saying by the time s/he enters secondary school.

One type of sentence that is particularly important in science and history for example (and actually in life in general) is complex conditionals: 'What would have happened if Hitler had not invaded Poland?'; 'If you mixed potassium with water would it ignite?' Understanding conditionals requires hypothetical thinking. Even some adults find this difficult. For example, Evans et al.[19] investigated this in 160 university students and related this to 'intelligence' (as measured by AH4; Heim 1970[20]). They showed, using 'concrete' examples, that a proportion of the students with lower measured 'intelligence' interpreted conditionals of the form 'if p then q' as meaning the opposite, 'if q then p'. We do not know whether this demonstrates a direct limitation caused by poor working memory, since the questions require information to be held in working memory and manipulated (and we know this ability is related to measures of intelligence; see Chapter 5) Alternatively, it could be a purely linguistic limitation, resulting from the student's not having acquired the use of the conditional. It is also possible that the two are related in that the ability to acquire the conditional may be dependent on the development of working memory. Elena Svirko[21] has recently carried out a

> **Box 3.3**   Type 3 conditionals
>
> A type 3 conditional is a sentence about something in the past e.g. *'if you had put the kettle on, we would have been able to have tea'*; or *'if you had not put the kettle on you would not have burnt your hand'*; or *'if you had not dirtied your boots the carpet would not have been muddy'*).

longitudinal study on 128 children over a period of four years (from age 5) in which she has measured the acquisition of complex grammar, in particular reversible passives and type 3 conditionals (see Box 3.3).

Linguistically, type 3 conditionals are considered to be the most complex type of conditional. Children do not produce complex conditionals early and it has been shown[22] that young children are much more likely spontaneously to produce simple conditionals concerning future rather than past events. Interestingly, children even as young as 3[23] can, however, demonstrate *understanding* of hypotheticals, even counterfactual ones, where they are acted out in front of them with toys. Svirko tested children's ability to *produce* type 3 conditionals using a repetition test where the tester reads out a sentence to the child who simply has to repeat it exactly. It has been shown[24] that in order to do this, the child needs to reconstruct the sentence. If s/he has not yet acquired the relevant grammatical structure then s/he cannot do this accurately and rather than saying 'if you had not put the kettle on, you would not have been burnt' may say something simpler such as *'if you put the kettle on, you will be burnt'*, or for 'if you had not dirtied your boots, the carpet would not have been muddy' 'if you *would have* not dirtied your boots, the carpet would not be muddy'. These examples show that whilst the child apparently can understand the hypothetical concepts s/he incorrectly reconstructs the verb. In the second case, where the child makes the verb in the conditional clause the same as that in the consequence clause, Svirko argues that the child is on the way to acquiring the conditional but has not yet got the full structure. She found that by the end of year 2 in primary school (age 6) there was wide variation in whether children were able to produce type 3 conditionals. Thus 32% could do this in Year 2, and this had risen to 68% by Year 4. However, a further study of Year 7 pupils showed that even at age 11, not all children had acquired this sentence structure. Importantly, she found that acquisition of these grammatical forms in Years 2 and 3 predicted how well the children performed on tests of spelling and reading comprehension in Year 4 and also predicted mathematical performance in problems presented in words e.g. 'if John has four sweets and he gives two to Mark, how many sweets has he now?'. Further work on this cohort of children has shown that the early acquisition of the conditional predicts reading comprehension in Year 6 (age 10 years). In this study, the above predictions were statistically significant even when non-verbal intelligence had been controlled for. So it was not just that 'brighter' children had better grammar and were better at literacy and numeracy; their previous level of grammar acquisition also contributed. This finding suggests that it would be advantageous to detect which children may be falling behind in the acquisition of complex grammar early in primary school and to devise ways of helping them to acquire it.

Can we improve children's mastery of their first language?

So what should we be doing to improve children's linguistic ability, both their vocabulary and their grammatical production and understanding? One apparently obvious solution lies in teaching grammar explicitly. Many British children are typically not taught English grammar explicitly. Knowing the names of different tenses and parts of speech is probably not of great value in terms of understanding content. However, awareness of the grammatical structure of language might be expected to help comprehension. Typically, children in schools in France, the Netherlands, Germany and many other European countries are taught explicitly about the structure of their language. Most British children will only encounter a fully developed concept of grammar in their modern language lessons. As we mentioned in Chapter 1, a common feature of many past educational systems, including those of Ancient Greece and Rome, medieval monastic schools, and fifteenth-century and later grammar schools, was emphasis on the understanding of the structure of language. Educationalists in nineteenth- and early twentieth-century Britain considered the teaching of Latin to be important in acquiring this linguistic understanding and indeed it was thought that the rote-learning followed by the use of this knowledge to translate and to write Latin prose and poetry was an important endpoint of education. Would the reintroduction of Latin into the British school curriculum help with children's understanding? Learning grammar through the study of Latin has several advantages over learning it during English lessons. Firstly, Latin is an almost entirely regular language and illustrates all the grammatical forms present in English. Because it is not a living language, the emphasis in teaching can be on language structure and how this leads to meaning. At the same time, it can be easier to make this interesting (a sort of logical detective work) than just parsing passages in English which, when you already understand the passage, seems like a big waste of time. Furthermore, because pupils are not learning the language for purposes of practical application, they are less likely to be distracted by wanting to know how to write an email or order a sandwich in the language. It can be argued that composing Latin, requiring the formation of structures based on rote-learnt grammatical knowledge (*mensa, mensa, mensam, mensae, mensae, mensa; hic, haec, hoc*) is a task requiring extensive use of working memory and it is therefore possible that doing this might actually increase working memory (see Chapter 2). At any rate, EL Thorndike (at a time long before the research identifying working memory) actually carried out a study in 1901 to see whether learning Latin improved performance in mathematics or science. He found that it didn't and based on this and subsequent research put forward his theory of transfer – that for there to be transfer between tasks, there has to be some commonality of content. He argued that there is not much in common between Latin and science and mathematics apart from some scientific words derived from Latin. During the early part of the twentieth century, many other studies were carried out in schools on the effect of Latin teaching on reading, spelling and comprehension. These mainly showed positive results (for a review see Douglass and Kittelson[25]). However, after the Second World War, the importance of Latin was doubted in the context of the drive for more 'relevant' (to everyday life) subjects to be taught in school. Once Oxford and Cambridge universities abolished their requirement for undergraduates to have a qualification in Latin (Oxford: 1960 for scientists, 1970 for arts students), it became very much a minority subject in British schools, taught only in some selective grammar schools and in independent schools. However, in the United States in the 1970s, a considerable number of studies in schools were undertaken to see whether Latin learning had positive benefits on language and literacy (see Masciantonio[26] for a review). Most of these studies controlled for intelligence between the Latin and non-Latin groups and in many cases involved quite large numbers of pupils (hundreds to several thousands). Most of them showed positive effects. However, the majority were only published in reports rather than in widely available journals and so the work was not widely disseminated and is therefore almost inaccessible today.

The possible advantageous effects of teaching Latin have more recently been investigated by Haag and Stern[27] in Germany. They did not obtain positive results. However, it should be noted that German, the native language of their participants, has a much more rule-based grammar than English and so the benefits of learning a rule-based language such as Latin would not necessarily be additive. Interestingly, Haag and Stern actually found that Latin was detrimental to the learning of a third language, Spanish. They suggested that this supported Thorndike's theory of transfer because whilst Latin is a highly inflected language (endings denote tense and case), Spanish depends more on word order and the insertion of prepositions.

Almost 20 years ago, we tested an intervention aimed at improving secondary school children's explicit understanding of grammar by teaching a course in simple Latin to 11-year-olds in a comprehensive secondary school. The teaching of Latin in schools was regarded by many teachers as an 'elitist' area of study not relevant to the current way of life. We chose to introduce Latin, rather than, say, German, on the very grounds that we were not teaching it in order to aid communication directly (to teach the child how to buy a bun from the baker) but to produce awareness of the structure of language. We hypothesized that this should help understanding of complex language, and thereby should improve verbal cognitive ability. The Latin teaching was delivered to three of the school's parallel mixed ability forms of 11-year-olds by the children's usual English class teacher over nine sessions and was based on the Cambridge Latin Course (Cambridge University Press). The teaching also included some work with word webs and relating the words to Latin roots and some simple instruction in deducing meaning from short paragraphs of information. The children were tested on verbal, quantitative and non-verbal reasoning (CAT[28]) and on reading before and soon after the intervention. The other three forms, the control group, received the regular humanities teaching. The main finding was that, for children who could already read well, the intervention did indeed produce a significant increase in verbal reasoning relative to no change in the control group. We did this intervention on two consecutive years on year 7 pupils. In the first, the classes were all mixed ability; in the second year they were put into sets according to reading age. The effect was greatest with the selected group of good readers. Table 3.1 illustrates the finding from the second study.

It can be seen that there was no significant increase in quantitative or non-verbal reasoning, thus showing that the result was not just a 'tender loving care' effect. However, there was no increase in children whose reading age was below their chronological age. A further finding was that nine months after the training, the reading level of the intervention group was significantly higher than that of their controls (rising to a mean standardized age score on single-word reading of 94.6 ($\pm$6.8) from 90.2

Table 3.1   The effect of a teaching programme centred on Latin on verbal reasoning

Group	VCAT gain	QCAT gain	NVCAT gain	n
Intervention	4.0 (±6.4)*	1.0 (±8.2)	0.9 (±6.1)	42
Controls	1.3 (±4.0)*	1.7 (±7.3)	2.3 (±5.8)	37

Cognitive Abilities Test: VCAT verbal CAT, QCAT quantitative CAT, NVCAT non-verbal CAT.[28]
* p < 0.02.

(±9.8) p = 0.027.). This preliminary study supported the idea that explicit knowledge of grammatical structure might promote educational achievement. Perhaps the most interesting result was that the children really enjoyed the Latin course and after it was finished they set up a Latin lunch club where they could learn more! We were not able to investigate whether the course had longer-term effects because for ethical reasons, as a result of its success, the course had then to be taught to the controls too.

A second approach to improving children's grammatical and vocabulary knowledge is simply to expose them to it in an interesting context and draw their attention to the structure used. This requires both identifying children whose language development is lagging behind and then devising methods for the remediation of the problem such as the use of extension and restatement of relevant types of sentence (see earlier re mothers' influence on language development). Such intervention will depend mainly on teachers, since in families where resources are short parents may simply not have the time to give to the child's language development. Furthermore, where the parent's own literacy skills are not very good, they may not be (or at least feel) capable of adapting their parent–child interactions. A further point is that governments who encourage parents to return to work once their children are a few months old when they cannot afford or find one-to-one childcare may be contributing to depriving the young children of the necessary one-to-one interaction needed to foster early language development. Also, it is often found that those families who are deemed most in need of help with their children's upbringing are often amongst the most reluctant to make use of it; uptake of programmes such as Sure Start is not always highest amongst the most deprived. If the educational achievement gap between children from lower- and higher-SES backgrounds is to be prevented from widening any further (see government papers), this discrepancy in level of language acquisition in the early primary school years must be urgently addressed in schools.

Teaching Second Languages

In 2004 the government made it optional to study a second language at GCSE in England and by 2009 the numbers of pupils taking these GCSEs had dropped by over a third. You might think this poor uptake of foreign language GCSEs at 16 in Britain indicates that learning another language is a difficult and unusual thing to do. Actually, across the world there are more bilingual than monolingual people and there are indeed many who can speak more than two languages fluently.[29]

The easiest way to become a native speaker in two languages is to be brought up from birth in a home where two languages are habitually spoken, usually by each parent speaking his or her native language to the child. In this case, the acquisition of both languages is like the acquisition of any first language – it is an implicit process. Children who are immigrants from another country will need to acquire a second language from the time of entry into their new country. Even though their native language is likely to continue to be spoken at home, they will be immersed in the new language when they go to school and with the new friends that they make. The evidence on whether it is better to learn a second language (L2) earlier than later (the age of acquisition effect) has mainly been addressed to these types of 'immersion' situations. We must realize, however, that this might not be relevant to teaching of L2 in the classroom. We have discussed above whether there may be a sensitive period for the acquisition of grammar of the first language by immersion. There has long been discussion in the literature as to whether there is also a sensitive period for the acquisition of L2.

Learning a second language by 'immersion'

It appears that in the case of Chinese or Korean children learning American English, such immersion is indeed more effective the younger it occurs; Johnson and Newport[30] showed that when the immersion takes place after the age of 3 years, even when people were tested at least 12 years later, the acquisition of English grammar is not perfect and there appears to be a linear relationship between age of exposure and level of acquisition during childhood. Chinese and Korean are very different languages from English (or from sign language) and do not have the sort of grammar that is found in English: there are no tenses or cases, for example. Thus one could argue that the Chinese or Korean child's brain has not been 'prepared' for the acquisition of this sort of grammar and the child in this respect is rather like the congenitally deaf child who as not been exposed to any language. This idea is in a way supported by a study by Birdsong and Molis[31] who showed, in children whose native language was Spanish, that there was no age of exposure effect for learning English grammar. Spanish has a grammar that is more like that of English. Thus Spanish has already pre-pared the brain for the acquisition of English grammar. This is only a speculation, however, and it may be that there is a different explanation, perhaps a social one, for the imperfect grammar of Chinese and Korean late learners of English. Birdsong and Molis's work suggests that, in prin-ciple at least, if both languages have a comparably complex grammar, a second language may be learnt by immersion to a high level at least up to early adulthood. After that, since many sorts of learning ability begin to decline, the lesser ability of older people to learn a new language may just be a further example of this general decline.

It appears that what is important for allowing the implicit acquisition of a second language after infancy is that the ability to acquire language grammar has already been 'switched on'. And this switch can be activated by any language with a grammatical structure, including sign language.[32] If a second language can be acquired implicitly after puberty, this suggests that the mechanism for language acquisition that is employed for the first language is still usable in adulthood – if one subscribes to the Chomskyan view, then the universal grammar module is still accessible. This has been tested with the use of artificial languages containing grammatical forms that are not present in the first language. These should not be learnt implicitly if the module is no longer accessible. Rothman[33] found that they could be learnt and this finding could be interpreted to favour the acces-sibility of the grammar production module. However, it can also be argued that learning some new sequences in an artificial grammar is surely a much simpler task than acquiring a whole new set of grammatical rules for an unfamiliar natural language. So the discussion as to whether there is or is not a 'sensitive' period for the acquisition of a structurally very different second language by immersion is not yet resolved.

Learning a second language in the classroom

However, the child of native English speakers, born in Britain and attend-ing an average British school, will not normally have the opportunity for full immersion in a second language. This child will be taught a second language in the classroom, with just a few hours of such teaching per week. A 'direct' method of teaching in the classroom would involve the teacher using only the new language. The idea here is that the teacher is trying in some sense to mimic the immersion situation, thus trying to initiate implicit learning of the new language. The question is then how much immersion is enough for implicit acquisition to occur? In international schools, where there will be a mixture of children from different nationalities, many subjects will be taught in a language that is not a child's native language. Additionally, s/he may make friends whose native language is that language. This exposure may well be adequate to constitute an immersion experience. But this is very different from the few hours per week exposure to L2 in an ordinary British school.

There are several questions that we need to ask about the teaching of L2. Firstly, should it be taught in the classroom as if it were the first language, i.e. without recourse to L1? In which case, does L1 in the classroom interfere with automaticity? Secondly, should grammar be taught explicitly and if so what role might metacognitive strategies play? Thirdly, does it matter at what age teaching is started – is earlier really better?

How should the second language be taught in the classroom?

In the 1980s the work of Stephen Krashen,[34,35] presented in several books designed for consumption by teachers, had a large influence on second-language teaching. He considered that the primary goal of such teaching was for people to be able to communicate orally in the second language; a secondary goal would be to read and write it. He made a clear distinction between language acquisition (an implicit process) and language learning (i.e. grammar) through the teaching of rules. His theoretical approach assumed that the language acquisition device (Chomsky) was still active into adulthood and proposed that a form of immersion acquisition could be produced in the classroom. His view was that for acquisition to occur, the nature of the teacher's input to the class was crucial. This speech should all be in the second language – that is, the teacher should not use the first language at all in the classroom. Secondly, this input needs to be comprehensible to the listener. This can be achieved in the early stages by using visual and other aids and language structure that is simplified in much the same way as the language we naturally use when talking to young children is simplified. Thirdly, the input needs to be of interest to the listener; otherwise s/he will simply switch off. I have seen this happen in many foreign language classes in school when the content of the teacher's speech is either incomprehensible or on a topic that the children find boring. Fourthly, and this is perhaps the main problem with this approach, a great deal of this comprehensible, simplified, interesting input is needed. Given these conditions, the student should automatically acquire competence in the target language. Since this method of acquisition is similar to the acquisition of a first language, correction by the teacher would be expected to be ineffective, as is found in that case. The role of any grammar teaching would be with respect to self-monitoring of language production and in literary work: in carrying out a translation, if a reader does not extract the meaning from a text automatically, s/he may require to apply grammatical rules in order to deduce meaning. Krashen's theoretical and practical approach to classroom teaching of foreign languages was hugely influential in the United States and United Kingdom and led to wide acceptance that in principle the teacher should use only the target language in the classroom.

However, there is really very little evidence to support the sole use of L2 in second-language teaching in the classroom. Ernesto Macaro[36] has looked at what actually goes on in the lessons and has shown that what appears to happen in the most successful classrooms is a mixture of first language (L1) and L2. He has argued that use of L1 should not interfere with acquisition on several grounds: within the mental lexicon, the L1 connections will be stronger than the L2 and so can be used to aid comprehension; and we know from experience that often the inner voice and private speech even in someone who is bilingual at a native level in both languages actually switches between languages.

However, there is to date not much research on the subject. Jacobs et al.[37] looked at whether teaching vocabulary by putting definitions into texts in either L1 or L2 made a difference to their effectiveness, and whether putting in such 'glosses' was more effective than having none. They found glosses in either language improved vocabulary knowledge when tested immediately, supporting the view that L1 intervention is not actually harmful. The effect was greatest in the most proficient students. Macaro looked at the question in the context of 159 Chinese native speakers learning new English words. He also found that using the first language whilst teaching the second did not do any harm to the process of learning new words.

The effect of correcting children's L2 grammar whilst they are speaking in the classroom was investigated by Dekeyser.[38] In theory, if the process of acquisition is implicit, then correction should not improve performance; if it is explicit, it should improve performance. The finding was that for a whole class, correction had no effect on outcome but that what it did for individual children depended on individual differences in the child's personality: the performance of the most proficient pupils, those who were extrinsically motivated and those with low anxiety improved with error correction, whilst performance of those with low proficiency and/or the opposite characteristics was unaffected or actually impaired. This result and that of Jacobs et al. have little bearing on the implicit/explicit controversy but do prompt suggestions with respect to classroom practice.

At what age should second-language learning in the classroom start?

We still do not know the age at which it is best to start teaching a second language: whether we should start as early as possible or wait for children to reach a higher level of cognitive maturity. It seems that if there is some element of implicit learning, then earlier would be better. However, if explicit grammar rule teaching is involved then it would seem reasonable to assume that older children would learn these more easily.

There are surprisingly few controlled studies of this subject. Victoria Murphy[39] has recently elegantly summarized relevant studies (in a book edited by Ernesto Macaro from the Department of Education in Oxford). Most studies appear to show that second-language instruction is most effective if started later rather than earlier. For example, Cenoz[40] compared English proficiency after 600 hours of English instruction in Basque/Spanish bilingual children who had started to learn English at 4, 8 or 11 years old. She found that the later learners were better on all measures of English proficiency (oral production, listening and reading comprehension, a cloze test based on the story of Little Red Riding Hood, and a grammar test). The results of this study and most others of a similar nature are, however, confounded by the different ages at which the children were then tested – in this case Year 2 of primary school for the youngest learners, and Year 2 or Year 5 respectively of secondary school for the two older groups. In any test situation younger children are likely to be at some disadvantage, partly because of their relative cognitive immaturity but also because they may have more difficulty in concentrating and will have had less experience of test situations. A similar caveat can be entered for a study by Garcia Mayo[41] which showed that children tested after the same number of hours of English teaching, 396 hours, and then again after 594 hours, performed better at both times on a grammaticality judgement test if they had started instruction at age 11/12 years rather than 8/9 years.

One study that has attempted to overcome this criticism was carried out by Larson-Hall[42] who tested 200 Japanese university students aged at least 18 years on English proficiency and asked them to provide information on when they started English lessons. She found that there was some advantage for those who had started at the youngest age but pointed out that the conflict between her study and the previous ones could be due to the much greater amount of teaching that these children would have received by the time they were tested at 18. We must also remember that the structure of the Japanese language differs profoundly from English (see earlier, re Chinese). Munoz[43] took a different approach and compared rates of learning English (again in a Basque/Spanish bilingual group) in children who started English at 8, 11, 14 or 18 years of age. Munoz found that the 14-year-olds learnt faster than the 11- or 8-year-olds. The oldest group (18+) initially showed a faster rate of learning but then slowed down relative to the younger groups. Overall, it appears that the view that earlier is better for classroom teaching of a second language is not supported with respect to proficiency. However, one finding that is of importance educationally is that children who experienced second-language teaching earlier were more motivated later to continue with the learning.

With respect to learning the grammar of a second language in adulthood, Macaro and Masterman[44] did a most interesting study on Oxford undergraduates. They selected a group of students who had obtained places to read modern languages including French, but who had scored poorly in the French language test for entrance. They attended an intensive course of learning French grammar explicitly before starting their university course. When they were tested at the end of this course it was found that they had improved in their ability to detect grammatical errors and to explain grammatical rules but there was no improvement in their ability to produce the French language. This supports a distinction between production as an automatic process and explicit understanding of rules, which is a conscious, controlled process that does not necessarily impact on the ability to speak the language. The experiment of course also illustrates that young adults are well able to learn grammatical rules explicitly.

Acquiring the correct accent of a foreign language

One further aspect of second-language acquisition concerns the accent of the speaker. Some people seem able to learn a new language with a near-native accent whilst others find it more difficult. Anecdotal accounts appear to show that it is easier to get the accent right if you learn the second language earlier, at least if you are learning the language by immersion; and it is generally suggested that this is more effective if the new language is learnt before puberty. This anecdotal view has been supported by quite a lot of research on immigrant populations. Thus it is argued that for the implicit learning of the pronunciation of a new language, there may be support for a critical period hypothesis.

In contrast to this widely held view for language acquisition by immersion, Garcia Lecumberri and Galliardo[45] found that with classroom teaching, correct accent could be acquired more readily later. They carried out a longitudinal study on Basque/Spanish bilingual children learning English. Their three groups of 20 children were first exposed to English classroom teaching (around three hours per school week) at ages 4, 8 or 11 and were then tested 6 years later in each case. So the children were 9–11, or 13–15, or 16–18 at final testing. The authors looked at pronunciation as judged by a native English speaker and also looked at the children's ability to perceive the difference between sounds in English. They found that the older learners were judged as having more native-like English pronunciation and greater general intelligibility than either of the two groups of younger learners. For the perception test, the children would hear a monosyllabic word spoken (by a native English speaker) and would have to point to the appropriate one out of two pictures e.g. 'goat' and 'coat'. Those who had started learning at 4 or 8 years did not differ much but those who had started at 11 were significantly better than either of the earlier groups. Since these tests did not require sophisticated cognitive ability, the better performance of those who learnt later is unlikely merely to reflect greater cognitive maturity. This finding contrasts with the results of testing the ability of babies to discriminate between sounds. Kuhl et al.[46] found that whilst babies under 12 months can discriminate between many sounds that do not occur in the native language to which they are daily exposed, this ability has waned by the end of the first year. However, this ability was tested by observing habituation in babies which may be tapping into something very different from what is involved in the sound perception choice experiment.

It is a common observation that the nature of the first language seems to affect the ease with which a national accent can be eradicated from spoken English: for example, the Scandinavians and the Dutch are more likely than the Russians to speak accent-free, or almost accent-free, English. This may be related to the different way in which speech sounds are articulated in Russian as compared with most European languages. It also may be related to the amount of inadvertent exposure (as seen with

English in the Netherlands and Scandinavia, where a majority of the population can and do speak English, and English language television and radio are widely available). A reason that German and French speakers of English are more likely than Dutch or Scandinavians to retain their accent is probably because English language films in the Netherlands and Scandinavia tend to be subtitled only, whilst in France and Germany they are usually dubbed.

Summary

First-language acquisition

- The apparent inability to acquire grammar correctly of (the fortunately rare) children deprived of language until puberty has supported the view that there is a 'critical' or more correctly a 'sensitive' period for the acquisition of grammar in a first language. This view is supported by research on congenitally deaf children who have not been exposed to sign language until entering school or later. A sensitive period would mean that the Chomskyan language acquisition module loses its potency as children grow up. However, there is some evidence from the ability of adults to acquire grammatical forms not present in their first language implicitly that this may not be the case.
- Whilst by the age of 4, children will be using largely correct grammar (for the language or dialect to which they are exposed), there are wide variations in the complexity of their grammar and in their vocabulary. These differences are related to the linguistic exposure in their environment (at home and/or in daycare). On average, children from lower-SES status backgrounds enter school with lower language levels.
- Certain kinds of complex grammar, particularly the use of conditionals, are not fully developed in all children until at least the middle primary years.

Second-language acquisition

- The distinction between learning a second language by immersion and by classroom teaching needs to be widely appreciated. With immersion, the acquisition of the second language is implicit and automatic and hence might depend on use of the Chomskyan grammar module. With teaching, it is likely to be explicit and will only become automatic with much practice.

- There is evidence that with immersion in a second language (for example, for immigrant children to a country with another language at school and in the community), younger is better, at least for very dissimilar languages (such as Chinese and English). For rather similar languages, such as Spanish and English, it is possible that age of acquisition may not be relevant.

Implications for educators

First-language acquisition

- There is a need for the teaching of more complex grammar and wider vocabulary at an early stage in primary school education to help overcome the linguistic disadvantage that many children from lower-SES homes demonstrate. If teachers are aware of this need then they can supply the necessary interactive input.

    It is likely that extending and expanding the children's own utterances may be the best way to introduce new grammatical forms.

- The realization of this linguistic disadvantage is behind the last Labour government's introduction of checklists on behaviour including verbal development for childminders and nursery schools (see Chapter 10). The problem of course with such extensive checking procedures is that they take up teachers' and carers' time which could perhaps be more profitably used in direct interaction with the children.

Second-language acquisition

- An interim conclusion concerning the best age at which to introduce second-language *teaching* seems to be that it probably doesn't matter much in terms of eventual proficiency. It could therefore be argued that second-language teaching in primary school will take up a lot of valuable time which might be used to more advantage teaching other things. On the other hand, some familiarity with the concept of other languages probably ought to be introduced in primary schools, possibly by playing games to acquire vocabulary and learning useful phrases by rote (see Chapter 2) and perhaps listening to recorded speech to familiarize the children with the sounds of a different language.

- In order for a clear educational policy concerning the age at which second-language teaching in the classroom should be introduced, robust, carefully controlled longitudinal studies of the age at which classroom teaching is most effective for ultimate performance are needed. However, it is difficult to set these up for both ethical and practical reasons.

- Where the teaching involves explicitly introducing the rules of grammar, this probably is best taught in secondary school when the children are more cognitively mature.
- It appears that use by the teacher in the classroom of the first language as well as the second language is not detrimental to second-language learning.

References

1   Ullman MT. A neurocognitive perspective on language: The declarative/procedural model. *Nature Reviews: Neuroscience*. 2001;2:717–724.

2   Chomsky N. *Aspects of the Theory of Syntax*. Cambridge, MA: MIT Press; 1965.

3   Pinker S. *The Language Instinct*. London: Penguin Books; 1994.

4   Plunkett K, Davies M. Theoretical issues in the study of language. *Language & Cognition*. 1996:1–6.

5   Plunkett K, Juola P. A connectionist model of English past tense and plural morphology. *Cognitive Science*. 1999;23:463–490.

6   Sirois S, Spratling M, Thomas MSC, Westermann G, Mareschal D, *et al*. Precis of neuroconstructivism: How the brain constructs cognition. *Behavioral and Brain Sciences*. 2008;31:321–356.

7   Bernstein B. *Class, Codes and Control*. 2nd ed. St Albans, UK: Granada Publishing; 1973.

8   Hart B, Risley TR. American parenting of language-learning children: Persisting differences in family–child interactions observed in natural home environments. *Developmental Psychology*. 1992;28:1096–1105.

9   Hoff E. How social context support and shape language development. *Developmental Review*. 2006;26:55–88.

10 Nelson KE, Carskaddon G, Bonvillian JD. Syntax acquisition: Impact of experimental variation in adult verbal interaction with the child. *Child Development*. 1973;44(3):497–504.

11 Hoff-Ginsberg E. Function and structure in maternal speech: Their relation to the child's development of syntax. *Developmental Psychology*. 1986;22(2):155–163.

12 Hoff-Ginsberg E. Mother–child conversation in different social classes and communicative settings. *Child Development*. 1991;62:782–796.

13 Hoff E. The specificity of environmental influence: Socioeconomic status affects early vocabulary development via maternal speech. *Child Development*. 2003;74(5):1368–1378.

14 Huttenlocher J, Haight W, Bryk A, Seltzer M, Lyons T. Early vocabulary growth: Relation to language input and gender. *Developmental Psychology.* 1991;27(2):236–248.

15 Vasilyeva M, Huttenlocher J, Waterfall H. Effect of language intervention on syntactic skill levels in preschoolers. *Developmental Psychology.* 2006; 42(1):164–174.

16 Huttenlocher J, Waterfall H, Vasilyeva M, Vevea J, Hedges LV. Sources of variability in children's language growth. *Cognitive Psychology.* 2010;61: 343–365.

17 Bruer JT. Critical and sensitive period primer. In: *Critical Thinking about Critical Periods.* London: Pul Brookes Publishing; 2001:3–26.

18 Curtiss S. *Genie: A Psycholinguistic Study of a Modern-Day "Wild Child".* Boston: Academic Press; 1977.

19 Evans JStBT, Handley SJ, Neilens H, Over DE. Understanding causal conditionals: A study of individual differences. *Quarterly Journal of Experimental Psychology.* 2008;61:1291–1297.

20 Heim, AW. *Intelligence and Personality: Their Assessment and Relationship.* Harmondsworth, UK: Penguin; 1970.

21 Svirko E. Individual Differences in Complex Grammar Acquisition. DPhil Thesis, University of Oxford; 2011.

22 Kuczaj SA, Daly MJ. The development of hypothetical reference in the speech of young children. *Journal of Child Language.* 1979;6:563–579.

23 Harris PL. *The work of the imagination.* Oxford: Blackwell; 2000.

24 Lust B, Flynn S, Foley C. What children know about what they say: Elicited imitation as a research method for assessing children's syntax. In: *Methods for Assessing Children's Syntax.* Cambridge, MA: MIT Press; 1996:55–76.

25 Douglass HR, Kittelson C. The transfer of training in high school Latin to English grammar, spelling, and vocabulary. *Journal of Experimental Education.* 1935;4:26–33.

26 Masciantonio R. Tangible benefits of the study of Latin: A review of research. *Foreign Language Annals.* 1977;10(4):376–382.

27 Haag L, Stern E. In search of the benefits of learning Latin. *Journal of Educational Psychology.* 2003;95(1):174–178.

28 Thorndike RL, Hagen EP, Lorge I. Cognitive Abilities Test. 2001.

29 Bialystok E. *Bilingualism in Development: Language, Literacy and Cognition.* Cambridge: Cambridge University Press; 2001.

30 Johnson J, Newport E. Critical period effects in second language learning: The influence of maturational state on the acquisition of English as a second language. *Cognitive Psychology.* 1989;21(1):60–99.

31 Birdsong D, Molis M. On the evidence for maturational constraints in second-language acquisition. *Journal of Memory and Language.* 2001;44(2): 235–249.

32   Mayberry RI, Lock E. Age constraints on first versus second language acquisition: Evidence for linguistic plasticity and epigenesis. *Brain and Language.* 2003;87(3):369–384.

33   Rothman J. Why all counter-evidence to the critical period hypothesis in second language acquisition is not equal or problematic. *Language and Linguistics Compass.* 2008;2(6):1063–1088.

34   Krashen SD. *Second Language Acquisition and Second Language Learning.* Oxford: Pergamon Press; 1981.

35   Krashen SD. *Language Acquisition and Language Education: Extensions and Applications.* London: Prentice-Hall International; 1989.

36   Macaro E. *Continuum Companion to Second Language Acquisition.* London; 2010.

37   Jacobs GM, Dufon P, Hong FC. L1 and L2 vocabulary glosses in L2 reading passages: Their effectiveness for increasing comprehension and vocabulary knowledge. *Journal of Research in Reading.* 1994;17(1):19–28.

38   Dekeyser RM. The effect of error correction on L2 grammar knowledge and oral proficiency. *The Modern Language Journal.* 1993;77:501–514.

39   Murphy V. The relationship between age of learning and type of linguistic exposure in children learning a second language. In: *Continuum Companion to Second Language Acquisition.* London: Continuum International Publishing Group; 2010.

40   Cenoz J. The influence of age on the acquisition of English: General proficiency, attitudes and code mixing. In: *Age and the Acquisition of English as a Foreign Language.* Clevedon: Multilingual Matters; 2003:77–93.

41   Garcia Mayo ML. Age, length of exposure and grammaticality judgements in the acquisition of English as foreign language. In: *Age and the Acquisition of English as a Foreign Language.* Clevedon: Multilingual Matters; 2003: 94–114.

42   Larson-Hall J. Weighing the benefits of studying a foreign language at a younger starting age in a minimal input situation. *Second Language Research.* 2008;24:35–63.

43   Munoz C. Variation in oral skills development and age of onset. In: *Age and the Acquisition of English as a Foreign Language.* Clevedon: Multilingual Matters; 2003:161–181.

44   Macaro E, Masterman L. Does intensive explicit grammar instruction make all the difference? *Language Teaching Research.* 2006;10(3):297–327.

45   Garcia Lecumberri ML, Galliardo F. English FL sounds in school learners of different ages. In: *Age and the Acquisition of English as a Foreign Language.* Clevedon: Multilingual Matters; 2003:114–135.

46   Kuhl P. A new view of language acquisition. *Proceedings of the National Academy of Sciences.* 2000;97(22):11850–11857.

Chapter 4

Reading

How Do We Learn to Read and Why Is It Sometimes so Difficult?

Figure 4.1   Adult/child interaction in reading. Photograph by rSnapshotPhotos/Shutterstock

The acquisition of fluent reading ability is almost universally agreed to be an essential component of education. Reading is a particularly efficient method of communication, as it is much faster than speech and hence the need to learn to read is not obviated by the development of technology that converts the written word into speech. The outcome of successful reading is to extract meaning from printed/written text. In fluent readers, the process is automatic – we do not usually need to 'sound out' the letters

Education and Learning: An Evidence-Based Approach, First Edition. Jane Mellanby and Katy Theobald.
© 2014 John Wiley & Sons, Ltd. Published 2014 by John Wiley & Sons, Ltd.

MS 1275/28
Square notation, , The Hymn to St. John;
line beginnings are the origins of Ut-Re-Mi-Fa-Sol-La.

Figure 4.2   An example of a psalter used for singing psalms in churches. (The syllables of the words are related precisely to the notes of the music.) Reproduced with permission from The Schøyen Collection, Oslo and London (MS1275/28).

in words: we recognize them from long-term memory and predict them from our knowledge of syntax and the context, which speeds up the process. It is only when we meet an unfamiliar word that we may resort to sounding it out. However, in the process of learning to read, a role for first learning the sound of letters has been considered central for many generations, probably going back at least to the twelfth century: John of Salisbury (1115–1180) is attributed with promoting the order of learning: first the letters as shapes representing sounds, then syllables, then words, then phrases.[1] This view was strongly promoted during the second half of the nineteenth century and until the mid-twentieth century.

There is abundant evidence that the currently promoted practice of synthetic phonics involving first learning the sounds of 'c' and 'a' and 't' and then blending them together to make 'cat' is a successful way of starting to teach reading for most children. However, the central importance of phonics has been disputed. Indeed, there has been a very long-running disagreement between those who advocated teaching reading using larger units such as words and sentences and letting children deduce meaning from context, and those who favoured a phonological approach.[2,3] From the 1930s to the 1960s, the most widely accepted view was that the 'whole word' approach should be used for beginning reading and that phonics should only be introduced when sight reading of common words was well established. It is not clear where the pressure to use this method in place of phonics originated. It is reasonable to assume that it was based on two common observations: firstly, very young children can often be taught to recognize whole words; secondly, this is how fluent readers read. So why not teach this way from the beginning? Indeed, many parents bought flash cards with single words printed in a large font and proudly reported their 18-month-old's progress in 'reading' them. There are also many anecdotal accounts of individual children who have taught themselves to read through having memorized a story, word for word, having had it read to them many times, and then matching the whole word sounds with the written text. In the classroom, this 'look and say' method worked for some children, but for others it did not – and they remained puzzled by what they were supposed to be doing. Stuart, Stainthorp and Snowling[4] have shown that this early logographic 'reading' is not a necessary step in learning to read and success in it in the very early years does not predict better reading fluency later. At least with the phonic approach, the child rapidly discovers the concept of reading: the relation between the structure of a string of letters and a word. Furthermore, once reading is established, there is a reciprocal effect of reading on awareness of the sound of letters which of course further facilitates reading. Research in the 1970s had proposed a relationship between phonological awareness, that is, the ability to segment speech into syllables and phonemes, and reading acquisition.[5] In 1983, Peter Bryant and Lynette Bradley,[6] in Oxford, showed that reading could be predicted from pre-school children's awareness of onset and rime (that is, detecting that 'log' and 'light' start with the same sound or that 'pig' and 'fig' end with the same sound). Furthermore, they reported that teaching this skill improved the children's ability to spell. The recognition of the importance of phonological awareness in predicting reading success influenced the swing of the pendulum back from the whole word method to phonics teaching.

Box 4.1   Phonics

Rose:[8] 'Phonics consists of the skills of segmentation and blending, knowledge of the alphabetic code and an understanding of the principles which underpin how the code is used in reading and spelling.'

Synthetic phonics involves teaching the correspondence between letters and sounds, and then between phonemes and sounds. Phonemes may be single letters or combinations of letters, such as 'sh', 'ch', etc. The children learn to build up (synthesize) words from phonemes. An alternative has previously involved analytic phonics, where a child would be made aware of onset (first sound) and rime (end sound e.g. b-it, s-it etc.). This is a slightly different way of looking at phonology and is not the one recommended to schools at present. However, it was from looking at the predictive value for later reading of recognizing onset and rime and also the familiarity with nursery rhymes that Bradley and Bryant proposed the importance of phonological awareness for learning to read.

Ehri:[9] 'Systematic phonics is a method of instruction that teaches students correspondences between graphemes in written language and phonemes in spoken language and how to use these correspondences to read and spell words.' Phonics instruction is systematic when all the major grapheme–phoneme correspondences are taught and they are covered in a clearly defined sequence.

The majority of the content of this chapter concerns how children learn to read English. It must be emphasized that English is the most difficult of the European languages to learn to read because for the 26 letters of the alphabet there are about 200 different letter–sound correspondences. In contrast, there are very many fewer in 'transparent' languages such as Italian, Spanish or Finnish. (See Goswami[7(p346)] *et seq.*) The Rose Review,[8] itself based heavily on the American meta-analysis of reading research (NICHHD; National Institute for Child Health and Human Development, 2000), strongly reinforced the case for the teaching of phonics. We now have firm instructions in place in schools for the use of synthetic phonics (see Box 4.1) for the teaching of reading in Reception through years 1 and 2 at primary school. The Rose Review supported a Phonics plus Reading approach (P+R) which includes also the direct 'sight' teaching of common words that cannot be decoded (such as 'said' and 'the') and exposure to words within the context of age-appropriate stories read aloud to, and read by, the children.

The government has decided that all children are to be checked in the first years of primary school for their ability to decode. Unfortunately, at present this is viewed by many teachers as yet another test for discrediting 'poor' schools. However, the intention is to screen for children who are having difficulty in developing phonological awareness so that they can receive early help – it is a diagnostic tool, not a test (see Chapter 10).

Decoding and blending of sounds allows a whole word to be read. Practice will then lead to automatic recognition of single words. Meaning must then be extracted from the memorized lexicon. However, this does not necessarily lead directly to comprehension of what is being 'read' in a passage of text. For comprehension to be achieved, the words read must be understood within their syntactic context and within the overall meaning of what is being read. Reading aloud involves coordination of visual input with auditory representation and vocal production; it does not necessarily interact with meaning – most of us have at some point realized that we have been reading something aloud without noticing what it is about (particularly perhaps when reading the same story for the umpteenth time to our children!).

Obviously, success in reading will depend not only on word recognition but also on a child's level of oral language production and comprehension. As Stuart et al. (2008) put it: 'It is imperative to develop children's language comprehension abilities before and alongside their development of their word recognition skills.' Muter et al.[10] demonstrated the separability of the phonological and oral language inputs to reading in a two-year longitudinal study of 90 children from their entry to school in the Reception class (age range 4 years 9 months to 5 years 2 months). They showed (using a statistical analytical method called path analysis) that word reading was predicted by phonological skills, particularly letter knowledge and to a lesser extent knowledge of onset and rime, and not by oral language. In contrast, reading comprehension was predicted by vocabulary and grammatical knowledge, and of course by word reading, but not by phonological measures. This separation is supported by work on a different sort of poor readers: the poor comprehenders.[11] These children can actually read fluently, show no phonological impairment and are in the normal range for non-verbal intelligence (though usually at the lower end), but have difficulty extracting meaning from what they read.

Some of the evidence concerning the mechanism of learning to read comes from the study of effective remediation of difficulties with learning to read: if a specific difference is observed between suitably matched poor and good readers, and if remediating the specific difference can improve reading or indeed prevent reading difficulties in 'at-risk' children, then it is reasonable to suggest that this supports the view that this factor is an integral part of the normal process of learning to read. Studies of this sort, involving a randomized control design, have been used both for developmental dyslexia and for poor comprehenders. Snowling and Hulme[12] and their colleagues[13] have carried out elegant RCTs (randomized control trials) investigating the role of phonological knowledge in learning to read. They selected a group of 152 children (mean age 4 years 9 months; from 19 different schools) whom they considered to be 'at risk' of reading problems on the basis of poor vocabulary and verbal reasoning. They[13] compared the effect of either phonological training or oral language training on the development of word recognition and reading comprehension. They used the 'Phonology plus Reading' (P+R) intervention procedure used in primary schools for the Literacy Hour and compared this with instruction in vocabulary, expressive language, listening skills and inferencing. Their predictions were borne out in that the P+R improved single-word reading whilst the oral language teaching improved reading comprehension. Hulme et al.[14] further analysed the data from the group receiving P+R training and showed that the improvement in word reading was fully mediated (a statistical term meaning 'could be fully explained by') by the training effects of letter–sound correspondence and phonemic awareness (the ability to relate letters, or letter combinations such as 'ch', to sounds). This study showed the benefit of phonics and language teaching in the early primary school years, which supports the belief that both phonological awareness and oral language are components of the process whereby normally developing children learn to read. However, a proportion of children did not respond to the intervention. Snowling and Hulme[15] quote a figure of about a quarter of children as being 'non-responders', in that whilst they may have improved in absolute terms, their standardized age scores (scores relative to their normally developing peers) did not advance. We will, however, discuss methods of remediation later in this chapter.

So, the acquisition of successful, fluent reading requires the ability to decode phonologically, to recognize words automatically and to deduce meaning. Skilled readers do not need to decode words phonologically, since they recognize them visually direct from their lexicon. How this automatic recognition of words is acquired remains something of a mystery. Whilst work on acquired dyslexias (that is, those caused in adulthood by brain damage; Coltheart et al.[16] has provided evidence that the phonological and lexical (word recognition) routes to reading are separable in adults, in the process of learning to read and in the normal functioning of skilled reading these 'routes' of necessity interact. (Indeed, a connectionist view of reading dispenses entirely with the concept of two routes[17]). It is interesting that whilst the order in which children naturally (without teaching) acquire phonological awareness in spoken language is in the order of syllables, then onset and rime, and lastly phonemic awareness (see Goswami 2008), in teaching we are recommending the reverse order.

Learning to read changes the connections within the brain. Work on illiterate adults showed that they were much less good at phonological tasks in spoken language than age- and culture-matched literate adults. Furthermore, PET scanning demonstrated that their brains were differently organized,[18,19] particularly with respect to the amount of activation in the left parietal cortex when processing spoken words. Additionally, the area of the corpus callosum involved in the transfer of information between the parietal cortices of the two hemispheres was smaller in the illiterate subjects. Carreiras et al.[20] investigated the effects of late-acquired literacy in one of those useful (if unfortunate) natural experiments: they were able to investigate the effect of learning to read in adulthood in Colombian men in their twenties who had previously not received any formal education because they had been members of guerrilla fighting forces. The authors compared structural brain scans of these late-literates with early-literates and illiterates and showed that having learnt to read was associated with an increase in the density of grey matter in areas associated with higher-level visual processing, phonological processing and semantic processing. They also confirmed Castro-Caldas and colleagues' finding that literacy was associated with increased thickness of the splenium area of the corpus callosum. These findings show that learning to read, either in childhood or in adulthood, produces profound changes in brain structure. Carreiras and colleagues point out that these results are relevant to the interpretation of structural differences in the brains of dyslexic people: these may reflect lack of reading rather than provide evidence for a structural cause of dyslexia.

Problems with Learning to Read

What is dyslexia (specific reading disability)?

Reading is, of course, a complex process and one which needs to be taught. Since the history of writing suggests that it originated only about

3000 years ago, there has not been enough time for reading ability to have resulted from direct evolutionary pressure. Furthermore, it is unlikely that it confers a reproductive advantage; in the past it was usually restricted to an elite, who are not necessarily the most reproductively successful. Indeed, in at least European medieval times it was mainly the preserve of monastic orders who were, or at least were expected to be, celibate. It is interesting therefore that there is a genetic element in dyslexia – children with first-degree relatives exhibiting dyslexic symptoms are much more likely to be dyslexic than their matched controls without such relatives. The genetically determined process must involve some structure/process relevant to reading but which originally served some other function of the brain.

Five to ten per cent of children are diagnosed as dyslexic. The original definition of dyslexia involved a discrepancy between a person's measured intelligence and their reading ability: their reading was much less good than would be predicted from their measured intelligence.[21] This definition of the condition has more recently been scrapped, and dyslexia is diagnosed primarily by a specific difficulty in learning to read that is not explicable by lack of educational opportunity or by severe physical or mental disability. The reason for this change lay in the finding that there did not seem to be any specific behavioural or neurological difference between children with low intelligence scores who were poor readers (so-called 'garden-variety poor readers') and those with average or above average intelligence who were poor readers (discrepants).[22] It is important when examining studies on the cause of dyslexia to note the criteria for selecting the dyslexic and control groups. Whether deficits are considered as contributing to dyslexia depends on the definition of the disorder: for example, if it necessarily involves a phonological deficit, then there may well be poor readers who have a visual problem who are not classified as dyslexic on this criterion but are dyslexic on a discrepancy criterion. Where differences in behaviour or neurophysiology are found between typically developing readers and those who are dyslexic (by whatever definition), it is important to consider whether the differences might be the result rather than the cause of poor reading. The use of reading age-matched controls who have been matched for reading age rather than for chronological age for comparison to some extent removes this criticism.

Dyslexia comprises a range of psychological problems (see Box 4.2) and individuals diagnosed as dyslexic may show a variety of combinations of these.

Castles and Colheart[23] argued 20 years ago that there are two sorts of dyslexia: phonological and orthographic. The orthographic variety

Box 4.2

Those diagnosed as dyslexic may show problems with one or more of the following:

- Phonological awareness (e.g. as detected in orally presented awareness of onset and rime)
- Grapheme to phoneme translation (e.g. as detected by ability to read nonsense but decodable words such as grikimest or tolb)
- Short-term verbal memory (e.g. ability to recite back a series of numbers presented orally)
- Speed of rapid automatic naming (in which the person has to name as fast as possible a large number of pictures, letters, numbers or colours presented in a grid)
- Reading fluency
- Reading comprehension
- Spelling
- Visual tests involving eye movements (e.g. control of vergence of the eyes on a fixation point), control of visual attention, detection of movement
- Auditory tests detecting changes in frequency such as are found in normal speech
- Tactile detection of slow pressure changes.

involved problems with reading irregular words (such as yacht and pint) rather than a problem with decoding letters in words to sounds. Children might have one or the other of these problems or both.

There is evidence that those diagnosed as dyslexic may often also have a diagnosis of ADHD or SLI (specific language impairment[24]). The presence of such co-morbidities means that if there is a difference identified between dyslexics and their controls, these might actually be related to the co-morbid condition rather than to dyslexia specifically.

Dyslexia occurs in the acquisition of all languages, but there are differences in its manifestation depending on the regularity of the correspondence between sounds and letters/combinations of letters (phonemes) in the language being learnt, and on the complexity of syllables in the language.[25] Thus Italian, Spanish and Finnish, for example, where each letter has only one sound, and German which is almost as regular, are much easier to learn to read than English, Danish or French where most letters correspond to more than one sound. Also, in Italian and Spanish, for example, syllable structure is mainly of the simplest CV type (Consonant followed by Vowel). In English or German, syllables may be much more complex e.g. CCVCC such as 'grant'). Reading acquisition may not be as fast in German as in Italian, but children do learn to decode much more quickly than those learning English. Children acquiring the more regular languages demonstrate dyslexia in terms of slow and effortful decoding rather than inaccurate decoding and are mostly diagnosed through being poor spellers and non-fluent readers. Dyslexia is not confined to languages with an alphabetic writing system but is also found in those languages where a symbol represents a word, as in Chinese and in Japanese *kanji*, or a syllable, as in Japanese *hiragana*.

Dyslexia causes

It is important to emphasize that since dyslexia (specific reading disorder) encompasses several different problems (see Box 4.2), there are probably several different causes. As we have discussed, successful reading of single words depends on both visual and auditory processing: for regular words, firstly letters have to recognized by sight, then the sounds with which they are associated need to be learnt, and then their combinations into syllables and then words need to be acquired. For irregular words, a direct connection has to be made between the appearance of the word as a unit and the mental lexicon.

There has been a vast amount of research on the nature and causes of dyslexia and considerable disagreement as to the causes of the condition. Questions regarding the neurological basis have so far evaded resolution.

Neurological basis A major question is whether dyslexia (by whatever definition) is a 'top-down' problem, originating at higher cortical levels where inputs from auditory and visual (and other) sensory systems are integrated, or whether it is 'bottom-up' problem, originating at a lower level with differences in the sensory inputs themselves. It might be expected a priori in view of the need to translate visual input into sound (and meaning) that deficits in visual or auditory processes alone could cause reading problems. Furthermore, learning to read requires focused attention, and hence there is an expectation that abnormal function of brain areas involved in visual or auditory attentional processes could be involved

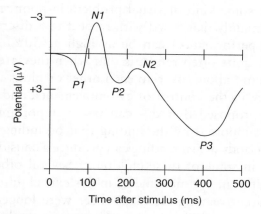

Figure 4.3 Evoked response potential.

in poor reading. In order to determine the causes of reading problems, longitudinal studies are needed that investigate which factors predict the various components. However, the majority of studies have involved comparing age- or reading-age-matched groups of dyslexic children or adults with control children or adults (a cross-sectional approach).

One type of study of the 'dyslexic brain' has involved measuring event-related potentials (ERPs). These are electrical signs in the electroencephalogram (EEG) recorded from the scalp in response to discrete stimuli, such as a single tone or a flash of light. The electrical waves recorded can be analysed with respect to their latency after the stimulus, their polarity (positive or negative), their amplitude and their site of origin (Figure 4.3).

Particular parts of the recorded waves from particular pairs of electrodes relate to the brain response to visual or to auditory stimuli. It has been found that in poor readers certain responses occur later than in 'normals' – that is, the transmission within the brain is slowed. A longitudinal study has shown that this difference is detectable in infants who later develop reading problems, and hence could have a causal role.[26] One way in which slowing of processing of signals related to vision or hearing might impact on the acquisition of reading is that it could increase the load on the working memory (see Chapter 2).

Visual problems in dyslexia

It is natural to assume that since the sensory input for reading is visual, problems with reading would be likely to result from visual problems.

The incidence of some kind of visual problem in poor readers attending dyslexia clinics (mainly diagnosed with respect to a discrepancy between IQ and reading performance) can be as high as 50%. One thing that dyslexic children quite often report is that when they are trying to read, letters seem to jump about, overlap each other or blur.[27] These problems suggest deficiency in the control of eye movements, and John Stein and colleagues have proposed that this can be an important cause of poor reading. This is supported by the finding that occluding one eye with a patch for short periods whilst reading can produce a considerable improvement in reading in some of these children.[28] Several other authors have found abnormalities in eye movements in dyslexic children; for example, in German children (reading German) there were longer and more frequent fixation patterns.[29] Biscaldi et al.[30] demonstrated that about 50% of dyslexics (diagnosed on the discrepancy criterion) showed a deficit in an antisaccade task. This is a task specifically designed to detect problems in the control of eye movements: the child is requested to direct his/her gaze to the side opposite to that on which a stimulus has suddenly been presented. It has been argued that because this deficit is also seen in some patients with schizophrenia and in some children with ADHD, it should not be considered a cause specifically of reading problems. However, this does not mean that problems with eye movements might not at least contribute to the development of dyslexia.

Forty years ago, Stanley and Hall[31] reported a difference in early visual processing in dyslexics. Their sample of 33 dyslexics aged 8–12 years were diagnosed by remedial teachers as having reading ages at least 2.5 years below their chronological age whilst performing in class in other subjects at or above average, and did not present with behavioural problems. By presenting the children with pairs of stimuli separated at various intervals, they showed that the short-term visual store lasted for 30–50% longer in the dyslexic children than in controls. One can hypothesize that such persistence might interfere with reading by making it more difficult to proceed linearly from letter to letter and word to word.

There are also problems in some dyslexics with the detection of visual motion. Stein and colleagues have used random dot kinetograms to investigate this. The test is delivered on a computer screen as two panels of moving dots. In one panel the dots are moving randomly and in the other they are moving coherently. The number of dots moving coherently or the speed of movement of dots can be graded and the child has to detect whether such coherent movement is occurring. A threshold is then determined and it is found that this threshold is higher for some dyslexics.[32,33]

Recently, Anne Castles and colleagues[34] have investigated temporal processing of visual stimuli in dyslexics. They found that over 40% of a sample of 40 (discrepancy-diagnosed) dyslexic children scored in the bottom 15% on a task to detect high-frequency flicker – in contrast, only 14% of their controls performed this poorly (a statistically significant difference in incidence).

Visual attention span – the number of individual visual elements, which would include letters, that can be processed simultaneously – has been investigated by Sylvie Valdois and colleagues, working with French children in Grenoble.[35,36] Recognizing irregular words requires a wide ('global') visual attention span; a more focused span is needed for identifying individual phonemes. Hence they predicted that reduced attention span could contribute particularly to problems with reading irregular words, since they need to be recognized as a whole, but could also impair reading pseudo-words (e.g. prabendent; a skill usually thought of as being a symptom of impaired phonological processing). They found that visual attention span (as well as phonological ability) is predictive of reading proficiency both in normally developing and in dyslexic children (diagnosed as having normal or superior IQ but reading delayed by 20 to 87 months). In a subset of the dyslexic children, a reduced visual attention span occurred independently of a phonological problem. This supports the view that dyslexia may involve either a visual[37] or a phonological problem or both. This conclusion has recently been confirmed.*

Auditory problems in dyslexia

Since the visually presented material has to be translated into sounds in order for words to be recognized, it was a reasonable assumption that problems in reading could result from auditory problems. Paula Tallal[38] in the 1980s proposed that a deficit in non-verbal auditory perception was related to phonological reading difficulties. She used two tests in which the ability of the children to perform correctly was tested at different rates of presentation of the stimuli. In one test the children had to repeat a sequence of panel-pressing depending on the sequence of two presented sounds; in the other, children had to tell whether pairs of sounds presented at different intervals were the same or different. She found that when the sounds followed each other in rapid succession, dyslexic children had more

---

* Recent work has supported this view and found that the combination of problems is the most difficult to remediate. Talcott, JB, Witton, C, Stein, JF. Probing the neurocognitive trajectories of children's reading skills. *Neuropsychologia*. 2014;31:472–481.

difficulty in performing accurately. Since then, she has developed a training programme, 'Fast for Word', incorporating the type of acoustic rapid changes that take place in normal speech and has found improvements in both the auditory discrimination and in reading.[39] She compared brain activity (using fMRI) in response to fast and slower acoustic changes. She found that whilst typically developing children showed a clear difference, with greater activity in left prefrontal cortex to the rapid changes, the responses of dyslexics were the same for fast and slow. Apparently, training could ameliorate this and at the same time improve reading.

The finding that some dyslexics have problems in the discrimination of the types of sounds found in normal speech (e.g. 'ba' and 'da') supports a 'bottom-up' auditory explanation of dyslexics' phonological impairment.

Another approach to auditory processing in reading disability was used by Witton et al.[40] They showed raised thresholds for dyslexic adults (n = 21; discrepancy-diagnosed) in discriminating auditory frequency modulation at low but not high frequencies. (Frequency modulation involves producing a 'wobble' in a regular-frequency background tone.) However, Halliday and Bishop[41] demonstrated that this is not specific to dyslexia. They showed that children with mild to moderate hearing loss showed a similar problem in auditory processing, and found that only in this group did the threshold correlate with phonological ability.

Magnocellular theory of dyslexia

The finding in the Witton et al.[40] study that the threshold for detecting frequency modulation correlated not only with the ability to decode non-words but also with the ability to detect coherent visual movement led to an attractive hypothesis which combines the auditory and visual explanations. This involves a defect in magnocellular pathways (Figure 4.4) from the eye and the ear (via the lateral and medial nuclei of the thalamus, respectively) to the cerebral cortex. Within the cortex the visual input to the so-called 'dorsal stream' involved in visuomotor control is mainly provided by magnocellular neurons.[42]

There is actually some anatomical evidence of disorganization of the relevant cell layers in the thalamus and in the cortex in dyslexics.[43] The present status of the magnocellular hypothesis as a primary sensory deficit in dyslexia dysfunction is still controversial (see Box 4.3) but it probably is a contributory cause of dyslexia.[44]

Anne Castles' group has looked specifically at the involvement of the magnocellular visual system in dyslexia (McLean et al.[34]). The flicker detec-

Visual magnocellular system directs visual attention and eye movements.

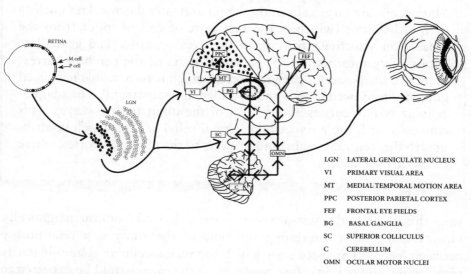

LGN	LATERAL GENICULATE NUCLEUS
VI	PRIMARY VISUAL AREA
MT	MEDIAL TEMPORAL MOTION AREA
PPC	POSTERIOR PARIETAL CORTEX
FEF	FRONTAL EYE FIELDS
BG	BASAL GANGLIA
SC	SUPERIOR COLLICULUS
C	CEREBELLUM
OMN	OCULAR MOTOR NUCLEI

Figure 4.4 The diagram shows the retina of the eye on the left. The dark dots denote the magnocells (the light dots are the more abundant parvocells). The nerve axons from the retina pass to the lateral geniculate nucleus (LGN, in the thalamus of the brain) and thence the pathways divide: one pathway goes to the primary visual area (V1) in the occipital cortex (at back of the brain) and on to the medial temporal motion area and posterior parietal cortex; the other goes to the superior colliculus which has connections with areas involved in the control of eye movements. This is indicated by the pathway to the eye muscles indicated on the eye on the right hand side of the diagram. *Source*: Adapted from Stein JF. *Neuroscience: An Introduction.* Chichester: John Wiley & Sons; 2006

tion test they use is designed to discriminate between the parvo- and magno-cellular systems originating in the retina (see Box 4.3). They found that lowered ability to detect high-frequency flicker (a property of the magnocellular system) was accompanied by lowered ability to detect low-frequency flicker (via the parvo system) in some cases but in a minority the magnocellular deficit occurred alone. The magnocellular raised threshold correlated weakly with measures of reading. The only one of these correlates that reached statistical significance was with orthographic reading. Thus it is possible that the magnocellular system is specifically involved in reading irregular words. This idea fits with the finding (see above) that some dyslexic children have a specific problem with visual attention span

Box 4.3   Magnocellular system

Magnocells are large cells in the retina and lateral geniculate nucleus of the thalamus (which is the first port of call of input from the senses) on which neurons from the eyes synapse. The geniculate axons carry information to the visual parts of the cerebral cortex, thence to the posterior parietal cortex which is responsible for visual guidance of movement via the so-called 'dorsal stream'. The magnocellular system carries about 10% of the input from the eyes. This contrasts with the parvocellular (small cells) system which contributes to the 'ventral stream' and projects to the temporal cortex where letters are identified.

since this involves the 'dorsal visual stream' derived from the magnocells. However, the most interesting outcome of the study is a relationship between 'perceptual speed', for which the magnocellular system is partly responsible, and reading. Just how these differences would be expected to produce their impact on reading is open to many interpretations.

The magnocellular systems also project, via the parietal cortex, to the cerebellum. The cerebellum has been described as the brain's autopilot,[45] being involved in the control of processes that have become automatic. It is therefore possible that abnormal magnocellular input to the cerebellum (via the parietal cortex) could result in difficulty in those processes in reading that involve automatization – that is, both the mapping of letters onto sounds and hence in word recognition and the automatic retrieval of word meanings and the establishment of fluency.[46] Acquisition of skilled fluent reading is an automatic implicit rather than an explicit process – it occurs through practice in reading.

It is to be expected that different factors will contribute to different facets of reading. We have discussed the contribution of phonological and visual problems to reading failure. Both of these primarily affect reading accuracy. However, reading fluency is independently related to a different measure: rapid automatic naming (see Box 4.2). Thus Torgesen et al.[47] showed that in fourth-grade children whose reading scores fell in the bottom quarter, 39% of the variance in reading speed could be accounted for by rapid automatic naming speed as measured two years earlier, whilst a phonological measure accounted for only 9% of this variance.

In German, which is a language with a regular mapping of letters and sounds (see above), accuracy of word reading is not really a problem in dyslexic children – their problem is in reading speed. Wimmer[48] showed that rapid automatic naming accounted for about 30% of the variance in speed of reading compared with around 10% accounted for by phonological awareness. Hence, rapid automatic naming is tapping into a process that has a large effect on the automatization of reading, which, as we have pointed out, is an implicit process.

Several authors have obtained evidence for a more general deficit in implicit learning in dyslexics. Again, this is not specific to dyslexics since a similar deficit has been found in people with schizophrenia. Using a measure of implicit learning, Stoodley and Stein[49] (and see Stoodley and Stein[50]) showed that in a group of 45 discrepancy-diagnosed dyslexics, the degree of impairment correlated with the degree of discrepancy between cognitive and literacy scores. Furthermore, they showed that this implicit learning deficit was not shared by a group of 'garden-variety' poor readers. This latter observation counters the argument that the poor implicit learning could be a result rather than a cause of poor reading. The further observation that it is the sequencing component of implicit learning that is impaired in dyslexics supports a role for cerebellar involvement, since this component has been firmly attributed to the cerebellum.[51] Some dyslexics show abnormalities in more general cerebellar functions, such as balancing on one leg, but whether this is specific to dyslexia or is only seen where there is co-morbidity with ADHD is disputed.[24]

Testing the different hypotheses concerning a primary sensory deficit in dyslexia (rather than a primary linguistic deficit) has mainly involved comparing groups of diagnosed dyslexic children or adults with matched controls (either for age or for reading age) on a variety of tasks. The results have been variable but overall group differences (usually quite small) have been observed. Where dyslexic children have been selected from a population of poor readers as those also having visual problems (such as ocular instability and 'visual stress'), it has been shown that they are significantly less good at detecting visual motion.[52]

Ramus et al.[53] attempted to decide between these different hypotheses (visual, auditory, cerebellar, higher-level phonological) by looking in detail at the abilities of 16 dyslexic university students who had been diagnosed by educational psychologists. They compared them with well-matched non-dyslexic controls. They found strong support, in this small group of high-achieving (hence compensated) dyslexics, for the phonological theory of dyslexia and also in some individuals found mild auditory or visual sensory deficits. A later paper from the same group[54] on children also looked at the incidence of sensory or motor problems in dyslexics (referred from chartered educational psychologists, but specifics of diagnosis not given; n = 22) and their controls (n = 23). Interestingly, at least one sensory or motor problem (defined as outliers) was seen in an equal proportion of dyslexics and controls (14/23 dyslexics; 13/22 controls). However, the tests used for identifying visual problems were less sensitive than those used by Stein and colleagues, which may explain why they found such a low incidence of visual problems in the dyslexics.

Dyslexia often runs in families and there is much evidence for a complex genetic component. This is certainly not a single gene, but a number of gene clusters that, when present in combination, increase the likelihood of dyslexia.[55,56] Interestingly, Castles and colleagues[57] have looked at the heritability of phonological dyslexia compared with orthographic dyslexia in a large study of twins in Australia. They reported that the direction of the heritability effect is opposite between the two: phonological is 67% genetic and 27% shared environment whilst orthographic is 31% genetic compared with 63% shared environment. This suggests that some innate structural and/or functional difference underlies phonological problems, whereas word recognition may be more related to experience with print. It is possible that the brain networks that Castro-Caldas et al.[58] have shown are activated by learning to read are constitutionally malfunctioning in phonological dyslexics who do not respond even to intensive training. However, it is important to remember that most reading delay is probably not caused by hereditary factors but results from lack of exposure to print and poor oral language skills – both of which are commoner in children from deprived backgrounds. These predisposing factors can be overcome for most children by the appropriate teaching within the normal school curriculum.

Overall, research in dyslexia has lead to a great deal of controversy with respect to both symptoms and causes. However, it has at least resulted in the general appreciation that 'specific reading disability' is a real condition, though it comprises a variety of symptoms and causes. This contrasts with the attitude taken in the not-so-distant past that it was just an excuse given by parents, particularly middle-class parents, for 'stupidity' in their children.

Dyslexia

Is there a spatial advantage?

Although dyslexia makes reading and writing more challenging, it does not stop some dyslexic people from becoming very successful in certain

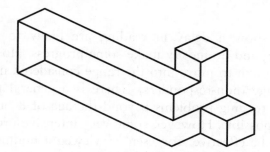

Figure 4.5 The impossible trident illusion. If one looks at this part by part, then it is not immediately obvious that the figure is impossible. To realize that, one must scan it as a whole. *Source*: From von Karolyi *et al. Brain and Language.* 2003;85:427–431. Reproduced with permission from Elsevier.

fields. We can probably cite from our own experience architects, graphic designers or IT experts who are dyslexic. Wolff and Lundberg[59] found that art students had a statistically significantly higher incidence of phonological problems and diagnosed dyslexia than their contemporaries at the same institution studying economics, commercial law, political science, civil engineering or psychology. This might just be because highly intelligent dyslexics are likely to divert their energies towards fields that do not depend on reading and, consequently, to excel in such areas. However, if dyslexia is actually the result of fundamental differences in how the brain develops, it may be that deficits in the verbal domain (more dependent on left hemisphere function) might be compensated for by improved functioning in the visuo-spatial domain (more dependent on the right hemisphere). Not all of the studies investigating this idea have confirmed it, but an exception is the finding that dyslexics are quicker to recognize 'impossible figures'[60] (see Figure 4.5).

The authors argued that this particular task involves global visuo-spatial ability – a holistic process. Probably somewhat prematurely, such differences in 3D processing were seized on enthusiastically by the media, which has led to the production of training programmes for dyslexics that capitalize on this idea (e.g. the Davis Dyslexia Correction Programme). However, there are many anecdotal examples of children, who have become frustrated and demotivated by the usual methods of trying to teach them to read, being helped by this approach. Brunswick and colleagues[61] have recently addressed whether the 3D advantage is myth or reality and have reported that the advantage may only be present in males.

Remediation

Children who show a delay in reading are likely to receive further phonics training and do mostly make some progress. However, some do not improve enough to move into the range considered normal for their chronological age (non-responders). There is a general perception that remediation of reading problems beyond the age of 8 or so is very difficult if not impossible. However, some very intensive programmes have been shown to be effective. Torgesen[62] reviewed a number of studies of remediation of reading difficulties in severely or moderately dyslexic children aged between 8 and 12 years. This showed that skilled, very intensive teaching, including a mixture of phonological training, sight word training and reading continuous text, could produce improvements that led to the majority of the children's phonological decoding ability rising substantially. The training used ranged from 35 to 100 hours typically administered 1:1 or 1:2 for an hour a day on at least four days a week – a hugely labour-intensive and of course therefore expensive process. Torgesen reported a study carried out by his group with 67.5 hours of intensive teaching to children between 8 and 12 years (who had already been receiving instruction for 16 months in a special education unit) which did produce a dramatic improvement in literacy. Torgesen compared two different teaching regimens, differing in the proportion of different content: 85% versus 20% phonological training; 10% versus 30% direct word recognition training; 5% versus 50% reading meaningful text. Interestingly, he found that they were equally effective in raising a composite reading accuracy plus comprehension score to within the normal range of standard age score. This supports the view that concentrating mainly on phonological training for poor readers, which is generally very boring, is not necessarily the most effective approach.

Unfortunately, whilst the majority of children in Torgeson's programme maintained their gains over the next two years, about a quarter of the children did not. Furthermore, whilst the components of reading had all improved, reading fluency did not reach the normal range. This could be because the children had not yet had enough practice in reading for it to become fully automatic, or it could result from a basic defect in cerebellar processing (including one related to the magnocellular input to the cerebellum). It will be important to investigate whether there are specific characteristics of the children who do not maintain their progress in reading, in order to be able to find further methods for their remediation.

Snowling and Hulme[12] point out that non-responders, in addition to their severe phonological impairment, often have poor vocabulary and a tendency for problems with attentional control (ADHD). However, one of the effects of an inability to learn to read is frustration and this itself might explain some of the problems seen in these non-responders. Indeed Hagtvet[63] (1993), in a longitudinal study of the acquisition of reading, emphasized the importance of social factors and in contrast showed that a characteristic of the background of particularly early readers was an emotionally warm home environment.

Poor comprehenders

Causes

It appears that a major problem with these children lies in the understanding of grammar and in the acquisition of vocabulary. There has been considerable progress in the study of poor comprehenders. Nation et al.[11] carried out a longitudinal study in children from age 5 to age 8, measuring a range of oral language abilities at yearly intervals. They selected 15 children who at age 8 qualified for their definition of poor comprehenders and then looked retrospectively at their scores on previous tests and compared them with a typically developing group matched for age and non-verbal intelligence. They found that the poor comprehenders showed oral language scores that were significantly lower than those of the controls. In particular, their understanding of grammar (measured with TROG[64]) at age 5, their verbal memory (measured as their ability to recall orally presented sentences accurately) and their listening comprehension were significantly lower. A poorer vocabulary was not seen at age 5 but did emerge in the later measures.

Remediation

Interestingly, Clarke et al.,[65] in a carefully constructed randomized control interventional study, showed that teaching vocabulary through a 'multiple context learning approach', where children are taught the use of new words in relevant and familiar contexts, could produce a marked improvement in the reading comprehension skills of poor comprehenders. This then further supports the view that oral language skills are important in the development of reading comprehension.

Summary

Reading acquisition

- Phonological awareness, firstly of letter–sound correspondence and then of phonemes, is an important part of learning to read individual words. Once this is well practised, word recognition will become automatic.
- Words that cannot readily be decoded need to be learnt by sight reading (orthographic) directly.
- The phonological and orthographic processes interact in the acquisition of fluent reading. We do not fully understand how the process of word recognition becomes automatic.
- In order to be able to understand passages of written text, vocabulary and grammatical understanding need to be acquired in addition to the basic ability to read single words.
- Reading comprehension and phonological decoding can be considered as two orthogonal processes which necessarily interact to produce fluent reading with understanding.
- Reading practice is very important in producing automatization of the reading process so that the reader can concentrate on comprehension.

Dyslexia

- Children can be considered to be dyslexic if their reading level is well below that of children of a similar age and background, if they have had adequate opportunities to learn to read and do not have serious physical or mental handicaps. A majority of such children have a deficit in their ability to decode phonologically. The presence of a phonological deficit is sometimes used as the basis for diagnosis; however, where the more general diagnosis is used, as many as 50% of dyslexics have visual problems.
- There is a wide variety of symptoms associated with dyslexia. These include low-level visual and auditory problems and higher-level deficits such as problems with visual attention, rapid automatic naming and short-term memory. Reduced visual attention span can occur independently of phonological problems. Dyslexia is a heterogeneous disorder and we should not expect to find just one cause.
- Dyslexia can show co-morbidity with ADHD or specific language impairment (SLI).

- Behavioural problems in dyslexic children may be as much related to frustration as to co-morbidities.
- About three-quarters of children diagnosed as dyslexic can succeed in advancing their reading accuracy to within the normal range for their age with very intensive training, including phonological and sight word training and reading embedded in book reading. About a quarter of the children who undertake such an intensive remediation problem do not improve their reading skill to within the normal range for their age group. More research is needed to identify the specific problems of these children. It is likely that they suffer from several co-morbidities.
- The neurological basis of dyslexia is not understood. The evidence concerning a deficit in the magnocellular systems involved in vision and hearing suggests that this is unlikely to be a universal cause of dyslexia but is probably contributory to the problem in many cases.
- The cerebellar theory that dyslexia involves dysfunction in the acquisition of automatic processes involved in reading has some support. This theory does not necessarily imply that all cerebellar functions, such as those involved in balance, should be affected in all dyslexics, just that they might sometimes be. Studies showing impairment in implicit learning support the possibility of dyslexics having problems that could involve the cerebellum, though many other areas of the brain are also involved in implicit learning (see Chapter 2). The cerebellum receives input from magnocellular neurons so the cerebellar deficit theory might support a theory of magnocellular deficit in dyslexia.

Educational implications

(All of these points will be familiar to those involved in teaching children to read.)

- Systematic synthetic phonics involving teaching letter–sound correspondence in a prescribed order, followed by segmentation and blending, is a highly successful method for teaching reading in Reception and years 1 and 2.
- This approach needs to be combined with some 'sight reading' instruction of common words that cannot be directly decoded.
- The teaching needs to be embedded in classes where stories involving the words that have been learnt are read to and with the children.
- Children who have not responded to intensive phonological remediation need to be exposed to alternative methods of learning to read rather then just be exposed to more phonics.

- Young children with visual problems in reading may benefit from the occlusion of one eye (during reading) to help stabilize binocular control.
- Fluent reading is achieved through practice. Hence encouragement to use libraries and/or to own books, read magazines and newspapers should have high priority.
- Delay in learning to read needs urgent remediation since it frustrates children and often demotivates them towards education in general. Reading remains effortful and therefore not really enjoyable unless there has been adequate practice to render it automatic. Actively promoting reading in the early primary school years should be a major force in removing the socioeconomic disparities in school achievement.
- Teachers have an important role in widening children's vocabulary and use of complex grammar. This will help the development of comprehension of what the children read.

References

1   Reynolds S. *Medieval Reading, Grammar and the Classical Text*. Cambridge: Cambridge University Press; 1996.
2   Chall JS. *Learning to Read: The Great Debate*. New York: McGraw-Hill; 1983.
3   Snow CE, Juel C. Teaching children to read: What do we know about how to do it? In: *The Science of Reading: A Handbook*. Chichester, UK: John Wiley & Sons; 2007:501–520.
4   Stuart M, Stainthorp R, Snowling MJ. Literacy as a complex activity: Deconstructing the simple view of reading. *Literacy*. 2008;42(2):59–66.
5   Liberman IY, Shankweiler D, Fischer FW, Bonnie C. Explicit syllable and phoneme segmentation in the young child. *Journal of Experimental Child Psychology*. 1974;18:201–212.
6   Bradley L, Bryant PE. Categorizing sounds and learning to read: A causal connection. *Nature*. 1983;301:419–421.
7   Goswami U. *Cognitive Development: The Learning Brain*. Hove, East Sussex, UK: Psychology Press; 2008.
8   Rose J. Independent Review of the Teaching of Early Reading. 2006.
9   Ehri EC. Teaching phonemic awareness and phonics: An explanation of the National Reading Panel meta-analyses. In: *The Voice of Evidence in Reading Research*. Baltimore: Paul H Brookes; 2007:153–186.
10 Muter V, Hulme C, Snowling MJ, Stevenson J. Phonemes, rimes, vocabulary, and grammatical skills as foundations of early reading development:

evidence from a longitudinal study. *Developmental Psychology*. 2004;40(5): 665–681.

11   Nation K, Cocksey J, Taylor JSH, Bishop DVM. A longitudinal investigation of early reading and language skills in children with poor reading comprehension. *Journal of child Psychology and Psychiatry*. 2010;51(9):031–1039.

12   Snowling MJ, Hulme C. Evidence-based interventions for reading and language difficulties: Creating a virtuous circle. *British Journal of Educational Psychology*. 2010;81:1–23.

13   Bowyer-Crane C, Snowling, MJ, Duff FJ, *et al*. Improving early language and literacy skills: Differential effects of an oral language versus a phonology with reading intervention. *Journal of Child Psychology and Psychiatry*. 2008;49(4):422–432.

14   Hulme C, Bowyer-Crane C, Carroll JM, Duff FJ, Snowling MJ. The causal role of phoneme awareness and letter-sound knowledge in learning to read: Combining intervention studies with mediation analyses. *Psychological Science*. 2012;23(6):572–577.

15   Snowling MJ, Hulme C. *The Science of Reading: A Handbook*. Chichester: John Wiley & Sons; 2007.

16   Coltheart M, Masterson J, Byng S, Prior M, Riddoch J. Surface dyslexia. *Quarterly Journal of Experimental Psychology Section A*. 1983;35(3):469–495. doi:10.1080/14640748308402483.

17   Plaut DC. Connectionist approaches to reading. In: Snowling MJ and Hulme C. *The Science of Reading: A Handbook*. Wiley-Blackwell; 2007:24–38.

18   Castro-Caldas A, Petersson KM, Reis A, Stone-Elander S, Ingvar M. The illiterate brain. Learning to read and write during childhood influences the functional organization of the brain. *Brain*. 1998;121(6):1053–1063.

19   Castro-Caldas A, Cavaleiro P, Carmo I, *et al*. Influence of learning to read and write on the morphology of the corpus callosum. *European Journal of Neurology*. 1999;6:23–28.

20   Carreiras M, Baquero S, *et al*. An anatomical signature for literacy. *Nature*. 2009;461:983–986.

21   Rutter M, Yule W. The concept of specific reading retardation. *Journal of Child Psychology and Psychiatry*. 1975;16(3):181–197.

22   Fletcher JM, Shaywitz SE, Shankweiler, *et al*. Cognitive profiles of reading disability: Comparisons of discrepancy and low achievement definitions. *Journal of Educational Psychology*. 1994;86(1):6–23.

23   Castles A, Coltheart M. Varieties of developmental dyslexia. *Cognition*. 1993;47:149–180.

24   Bishop DVM. The underlying nature of specific language impairment. *Journal of Child Psychology and Psychiatry*. 1992;33(1):3–66. doi:10.1111/j.1469-7610.1992.tb00858.x.

25   Ziegler JC, Goswami U. Reading acquisition, developmental dyslexia, and skilled reading across languages: A psycholinguistic grain size theory. *Psychological Bulletin*. 2005;131(1):3–29.

26   Leppanen PH, Hamalainen JA, Guttorm TK, *et al.* Infant brain responses associated with reading-related skills before school and at school age. *Neurophysiologie clinique.* 2012;42(1–1):35–41.

27   Stein JF, Fowler S. Visual dyslexia. *Trends in Neurosciences.* 1981;4: 77–80.

28   Stein JF, Richardson AJ, Fowler MS. Monocular occlusion can improve binocular control in dyslexics. *Brain.* 2000;123:164–170.

29   Hutzler F, Wimmer H. Eye movements of dyslexic children when reading in a regular orthography. *Brain and Language.* 2004;89(1): 235–242.

30   Biscaldi M, Fischer B, Hartnegg K. Voluntary saccadic control in dyslexia. *Perception.* 2000;29:509–521.

31   Stanley G, Hall R. Short-term visual information-processing in dyslexics. *Child Development.* 1973;44(4):841–844.

32   Cornelissen PL, Richardson A, Mason A, Fowler S, Stein J. Contrast sensitivity and coherent motion detection measured at photopic luminance levels in dyslexics and controls. *Vision Research.* 1995;35:1493–1494.

33   Talcott J, Witton C, McLean MF, *et al.* Dynamic sensory sensitivity and children's word decoding skills. *Proceedings of the National Academy of Sciences.* 2000;97:2952–2962.

34   McLean GMT, Stuart GW, Cotlheart V, Castles A. Visual temporal processing in dyslexia and the magnocellular deficit theory: The need for speed? *Journal of Developmental Psychology: Human Perception and Performance.* 2011;37(6):1957–1975.

35   Bosse M-L, Tainturier MJ, Valdois S. Developmental dyslexia: The visual attention span hypothesis. *Cognition.* 2007;104:198–230.

36   Lobier M, Zoubrinetzky R, Valdois S. The visual attention span deficit in dyslexia is visual not verbal. *Cortex.* 2012;48:768–773.

37   Vidyasagar TR, Pammer K. Dyslexia: A deficit in visuo-spatial attention, not in phonological processing. *Trends in Cognitive Science.* 2010;14(2):57–63. doi: 10.1016/j.tics.2009.12.003.

38   Tallal P. Auditory temporal perception, phonics, and reading disability in children. *Brain and Language.* 1980;9:182–198.

39   Tallal P. Improving language and literacy is a matter of time. *Nature Reviews: Neuroscience.* 2004;5:721–728.

40   Witton C, Talcott JB, Hansen PC, *et al.* Sensitivity to dynamic auditory and visual stimuli predicts non-word reading ability in both dyslexic and normal readers. *Current Biology.* 1998;8:791–797.

41   Halliday LF, Bishop DVM. Is poor frequency modulation detection linked to literacy problems? A comparison of specific reading disability and mild to moderate sensorineural hearing loss. *Brain and Language.* 2006;97: 200–213.

42   Stein JF, Walsh V. To see but not to read: The magnocellular theory of dyslexia. *Trends in Neurosciences.* 1997;20(4):147–152.

43 Galaburda AM, Sherman GF, Rosen GD, Aboitiz F, Geschwind, N. Developmental dyslexia: Four consecutive patients with cortical anomalies. *Annals of Neurology*. 1985;18(2):222–233.

44 Laycock R, Crewther SG. Towards an understanding of the magnocellular advantage in fluent reading. *Neuroscience and Biobehavioral reviews*. 2008; 32:1494–1506.

45 Miall R, Weir DW, Stein J. Is the cerebellum a smith predictor? *Journal of Motor Behavior*. 1993;25:203–216.

46 Nicolson RI, Fawcett AJ. Do cerebellar deficits underlie phonological problems in dyslexia? *Developmental Science*. 2006;9(3):259–262.

47 Torgesen JK, Wagner RK, Rashotte CA, Burgess S, Hecht S. Contributions of phonological awareness and rapid naming ability to the growth of word-reading skills in second to fifth graders. *Scientific Studies of Reading*. 1997;1(2):161–185.

48 Wimmer H. Characteristics of developmental dyslexia in a regular writing system. *Applied Psycholinguistics*. 1993;14(01):1–33. doi:10.1017/S0142716400010122.

49 Stoodley CJ, Ray NJ, Jack A, Stein JF. Implicit learning in control, dyslexic and garden-variety poor readers. *Proceedings of the National Academy of Sciences*. 2008;1145:173–183.

50 Stoodley CJ, Stein JF. The cerebellum and dyslexia. *Cortex*. 2011;47: 101–116.

51 Molinari M, Chiricozzi FR, Clausi S, Tedesco AM, De Lisa M, *et al*. Cerebellum and detection of sequences, from perception to cognition. *Cerebellum*. 2008;7:611–615.

52 Stein J. Visual motion sensitivity and reading. *Neuropsychologia*. 2003; 41:1785–1793.

53 Ramus F, Rosen S, Dakin SC, Day BL, Castellote JM, *et al*. Theories of developmental dyslexia: Insights from a multiple case study of dyslexic adults. *Brain*. 2003;126:841–865.

54 White S, Milne E, Rosen S, Hansen P, Swettenham J, *et al*. The role of sensorimotor impairments in dyslexia: A multiple case study of dyslexic children. *Developmental Science*. 2006;9(3):237–269.

55 Stein JF. Dyslexia genetics. In: *Dyslexia in Context*. London: Whurr; 2004:76–90.

56 Pennington BF. Genetics of dyslexia. In: *The Science of Reading: A Handbook*. Wiley-Blackwell; 2005:454–472.

57 Bates TC, Castles A, Luciano M, Wright MJ, Coltheart M, *et al*. Genetic and environmental bases of reading and spelling: A unified genetic dual route model. *Reading and Writing*. 2007;20(1–2):147–171.

58 Castro-Caldas A, Reis A. The knowledge of orthography is a revolution in the brain. *Reading and Writing*. 2003;16:81–97.

59 Wolff U, Lundberg I. The prevalence of dyslexia among art students. *Dyslexia*. 2002;8:34–42.

60   Von Karolyi C, Winner E, Gray W, Sherman, GF. Dyslexia linked to talent: Global visual spatial ability. *Brain and Language*. 2003;85:427–431.

61   Brunswick N, Martin GN, Marzano L. Visuospatial superiority in developmental dyslexia: Myth or reality? *Learning and Individual Differences*. 2010;20(5):421–426.

62   Torgesen JK. Recent discoveries in remedial interventions for children with dyslexia. In: Snowling MJ and Hulme C. *The Science of Reading: A Handbook*. 2nd ed. Oxford: Blackwell; 2007:521–537.

63   Hagtvet B. From oral to written language: A developmental and interventional perspective. *European Journal of Psychology of Education*. 1993; VIII(3):205–220.

64   Bishop DVM. *Test for Reception of Grammar – Electronic*. London: Harcourt Assessment; 2005.

65   Clarke PJ, Snowling MJ, Truelove E, Hulme C. Ameliorating children's reading comprehension difficulties: A randomized controlled trial. *Psychological Science*. 2010;21(8):1106–1116.

Chapter 5

Intelligence and Ability
How Does Our Understanding of These Affect How We Teach?

> *Genius is one percent inspiration, ninety-nine percent perspiration.*
> *Thomas Edison*

The word 'ability' is used all the time in education, but it does not always refer to the same thing. If a teacher describes a pupil as 'able' it could mean that the child is intelligent, capable, mature or focused. If a sports coach divides some pupils into ability groups this usually reflects their current level of performance, rather than their physiological aptitude for that sport. In general conversation, we might talk about a young person's ability to empathize, or their emotional intelligence.

Ability is domain specific: mathematical, verbal, physical. Some people also regard it as heritable, believing that certain individuals have a greater level of innate ability, for example to do maths or to paint, than others. It should not be confused with attainment, because as Thomas Edison's quote suggests, ability is only one factor affecting an individual's day-to-day performance. Effort, motivation, focus, personality and mood can all have independent effects. For this reason, ability can be described as 'current capacity that limits the effect of effort during test performance on how well an individual can perform relative to others'[1(p637)].

In some research the words ability and intelligence are used interchangeably. This partly reflects the fact that there is no universal theory or definition of intelligence. When some people talk about intelligence

Education and Learning: An Evidence-Based Approach, First Edition. Jane Mellanby and Katy Theobald.
© 2014 John Wiley & Sons, Ltd. Published 2014 by John Wiley & Sons, Ltd.

they are referring to *g*, the general factor of intelligence.[2] However, *g* is essentially a statistical creation, based on the observation that people's performance tends to correlate across different tests and tasks. Some psychologists differentiate fluid (Gf) and crystallized (Gc) intelligence, Gf being similar to *g*, or very general underlying potential and Gc being the culturally relevant knowledge and skills one can acquire by applying Gf, such as vocabulary or mathematical strategies.[3] Finally, another group of psychologists see intelligence in terms of individual mental abilities such as creative, social and practical intelligence. This chapter incorporates research conducted from each of these perspectives, so it is important to remember that when different studies use the terms 'intelligence' and 'ability' they might not always mean the same things.

Before reading this chapter it is worth considering your own views about the following:

How would you define intelligence?
Do you believe abilities and intelligence are fixed or changeable?
Do you think that intelligent people have different brains?
Do you believe that people inherit certain abilities or a certain level of intelligence?

In this chapter these questions are addressed by presenting theoretical, experimental and neuropsychological evidence. It finishes with a discussion of how different conceptions of ability can affect the way in which education is delivered.

Definitions of intelligence

There is no single definition of intelligence. However, when multiple definitions from different researchers are compiled (see Legg and Hutter[4]), there is general agreement that intelligence involves a capacity to:

- learn quickly;
- problem-solve effectively;
- adapt to and succeed in one's environment.

As explained earlier, psychologists are divided as to whether intelligence reflects a single or multiple capacities and whether it is a wholly cognitive characteristic or includes non-cognitive abilities.

Researchers such as Binet, Simon, Cattell and Thurstone have all treated intelligence as a purely cognitive trait.[5] This is the traditional academic perspective and explains why many intelligence tests are designed to assess only cognitive skills such as problem-solving, verbal and mathematical abilities. This view of intelligence as purely cognitive partly reflects early research in the field. In 1904, Charles Spearman published his seminal paper outlining the 'positive manifold' effect, the positive correlation between the performances of school pupils on apparently unrelated tests. Using the newly developed statistical technique of factor analysis, Spearman later showed that there seemed to be a common factor contributing to variations in performance across these tests, which he termed g, the general factor of intelligence.[2] Shortly afterwards, Binet and Simon developed the first standardized intelligence tests, intended for identifying school pupils requiring additional academic support. Reflecting this purpose, these tests focused on the assessment of academic abilities. So from the start, measures and tests of intelligence gave weight to the cognitive skills favoured by the Western education system rather than practical, creative or interpersonal qualities.

This Western view of intelligence as being predominantly cognitive may also reflect our socioeconomic hierarchy, which financially rewards professional activities more than skilled manual labour. However, in rural communities and non-Western cultures, people often view practical or social skills as an important aspect of intelligence. An oft-cited example of this is the experience of some American researchers who travelled to Liberia in the 1960s to work with the Kpelle tribe. They gave the tribespeople an object-sorting task which Americans would complete by sorting the objects into four groups according to their linguistic categories: foods in one, implements in another and so on. The Kpelle instead made functional pairings, such as a vegetable with a knife. The researchers tried to persuade them to sort differently, but the Kpelle asserted that they were answering as a wise man would do. Eventually the frustrated researchers resorted to asking what a fool would do. At this point the Kpelle finally placed the objects into the four expected, taxonomic groups.[6] What the American researchers thought to be the intelligent response was in this culture completely foolish.

Okagaki and Sternberg[5] have shown similar differences amongst parents from different cultures. They directly asked an ethnically diverse group of 359 parents to rate characteristics they associated with intelligence in first-grade pupils. Anglo-American parents rated cognitive skills (problem-solving, verbal and creative abilities) as equally or more important than non-cognitive skills (motivation, self-management and social skills). However, Cambodian, Filipino and Vietnamese parents rated non-cognitive skills as equally or more important. Parents from these cultures regarded practical and social skills as fundamental aspects of intelligence.

Sternberg and colleagues[7] demonstrated this when they compared the characteristics that 122 laypeople and 144 academic experts considered fundamental to conceptions of intelligence. Both the experts and laypeople thought problem-solving skills and verbal abilities were reflective of academic intelligence. However, laypeople also emphasized social skills as an aspect of intelligence whereas academics placed more emphasis on motivation. In combination with a wider survey that they conducted, this research indicated that academic experts might give less consideration to social aspects of intelligence than 'ordinary' people. Since it is academics who define intelligence for research purposes, this could also explain why many theories and tests of intelligence focus so narrowly on cognitive skills.

Some Western psychologists do take a broader view. For example, Philip Vernon[8] proposed that, after accounting for general intelligence, g, the structure of intelligence could be divided into two main areas: $v{:}ed$, verbal and educational abilities; and $k{:}m$, spatial, practical, and mechanical abilities. The American psychologist David Lubinski argues strongly for greater recognition of the role that spatial abilities play in certain occupations. He often draws on longitudinal data from a study of over 400,000 American pupils who completed measures of mathematical, verbal and spatial ability as well as reporting interests, hobbies and background information. The first data were collected during the 1960s when the pupils were aged 14–18, with further information about their education and occupations recorded 1, 5 and 11 years later. Pupils with strong spatial abilities exhibited a distinctive pattern of educational and occupational outcomes: they were more likely to leave education after high school than those who had high verbal abilities,[9] but if they progressed to higher education they seemed drawn to STEM (Science, Technology, Engineering, Mathematics) subjects. Of the pupils who went to university, those who pursued STEM subjects had relatively higher spatial and mathematical abilities whereas those who studied arts and humanities had relatively higher verbal and mathematical abilities.[10] Forty-five per cent of individuals with doctorates in STEM subjects ranked in the top 4% of spatial ability, yet as the authors note, this ability is rarely utilized in school lessons or measured in standardized tests.

Some researchers such as J.P. Guilford,[11] Howard Gardner,[12] Stephen Ceci[13] and Robert Sternberg[14] include non-cognitive skills in their theories of intelligence. Howard Gardner's theory of Multiple Intelligences (MI Theory) began with seven intelligences and has now expanded to incorporate nine:

- Visual/spatial
- Bodily/kinaesthetic
- Intrapersonal
- Interpersonal
- Mathematical/logical
- Verbal/linguistic
- Naturalistic
- Musical/rhythmic
- Existentialist.

Gardner developed Multiple Intelligences Theory as a reaction to the narrow academic view of intelligence as *g*. He argues that each of the multiple intelligences is independent, based on autonomous computational modules in the brain, so people are not simply intelligent or unintelligent. Someone may have low musical intelligence but high verbal intelligence, others may have high interpersonal intelligence but low mathematical intelligence.[15] This theory is often popular with educators because it recognizes and values diversity, rather than favouring academic performance at the expense of other aptitudes.

However, Multiple Intelligences Theory has faced much criticism (see Armstrong[16]). Firstly, it has been argued that there is minimal empirical evidence to support Multiple Intelligences Theory, whereas alternative theories such as Spearman's are based on strong evidence. More recently, there have been attempts to measure the different intelligences and therefore test whether they are independent. Visser and colleagues[17,18] have argued that there is some common variation in performance across measures of the individual intelligences and that the multiple intelligences are therefore better viewed as talents, underpinned partly by a common *g* factor. Similarly, Waterhouse[19] has argued that it is almost impossible to test each intelligence individually because, for example, demonstrating naturalistic skills like labelling, grouping and conceptualizing objects relies on at least four intelligences: naturalistic, verbal, visual spatial and interpersonal.

In some ways, one can view this as a matter of semantics: whether one restricts definitions of intelligence to the cognitive domain and to a general factor or whether one uses the term 'intelligence' to refer to multiple cognitive and non-cognitive characteristics. Possibly, as Visser and colleagues suggest, it would be more appropriate to label the nine skills identified by Gardner as something other than 'intelligences'. Beyond this debate, though, it is worth considering how learners can be affected by the way that intelligence and ability are framed. As discussed in the next section, the way that adults characterize ability may actually affect the learning strategies pupils employ and the ways they respond to failure. Pupils who are weak in pure academic subjects can easily come to believe they are 'unintelligent' and therefore likely to fail in education. If Multiple Intelligences Theory offers a framework for challenging these beliefs and encouraging children to appreciate alternative skills, it may have value even if it is not underpinned by strong empirical evidence.

Beliefs about ability and intelligence

Traditional, Western views of intelligence typically treat it as a fixed characteristic which can limit people's potential for success in a certain field. Again, this has a historical basis. In the 1800s, Western understanding of evolution and heredity was growing as a result of the work of scientists like Charles Darwin and Gregor Mendel. Inspired by such works and his own lay-theories of eminence, Francis Galton mapped out the family trees of individuals who were prominent in fields such as the law, religion, the military, science and the arts and presented a thesis outlining the hereditary nature of innate ability. This thesis largely overlooked the social advantage gained by having family members who are eminent in a certain field and meant that at the turn of the twentieth century, as more rigorous scientific research into intelligence began, the dominant Western view was that intelligence was innate and that eminence in a given field resulted as much from the inheritance of abilities as the investment of effort. As discussed in Chapter 11, this perception of ability as largely predetermined is not universal. In East Asian cultures ability is often viewed as being much more malleable, and people are more likely to explain their performance in terms of effort and hard work than innate ability.

Carol Dweck and her colleagues have proposed a theory of achievement based on the idea that individuals have different implicit theories of intelligence.[20] It is worth noting that Dweck uses the terms 'intelligence' and 'ability' relatively interchangeably, rather than establishing a clear distinction between general potential and specific areas of achievement. Dweck argues that some individuals adhere to entity theories where they view intelligence as a relatively fixed characteristic, but that other people hold incremental theories, viewing intelligence as malleable and open to development. Depending on whether they follow an entity or incremental theory of ability, people may then express different beliefs and exhibit different behaviours as detailed in Table 5.1.

Importantly for educators, the ability theory endorsed by pupils and students may affect their achievement. Blackwell, Trzesniewski and Dweck[21] monitored a group of ethnically diverse American pupils as they

Table 5.1 Entity and incremental theories of ability

	Entity theorists	Incremental theorists
Goal setting	Set performance goals – focused on documenting their ability	Set mastery goals – focused on developing their ability
Explanations for failure	Tend to explain failure in terms of a lack of ability	Tend to explain failure in terms of lack of effort
Beliefs about effort	Believe that additional effort is pointless since ability is fixed	Believe that with additional effort performance can improve
Responses to failure	Tend to stop trying or persevere with the same strategy	Tend to try harder or change strategy

Source: Blackwell et al.[21]

made the transition from elementary to junior school at ages 12 and 13. In their first study of 373 pupils they found that those who advocated an incremental theory of intelligence also expressed more positive beliefs about the power of effort to improve performance, set more mastery goals, made fewer helpless attributions about their attainment and employed more positive strategies to improve their performance. Controlling for prior attainment they then found that pupils who held these beliefs had higher attainment at the end of their second year. In the second study, they worked with new pupils who were in their first year of junior school. Forty-eight pupils were given classes in which they were taught about incremental theories of intelligence whilst a control group of 43 pupils was taught about memory and memorization strategies. Whilst the control group's mathematics attainment declined throughout their time at junior school, the intervention group's attainment stopped declining and their predicted grades were significantly higher ($p < 0.05$) after the intervention (see Figure 5.1).

Dweck's research suggests that encouraging pupils to view intelligence as something that can change and develop over time – to endorse incremental theories of intelligence – may be one way to promote perseverance and effort, and therefore boost attainment. There is tentative evidence to suggest that one way in which entity theories of intelligence are reinforced is through the language that adults use. For example, Mueller and Dweck[22] conducted a number of studies looking at the impact of praising pupils

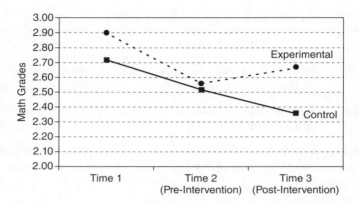

Figure 5.1 Predicted maths grades for the experimental and control group. *Source*: Blackwell LS, Trzesniewski KH, Dweck CS. Implicit theories of intelligence predict achievement across an adolescent transition: A longitudinal study and an intervention. *Child Development*. 78(1). Copyright © 2007 John Wiley & Sons. Reproduced by permission of John Wiley & Sons.

for their effort or intelligence. In one study with 51 children aged 9–11 they found that pupils praised for their intelligence rather than effort were more likely to rate ability as a fixed trait. In another study detailed in the same paper they gave 88 10-year-old pupils problem-solving tasks and varied the feedback they received. After the first set of tasks a third of the participants were praised for their effort, a third for their intelligence and a third received no additional praise. All the participants were then told they had performed poorly on the next set of tasks. Participants who had been praised for their intelligence were then more likely to explain their poor performance in terms of low ability rather than low effort and less likely to enjoy subsequent tasks. They were also significantly more likely to set performance goals – to focus on doing tasks where they could raise their performance rather than necessarily learning anything.

Categorizing pupils by ability may also encourage them to view ability as a fixed entity. Heyman[23] presented a scenario to 80 pupils aged 8–12 where a pupil was described as doing well on a test. In one version the pupil was labelled a 'math whizz' or 'spelling master' whereas in the other this label was not used. Pupils presented with the former condition were significantly more likely to agree that:

- the pupil was born with special maths or spelling ability;
- the pupil would still do well in the future even without much practice.

Later, in a study with 192 younger children aged 4 to 7, Cimpian and colleagues[24] found that describing a task as something that a certain group – in this case boys or girls – were particularly good at reduced the average performance of pupils whether or not they belonged to that group.

In many British schools it is common to sort pupils into academic groups for teaching and to select high-attaining pupils for gifted and talented programmes (see Chapter 8). However, the studies described above suggest that using noun labels such as 'gifted' to describe successful pupils encourages an entity view of ability. This may have negative consequences for pupils both within and outside the programme because they see their performance as dependent on fixed ability rather than changeable effort, and therefore beyond their control.

Measuring intelligence

No test is a perfect measure of intelligence (not least because no one has categorically defined what intelligence is). Hence the words intelligence and IQ should not be used interchangeably: intelligence is a concept, general potential underlying performance in many areas of life, whereas IQ is a score on a test that is supposed to reflect one's intelligence. Intelligence tests fall into two main groups, those which have a large verbal component such as the Wechsler intelligence scales (the WISC-R for children and WAIS for adults) and those which draw predominantly on spatial abilities such as the Raven's Progressive Matrices (Raven's) and Cattell's Culture Fair test. Figure 5.2 shows some examples of such tests.

Different tests vary in their *g*-loading, the extent to which the scores reflect this general factor of intelligence rather than abilities or knowledge that are specific to that test. Raven's Matrices have one of the highest *g*-loadings amongst all the intelligence tests. The Wechsler scales include both verbal and spatial subtests, each with different *g*-loadings. There is good evidence to support some independence between verbal and spatial abilities, and also between verbal and spatial IQ. Individuals with learning difficulties can often be differentiated into two categories: those with nonverbal learning disabilities and those with basic phonological processing difficulties. The former have particularly low non-verbal IQ scores and exhibit problems with non-verbal problem-solving and visual-spatial organization. The latter have particularly low verbal IQ scores and exhibit poor reading and spelling skills. This dissociation between different types of learning difficulties suggests that verbal and spatial abilities have some level of independence. As explained in Chapter 6, there are also sex differences in these abilities: males tend to outperform females on tests of spatial ability whereas females often perform better on verbal tests.

Box 5.1   How are IQ scores calculated?

All reputable IQ tests will have been taken by a large, representative sample of people from the population for which it is designed. We expect their test scores to be normally distributed, in other words to be distributed along a bell curve, with more people scoring around the average than at the extremes:

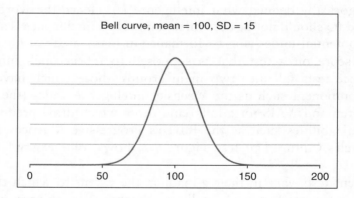

Bell curve, mean = 100, SD = 15

The test's developers will convert each of the raw scores from the test to a standardized score. This means that the average score becomes 100, and a range of scores (for the WAIS between 85 and 115) is selected to fall within one standard deviation above or below the mean (average) score. This means that 68% of people are expected to score between 85 and 115 on the test. People will get slightly different IQ scores from different tests depending on how the test's developers have carried out this conversion process. Children's IQ scores also take account of their age, because we would not expect equally intelligent 8- and 12-year-olds to be able to complete the same proportion of questions on a test.

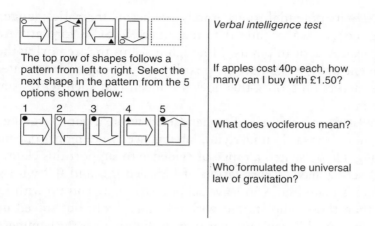

The top row of shapes follows a pattern from left to right. Select the next shape in the pattern from the 5 options shown below:

Verbal intelligence test

If apples cost 40p each, how many can I buy with £1.50?

What does vociferous mean?

Who formulated the universal law of gravitation?

Figure 5.2   Examples of non-verbal and verbal intelligence scale question styles.

Tests such as the Wechsler Scales have large verbal components. Answering questions like 'cow is to herd as geese is to (a) bird, (b) gaggle, (c) fly' requires general knowledge and a fairly good grasp of the English language as well as the logical skills that the question is intended to test. Hence differences in linguistic skills can become conflated with differences in intelligence. This can put ethnic minority and lower-SES individuals at a disadvantage. Indeed, one often finds that when these groups produce lower average IQ scores than middle-class, Western English speakers, it is mainly attributable to their scoring lower in the verbal components of the tests. Tests such as the Raven's do not use verbal instructions or questions, but measure non-verbal reasoning. Ethnic minority and lower-SES individuals therefore often score higher on these tests and hence they are described as 'culture fair'. However, it is worth reading Chapter 6 for a discussion of whether these tests are also 'gender fair'.

The differing cultural sensitivity of IQ tests has implications for their use in academic selection. Saccuzzo and Johnson[25] compared the utility of the Revised Wechsler Intelligence Scale for Children (WISC-R) and the Standard Raven's Progressive Matrices (SPM) for identifying gifted and talented children in San Diego. When the WISC-R was used to select children, white American children were over-represented in the gifted and talented programme. This difference was much reduced when the SPM was employed, and the authors also found that the predictive validity of the SPM – its potential to accurately predict mathematics, language and reading scores – was greater than that of the WISC-R for Latin American and African American pupils. Although it seems that removing the verbal component of IQ tests does help to limit the impact of unrelated background factors on scores, this does not mean that such IQ tests are truly culture fair.

In 1991, the psychologist Stephen Ceci[26] wrote a paper arguing that IQ scores (not necessarily underlying intelligence) were highly dependent on schooling. He presented a range of evidence to support this claim, including: IQ scores have a correlation of between 0.6 and 0.8 with years of schooling, so children who leave school early may end up with lower IQ scores than those who started with the same score but stayed in school for longer; and children's IQ scores drop slightly over the summer months when they are on vacation. Ceci explained these differences in terms of the skills which schooling confers and which are required for good performance on IQ tests. For example, IQ tests require good memory and taxonomic categorization skills as well as an understanding of the principle that closed questions in tests require a single, correct answer. The WISC-R also includes basic general knowledge such as the geographical location of famous rivers.

This dependence of IQ scores on schooling is a major reason why people from very different backgrounds such as rural, tribal cultures often register lower IQ scores. In the early part of the twenty-first century, researchers were very interested in investigating whether these low IQ scores were genuinely reflective of intelligence differences or could be otherwise explained. Many found that with appropriate training in the nature and demands of IQ tests, scores comparable to Western norms could be obtained. For example, Nicolas Hawkes[27] used a four-day training regime where the basic principles of the Raven's were explained to Primary 6 (typically age 10 and 11) schoolchildren in Ghana and practice questions were then completed. On the final day, 436 children were given three subtests from the Raven's. Their average scores were 9.1, 4.5 and 3.9 as compared to Western norms of 8.4, 5.4 and 3.7, supporting the idea that it is differences in experience rather than intelligence which underpin cultural differences in IQ scores. Indeed, IQ test scores can be seen to improve with practice even amongst Western test-takers.[28]

Another phenomenon that can affect people's performance in any test situation is stereotype threat. If an individual is aware of a certain stereotype, then their performance can reflect it. Steele and Aronson[29] first identified this effect in white and black American college students. They gave the same tests to different groups of participants, but in one condition the instructions for participants emphasized that verbal ability was being tested. Black Americans performed notably worse in this condition, reflecting the stereotype that Black Americans have poorer intellectual, and particularly verbal, ability. The impact of stereotype threat is also evident for gender stereotypes and other racial stereotypes such as Asian students being better at maths.[30] Notably, stereotype threat has been shown to affect the scores of African American participants taking the apparently 'culture fair' Raven's, such that they are significantly lower in a high-threat condition ($p < 0.01$, $d = 1.00$) but non-significantly higher in a low-threat condition than those of white American participants.[31]

If intelligence tests have so many flaws you may wonder why psychologists still make use of them. Well, measures of g extracted from IQ tests do correlate with diverse outcomes, including educational attainment, occupation and income. Taking a sample of 98 UK school children, Alloway and Alloway[32] found that non-verbal IQ measured at age 4–5 predicted 17% of the variation in numerical ability at age 10–11, whilst verbal IQ measured at age 10–11 predicted 11% of the variation in verbal ability at the same age. Looking at the GCSE scores of 334 pupils from the South East of England, Furnham and Monsen[33] found that general intelligence as measured using the Wonderlic Personnel Test explained 21% of variation in GCSE grades. Of course, this leaves roughly 80% of variation in academic performance to be explained by other factors (hence the distinction between intelligence, which affects performance in many areas, and ability or skills, which are measured in a specific area). Nevertheless, as humans we naturally want to understand what makes some people better at certain tasks than others, and whatever it is that IQ tests measure, this factor seems to play a role.

The Brain, Intelligence and Ability

The brain is the seat of intellectual functioning and therefore if people differ in their intelligence and abilities, one would expect to find some difference in their brains as well. However, the brain is incredibly complex, so identifying individual differences is only the beginning. One then needs to understand which differences are important and why.

Box 5.2   Areas of the brain

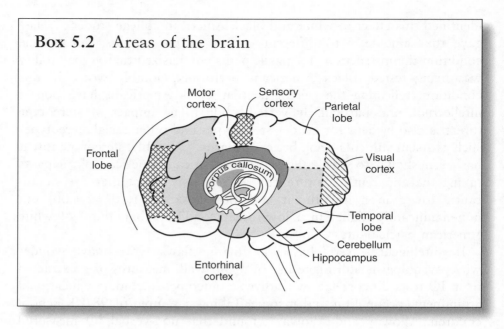

There is now a considerable amount of evidence to show that adults' brain structures vary according to their abilities. Drivers of London black cabs who have to memorize The Knowledge (the layout of all the routes in London) have been found to have greater grey-matter volume in the posterior hippocampus, which is an area of the brain linked with spatial memory. Meanwhile, non-taxi drivers have greater grey-matter volume in the anterior hippocampus.[34] Similarly, professional keyboard players have different grey-matter volumes in auditory, visual-spatial and motor areas compared to amateur musicians and non-musicians.[35] It appears that people's brain structures do specialize in response to the type of environmental inputs they receive.

One might argue that these individuals could have had different brain structures to begin with, which predisposed them to become taxi drivers or musicians. However, two factors argue against this as the sole explanation for the differences. Firstly, Maguire and colleagues have shown that the difference in anterior and posterior hippocampal volume of taxi drivers varies according to the length of their experience.[36] Second, Hyde and colleagues[37] have specifically shown that 5–7-year-olds who receive musical training for 29 months develop a larger anterior midbody of the corpus callosum than other children who receive no such training, despite there being no difference at baseline. Similarly, Ilg and colleagues[38] identified an increase in the density of grey matter in certain visual processing areas after adult participants practised a mirror-writing task every day for two weeks, something they believed reflected the involvement of these processing areas in learning or executing the task.

Such studies also offer evidence for the notion of 'use it or lose it'. Draganski and colleagues[39] took 24 young adults who did not know how to juggle and had half of them learn a simple juggling routine. They took MRI scans at the start of the study, after the training group had learned the routine and three months later, when many of this group could no longer juggle. Initially the groups showed no significant difference in their brain structures. Directly after learning the routine, the training group exhibited a significant expansion of grey matter in two brain areas ($p < 0.05$), the mid-temporal area and left posterior intraparietal sulcus. This difference was much smaller after three months without practice, suggesting that without continued use of the newly learned skill these neural adaptations were not maintained.

All of these studies indicate that our brains are adaptive structures; that their formation is not wholly predetermined but also responds and adapts to inputs. Even more interesting, however, is evidence that such inputs interact with typical development. Magnetic resonance morphometry, a type of brain imaging, has been used to show that musicians who learned their instrument before the age of 7 have a larger anterior corpus callosum than non-musicians or those who began learning after the age of 7,[40] although this difference may be restricted to males.[41] In Chapter 3 the notion of critical periods with respect to language learning is discussed. These imaging studies demonstrate that the teaching of specific skills interacts with typical brain development. Different brain areas are affected depending on the age at which one learns them. Over time we may be able to use such studies to determine the optimal time to teach different skills in order for the best possible levels of performance to be achieved.

This interaction of genes and environment is addressed by the theory of neuroconstructivism, which builds on Piaget's constructivist theory of development – that children purposefully interact with the environment to develop their knowledge, but that such interactions are bound by the limits of their mental maturity. Neuroconstructivism considers how both brain and cognition develop within environmental and biological limitations. The whole theory is one of interaction and mutual constraint:[42]

- Genes: expression of genes is not wholly predetermined but depends in part on environmental inputs; however, the expression of certain genes may increase the likelihood that an individual may seek out or experience certain inputs.

- Encellment: the activity of neurons shapes neural networks but the existing structure of neural networks also shapes that activity.
- Enbrainment: regions of the brain become functionally specialized by interacting with other brain areas that have different functions.
- Embodiment: physical limitations constrain the sensory inputs that the brain receives, but the brain's processing of these inputs may also affect how the body goes on to act.
- Ensocialment: the social environment affects whether individuals develop typical social attachment, mental health and cognition.

Neuroconstructivism suggests that our brains do not develop wholly according to some pre-determined genetic programme, nor do they begin as 'blank slates' and develop wholly in response to environmental inputs. Instead, children interact with their environment and environmental inputs affect the expression of genes, so that the brain shapes and is shaped by experiences. However, one can still ask whether some people start out with specific genes that cause their brains to develop in a way that means they can naturally acquire certain skills more easily than other people. For example, are some people predisposed to have a good sense of pitch or rhythm, or are some people predisposed to be more intelligent?

A particularly interesting study was conducted by Shaw and colleagues[43] who took brain scans from 307 participants between the ages of 3 and 29 years. The subjects also completed an age-appropriate Wechsler intelligence scale and were thereby divided into three groups: average intelligence (IQ 83–108), high intelligence (IQ 109–120) and superior intelligence (IQ 121–149). Although there was a modest correlation of cortical thickness and IQ, the main finding was that the developmental trajectory of cortical thickness varied with IQ score. Participants with superior IQs started with a thinner cortex in earlier childhood but then exhibited a long increase in cortical thickness up until early adolescence, followed by a prolonged decline. In participants with average IQs there was less or no initial cortical thickening and then a slow decline in cortical thickness over the same developmental period. This indicates that the brains of people with higher IQs might actually follow a completely different developmental trajectory.

So what variations do we see in the brain structure of adults with high and low IQs? McDaniel[44] conducted a meta-analysis of studies where IQ and brain size were reported and found that the two were significantly correlated. For males, IQ correlated 0.34 with brain size and for females

Box 5.3   Basic structure of the brain

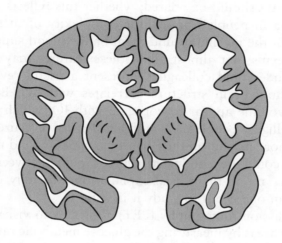

The picture shows a *coronal cross-section* of the brain; the view you would get if the brain were split in half from one ear to the other. You can see that it is divided into *grey* and *white matter*. The outer band of grey matter is the *cortex*, which is where the main bodies of all the *neurons* (nerve cells) in the brain are located, surrounded by non-neuronal supporting cells called *glia*. The white matter is where the long *axons* of these neurons extend to connect different areas of the brain to each other and to the central nervous system. These axons are covered in a fatty layer called *myelin*, which is why they appear white in this image. Myelin acts a bit like insulation on an electrical cable; it increases the speed with which *action potentials* – the electrical signals with which cells communicate – are conducted.

In the middle of the picture you can see a white bridge connecting the two hemispheres of the brain. This is the *corpus callosum*, a bundle of axons via which the two sides of the brain communicate.

the correlation was 0.40. The relationship was also stronger in adult samples. Although this is an interesting finding, it does not tell us why brain size and IQ should be related; whether this reflects the number of neurons or glia in people's brains, the complexity of their connections, the thickness of the myelin around them or the blood supply to them.

In fact, it seems that almost all of these features may correlate with intelligence. Luders and colleagues[45] present a useful review of studies investigating how brain structure correlates with IQ. Both grey- and white-matter volume appear to correlate with IQ, which could indicate that more intelligent people have a higher density of neurons or glia and that there is more myelin on their neurons, which would mean that neuronal signals could be conducted more rapidly between brain areas. However, these are all theoretical explanations. To fully understand the intelligent brain one needs to study it in action.

Positron emission tomography (PET) allows us to visualize activity in different brain areas by measuring the glucose metabolic rate (GMR) – the amount of energy the neurons and glia require to complete a task. Haier and colleagues[46] showed that people who scored higher on the Raven's actually had a lower GMR as they completed this test. In another small study with eight participants, they showed that individuals with the highest Raven's scores also showed the greatest decline in GMR as they learned to play the computer game Tetris.[47] This suggests that although people with higher IQs might have a higher volume of grey matter, intelligence is not just the result of using more brain cells to complete a task. These cells actually seem to work more efficiently – they can produce the same output whilst expending less energy.

There is also evidence to suggest that the brains of people with higher IQs might be better connected: the IQ scores of both children and adults correlate with measures of white matter[48,49] and there is a correlation between declines in white matter and cognitive ability in older people (see Charlton et al.[50]). Van den Heuvel and colleagues[51] used fMRI to monitor the spontaneous brain signals of 19 adults over 8 minutes, all of whom had completed the Dutch version of the WAIS-III. They used the fMRI data to calculate three measures: the extent to which neural activity was clustered in the brain; the number of connections between active areas; and the level of global communication efficiency between nodes of activity. Neither the number of connections nor the clustering of activity was significantly related to IQ scores. However, they found that nodes of activity were better connected in people with higher IQs, indicating that 'more efficiently functionally connected brains show a higher level of intellectual performance'.

These results fit with the work of Rex Jung and Richard Haier, who have attempted to bring together different neuropsychological evidence and produce an overarching theory of intelligence in the brain, which they term P-FIT: parietal-frontal integration theory.[52] Parietal and frontal brain areas are both shown to be active when individuals undertake tasks with high *g*-loadings: those that apparently rely heavily on intelligence rather than learned skills. Jung and Haier propose that the parietal areas take basic sensory inputs and abstract them so that they can be related to alternative 'cognitive sets'. These parietal areas then interact with frontal areas that test out different solutions to the given problem. Finally the anterior cingulate is engaged to initiate the correct response to the problem whilst inhibiting alternative responses. All of this relies on fast and reliable connectivity between brain areas, hence the importance of white matter, and indeed van den Heuvel and colleagues found some of the strongest associations between functional connectivity and IQ in frontal and parietal areas.

One finding that any neuroscientific theory of intelligence must eventually account for is that of sex differences in neural activation during the same tasks and in the relationship between white- and grey-matter densities and *g*. Females appear to have a higher proportion of grey matter than males, which may be explicable by the fact that their brains are smaller, so less extensive white matter is needed to connect different areas.[53] Gur and colleagues[53] gave 80 adults age 18–45 tests of verbal and spatial ability: the California Verbal Learning Test, verbal and spatial tests from the WAIS-R and the Judgment of Line Orientation test. They found that intracranial volume correlated with overall and spatial performance for both males and females, but only correlated significantly with verbal performance for females (r = 0.40). The relationship between white-matter volume and test performance (spatial, verbal and overall) was stronger for females than males. More recent work by Haier and colleagues[54] supports this finding. IQ correlated with the volume of white matter in more brain areas of females, and with the volume of grey matter in more brain areas of males. Furthermore, the areas where grey- and white-matter volumes correlated with IQ differed between males and females. Since males and females do not differ in their overall IQs, this led the researchers to suggest that 'different types of brain designs may manifest equivalent intellectual performance' (p320).

Much more research is needed before we can understand just how differences in neural structures relate to task performance and underlying cognitive potential. Apart from anything else, any future work needs to account for possible sex differences in these patterns. However, existing studies do suggest that people with different IQs may have different brain structures and this begs the question of whether genes or environment caused these differences.

Nature and nurture

As already discussed, Galton's early interest in intelligence arose because he thought it was a hereditary trait. Over a decade later, however, researchers are still trying to understand exactly how any genetic component of ability expresses itself and interacts with environmental factors. The heritability of intelligence appears to increase with age, with genetic factors explaining about 30% of variation in the IQ of children and up to 80% of the variation in adult IQs.[55] Davis, Haworth and Plomin[56] drew 8791 twin pairs from the Twins Early Development Study (TEDS) and assessed the verbal and non-verbal ability of a subset of this sample at different ages. They found that in early childhood (age 2–4) the heritability of *g* was 26% whereas in middle childhood (age 7–10) this rose to 54%. Meanwhile, the influence of shared environment declined from 68 to 28%. Two possible reasons for the increase in heritability were suggested. Firstly, the influence of genes may vary across development, which fits with Shaw *et al.*'s[43] finding that the correlation of *g* with cortical thickness increases during development. Secondly, it may be that as children develop they seek out stimuli that suit their genetic predispositions and hence the impact of these genetic factors is enhanced (gene–environment co-variation).

A number of studies indicate that there is a genetic component underlying some of the individual differences in brain structure that correlate with IQ. For example, Posthuma and colleagues[57] have provided evidence for high heritability of total grey- and white-matter volume in the brain. Meanwhile, Chiang and colleagues[58] compared the brain structure of 92 twins to show that differences in white-matter structure of key brain regions had a heritable basis. Since then, by comparing the genetic makeup of 571 twins and siblings, they have actually identified single nucleotide polymorphisms (DNA sequences) that seem to modulate the relationship between white-matter structure and IQ.[59] This suggests that there is a genetic basis for some IQ differences; however, the fact that IQ is not 100% heritable also indicates that environmental factors must have an influence.

You only have to compare identical twins to see that even if people have an identical genotype (genetic code), their phenotype (the characteristics and behaviours resulting from these genes) varies with subtle differences in experience. This interaction of genes and environment is what makes it so hard to determine quite how much our cognitive abilities

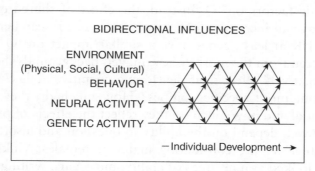

Figure 5.3   The bidirectional influences of environment, behaviour, neural and genetic activity on one another. *Source*: Gottlieb, G. Experiential canalization of behavioural development: Theory. *Developmental Psychology*. 1991;21(1): 4–13. Copyright © APA. Reprinted with permission.

are pre-determined. It used to be thought that genes worked like a video: each person was born with their genetic code which then played out along pre-determined lines. However, we now think of genes as being more like a video game that starts with a certain level of pre-programming but also adapts to the inputs of the user. This more modern theory can be described as probabilistic epigenesis,[60] where there are 'bidirectional influences within and between levels of analysis'; these levels of analysis are shown in Figure 5.3. The implication is that although we are born with a certain set of genes, different ones may be activated in different conditions, so may be more or less influential depending on our environment. For example, we have genes in our skeletal muscle that are only activated with exercise and therefore help us to adapt to such physical exertion. Similarly, it is possible that even if someone is born with genes that predispose them to have more grey matter or highly myelinated axons, these genes might only be activated in certain environments.

One of the main factors correlated with variations in early childhood environment is socioeconomic status. Hanscombe and colleagues[61] review a range of studies, some of which suggest that intelligence is more heritable amongst higher-SES groups and others that indicate it is more heritable amongst lower-SES groups. In their own study, they used 8716 twin pairs from TEDS and measured their SES by parental income, occupation or education. They also calculated g from a number of age-appropriate tests of cognitive ability. As expected from prior research, the correlation of IQ with SES increased from r = 0.08 at age 2 to r = 0.37 at age 14. IQ was also more variable amongst lower-SES participants. Contrary to existing findings, however, there was no consistent impact of shared genetic factors on IQ. Instead, the effect of shared environment seemed to have an increasing impact with age. The researchers suggested that, in the UK at least, genes have a similar impact on IQ across SES, but for children from the most disadvantaged backgrounds their environment can negatively affect their developing cognitive ability.

What about more specific abilities? How much do they depend on innate potential and how much do they reflect the effects of practice? The answer may well depend on the ability in question and also, to a certain extent, whether we are considering males or females. Vinkhuyzen and colleagues[62] looked at nine areas of ability: music; art; writing; languages; chess; mathematics; sports; memory; and knowledge. They used data from 1685 pairs of twins aged 12–24 who had completed a self-rating of their competence in each area, from 1 (below average) to 4 (exceptional). They found that dominant genetic factors explained 48% of variance in chess competence, 56% of variance in mathematical competence and 47% of variance in memory competence. However, there were also sex-specific findings: for example, for males 64% of variance in sports competence was explained by additive genetic factors, whereas for females 51% of variance in sports competence was explained by shared environmental factors. Although this might reflect genuine genetically based sex differences, it could also reflect sex differences in environmental inputs or simply in self-reporting. For example, the authors noted that self-report was a poor measure of language competence for this sample because languages are taught to a high level in the Netherlands and so many more respondents rated themselves as above average in this area than in other abilities. Second, the researchers did not control for IQ in this study, but from prior data suggested that this did correlate with the different abilities to varying degrees. Therefore part of the heritability of each individual ability may have actually reflected the heritability of IQ, which affects competency in many fields.

It is evident from these studies that even if IQ and specific abilities are partially heritable, there is also a considerable amount of variation explained by environmental influences. Therefore the next question is whether environmental interventions can actually be used to boost people's intelligence.

Interventions to Affect Abilities and Intelligence

It is common sense that practice will tend to improve performance and neuro-imaging shows us that this can also alter the grey matter in our brains. However, intuition also tells us that some people tend to reach a certain level of performance with less practice than others, and this is usually considered to reflect their intelligence. Therefore a popular question is whether specific interventions can actually boost intelligence (and not just IQ scores). Three interventions are addressed here: learning a musical instrument; changing what you eat; and 'brain training'.

A correlation between childhood intelligence and the learning of a musical instrument is relatively well established; however, as the saying goes, correlation does not equal causation. Despite a popular idea that musical training may boost IQ, the evidence for this is variable. In a study comparing 114 six-year-olds divided into piano, voice, drama and no-lesson groups, Schellenberg[63] found that after 36 weeks of teaching the WISC-III scores of the combined piano and voice groups had increased more than those of controls (d = 0.35). However, the very fact that these groups had to be combined for the difference to reach significance indicates that the impact of musical training was very small. Other studies have found no such difference on WISC-III or Raven's scores after training on musical instruments.[37,64] Musical training – that is, training in rhythm, pitch, melody, voice, and basic musical concepts – has been shown to boost the verbal IQ of 4–6-year-olds[65] but this is not the same thing as learning to play an instrument. Overall, the message seems to be that most of the correlation between learning a musical instrument and IQ scores is not causal: higher-achieving pupils are simply more likely to take music lessons as well. As Schellenberg[66] points out, undergraduates studying music do not have particularly high IQs, which contradicts the idea that advanced instrumental training can boost intelligence.

The idea of 'brain food' is popular in the media; we are constantly hearing about new foods that might boost brain power. So is there empirical support for any of these claims? Omega-3 fatty acids are found in oily fish and certain nuts and are often linked with brainpower. However, in a recent review of intervention studies where participants of different ages were given either omega-3 dietary supplements or placebos, Karr[67] suggested that the power of such interventions is limited. Whilst there is good evidence that maternal consumption of omega-3s during pregnancy may boost cognitive abilities in early childhood (up to about 4 years of age), the evidence linking intake of omega-3 supplements and increases in IQ amongst typically developing school children is much less consistent. This could be because DHA is a component of cell membranes and many new synapses are being formed during infancy, whereas later there is more emphasis on synaptic pruning.

The Avon Longitudinal Study of Parents and Children has tracked thousands of children in the Avon area since they were born in 1991 and 1992. As part of the study, parents were asked to complete a checklist indicating what their children were eating at ages 3, 4, 7 and 8½. Three dietary groups were thereby identified: processed (high in fat and sugar), traditional (high in meat, potatoes and vegetables) and health conscious (high in salads, pasta, rice, fruit and vegetables). The children's attainment at each Key Stage in school was recorded and at age 8½ they took a short form of the WISC-III. Longitudinal comparisons of data from 3966 children showed that those who had a diet high in processed foods at age 3 had significantly lower IQs at age 8½ ($p < 0.0001$), even after controlling for background factors such as SES. Those who were eating a more health-conscious diet at age 8½ had significantly higher IQs ($p = 0.001$).[68] The consumption of processed foods at age 3 was also linked to significantly lower school attainment at the end of Key Stages 1 and 2 for 5741 of the children.[69] Again, it is worth noting how children's diet in early childhood actually seems to have a stronger impact on their cognitive ability than their diet at the time of testing.

Finally, what about brain training? Plenty of books and computer games are now available that claim to be able to boost the intelligence of the reader or player and we discuss the evidence relating to these training programmes in Chapter 2. To summarize very briefly, there are studies showing that sustained training on some tasks (e.g. five days a week over at least a month) can boost IQ scores. For example, Jaeggi and colleagues[70] gave primary-age children an attention-related *n*-back task and reported a significant increase in the IQ scores of those children who improved most on the task. Meanwhile, Karbach and Kray[71] showed that children and adults who trained on task-switching paradigms ended up with significantly higher Raven's scores ($p < 0.05$) than those who trained on a single task that did not place high demands on executive functions. However, further work is needed to prove that it is underlying intelligence, not just IQ test performance, which is affected by this training and that any intelligence gains, independent of gains in other executive functions, actually impact on future academic performance.

Psychologists have not yet identified simple interventions that consistently and universally boost the intelligence of typically developing children. However, it is worth remembering that some interventions have a bigger impact on lower-performing children; they may be particularly beneficial for children who have below average cognitive abilities rather than affecting all children equally. Also, even if some of these interventions do not affect IQ scores they may still have other positive cognitive or behavioural effects. Finally, it is important to remember that IQ is a statistical creation; if everyone's intelligence were to be boosted by some intervention then IQ tests would simply be re-standardized so that a new absolute score became the average IQ of 100. Indeed, this is what we have seen as overall living standards improve in developed countries.

Attitudes to Ability in the Education System

No teacher would deny that they want every child to reach their full potential. However, existing empirical research still has not clarified quite how much of this potential is genetically determined from birth and how much it can vary with experience. Furthermore, it is unclear whether, as the brain's structure matures, our intelligence and abilities become increasingly fixed.

The structure of an education system and the pedagogical approaches of its teachers actually speak volumes about dominant cultural beliefs regarding intelligence and ability. For example, identifying 'gifted and talented' pupils indicates that educators believe that ability is a relatively fixed trait, unlikely to change. Placing pupils in academic streams (see Chapter 8) implies that general intelligence has more impact on academic performance than subject-specific abilities, whilst setting by subject suggests the reverse.

The use of setting, streaming and ability grouping also reflects a cultural belief that intelligence is predetermined and relatively static. In UK primary schools children are often seated according to their current attainment, with the idea that slower learners can easily receive additional support whilst more able pupils will not be held back. In secondary schools, setting is quite commonplace, which firmly reinforces the idea that some pupils are inherently more academically able than others. Crucially, the UK curriculum is set and taught according to year group. This means that even if some learners have not picked up all of the basics in a subject, they are swept along to be taught more complex topics the next year. Learners are also allowed to drop some subjects at age 14 and more at 16, regardless of their attainment to date, the implication being that no matter how much they persevere they would not be able to acquire this knowledge (or that it would not be worth the additional time).

In contrast, in Japanese elementary schools the whole class is expected to progress together, until every child has acquired a new concept (see Chapter 11). The assumption is that all learners are able to acquire the knowledge but some will take longer than others. Hence ability is seen as a reflection of effort and application more than innate intelligence. Of course, there is still highly competitive academic selection at a later stage in the Japanese system, which suggests that educators believe that ability becomes less malleable with age.

So how do effort, application and genetics balance out? The evidence in this chapter identifies a heritable element to intelligence and suggests that there are differences between the neural development of people with high and average IQs. Therefore it is not entirely wrong to talk about intelligence as predetermined, or ability as fixed. Nonetheless, neuroconstructivist theory and studies of socioeconomic differences in IQ and of the impact of early childhood diet on later attainment tell us that the environment also has an influence on how our abilities develop. In fact, the early interventions described in Chapter 10 rely on this being the case. What research is yet to determine is quite how genes and environment interact, and how much the influence of one can outweigh the other.

Consider identical twins, separated at birth, who have inherited genes that predispose them to high academic intelligence. Say the first twin, A, lives in a home where there is nothing to read (either in print or online), so spends her days outside climbing and building dens, hence developing her spatial abilities. The second twin, B, meanwhile, grows up in a flat with adults reading and talking to her and playing interactive word and number games. When they start school, Twin B exhibits exceptional verbal and numerical abilities, whilst Twin A has average verbal and numerical abilities but good spatial skills and coordination. We do not know whether it is too late to change things around. Given her genetic advantage, and relatively young age, it is possible that Twin A could still catch up with Twin B. However, at some point Twin A's brain might have adapted so much to the spatially rich but linguistically poor environment that no amount of studying can close the gap. Furthermore, Twin B is not going to stop learning during this time, so her head start might put her at an advantage for the rest of her life.

Empirical research has not yet resolved these questions. We do know that even the adult brain changes in response to learning, suggesting that it is never too late to intervene. On the other hand, we know that experiences like learning a musical instrument interact with the genetically determined process of neural development, suggesting that the early childhood environment may have a lasting impact on the structure of the brain. The tendency in many education systems to sort adolescents by attainment would imply that by this age we think their abilities are relatively fixed. Actually, we still do not know how much genes determine academic potential and whether there is an age at which no amount of additional support can fully compensate for disadvantage in early life.

Summary

- There are many definitions of intelligence, the common elements of which are a capacity to learn quickly, problem-solve effectively and adapt and succeed in one's environment. Some psychologists restrict their theories of intelligence to cognitive characteristics but others include other factors such as interpersonal skills. In non-Western cultures, social and practical skills may also be more central to conceptions of intelligence.
- The traditional Western view of intelligence as a heritable trait can result in teachers and parents making the implicit assumption that some pupils are inherently more academically able than others. In other countries ability is considered more reflective of effort. Carol Dweck has shown that portraying ability as an incremental rather than a fixed entity can encourage pupils to adopt more positive learning goals and raise their attainment.
- IQ scores correlate with future attainment, occupation and income. Many intelligence tests rely on good literacy skills, which can result in the IQs of lower-SES pupils and those with English as an additional language being underestimated. 'Culture fair' tests such as the Raven's Progressive Matrices help to mitigate this bias, but still reward other school-taught skills such as convergent (rather than creative) thinking and general knowledge.
- The structure of both children's and adults' brains can alter with the acquisition of new abilities, although the precise areas that change can vary with the ongoing process of neural maturation. It is still uncertain precisely whether and how neural maturation constrains our acquisition of new skills and abilities.
- Empirical research suggests that individuals with higher IQ scores have: a different pattern of neural maturation; larger brains; greater grey- and white-matter volume; more efficient neural use of glucose in the brain during well-practised tasks; and more efficient neuronal connectivity. These structural differences indicate that it is reasonable to employ the concept of IQ and to expect IQ variations to be reflected in other tests of cognitive performance, including academic measures.
- The heritability of IQ ranges from about 25% in early childhood to 80% in adulthood, whilst the heritability of specific abilities varies

widely. The impact of genes co-varies with the environment, so that people with similar genes may have differing IQs depending upon their experience.

- Amongst interventions purported to boost children's IQs, there is little evidence that learning a musical instrument or taking dietary supplements in later life is effective. Early childhood diet may be important, however, and sustained brain training programmes may also have some impact on IQ test scores, if not on intelligence itself.

Educational implications

- Some theories of intelligence that are popular with educators, such as Multiple Intelligences, do not actually have strong empirical support, and should therefore be employed with caution. Nonetheless, adopting a broad view of intelligence can ensure that pupils with non-academic strengths still feel valued and successful in an educational environment.
- A predominant focus on verbal and mathematical skills in schools can result in the strong spatial abilities exhibited by some pupils being overlooked and undervalued. Pupils with strong spatial abilities excel in STEM subjects, so educators and politicians should consider how to adapt the modern curriculum and teaching methods to use and reward these skills more frequently.
- Given the academic benefits of pupils adopting incremental theories of ability, teachers should be careful to praise effort rather than intelligence. Educators might also try to avoid signalling that ability is fixed, for example by not explicitly labelling 'gifted and talented' pupils and by not grouping pupils by ability from a young age.
- Consuming a diet high in processed foods in early life has been linked to lower attainment in primary school, which suggests that primary schools should be particularly careful to provide nutritious, un-processed meals since this might actually affect pupils' future academic performance.
- We do not know how the relative influences of genes and environment on IQ play out over the lifespan. However, since environmental variation during childhood explains socioeconomic differences in IQ and since neural changes with learning interact with ongoing neural development, we might conclude that early interventions will have more impact than adolescent interventions for addressing socioeconomic inequalities in attainment.

Note: Answer to Figure 5.2: The large arrow and small circles and triangle follow a different pattern. The arrow rotates counter-clockwise, therefore the next shape is either 1 or 4. The small circles and triangles move clockwise from the top left, to top right, to bottom right etc. Therefore the next shape must be in the top left. Finally, the circles are all white and the triangles are all black. Therefore the answer cannot be 1 as the circle is black. This leaves option 4 as the correct answer.

References

1　Nicholls JG, Patashnick M, Mettetal G. Conceptions of ability and intelligence. *Child Development*. 1986;57(3):636–645. doi:10.2307/1130342.

2　Spearman C. *The Abilities of Man, Their Nature and Measurement*. New York: Macmillan; 1927.

3　Horn JL, Cattell RB. Refinement and test of the theory of fluid and crystallized general intelligences. *Journal of Educational Psychology*. 1966; 57(5):253.

4　Legg S, Hutter M. A collection of definitions of intelligence. 2006. Available at:www.vetta.org/documents/A-Collection-of-Definitions-of-Intelligence.pdf. Accessed 2 December 2013.

5　Okagaki L, Sternberg RJ. Parental beliefs and children's school performance. *Child Development*. 1993;64(1):36–56.

6　Cole M, Gay J, Glick JA, Sharp DW. *The Cultural Context of Learning and Thinking: An Exploration in Experimental Anthropology*. New York: Basic Books; 1971.

7　Sternberg RJ, Conway BE, Ketron JL, Bernstein M. People's conceptions of intelligence. *Journal of Personality and Social Psychology*. 1981;41(1):37–55. doi:10.1037/0022-3514.41.1.37.

8　Vernon PE. *The Structure of Human Abilities*. New York: Methuen; 1950.

9　Humphreys LG, Lubinski D, Yao G. Utility of predicting group membership and the role of spatial visualization in becoming an engineer, physical scientist, or artist. *Journal of Applied Psychology*. 1993;78(2):250–261. doi:10.1037/0021-9010.78.2.250.

10　Wai J, Lubinski D, Benbow CP. Spatial ability for STEM domains: Aligning over 50 years of cumulative psychological knowledge solidifies its importance. *Journal of Educational Psychology*. 2009;101(4):817.

11　Guilford JP. Intelligence: 1965 model. *American Psychologist*. 1966;21(1): 20–26. doi:10.1037/h0023296.

12　Gardner HE. *Frames of Mind: The Theory of Multiple Intelligences*. New York: Basic Books; 1985.

13　Ceci SJ, Liker J. Academic and nonacademic intelligence: An experimental separation. In: Sternberg RJ, Wagner RK, eds. *Practical Intelligence: Nature and Origins of Competence in the Everyday World*. New York: Cambridge University Press; 1986.

14 Sternberg RJ. Patterns of giftedness: A triarchic analysis. *Roeper Review.* 2000;22(4):231–235. doi:10.1080/02783190009554044.

15 Gardner HE. On failing to grasp the core of MI theory: A response to Visser *et al. Intelligence.* 2006;34:503–505.

16 Armstrong T. *Multiple Intelligences in the Classroom*. Alexandria, VA: ASCD; 2009.

17 Visser BA, Ashton MC, Vernon PA. *g* and the measurement of multiple intelligences: A response to Gardner. *Intelligence.* 2006;34(5):507–510.

18 Visser BA, Ashton MC, Vernon PA. Beyond *g*: Putting multiple intelligences theory to the test. *Intelligence.* 2006;34(5):487–502. doi:10.1016/j.intell. 2006.02.004.

19 Waterhouse L. Multiple intelligences, the Mozart effect, and emotional intelligence: A critical review. *Educational Psychologist.* 2006;41(4):207–225.

20 Dweck CS. Motivational processes affecting learning. *American Psychologist.* 1986;41(10):1040.

21 Blackwell LS, Trzesniewski KH, Dweck CS. Implicit theories of intelligence predict achievement across an adolescent transition: A longitudinal study and an intervention. *Child Development.* 2007;78(1):246–263.

22 Mueller CM, Dweck CS. Praise for intelligence can undermine children's motivation and performance. *Journal of Personality and Social Psychology.* 1998;75(1):33–52. doi:10.1037/0022-3514.75.1.33.

23 Heyman GD. Talking about success: Implications for achievement motivation. *Journal of Applied Developmental Psychology.* 2008;29(5):361–370. doi:10.1016/j.appdev.2008.06.003.

24 Cimpian A, Mu Y, Erickson LC. Who is good at this game? Linking an activity to a social category undermines children's achievement. *Psychological Science.* 2012;23(5):533–541. doi:10.1177/0956797611429803.

25 Saccuzzo DP, Johnson NE. Traditional psychometric tests and proportionate representation: An intervention and program evaluation study. *Psychological Assessment.* 1995;7(2):183–194. doi:10.1037/1040-3590.7.2.183.

26 Ceci SJ. How much does schooling influence general intelligence and its cognitive components? A reassessment of the evidence. *Developmental Psychology.* 1991;27(5):703–722. doi:10.1037/0012-1649.27.5.703.

27 Hawkes NC. The written English of Ghanaian primary six pupils in relation to their exposure to English as the medium of spoken instruction. PhD Thesis, University of York; 1973.

28 Kulik JA, Kulik C-LC, Bangert RL. Effects of practice on aptitude and achievement test scores. *American Educational Research Journal.* 1984;21(2): 435–447. doi:10.2307/1162453.

29 Steele CM, Aronson J. Stereotype threat and the intellectual test performance of African Americans. *Journal of Personality and Social Psychology.* 1995; 69(5):797.

30 Aronson J, Lustina MJ, Good C, Keough K, Brown J, *et al.* When white men can't do math: Necessary and sufficient factors in stereotype threat. *Journal of Experimental Social Psychology.* 1999;35(1):29–46.

31 Brown RP, Day EA. The difference isn't black and white: Stereotype threat and the race gap on Raven's Advanced Progressive Matrices. *Journal of Applied Psychology.* 2006;91(4):979–985. doi:10.1037/0021-9010.91.4.979.

32 Alloway TP, Alloway RG. Investigating the predictive roles of working memory and IQ in academic attainment. *Journal of Experimental Child Psychology.* 2010;106(1):20–29.

33 Furnham A, Monsen J. Personality traits and intelligence predict academic school grades. *Learning and Individual Differences.* 2009;19(1):28–33. doi:10.1016/j.lindif.2008.02.001.

34 Maguire EA, Woollett K, Spiers HJ. London taxi drivers and bus drivers: A structural MRI and neuropsychological analysis. *Hippocampus.* 2006;16(12):1091–1101.

35 Gaser C, Schlaug G. Brain structures differ between musicians and non-musicians. *Journal of Neuroscience.* 2003;23(27):9240–9245.

36 Maguire EA, Gadian DG, Johnsrude IS, *et al.* Navigation-related structural change in the hippocampi of taxi drivers. *PNAS.* 2000;97(8):4398–4403. doi:10.1073/pnas.070039597.

37 Hyde KL, Lerch J, Norton A, *et al.* Musical training shapes structural brain development. *Journal of Neuroscience.* 2009;29(10):3019–3025.

38 Ilg R, Wohlschläger AM, Gaser C, *et al.* Gray matter increase induced by practice correlates with task-specific activation: A combined functional and morphometric magnetic resonance imaging study. *Journal of Neuroscience.* 2008;28(16):4210–4215. doi:10.1523/JNEUROSCI.5722-07.2008.

39 Draganski B, Gaser C, Busch V, Schuierer G, Bogdahn U, *et al.* Neuroplasticity: Changes in grey matter induced by training. *Nature.* 2004;427(6972):311–312. doi:10.1038/427311a.

40 Schlaug G, Jäncke L, Huang Y, Staiger JF, Steinmetz H. Increased corpus callosum size in musicians. *Neuropsychologia.* 1995;33(8):1047–1055.

41 Lee DJ, Chen Y, Schlaug G. Corpus callosum: Musician and gender effects. *Neuroreport.* 2003;14(2):205–209. doi:10.1097/01.wnr.0000053761.76853.41.

42 Westermann G, Thomas MSC, Karmiloff-Smith A. Neuroconstructivism. In: Goswami U, ed. *The Wiley-Blackwell Handbook of Childhood Cognitive Development.* 2nd ed. Chichester: John Wiley & Sons; 2010:723–748. Available at: www.psyc.bbk.ac.uk/research/DNL/personalpages/Westermann_Thomas_Karmiloff-Smith.pdf. Accessed 2 December 2013.

43 Shaw P, Greenstein D, Lerch J, *et al.* Intellectual ability and cortical development in children and adolescents. *Nature.* 2006;440(7084):676–679.

44 McDaniel MA. Big-brained people are smarter: A meta-analysis of the relationship between in vivo brain volume and intelligence. *Intelligence.* 2005;33(4):337–346.

45   Luders E, Narr KL, Thompson PM, Toga AW. Neuroanatomical correlates of intelligence. *Intelligence.* 2009;37(2):156–163. doi:10.1016/j.intell.2008. 07.002.

46   Haier RJ, Siegel BV, Nuechterlein KH, *et al.* Cortical glucose metabolic rate correlates of abstract reasoning and attention studied with positron emission tomography. *Intelligence.* 1988;12(2):199–217.

47   Haier RJ, Siegel B, Tang C, Abel L, Buchsbaum MS. Intelligence and changes in regional cerebral glucose metabolic rate following learning. *Intelligence.* 1992;16(3–4):415–426.

48   Narr KL, Woods RP, Thompson PM, *et al.* Relationships between IQ and regional cortical gray matter thickness in healthy adults. *Cerebral Cortex.* 2007;17(9):2163–2171.

49   Schmithorst VJ, Wilke M, Dardzinski BJ, Holland SK. Cognitive functions correlate with white matter architecture in a normal pediatric population: A diffusion tensor MRI study. *Human brain mapping.* 2005;26(2):139–147.

50   Charlton RA, Barrick TR, McIntyre DJ, *et al.* White matter damage on diffusion tensor imaging correlates with age-related cognitive decline. *Neurology.* 2006;66(2):217–222.

51   Van den Heuvel MP, Stam CJ, Kahn RS, Pol HEH. Efficiency of functional brain networks and intellectual performance. *Journal of Neuroscience.* 2009;29(23):7619–7624. doi:10.1523/JNEUROSCI.1443-09.2009.

52   Jung RE, Haier RJ. The parieto-frontal integration theory (P-FIT) of intelligence: Converging neuroimaging evidence. *Behavioral and Brain Sciences.* 2007;30(2):135–153.

53   Gur RC, Turetsky BI, Matsui M, *et al.* Sex differences in brain gray and white matter in healthy young adults: Correlations with cognitive performance. *Journal of Neuroscience.* 1999;19(10):4065–4072.

54   Haier RJ, Jung RE, Yeo RA, Head K, Alkire MT. The neuroanatomy of general intelligence: Sex matters. *Neuroimage.* 2005;25(1):320–327. doi:10.1016/j.neuroimage.2004.11.019.

55   Deary IJ, Penke L, Johnson W. The neuroscience of human intelligence differences. *Nature Reviews: Neuroscience.* 2010;11(3):201–211.

56   Davis OSP, Haworth CMA, Plomin R. Dramatic increase in heritability of cognitive development from early to middle childhood: An 8-year longitudinal study of 8,700 pairs of twins. *Psychological Science.* 2009;20(10):1301–1308. doi:10.1111/j.1467-9280.2009.02433.x.

57   Posthuma D, De Geus EJC, Baaré WFC, Pol HEH, Kahn RS, *et al.* The association between brain volume and intelligence is of genetic origin. 2002. Available at: http://psycnet.apa.org/psycinfo/2002-10756-001. Accessed 2 December 2013.

58   Chiang M-C, Barysheva M, Shattuck DW, *et al.* Genetics of brain fiber architecture and intellectual performance. *Journal of Neuroscience.* 2009;29(7):2212–2224. doi:10.1523/JNEUROSCI.4184-08.2009.

59 Chiang M-C, Barysheva M, McMahon KL, *et al.* Gene network effects on brain microstructure and intellectual performance identified in 472 twins. *Journal of Neuroscience.* 2012;32(25):8732–8745. doi:10.1523/JNEUROSCI.5993-11.2012.

60 Gottlieb G. Probabilistic epigenesis. *Developmental Science.* 2007;10(1):1–11. doi:10.1111/j.1467-7687.2007.00556.x.

61 Hanscombe KB, Trzaskowski M, Haworth CMA, Davis OSP, Dale PS, *et al.* Socioeconomic status (SES) and children's intelligence (IQ): In a UK-representative sample SES moderates the environmental, not genetic, effect on IQ. *PLoS ONE.* 2012;7(2):e30320. doi:10.1371/journal.pone.0030320.

62 Vinkhuyzen AAE, van der Sluis S, Posthuma D, Boomsma DI. The heritability of aptitude and exceptional talent across different domains in adolescents and young adults. *Behavior Genetics.* 2009;39(4):380–392. doi:10.1007/s10519-009-9260-5.

63 Schellenberg EG. Music lessons enhance IQ. *Psychological Science.* 2004;15(8):511.

64 Moreno S, Marques C, Santos A, Santos M, Besson M, *et al.* Musical training influences linguistic abilities in 8-year-old children: More evidence for brain plasticity. *Cerebral Cortex.* 2009;19(3):712–723.

65 Moreno S, Bialystok E, Barac R, Schellenberg EG, Cepeda NJ, *et al.* Short-term music training enhances verbal intelligence and executive function. *Psychological Science.* 2011;22(11):1425–1433. doi:10.1177/0956797611416999.

66 Schellenberg EG. Cognitive performance after listening to music: A review of the Mozart effect. *Music, Health, and Wellbeing.* 2012:324.

67 Karr JE, Alexander JE, Winningham RG. Omega-3 polyunsaturated fatty acids and cognition throughout the lifespan: A review. *Nutritional Neuroscience.* 2011;14(5):216–225. doi:10.1179/1476830511Y.0000000012.

68 Northstone K, Joinson C, Emmett P, Ness A, Paus T. Are dietary patterns in childhood associated with IQ at 8 years of age? A population-based cohort study. *Journal of Epidemiology and Community Health.* 2011. doi:10.1136/jech.2010.111955.

69 Feinstein L, Sabates R, Sorhaindo A, *et al.* Dietary patterns related to attainment in school: The importance of early eating patterns. *Journal of Epidemiology and Community Health.* 2008;62(8):734–739. doi:10.1136/jech.2007.068213.

70 Jaeggi SM, Buschkuehl M, Jonides J, Shah P. Short- and long-term benefits of cognitive training. *PNAS.* 2011;108(25):10081–10086. doi:10.1073/pnas.1103228108.

71 Karbach J, Kray J. How useful is executive control training? Age differences in near and far transfer of task-switching training. *Developmental Science.* 2009;12(6):978–990. doi:10.1111/j.1467-7687.2009.00846.x.

Chapter 6

Sex* Differences
Do They Matter in Education?

Many of us think of certain personality traits as being particularly masculine or feminine. Do you? Test yourself. Rate each of the following on whether you rate it as a feminine or a masculine attribute (or as neither).

Attribute	Masculine or feminine or neutral
Self-reliant	
Compassionate	
Gentle	
Competitive	
Reliable	
Friendly	
Sympathetic	
Assertive	
Independent	
Conventional	
Analytical	
Solemn	
Affectionate	
Conceited	
Understanding	

Check against Table 6.1, see later.
Source: Taken from Sandra Bem's 1974 paper.[21]

* Sex is biological, gender is a social construct, but the terms are often used interchangeably.

Education and Learning: An Evidence-Based Approach, First Edition. Jane Mellanby and Katy Theobald.

There are differences in the educational outcomes of boys and girls and men and women. In many cultures, boys perform somewhat better at mathematics than girls but are worse at reading. Overall, in the large PISA study (Programme for International Student Assessment, see Chapter 11) this amounted to an average 2% advantage in mathematics for 15-year-old boys compared with girls. In contrast, 15-year-old girls did 16% better than boys in reading. At universities in the UK, a higher proportion of women get 'good' degrees (in 2010, women 67%, men 61%); but a slightly lower proportion of women than men obtain top (first-class) degrees (in 2010, women 14.3%, men 14.9%). At the most prestigious universities, this sex difference in first-class degrees is greater, particularly in certain humanities subjects.

The question of whether the sexes have equal capacities to perform in all areas of academic endeavour is highly controversial and of great interest to the media today. There are deep-seated beliefs about the different capabilities of men and women and girls and boys and about the relative importance of those capabilities. Educating girls in a similar way to boys is a comparatively recent phenomenon. In the educational systems of the past – ancient Athens and Rome, Europe into the latter half of the nineteenth century, ancient China – it was usually only the boys who received formal education. Education was also restricted to the reasonably well off. Since people of higher social class would have had servants or slaves to do menial work, it cannot be argued that girls were not educated because they would be expected only to have time to do housework and look after children. No; the reason lies within those deep-seated beliefs about the capabilities of the two sexes. Thus, Pierre Dubois, a medieval educationalist, in his *De Recuperatione Terrae Sanctae* (1309) advocated teaching of Latin to both girls and boys but also proposed that it was necessary with girls to: 'Instruct them in a manner as far as possible more perceptible to the senses and plainer and easier because of the weakness of the sex, and because they run through their ages more quickly than men, attain more rapidly to such perfection as is possible for them, which is a sign of the weakness of their natural virtue. . . . Those that last less long grow more quickly.'

Charles Darwin (Figure 6.1), in *The Descent of Man and Selection in Relation to Sex*,[1] promoted the superiority of men, writing 'man attains higher eminence in whatever he takes up' in ways ranging from 'deep thought, reason or imagination or merely the use of the senses and hands', referring to Galton's work on genius. He considered that there were profound differences in personality such that 'Man is more courageous, pugnacious and energetic, and has more inventive genius' (p557); women have 'greater tenderness and less selfishness' (p563); in woman 'powers of intuition, of rapid perception, and perhaps of imitation, are more strongly marked than in man'; man 'delights in competition, and this leads to ambition which passes too easily into selfishness . . . his natural and unfortunate birthright'.

Box 6.1   Major theories and beliefs (not necessarily mutually exclusive) concerning causes of sex differences in behaviour and achievement

---

Evolutionary:	Males were the hunters, so needed to be better at navigation and fighting; hence selected for spatial skill, physical strength, speed and aggression.
	Females looked after the children and so needed to be better at communication; hence selected for language ability. (Charles Darwin)
Hormonal:	Male babies produce more testosterone than female babies. Testosterone in the womb causes the brain to develop as systematizer; with less testosterone the brain develops as empathizer. (Simon Baron-Cohen[2])
Brain size:	Males have bigger brains and this makes them more intelligent than females. (Richard Lynn)
Stereotype threat:	Women are generally stereotyped as being worse at certain skills, such as navigation, mental rotation, mathematics. They are aware of these perceptions, and this causes them to be anxious when performing relevant tasks, which impairs performance.
Discrimination:	Certain courses or occupations are considered more suitable for one sex or the other and conscious or unconscious bias is produced.

Figure 6.1   Portait of Charles Darwin by John Collier. © National Portrait Gallery, London. Reproduced with permission from The National Portrait Gallery.

But where did the attitude that women are intellectually inferior actually come from? Since in the societies mentioned women had no role in public life, educational provision was presumably deemed unnecessary for girls and hence women appeared stupid because they were less educated. A further point, though one not often mentioned for reasons of political correctness, is that in the past, many married women were almost continuously pregnant or breastfeeding, under which conditions women may be preoccupied with motherhood (partly because of the huge hormonal changes going on). Additionally, there may be a belief that women are subversive and dangerous. Certainly there are historical examples of the power that sexual attraction can have over men in important positions – think of Mata Hari or Christine Keeler. Think too of the story of Adam and Eve – 'the woman tempted me and I did eat'. Such an attitude may underlie the suppression of women in many countries today. Will they perhaps not obey their husbands, brothers and fathers if they have access to the wider intellectual world? One might draw a parallel with the eighteenth-century belief that it was unwise to educate slaves.

So we have to start this discussion aware that there is a dead weight of history against believing that women are as academically able as men. Of course, there have been exceptions – Queen Elizabeth I could read five languages by the time she was 16 (Latin, Greek, French, Italian and English; and later Italian; Neale[3(pp22–26)]); Catherine de Medici (1519–1589) had enormous political influence – but the point is that they were exceptions and that they came from the highest social echelons.

In this chapter we first present the evidence for different academic outcomes for males and females at school and university and then we shall discuss examples of sex differences in a variety of behaviours. There are of course innate sex differences in the structure of specific parts of male and female brains related to differences in sexual behaviour. However, the relation between sex differences in other sorts of behaviour and differences in brain structure is not strong. There is, however, some evidence that the sexes employ different strategies to solve the same problems and this may be associated with differences in the brain areas involved. We shall also show that differences in scores on tests do not necessarily stem from basic inborn sex differences in ability produced by the forces of natural selection but may result from the pressure of society's preconceptions. However, we need to acknowledge that since such preconceptions are often projected onto children from an early age (see Goldberg and Lewis[4]), restricting or encouraging what are considered to be sex-specific activities, the resulting differences in experience will themselves shape the developing brain. The resulting differences in the brain could then lead the child, and later the adult, to prefer and to excel in the kinds of sex-specific activities that had been promoted from early childhood.

Sex Differences in Educational Outcomes

It is perhaps surprising that whilst in Europe and America (and many other countries) it is nowadays taken for granted that girls will be educated to the same standard as boys, there are some marked differences in outcomes for males and females: there are differences in the school and university academic achievements of males and females and there are wide differences in career choice. The direction of these differences does not consistently favour one sex or the other. There has been ample evidence even in the twenty-first century that boys' achievement in maths exceeds that of girls; and conversely that girls do better than boys in tests of literacy.

Are boys better at mathematics?

In 2003, PISA used similar tests of mathematics and reading for 276,175 15-year-olds in 40 countries inside and outside the OECD. It was found that the boys showed on average a 2% lead in mathematics whilst the girls led in reading by 6.6%. For some years now, in England, whilst girls have consistently outperformed boys at GCSE (16+ school examination) in most subjects, it has usually been the case that a slightly higher proportion of boys has achieved the top grade (A*) in maths and physics.

The sex differences in maths achievement in the 2003 and 2009 PISA reports have led people to ask (as Larry Summers, erstwhile president of Harvard, so unfortunately did in public) whether there just are fewer women than men who are talented in mathematics and physical sciences. This was thought to support a biological basis for this difference and followed Charles Darwin's view that such differences resulted from very long-term sexual selection in evolution. The popular idea, which is quite widely accepted, is that this selection in hominids would have been related to the division of labour between the sexes whereby men became specialized hunters and navigators whilst women took the more domestic role, specializing in communicating with their offspring and each other.

The PISA sex differences in mathematics related to a difference in mean scores and, additionally, there was a wider distribution of scores in males than in females. Such a wider distribution has been reported in the past for many different types of ability test.

Alice Heim (working in the Psychology Department at Cambridge University), who designed intelligence tests suitable for different populations, in her 1970 book on ability even had a chapter entitled 'The Mediocrity of Women' demonstrating the smaller percentage of women obtaining top scores (and lowest scores) on her IQ tests. This wider distribution of men's scores has frequently been claimed with respect to mathematics as the explanation for the excess of men in top scientific careers. However, test scores do not only represent 'ability' because they may be affected by many other factors, including previous teaching, motivation, amount of work on the subject, and individual expectations (see Chapter 5).

The finding that the advantage for males is not present in all populations would suggest a cultural basis to the difference. This is strongly supported by further analysis of the PISA 2003 results which has looked at the relation between the 'gender gap' in the scores and the status of women in different countries. Status of women, or 'gender empowerment', in a country has been estimated by a variety of measures. These are firstly the GGI (Gender Gap Index) which looks at the economic level, the political opportunities and the level of education of women; secondly, an index of the cultural attitudes towards women in that country, obtained from World Value Surveys; thirdly, a measure of political empowerment of women from the World Economic Forum. What has emerged is that there is a strong relation between maths scores and status of women. Low status of women is associated with a large advantage for men in the maths scores (in, for example, Turkey), whereas where women's status is high, the male advantage disappears or is actually reversed (as in Iceland). In addition, there is a similar relationship between the status of women in different countries and the wider range of the maths scores: where the status of women is high, the greater range for men's scores is not present either (Guiso et al.).[5] These findings strongly support the view that the higher test scores of 15-year-old males than females in maths are dependent on cultural rather than biological factors.

There are several explanations that can be put forward for the effect of the status of women in society on their performance in maths. Firstly, there is likely to be a difference in the opportunity for women to study maths in those societies where women's status is very low and the opportunities for using maths in a career are limited for them. Secondly, if women themselves do not see a role in mathematics-related subjects as appropriate for their sex, they are unlikely to aspire to take up such roles. Thirdly, a popular explanation lies in the effect of what is termed 'stereotype threat': individuals who have the perception of low status in any specific field will show lowered performance in that field (see later).

Are girls better at reading?

A different story emerges when we look at the superiority of girls on measures of literacy in the PISA 2009 study. Interestingly, although the relative underachievement of boys in reading has only recently been a matter of public concern in the United Kingdom, it has been acknowledged, at least in the United States, for over a century (Ayers 1909 quoted in Bank et al.[6]). The PISA study showed that girls' scores in reading exceed those of boys in all countries studied (including China and Korea). Furthermore, there is no simple relation between the status of women in a country and the mean scores on reading – although it is noteworthy that

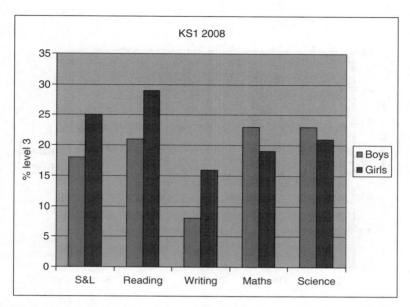

Figure 6.2   Key Stage 1 assessment results by gender. Percentage achieving Level 3 (S & L = speaking and listening).

in 2003 the largest female advantage was seen in Iceland, where women have the highest status.

Girls consistently outperform boys in England in language and literacy (but not necessarily in maths and science) at national assessments taken at age 6–7 years (KS1; see Figure 6.2), age 10–11 years (KS2; Figure 6.3) and age 14 (KS3; Figure 6.4). Strand, Deary and Smith[7] have carried out an analysis of the Cognitive Abilities Test scores in a very large sample of schoolchildren in Britain and found that whilst there was no sex difference in a 'general intelligence' factor that they extracted from the data, there was a sex difference in favour of girls in a literacy factor.

The fact that females seem universally to have higher levels of literacy suggests that this is more likely than the male advantage in maths to have at least some biological basis. However, many alternative explanations have been put forward, including a teacher bias in favour of girls: a 'response bias' amongst teachers because boys are naturally more active and girls quieter (see Bank et al.[6]). There may also be a stereotype threat acting here to the disadvantage of boys. Indeed, it can be argued that because, on average, girls' verbal skills develop earlier, they are likely to acquire reading skills earlier as well. If boys are aware of this early 'failure'

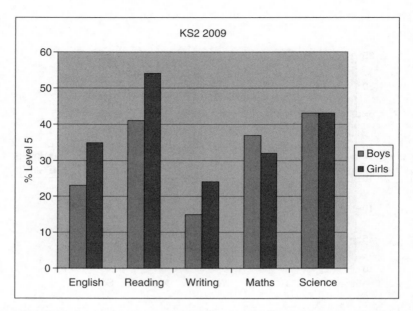

Figure 6.3 Key Stage 2 assessment results by gender. Percentage reaching Level 5.

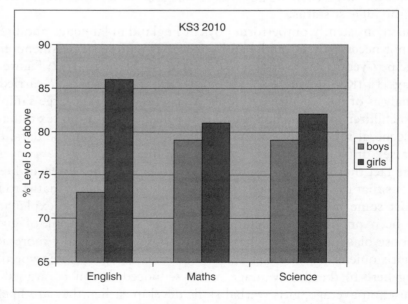

Figure 6.4 Key Stage 3 assessment results by gender. Percentage reaching level 5 or above.

it might be expected to demotivate them and may well lead to boys regarding reading as 'girlie' and hence their not paying it enough attention and thereby delaying their own development of literacy further. A further possibly relevant fact is that the vast majority of teachers in primary schools are women and hence the absence of male role models in education may give a discouraging message to boys.

There is a popular belief that the advantage for girls is carried on into adulthood. It has been widely reported that adult women obtain higher scores than men on a variety of tests of verbal ability. This could be the result of the early verbal encouragement of girls. However, this female advantage is hotly debated (see later).

Single-sex or co-educational schools?

People tend to have strong views on this subject. On the one hand, it is nowadays considered by many that single-sex education is 'unnatural' and will lead to problems in forming relationships with the opposite sex in later life. On the other hand, social pressures in co-educational schools are thought to lead to gendered stereotyping of behaviour and academic choices. What evidence is there that one or the other is better; and for what and for whom?

Obviously research is needed but there is a major problem in carrying out such research today. This is that single-sex schools are now in a small minority which is mainly confined to the independent sector, some state grammar schools and faith schools. This means that it is impossible to obtain a large, representative sample of children educated at a single-sex school who are matched demographically to a group of co-educated pupils.

The only large, carefully balanced study of the academic impact of single-sex schooling has been carried out by Alice Sullivan[8] (now at the Institute of Education in London) on the NCDS (National Childhood Development Study) cohort of all those children born in Britain in one week in 1958 (originally over 17,000 children). The physical and cognitive development, health, behaviour and achievements of these people, who are now in their 50s, have been followed up at intervals over their lives. When these children started secondary school, about a quarter of comprehensive schools were single sex. It was therefore possible to compare children that attended single-sex or co-educational comprehensives and produce reasonable demographic matching of the two groups. Additionally, Sullivan[9] ran more sophisticated statistics in which she was able to control for any differences between the groups in important factors such as parental education. She obtained some clear-cut answers on academic attainment: girls did better at O-level (age 16 examination) in science and maths if they were at girls-only schools; and boys did better at languages if they were at boys-only schools. As she states, 'coeducation was associated with greater gender differentiation in subject-specific attainment'. Sullivan showed that boys' and girls' academic self-concept with respect to different school subjects was related to whether their school was single sex or co-educational. She measured this by looking at the proportion of the children who regarded themselves as above average in their ability. Girls in girls' schools had greater confidence in their ability in maths and science than those in co-education; boys in boys' schools had greater confidence in their ability in English. Single-sex schooling actually reversed the gender effect on self-concept with respect to English, whilst for science and maths it markedly reduced it but did not reverse it since it had no effect on the boys' confidence in their ability. One long-term outcome difference was that girls from girls' schools were more likely to obtain a higher qualification in science or maths before they were 33 than those from co-educational comprehensives.

These finding are interesting, but of course it can be argued that if we could do a similar study now, more than 50 years later, we might not get the same results. We cannot come to definite conclusions about the benefits or otherwise of single-sex education today.

Sex differences in higher education

The situation at university level is more complicated. For the population of school-leavers that goes to university, women obtain a higher proportion of 'good degrees' (first and upper-second class). It is likely that this is due to a higher 'work ethic' in women[10] and their greater conscientiousness. However, when we consider top honours degrees (first class) then the opposite picture is the case – men do better. In the past, this gap has been considerably greater (men achieving at least a 30% higher proportion of Firsts) but the gap has now closed to less than 1%. There is, however, a bigger difference in the performance of men and women at the most 'research intensive' (most prestigious) Russell Group of universities and this is intensified at the most selective, that is, Oxford and Cambridge, where in certain subjects the proportion of men getting Firsts may be nearly twofold that of women. Surprisingly, in view of the better literacy performance of girls at school, the male 'advantage' is particularly marked in humanities subjects: English language and literature, philosophy and history. The reasons for this have been obscure: personality factors do not seem to be the answer, and perhaps surprisingly, the higher levels of trait anxiety in women seem to confer some advantage on them.[11] However, more negative reactions in women to serious unpleasant life events may contribute to their underperformance.[12] It is often argued that there may be some unconscious preference amongst examiners for a type of answer (perhaps more 'punchy') favoured by men in written examinations.[13,12,11] We have recently shown that an important factor appears to be that men are more likely to expect to do well (Mellanby, Zimdars and Cortina-Borja;[17] see later). However, the dead weight of history mentioned at the start of this chapter, coupled with the knowledge amongst students of the existence of the female disadvantage at Oxford and Cambridge, could produce what is known as stereotype threat.

There are many examples in the literature of stereotype threat – that is, underperformance on tests by particular groups that are commonly perceived as less talented in a particular field. These include comparisons of women versus men, black and some other ethnic minority groups versus white, white men versus Asian men. There are also many examples of the effect of experimentally manipulating stereotype threat on the performance of women on tasks in which they are generally believed to have less talent than men.[14] A particularly pertinent study where the effect of threat was substantial was carried out by Rydell et al.[15] on American university students. In this, telling the students that women were less good at maths was associated with the women attaining a 40% lower score on maths problems in the women, showing how readily a large effect can be induced. Additionally, women are likely to hold these stereotypes implicitly in relevant test situations without any explicit manipulation.

A very interesting experiment was carried out by Correll[16] to compare implicit beliefs in men and women about their capabilities. She gave men and women identical scores on a test of contrast sensitivity, which actually has no right or wrong answers. However, sometimes she told participants that men were typically better at this task. Female participants then assessed their performance as being worse than when they were told the sexes performed equally well. In addition, when asked what score they felt they would need to attain in order to feel that they had performed really well, the women said they would need a 10% higher score than the men said they would need. Correll concluded that 'men use a more lenient standard to assess ability'. Thus, for a given level of achievement, men had greater confidence in their ability in that area.

We have made a similar observation with students at Oxford University.[13,17] This university, like Cambridge, has a very long history as a male institution and although the student population is now fully mixed

Figure 6.5   Delegates of the Oxford University Press. (The delegates are appointed from the academic staff of the University and are actively involved in the publishing programme of the Press. This picture, taken around 1991, is typical of the absence of female academics in important offices in the university at that date. There are now four women delegates.) Courtesy of Professor L. Weiskrantz

with regard to sex, the majority of senior academics are still male (Figure 6.5).

We have found that an important determinant of whether a student obtains a first-class degree is his/her expectation of obtaining one.[13] This expectation is higher in men. An important factor determining this expectation is the mark obtained in first-year exams: men do better than women (despite women having equal or better school exam performance and equal verbal IQ). In addition, like in the Correll experiment, for a given level of exam performance (in the first year) the men have a higher expectation of doing well in Finals. So the two factors may work together to produce better Finals performance for men. It looks as if the university teaching and learning experience is more positive for men than for women

Figure 6.6   There are more female nurses. Photo by Monkey Business Images/ Shutterstock

and recent work has suggested that a more adversarial style of teaching, as can be encountered in tutorials, can have a negative effect on women's feelings of academic self-efficacy.[18] The results of the Mellanby et al. study[17] show that the 'gender gap' in first-class degrees at Oxford can be explained (statistically) by this interaction of negative factors.

Men and Women at Work

So far, then, we have discussed the different educational outcomes for boys and girls and the contribution of cultural factors to these. It is also well known that there are large sex differences in the proportion of women in certain occupations (see Radford 1998 for an extensive exposition of this subject).[19] Thus there are nowadays more female than male doctors, nursing has until recently been almost exclusively a female profession (Figure 6.6), there are more female teachers, whilst there are many more male physicists, chemists, mathematicians, engineers (Figure 6.7), computer experts and financiers. These differences are likely to be due to actual or perceived differences in abilities and personality characteristics which in turn will influence choice. In some cases, such as the building trade, the difference is obviously related to the average greater physical strength of men.

As a generalization, more women express interest in people-centred careers because they particularly enjoy social interaction and an environment in which they feel they can help others. In contrast, men are more interested in 'things'.[20] These differences in interest could be a major

Figure 6.7   There are more male engineers. Photograph by branislavpudar/ Shutterstock

reason that women are more likely to choose people-centred careers whilst men favour careers in the sciences.[19] Furthermore, for example within the legal profession, the different choices of men and women are probably related to perceived or actual sex differences in personality, such that there are more male barristers, a role which requires a degree of aggression, and more female family lawyers, a role which requires more empathy. Aggression is seen as a male characteristic,[21] whilst empathy is seen as feminine.[2]

It has been argued by Correll[16] and others that one of the reasons that there are more men in careers thought to require high ability is the tendency for women to assess their capabilities lower than men do (despite an equal level of previous achievement). Such an effect will depress the supply of women in the relevant labour market. Women's preference for working with people rather than things presumably contributes to their under-representation in the financial sector where money rewards are greatest: the traits needed to succeed there are very much those that are commoner in men.

It is well known that in academia, management, banking, the law and politics, whilst there are many women at lower levels, the proportion of women in top posts is low. However, this is at least in part a matter of choice. We must not ignore the fact that since women are the ones who have children, and childbearing is very important to many women, choices of mid-life career path may also be influenced by a need for flexibility in working hours and indeed not wishing to work the 100-hour weeks that many top scientists, bankers and lawyers work.

Sex Differences in Cognitive Ability

There is an extensive literature investigating whether there are differences in the test scores of males and females on a variety of cognitive tests. In general, where differences have been reported, they show higher scores for men on spatial tasks (and some sorts of advanced mathematics) and higher scores for women on many verbal tasks and on some aspects of perceptual sensitivity.

It is, however, important to realize that the previously discussed effects that cultural values and expectations can have on test scores in an educational context may well apply to any comparisons that are made of the behaviour of males and females. Bem[21] produced an inventory of sex differences in attributes by asking 100 students to rate a wide range of characteristics as socially desirable for a man or a woman. The resulting 20 items for each sex are shown in Table 6.1. (We presented a list at the start of the chapter: you can now check your attitudes.)

Whilst the gender-related social desirability of some of these traits is likely to have changed since 1974, many of them would probably still be classed as gender appropriate and hence could well exert a stereotype threat on either sex depending on the context.

Intelligence

An area in which there has been a great deal of research, and where there is most controversy, is in the measurement of differences between the sexes in 'intelligence'. Whilst IQ tests are designed specifically not to have sex differences in overall score (see Rushton and Ankney[22]), there is at least one strong believer in the inferiority of the intelligence of women – Richard Lynn from Ireland. He has argued that the difference is found in adults but is not seen in children because girls mature earlier; after the age of 15 or so, boys catch up and then surpass girls. He has published many papers showing a male advantage in IQ. He has proposed that there is a causal connection between the fact that men have larger brains than women (even after adjusting for body size[23]) and that brain size correlates with IQ ($r = 0.3$–0.4).

Much of Lynn's research showing a male advantage in IQ has been done on university students. This sex difference does not necessarily reflect a difference in the general population but rather some bias in the selection of students such that less 'intelligent' women have been selected. More recently, he and Paul Irwing have carried out a large meta-analysis of

Table 6.1　Bem[21] Sex Role Inventory

Masculine items	Feminine items
Acts as a leader	Affectionate
Aggressive	Cheerful
Ambitious	Childlike
Analytical	Compassionate
Assertive	Does not use harsh language
Athletic	Eager to soothe harsh feelings
Competitive	Feminine
Defends own beliefs	Flatterable
Dominant	Gentle
Forceful	Gullible
Has leadership abilities	Loves children
Independent	Loyal
Individualistic	Sensitive to the needs of others
Makes decisions easily	Shy
Masculine	Soft spoken
Self-reliant	Sympathetic
Self-sufficient	Tender
Strong personality	Understanding
Willing to take a stand	Warm
Willing to take risks	Yielding

university students' scores on Raven's Matrices (thought of as a measure of innate 'fluid intelligence') and concluded that there was a 4–5-point advantage in favour of men.[24] Irwing and Lynn calculated that this shift of the male distribution to the right would generate a large excess of super-bright males. Interestingly, the meta-analysis did not show the usual wider distribution for male scores. This study has, however, been subjected to some very cogent criticisms.[25] One major objection is their omission from their calculations of the largest study, carried out in Mexico, which showed no difference – it was discarded as being 'an outlier'. Steve Blinkhorn's critique of the article also points out that Irwing and Lynn's statistical procedures overemphasize the sex differences and that if his criticisms are taken into account then the male advantage reduces to a mere 0.15 of a standard deviation, which he dismisses as 'too small to be interesting'.

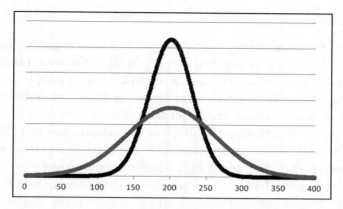

Figure 6.8 A comparison of two populations with the same mean value but different distribution (standard deviation, SD) of values.

Whilst it is thus by no means established that there is a difference in mean scores between men and women in the general population, the wider distribution of scores has been replicated on many occasions with many different tests (but not in Irwing and Lynn's meta-analysis). Where the wider distribution has been found, even with similar mean values, this would, of course, yield a higher number of men at the very top (see Figure 6.8).

However, in view of the cultural attitude in many countries that women are intellectually inferior, some or all of these differences may be due to status/stereotype effects. Furthermore, what is not known is whether those people with the very highest IQ scores are more likely to produce the very highest achievement than those with slightly lower scores – in other words, does the excess of males at the top end of the IQ distribution make any difference to academic or occupational outcomes? We have found at Oxford University that only 9% of the variance in the marks received in Finals examinations is accounted for by verbal IQ (and non-verbal IQ does not correlate with achievement).[13,26] Furthermore, in this study there were roughly equal numbers of males and females in the very highest verbal IQ category.

So it seems fair to conclude that differences between the sexes in IQ are small if they exist at all and cannot be used as an argument to explain the greater success of men than women in certain careers or in gaining first-class degrees at top universities. Sex differences in dispositional factors such as conscientiousness are more likely to be relevant to academic and career aspirations and achievement.

Verbal ability

As already discussed with respect to the PISA study, girls aged 15 score higher than boys on a measure of literacy in all of the wide range of countries studied. This does not come as a surprise to most people since there is an ingrained belief that females are generally better at verbal tasks. The evidence that adult women are better than men at tests of verbal ability is, however, not strong. Hyde and Linn,[27] in a meta-analysis in 1988, pointed out that the main evidence for this came from studies carried out before 1973. Between that date and 1987, when they published their paper, this difference diminished (d = 0.23 to d = 0.10). They concluded in their review that at that date (more than 20 years ago) in the United States the 'gender difference in verbal ability is currently so small that it can effectively be considered to be zero'. This view has been reinforced by a recent critical review by Wallentin.[28] His main point is that all the studies showing female advantage in verbal tests involve only small numbers of participants (fewer than about 100), whereas those showing no difference between the sexes involve larger samples. He believes that differences when found are artefacts due to lack of balancing of the samples with respect to age and educational level of the participants (both of which impact on verbal ability). One difference that has been reported quite often, and fits in with the public's view that it is always women who are chatting and making long telephone calls, is that verbal fluency is higher in females. Psychologists test verbal fluency by, for example, asking someone to produce as many words beginning with 'm', or as many animals or as many fruits as they can, within a minute. However, a large study carried out by Tombaugh et al.[29] found in an opportunity sample (i.e. those picked up in supermarkets etc. plus a group of those participating in an ageing study) of 1300 adults that when age and years of education were taken into account, there was no sex difference in verbal fluency.

The argument that girls develop earlier than boys and that any verbal advantage is a result of this is based on many studies showing that in early childhood the language of girls is more advanced by about 9 months on average. This difference in spoken language apparently declines as children mature. So this would not seem to be the simple explanation for the greater success in literacy in females at 15 years. We have already suggested that this may be due to boys giving up on reading earlier because they feel disadvantaged – maybe an early stereotype threat response. However, it is also likely to be related to the preferences that girls have (either innately or imposed by caregivers) for more sedentary activities (or maybe nowadays, less time spent playing video games) than

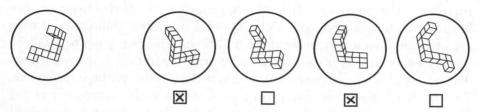

Figure 6.9 Test of mental rotation ability. Sample item, Vandenberg Test of Mental Rotation item. The task is to identify the two figures on the right that are rotated versions of the target. Correct choices are shown here.

boys, which gives them more time and inclination to read throughout childhood. The more you read, the better your reading skills and the higher your intelligence scores, as Stanovich[30] showed in a paper entitled 'Does reading make you smarter?'

Spatial skills

There is a general belief that women are poor at spatial tasks such as parking cars and reading maps – in the latter case the stereotypical woman has to turn a map upside down if she is travelling from north to south. So how much truth is there in this belief? One of the few consistently observed sex differences is male superiority in tests of mental rotation (see, for example, Linn and Peterson's[31] detailed meta-analysis of a large number of studies). A standard test of mental rotation involves deciding whether two figures, presented on a screen in two different rotations, are the same or mirror images of each other (see Figure 6.9). The main measure is speed since most answers will be accurate.

The task is intended to require the person tested to imagine the shapes and to rotate them in their mind until they are in the same orientation – then they can decide whether they are same or different. However, there is an alternative strategy for solving the problem and that is to attach verbal labels to parts of the figure and describe verbally (internally) what is happening. If there is a sex difference in which strategy is used, and if the strategy used by males, most likely the spatial strategy, is more efficient, then this might explain the sex difference in scores. This would then suggest that the difference in scores does not actually result from some basic difference in spatial ability but in the two sexes' preference for different strategies. An interesting study tested this hypothesis by looking at the effect of having people complete a simultaneous task during mental rotation.[32] The rationale behind this approach is that if two tasks require the same cognitive resources such as verbal or spatial skills, then if they are attempted simultaneously there will be interference – neither will be performed as well as if they were carried out separately; however, if they depend on different cognitive resources, there should not be interference. Two types of task were given to be carried out at the same time as the rotation task – either a verbal or a spatial task. The hypothesis was upheld since it was found that the simultaneous spatial task led to men's scores being lower than women's, whilst the verbal task reduced the women's scores more.

It has been proposed that one of the reasons for the poorer scores of women on the American SAT maths tests could be related to their lower ability at mental rotation. It is reasonable to assume that the skill required in a test of mental rotation might share something with the ability to do geometry, for example. Casey et al.[33] showed a consistent relation between mental rotation scores and SAT maths scores in three different groups of higher-ability female students and also in a group of lower-ability female students. In contrast, there was no consistent relation in the males of the same groups. They concluded that 'spatial ability may be responsible in part for mediating gender differences in math aptitude'. Casey and colleagues also showed that spatial perception was better in males. This was measured using a task originally designed by Piaget (the Swiss psychologist and philosopher, regarded as the 'father' of developmental psychology) where pictures of a container at various angles are shown with the water level either horizontal or at an angle. The observer has to say which picture describes how the water level would actually be. The relation between this ability and SAT maths scores was less strong than for mental rotation but still present.

We cannot disregard the possibility of stereotype/status threat influencing both maths ability and mental rotation. An interesting experiment by Wraga et al.[34] suggested a mechanism for stereotype threat reducing mental rotation ability. They compared brain activation (with functional magnetic resonance imaging, fMRI) in three small groups of women (about 18 in each) who carried out a mental rotation test under three different conditions: prior to the scanning, one group was given the negative stereotype, one was given a positive stereotype, and a control group was given a neutral statement. The two stereotype conditions were compared with the control and with each other. In the negative stereotype case there was specific activation of parts of the brain connected with the amygdala that are involved in processing emotion, whilst with the positive stereotype there was activation of visual processing areas and parts of the prefrontal cortex involved in working memory. The results are interesting because it is hypothesized that the emotion that the negative stereotype could be eliciting, which could be labelled 'worry', interferes with the performance of many types of task by impairing the functioning of working memory.[35]

Studies on navigation[36] suggest that women view the world slightly differently from men – that they define space more by the nature of the objects within it than by their relation to the framework. In other words, whilst men think in terms of north–south, horizontal–vertical, women think in terms of the telephone box round the corner from the café. Gron et al.[37] showed with fMRI that there are some sex differences in the areas of the brain that are activated during navigation of a virtual maze and so possibly this may be related to these differences.

Since there is some evidence that spatial ability improves in females when they study maths and physical sciences,[38] it is reasonable to suggest that girls should be actively encouraged to take part in activities that require spatial skills. Demonstrating that at least some of the lower spatial ability of females is due to stereotype threat, largely engendered by the feelings of inadequacy within the females themselves, suggests that counteracting this is of basic importance. Presenting an alternative stereotype, say females as excellent architects, might have the required effect.

Differences in brain structure and function

It is consistently found in both sexes that the left hemisphere is more involved in verbal tasks whereas both hemispheres, or more predominantly the right hemisphere, are involved in spatial tasks (though this is not always the case in left-handers). There is a long-established tradition that the brains of men are more lateralized than those of women – that is, that in the brains of men specific functions are more heavily biased towards one or the other side of the brain. This has been supported by a variety of clinical, behavioural, anatomical and functional studies.[39]

Gur et al.[40] have some structural evidence for men's brains being more asymmetric than women's. Using MRI, they looked at the amount and proportion of grey matter (neurons and their synaptic connections), white matter (myelinated axons) and cerebrospinal fluid (which fills the ventricles of the brain) in 40 men and 40 women well matched for age, education and parental education. Overall, women were shown to have a higher percentage of grey matter whilst the men had a higher percentage of white matter and cerebrospinal fluid. The left hemisphere of the male brains had a higher percentage of total grey matter and a lower percentage of cerebrospinal fluid relative to the right hemisphere (with no difference in white matter), whilst women's brains did not show any asymmetry on these measures.

Structural evidence for sex differences in the volume of specific brain areas is less compelling. Wallentin's review[28] concludes that there is no difference in the lateralization of areas involved in language or in the thickness or shape of the corpus callosum (the large connection between the left and right hemispheres). This conclusion was derived from consideration of a wide range of studies investigating the proposition that such differences in brain anatomy do exist between males and females. He points out that the differences, like those in verbal test scores (see above), have only been found in small groups of people who may not have been representative of the general population and that the groups may not have been balanced with respect to age and education (see above).

Functional evidence for sex differences in the brain has been found by Haier et al.[41] using fMRI. They studied males and females matched for IQ and showed that there were some sex differences in which areas of the brain were activated during particular tasks. Taken together with the finding that males and females may use different strategies to solve spatial tasks, this suggests that these differences in strategies might be related to the use of different systems in the brain.

Origins of sex differences in behaviour and anatomy

We have so far shown that there are some differences in abilities between males and females, though the differences for which there is really good evidence are considerably fewer than has been hyped by the media and public opinion. There are several possible origins of sex differences. These include direct and indirect genetic factors and the effect of environment from birth onwards. By direct genetic effects we mean the effect of males having one X chromosome and one Y chromosome whilst females have two X chromosomes. This already has an effect on brain development before the development of gonads in a foetus. After the development of the gonads, these start producing sex hormones, oestrogens (in females) and testosterone (in males), and these then also affect brain development. Male and female foetuses are thus exposed from quite early on *in utero* to different levels of these hormones. The brain is well known to be sexually dimorphic (that is, different between the sexes) in several areas, including the hypothalamus and the preoptic area, which are areas involved in the production and control of hormones involved in reproduction and in sexual behaviour directly. Simon Baron-Cohen and colleagues[2] believe that the level of testosterone to which a foetus has been exposed in the womb is directly related to the empathetic behaviour demonstrated by a child when s/he reaches 6 or so years of age. Hence he proposes that the differentiation of brain circuitry involved in this aspect of socialization has been programmed by the level of testosterone in the womb. Of course, the level of testosterone continues to be higher in males throughout childhood and has a major surge at puberty so this early effect is presumably maintained or magnified throughout the life-time. This difference could be one reason behind the gendered choice of careers.

As well as the differences in behaviour produced by these biological factors, there are the effects of environment on the brain. Neuroconstructivism[42] considers that interaction with environmental factors is what builds the differentiation of the brain: the brain is not strictly modular in the beginning, though different regions may be particularly suited to the processing of certain sorts of input. Thus the sensory cortices are not initially specialized for processing their preferred stimuli: they become more specialized during maturation through receiving a relevant input. If they do not receive the relevant input, the area of cortex can become specialized to process a different input instead (see Chapter 2).

It is likely that any early differences between the sexes in behaviour, presumably produced by differences in brain function, might be magnified by the response of the environment (e.g. the child's caregivers and peers) to these differences. For example, if young boys are more energetic than small girls, and they as a result explore more and take more exercise, this may well impact on their brain structure in areas relevant to spatial learning and hence on their spatial ability both as children and later in life. The earlier language development of girls may lead to their being talked to more in infancy and this may 'bootstrap' their linguistic development, magnifying the small advantage with which they start. We now know that structural brain development is affected by environmental influences after birth and throughout childhood, adolescence and into adulthood. Thus the behavioural history of each child will interact with any sex differences already set up by biological factors to construct the brain (Figures 6.10 and 6.11).

Recently, one way in which environment can influence development has been shown to be via the control of the transcription of genes. This effect may even be heritable – epigenetics (see Carey[43] [chapter 1] for an introduction to this concept).

Figure 6.10 Gender stereotypical activities in young children.

Figure 6.11 However, young children also act in ways that are opposite to stereotype.

Summary

- There are well-documented sex differences in the educational outcomes at school of boys and girls in a wide range of countries and these differences have not changed much during the twenty-first century.

- Internationally, boys are doing a little better than girls on maths at age 15. This male advantage appears to be related to cultural factors since it is greatest in countries where the status of women is low, but absent or even reversed where women's status is high. Furthermore, the wider distribution of boys' scores, which leads to the predominance of boys amongst the highest performers, is also related to the status of women. Thus it seems that the lower representation of women in careers requiring maths cannot be ascribed to lower innate mathematical ability of girls and women.

- Lower aspirations, based on females' own perception of their mathematical ability produced by stereotype threat, and lower educational experience of maths-related fields, are likely to account in part for the under-representation of women in most countries in science, technology, engineering and mathematics.

- Females score lower than males on tests of mental rotation. They are more likely than males to use a verbal rather than a visual strategy and this is apparently less efficient. There may be a relation between scores on maths tests and spatial tests.

- Girls are better at literacy in all countries studied. The causes of this may relate in part to innate differences in males and females leading to girls favouring more sedentary occupations, such as reading, and boys favouring more physical activity.

- There is excellent evidence from the National Child Development Study (NCDS) that in the 1960s/1970s single-sex schooling reduced gendered effects on subject choice and achievement – girls did more and better science and maths, boys did more and better work in languages. In addition, girls' belief in their capability in maths and science was greater in girls-only schools and boys' belief in their capability in English was greater in boys-only schools. It would be difficult, if not impossible, to repeat this study in Britain today because the small number of single-sex schools remaining serve a restricted part of the population, which precludes carrying out a balanced study.

- When Final exam results for all universities are combined, women obtain more 'good' degrees – first class and upper-second class – than men do. This seems to be related to better 'work ethic' in women; in particular, they are more conscientious. At the most selective universities, however, men obtain a higher proportion of Firsts in some subjects.

- Careers are still highly gendered, though much less so than in the past. Part of the reason for this may well be that women are more likely to have a preference for a career that involves social contact whereas more men are interested in 'things'.

- Differences in verbal cognitive ability (in favour of women) have probably been exaggerated by studies having small samples that were not fully matched with respect to factors such as level of education achieved, which can affect the psychological test scores.

- The average general intelligence of males and females is similar – any differences being 'too small to be interesting'. However, there is a wider distribution of scores for males than females on many tests, which leads to there being more very high-'ability' males in the general population (and more of very low 'ability' too).

- There are some differences in gross structure of male and female brains, including greater symmetry in the female brain, but there is not as yet any clear relation between these and sex differences in behaviour.

- Some of the origins of sex differences in behaviour are genetic and hormonal. Others originate in the environment – how the two sexes are treated differently in childhood. The malleability of the developing brain means that environmental influences can interact with any intrinsic differences, such as greater activity levels in males, and multiply or offset their effects.

Implications for educators

- There is a need for more people to enter careers in science, technology and engineering. One way to try to meet this need has been by encouraging more girls and women in this direction. There is nevertheless still a dearth of school-leavers, of either sex, qualified to read science and maths at university. Increasing the uptake of science by girls will need active measures, perhaps with the help of the media, to counteract sex stereotyping. And it will also require more encouragement for young girls to take part in and enjoy science and maths activities from the beginning of primary school. It may also be important to get girls to take part in activities that would be expected to expand their spatial abilities since these may affect brain processing in such a way as to impact on their mathematical achievement.

- The early advantage of girls in reading may lead to demotivation of boys. Reading needs to be promoted as an activity worthy of the attention of boys; unfortunately, programmes for overcoming this underachievement of boys have had little success in recent years in Britain. Maybe incorporating more reading into video games might help; at present they mainly involve visuo-spatial and motor skills.
- It should be acknowledged that there are differences in the interests of boys and girls. The greater interest that males show in 'things' and females in people means, for example, that books in primary schools should encompass an equal mixture of fact-related and people-related material.
- Instruction on the effects of stereotype threat on test scores should be given to all people when they take tests. It should be made clear at the time of testing that sex differences in any intellectual abilities are very small, and much smaller than the differences within the sexes.
- In the general population there may be an excess of males at the very top of some ability scales. It is important to emphasize that the highest scorers on intelligence tests are not necessarily the top performers in real-life situations or even in examinations – many other factors, particularly personality, are involved.
- More research is needed to determine whether there is a role for single-sex classes or schools.
- At university, it may help to show the young men the relationship between class of degree and conscientiousness and work ethic. New generations of university teachers need frequently to be reminded of the detrimental effect of negative criticism specifically on the academic self-concept of females, since this lowers academic performance. Teachers need to find ways of delivering it in a constructive way. Academics need to consider carefully whether open discussion of sex differences in Final marks will help address or in fact exacerbate the problem (through increased stereotype threat).

References

1   Darwin C. *The Descent of Man and Selection in Relation to Sex*. London: John Murray; 1894.
2   Baron-Cohen S. *The Essential Difference*. London: Allen Lane; 2003.
3   Neale JE. *Queen Elizabeth*. London: J. Cape; 1934.
4   Goldberg S, Lewis M. Play behaviour in the year-old infant: Early sex differences. *Child Development*. 1969;40(1):21–31.

5 Guiso L, Monte F, Sapienza P, Zingales L. Culture, gender, and math. *Science.* 2008;320:1164–1165.

6 Bank BJ, Biddle BJ, Good TL. Sex roles, classroom instruction and reading achievement. *Journal of Educational Psychology.* 1980;72(2):119–132.

7 Strand S, Deary IJ, Smith P. Sex differences in Cognitive Abilities Test scores: A UK national picture. *British Journal of Educational Psychology.* 2006; 76(3):463–480.

8 Sullivan A, Joshi H, Leonard D. Single-sex schooling and academic attainment at school and through the lifecourse. *American Educational Research Journal.* 2010;47(1):6–36. doi:10.3102/0002831209350106.

9 Sullivan A. Academic self-concept, gender and single-sex schooling. *British Educational Research Journal.* 2009;35(2):259–288.

10 Farsides T, Woodfield R. Individual and gender differences in 'good' and 'first class' undergraduate performance. *British Journal of Psychology.* 2007; 98:467–483.

11 Mellanby J, Zimdars A. Trait anxiety and final degree performance at the University of Oxford. *Higher Education.* 2011;61(4):357–370.

12 Surtees PG, Wainwright NWJ, Pharoah PDP. Psychosocial factors and sex differences in high academic attainment at Cambridge University. *Oxford Review of Education.* 2002;28:21–38.

13 Mellanby J, Martin M, O'Doherty J. The "gender gap" in final examinations at Oxford University. *British Journal of Psychology.* 2000;(91):377–390.

14 Steele CM. A threat in the air: How stereotypes shape intellectual identity and performance. *American Psychologist.* 1997;52:613–629.

15 Rydell RJ, McConnell AR, Beilock SL. Multiple social identities and stereotype threat: Imbalance, accessibility and working memory. *Journal of Personality and Social Psychology.* 2009;96:949–969.

16 Correll SJ. Constraints into preferences: Gender, status, and emerging career aspirations. *American Sociological Review.* 2004;69:93–113.

17 Mellanby J, Zimdars A, Cortina-Borja M. Sex differences in degree performance at the University of Oxford. *Learning and Individual Differences.* 2013;26:103–111.

18 Jackson C. Transitions into higher education: Gendered implications for academic self-concept. *Oxford Review of Education.* 2003;29:331–346.

19 Radford J. *Gender and Choice in Education and Occupation.* London: Routledge; 1998.

20 Su R, Rounds J, Armstrong PI. Men and things, women and people: A meta-analysis of sex differences in interests. *Psychological Bulletin.* 2009;135(6): 859–884.

21 Bem S. The measurement of psychological androgyny. *Consulting and Clinical Psychology.* 1974;42(2):155–162.

22 Mackintosh NJ. *IQ and Human Intelligence.* Oxford: Oxford University Press; 1998.

23   Rushton JP, Ankney CD. Brain size and cognitive ability: Correlation with age, sex, social class and race. *Psychonomic Bulletin and Review.* 1996; 3:21–36.

24   Irwing P, Lynn R. Sex differences in means and variability on the progressive matrices in university students: A meta-analysis. *British Journal of Psychology.* 2005;96:505–524.

25   Blinkhorn S. Intelligence: A gender bender. *Nature.* 2005;438:31–32.

26   Zimdars A. *Challenges to meritocracy? A study of the social mechanisms in student selection and attainment at the University of Oxford. DPhil. Dissertation*, University of Oxford. 2007.

27   Hyde JS, Linn MC. Gender differences in verbal ability: A meta-analysis. *Psychological Bulletin.* 1988;104(1):53–69.

28   Wallentin M. Putative sex differences in verbal abilities and language cortex: A critical review. *Brain and Language.* 2009;108:175–183.

29   Tombaugh TN, Kozak J, Rees L. Normative data stratified by age and education for two measures of verbal fluency: FAS and animal naming. *Archives of Clinical Neuropsychology.* 1999;14(2):167–177.

30   Stanovich KE. Does reading make you smarter? *Advances in Child Development and Behavior.* 1993;24:133–180.

31   Linn MC, Petersen AC. Emergence and characterization of sex differences in spatial ability: A meta-analysis. *Child Development.* 1985;56(6): 1479–1498.

32   Pezaris E, Casey MB. Girls who use "masculine" problem-solving strategies on a spatial task: Proposed genetic and environmental factors. *Brain and Cognition.* 1991;17:1–22.

33   Casey MB, Nuttall R, Pezaris E, Benbow CP. The influence of spatial ability on gender differences in mathematics College Entrance Test scores across diverse samples. *Developmental Psychology.* 1995;31(4):697–704.

34   Wraga M, Helt M, Jacobs E, Sullivan K. Neural basis of stereotype-induced shifts in women's mental rotation performance. *SCAN.* 2006;2:12–19.

35   Eysenck MW, Derakshan N, Santos R, Calvo MG. Anxiety and cognitive performance: Attentional control theory. *Emotion.* 2007;7:336–353.

36   Lawton CA. Gender differences in way-finding strategies: Relationship to spatial ability and spatial anxiety. *Sex Roles.* 1994;30:765–799.

37   Gron G, Wunderlich AP, Spitzer M, Tomczak R, Riepe MW. Brain activation during human navigation: Gender-different neural networks as substrate of performance. *Nature Neuroscience.* 2000;3(4):404–408.

38   Burnett SA, Lane DM. Effects of academic instruction on spatial visualization. *Intelligence.* 1980;4:233–242.

39   Kimura D. *Sex and Cognition.* Cambridge, MA: MIT Press; 1999.

40   Gur RC, Alsop D, Glahn D, *et al.* An fMRI study of sex differences in regional activation to a verbal and a spatial task. *Brain and Language.* 2000;74:157–170.

41   Haier RJ, Jung RE, Yeo RA, Head K, Alkire MT. The neuroanatomy of general intelligence: Sex matters. *NeuroImage*. 2005;25(1):320–327.
42   Sirois S, Spratling M, Thomas MSC, Westermann G, Mareschal D, *et al*. Précis of neuroconstructivism: How the brain constructs cognition. *Behavioral and Brain Sciences*. 2008;31:321–356.
43   Carey N. *The Epigenetics Revolution*. London: Icon Books; 2012.

Chapter 7

Metacognition
Can We Teach People How to Learn?

Sarah McElwee
(Cambridge English Language Assessment)

We do not learn from experience . . . we learn from reflecting upon experience.

John Dewey

Are you a crammer or a 'big-picture' learner? Are you highly structured in the way you choose to learn something new – making plans, setting targets and keeping an eye on your progress? Or are you more haphazard, looking at bits and pieces? Do you like to have a full overview of what you are about to learn, or do you memorize small chunks by heart as you go? Rate yourself out of five on the items in Box 7.1 – if you are not currently a student you can reflect on what your approach was like during your school or university days, or think about situations in your working life where you have to handle lots of new information.

The term for the capacity to think about our own thinking – 'metacognition' – was coined in the 1970s by an American researcher called John Flavell.[2] However, the notion itself can be traced from Ancient Greek philosophy, through the writings of the founders of modern psychology like James and Dewey, right up to the hugely influential developmental works of Piaget and Vygotsky. The broad philosophy behind teaching people how to learn stems from the idea of fostering a sense of agency and responsibility within learners, demonstrating how they can control their own cognitive and motivational processes in order to regulate their

Education and Learning: An Evidence-Based Approach, First Edition. Jane Mellanby and Katy Theobald.
© 2014 John Wiley & Sons, Ltd. Published 2014 by John Wiley & Sons, Ltd.

Box 7.1   Questions adapted from Study Process Questionnaire[1]

I find that at times studying gives me a feeling of deep personal satisfaction

1   2   3   4   5

I only study seriously what's given out in class or in the course outlines

1   2   3   4   5

I find I can get by in most assessments by memorizing key sections rather than trying to understand them

1   2   3   4   5

I come to most classes with questions in mind that I want answering

1   2   3   4   5

My aim is to pass the course while doing as little work as possible

1   2   3   4   5

I feel that virtually any topic can be highly interesting once I get into it

1   2   3   4   5

I find that I have to do enough work on a topic so that I can form my own conclusions before I am satisfied

1   2   3   4   5

I find it is not helpful to study topics in depth. It confuses, and wastes time, when all you need is a passing acquaintance with topics

1   2   3   4   5

I do not find my course very interesting so I try to keep work to a minimum

1   2   3   4   5

I make a point of looking at most of the suggested readings that go with lectures

1   2   3   4   5

Source: Questions adapted from the R-SPQ-2F[1]

time spent on-task and their overall task engagement. It also considers the right external and internal conditions for drawing students into a study topic, so that they are motivated to go beyond mere information acquisition to see its relevance further afield and to make critical evaluations and judgements on what they encounter.

Before we try to answer the question '*Can* we teach people how to learn?' it is worth taking a step back to consider first of all *why* we would want to teach people how to learn, and how that is different from teaching people *in order that* they learn. The answers probably lie in our own personal views on the purpose of education and, in particular, higher education. Palfreyman[3] suggests that the term 'higher' indicates a qualitative shift from what happens at primary and secondary school, describing it as 'the development of the individual's communication and critical facilities . . . over and beyond what would have happened by the person simply getting to be 3 or 4 years older . . . Higher education is not schooling for adults'. There is a shift in gears from accumulation of information to a focus on critical thinking, reflective practice, problem-solving, and the ability to see links between disparate subjects or to relate a narrow field of study to broader perspectives. These aims for 'higher' education need not be exclusive to university, however; some of the motivation behind teaching learners how to learn right across the education sector comes from a desire to impart these ideals to learners from a young age, not just to save them for high-attaining school-leavers.

Another more cynical view, related to the ongoing drive to raise educational standards, is that 'learning how to learn' initiatives are a longed-for magic bullet, a corner-cutting approach to success. Actually, however, beyond the immediate measurable output of exam results there is a hope that teaching students how to learn might create a climate of curiosity, and intellectual resilience, so that learners will come away from the experience of education not just with facts and figures but with a toolbox of skills and an attitude to learning that they can apply to new situations throughout their lives.

Presenting a coherent overview of the research on learning how to learn is tricky. In the early 1970s two distinct schools of research emerged in this field, and despite their similar focus, almost 40 years later there is still little overlap and few attempts have been made to integrate the findings. The questions they seek to answer are the same: what factors impact upon the way that a person learns? How can we support and foster attitudes and approaches that will support a learner to attain to the best of their potential? However, the techniques they use and the lenses with which they scrutinize the evidence differ.

The first, frequently termed *student approaches to learning* (SAL), is placed quite squarely in the education literature and is historically based on qualitative interviews that explore students' motivations and learning in a bottom-up, phenomenographic way. Researchers are interested in how students see themselves as learners, focusing particularly on a distinction

between so-called 'deep' and 'surface' learners. Deep learners are concep-
tualized as those who like to extract meaning from the material that they
study, and who search for links between topics and subjects to build
extended mental models. They focus on understanding. By contrast, surface
learners try to learn by rote and they are less concerned with gaining an
overall understanding for their own personal satisfaction than with 'getting
by' on a minimum amount of work. Geographically, SAL research has been
concentrated in Scandinavia, the United Kingdom and Australia.

North America and more recently central Europe, on the other hand,
have tended to focus on the self-regulated learning (SRL) approach, which
is based in the tradition of cognitive psychology and uses more quantitative research techniques. SRL research focuses more on the role of
individual differences and cognitive factors such as memory and attention
in learning situations. Self-regulated learners are students who employ
active techniques to monitor themselves as they learn and to direct their
attention, memory and behaviour towards the task at hand. Research in
this area focuses on the activity and strategy of the learner as they go
about the business of learning. This type of research is situated in the
broader field of research on 'metacognition' – the ability of humans to
think about their own thinking and to reflect upon their mental states and
cognitive processes. Psychologists and educators try to extract the most
successful strategies and make them explicit for pupils, modelling good
practice and creating interventions to teach these techniques and observe
their usefulness.*

In this chapter we will look at the evidence from these two approaches,
both of which propose that we can teach people how to learn. We will
investigate interventions used in the classroom to demystify the learning
process for students and encourage them to direct their own learning in
a variety of subjects. We shall see how the course of cognitive development, as well as preconceptions about particular subjects, affect which
interventions work best at certain ages. As ICT (information and communications technology) is now an unavoidable (if not yet integral) part
of the modern classroom, ways to maximize performance in online learning environments will be considered, as well as ways that ICT can be used
to support the learner. Of course, learning does not take place in a bubble;
students are affected by preconceptions of what it means to learn and the
value of particular subjects, by assessment demands, personality charac-

---

* Pintrich gives a more in-depth overview of these research strands in Pintrich PR. A
conceptual framework for assessing motivation and self-regulated learning in college
students. *Educational Psychology Review.* 2004;16(4):385–407.

teristics such as anxiety, and the type of teaching they receive. These factors determine whether students learn in a deep or surface way.

What Is Meant by Deep and Surface Learning?

One of the original works in this concept was instigated in Sweden by Ference Marton and Roger Säljö[4] in 1976. They decided to explore the way students approached one of the most basic tasks of university life – reading academic texts. Students were asked to read an article about reform of the education system in their own time and to answer some questions about the content. They also reported how they tackled the text and these accounts were used to illustrate the different levels of understanding that the students were able to extract from the text. The students' qualitative descriptions of their attempts to engage with the text ranged from admissions that they had tried to memorize the bits they thought were important, to descriptions of efforts to infer and abstract the author's meaning. There was a distinct relationship between students' reported interaction with the passage and the sophistication of meaning that they extracted from it, as well as their recall of the message of the text six weeks later. Those students who focused on the main arguments in the text gave the most coherent account of what they had read when asked to recall it immediately, and could still remember the gist of the article after six weeks. On the other hand, those who tried to rote-learn important bits divorced from the overall meaning had quite poor recall at both time points, and sometimes entirely misinterpreted the author's original meaning. The researchers emphasized both the intention of the student as they started the task, and the process by which they completed it, as central to the outcome.

> What we found was that the students who did not get the point failed to do so simply because they were not looking for it. The main difference we found in the process of learning concerned whether the students focused on the text itself or on what the text was about: the author's intention, the main point, the conclusion to be drawn.[4]

The term 'learning approaches' was adopted to characterize how students tackled the reading task. Surface learners tried to remember exact phrases from the text that they thought were important and focused in an atomistic fashion on small chunks of material. Deep learners, on the other hand, were more concerned with getting a sense of the overall argument, and relating what they had read to what they already knew. Marton and Säljö's characterizations of these types of learning approaches were corroborated by research groups internationally, who found strikingly similar results.[5-8]

Table 7.1   Approaches to learning, associated motivations and learning strategies

Approach to study	Motive for study	Strategy used
Surface	Gain qualification. Fear of failure.	Reproductive, rote-learning.
Deep	Intrinsic motivation. Self-actualization. Achievement of competence.	Meaningful, inter-related with prior knowledge.
Achieving	Competition and ego-control. High grades.	Organized, scheduled.

Measuring approaches to learning

The early studies of deep and surface learning approaches were distinctly qualitative in nature. However, Australian John Biggs[1] worked to devise a quantitative questionnaire-style instrument that could be used to gauge the extent of a student's dispositional learning style. You answered 10 of the items from the most recent version of his Study Process Questionnaire at the start of this chapter. You will be able to see which relate to deep and which to surface learning. Biggs found that students of English, chemistry and education responded to the questionnaire in similar ways, despite the apparent differences in their subjects of study. One subset of items has been shown to relate to rote-learning, pragmatic attitudes towards study as a means to an end, test anxiety and neuroticism. These students were motivated by a fear of failure and generally wanted to get their qualification and move on. A second set of items clustered around constructs relating to academic motivation, meaningful learning and openness, indicating students who were intrinsically motivated by enjoyment and a sense of fulfilment in what they were learning. A final group of questions related to study skills and low anxiety, describing competitive students who are organized and methodical and are motivated by obtaining high grades. Biggs initially labelled these approaches *reproducing, internalizing* and *organizing*. Around the same time, Entwistle and Wilson[9] had used cluster analyses to pick out specific student types within high- and low-attaining groups. Despite the different research methods used, the overlap between the researchers' findings was quite striking, and eventually the nomenclature of *surface, deep,* and *achieving* was adopted widely (see Table 7.1).

Box 7.2 Learner motivation and approaches to learning

Extrinsically motivated students are driven by rewards and praise. Surface learning is commonly associated with extrinsic motivation – learners who are not genuinely interested in a topic, but are given external incentives or feel forced to study it, are less likely to engage in deep learning. Extrinsic motivation is transient – when the reward disappears, often so too does the interest in the topic – and extrinsically motivated learners are less likely to be resilient to failure. One of the classic studies in social psychology showed that paying participants a lot of money to do boring tasks leads them to find the work significantly more tedious than unpaid or low-paid participants do; those receiving little financial reward find their own internal justification for carrying on the work.[10] The same is true for learning – not that we suggest learning is tedious! Students who have learnt to study for the external rewards that high attainment brings may have difficulty maintaining interest, or investigating their subject beyond the bare minimum needed to achieve that reward.

Intrinsically motivated students, on the other hand, will engage with a subject for the personal satisfaction it brings, and probably approach learning in a deep way. De Clercq et al.[11] (using the statistical technique of structural equation modelling) demonstrated that in a group of 110 first-year undergraduates, a mastery orientation to learning increased subsequent deep processing, which in turn increased self-regulation. Of course, given the extent to which they underpin deep and surface approaches to learning, it stands to reason that intrinsic and extrinsic motivation are highly context dependent and not stable traits in learners.

We must stress that the intention of this research and of the SPQ is not to label students as deep or surface learners as if it were a stable, immutable trait; rather students' approaches to learning depend on a wide range of interacting contextual factors (Box 7.2).[1] Their decisions on where and how to expend their study energies are based on (amongst other things) their personal abilities and motivations, the time available to them, and the demands of the task. Biggs illustrated where an approach to learning fits into the wider educational landscape with the 3P model – *Presage, Process, Performance* (Figure 7.1). Presage factors exist before the learning situation and affect how the learning is tackled in an ongoing way, which

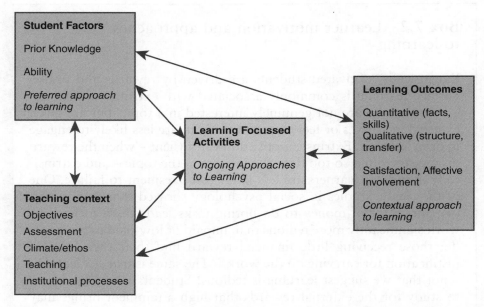

Figure 7.1   Biggs' Presage-Process-Performance model of learning processes. Reproduced with permission by John Wiley & Sons Ltd.

in turn affects the outcome/product. Each part of the model is linked with a double-headed arrow to indicate the constant interaction between these factors.

What are the effects of deep and surface approaches on learning?

Overall it appears that student performance correlates with a deep and/or strategic approach to learning.[12,13] McManus et al. found that deep and strategic learning approaches were positively correlated with final examination performance for medical students, and furthermore, those students who adopted deep approaches (measured both on entry to medical school and in the final year) seem to have gained most from their clinical experiences. Later on in their medical careers, students who adopted a surface approach to learning as an undergraduate also adopted surface approaches to working life. They were more likely to feel overwhelmed by work, and to work in a more disorganized way, which was in turn linked to lower levels of conscientiousness. The deep learning undergraduates also adopted deep styles in their work and were less likely to report feeling excessively stressed and 'burnt-out' by the age of 30.[14]

So far, so good. Deep learning is the approach that aligns philosophically with what educators would wish for their students, and it appears to yield results at exam time and in later life. So what can we do to inspire it?

Factors affecting use of deep learning

As the number of potentially interacting factors in Biggs' 3P model has probably already hinted to you, creating the conditions for deep learning is complex and research shows that some seemingly sensible attempts to inspire deep approaches to learning can backfire. Marton[15] asked 30 students of political science, economy and sociology to read an introductory chapter from a political science textbook. Half of the participants were prompted with questions about chapter content and the relationship between various sub-sections of text, of the sort believed to be used by students who engage in deep learning; the rest of the participants read the chapter without access to any prompts. Learning was measured by an immediate recall task, and then after eight weeks to see how information was retained. The data showed a clear influence of these prompt questions – but not in the way that the researchers expected! The questions had actually induced surface-type approaches to learning, with the control group performing significantly better on both immediate and delayed recall. Marton concluded that the external questions led the students to respond to the text in a rather superficial way, skimming just enough information to complete the task, rather than investing effort in extracting their own sense from it. The predictability of the questions allowed the students to trivialize the task, identifying the learning objectives and working solely to fulfil those criteria.

So, if we can induce surface learning with questions designed to keep students oriented in a text, is it then possible also to foster deep learning by exposing students to questions requiring evidence of judgement, understanding and argument? Säljö[16] asked students one of two sets of questions after they had read several chapters of an education textbook. One set was purely factual, while the other demanded comprehension of the arguments and judgements of reasoning. The students also had to recall and summarize the text. After the final chapter the students were given both types of questions to answer as well as a final summary exercise. While the factual questions clearly elicited a surface approach, backed up by the students' self-reports, the more complex questions did not necessarily inspire a deep approach – indeed, almost half of the students applied surface strategies to this task. Marton and Säljö[4,16] put this down to different interpretations of the task demands – where students believed summarizing to be the end goal of the task, rather than a supporting strategy to aid comprehension, they simply bypassed efforts to induce and scaffold deep learning approaches. The surprising twists in these early studies provide important information on structuring learning tasks for pupils to ensure they don't take cognitive short-cuts, and on efforts to identify 'quick fixes' to improving learning.

So which factors have been linked to a deep learning approach? For students, the perception of receiving high-quality teaching, including helpful feedback and explanations, and of teachers who empathize with difficulties and display a desire to see pupils succeed, frequently correlates with the adoption of deep learning styles.[17–19] Conversely, a teacher's desire to 'cover the topic' and ensure a good set of notes from which to study is more likely to foster surface approaches.[20,21] Trigwell, Prosser and Waterhouse[22] asked almost 4,000 science students to complete the SPQ to determine learning approaches, at the same time as surveying their teachers using the Approaches to Teaching Inventory.[23,21] Teachers rated their agreement with statements describing teaching as merely information transmission versus a view of the teacher as a classroom facilitator in learning activities that change students' conceptual understanding. Classes where teachers reported using information transmission approaches and where the teacher was the focal point of the room were more likely to have students who adopted surface/non-deep approaches to learning. While this might seem quite a promising endorsement of facilitative teaching styles over more traditional methods, caution is needed. The study does not show a causal link and teachers may well adopt one approach or another in response to the demands of their students for a particular kind of teaching, assessment demands, or their judgement of the capabilities of the students. Kember and Gow[24] report a similar finding. Aggregating lecturers' responses by department, they found that departments that endorsed 'knowledge transmission' over 'learning facilitation' saw a marked decline in students' use of deep approaches to learning (as measured by the SPQ) through the period of their course of study. It is worrying that Kember and Gow observed such a decline in deep learning, since university should ideally provide an extended time frame for students to pursue an area of real interest and to get really 'stuck in' to their subject. However, a number of other researchers have described a dip in deep learning scores over the duration of university study. Groves[25] reported a net shift towards an endorsement of the surface approach amongst pharmacy students during their first year and a significant decrease in deep learning scores. Pharmacy degrees are notoriously content-heavy but this finding was especially interesting as the students were following a mainly problem-based learning curriculum, which is generally believed to foster deep approaches.[26–28] Groves concluded that the problem-based learning focus could not overcome the demands of the sheer amount of information to be committed to memory.

While it is perhaps intuitive (though regrettable) that surface approaches would be adopted in vocationally oriented content-loaded degrees such as pharmacy, the effect is not limited to this subject. Gow and Kember[29] observed a similar shift amongst students of a range of subjects, including accountancy, diagnostic sciences and social studies. In particular, a surface-style approach to merely reproducing material was correlated with student perceptions of high workload measured by the Course Perception Questionnaire.[30]

Reid et al.[13] predicted that marks on in-course assignments, designed to test higher-level understanding, would correlate strongly with deep learning, while the relationship would be weaker for short essay questions and weakest for multiple choice questions. To their surprise, deep learning did not correlate with assignment success but was most often significantly related to multiple choice questions – perhaps due to an effort on the part of the examiners to devise complex multi-topic multiple choice questions. Much like Marton's[15] earlier study, relationships between task demands and deep learning were not at all straightforward and obvious. Further, students may not have been able to demonstrate deep learning in the short answers papers as many questions were devised to test basic competence rather than a deep understanding.

As you can probably tell by now, conclusions from the literature on which factors will stimulate deep learning are far from clear. The research findings on modes of teaching and assessment that seem plausible for coaxing students beyond rote-learning are often contradictory. However, in an extensive literature review, Baeten et al.[31] make a convincing argument that it is not so much the contextual factors themselves that affect deep learning but rather the students' perceptions of these factors. Echoing Gow and Kember's results, they find that student perceptions of excessive and inappropriate workloads have repeatedly been found to increase surface approaches to learning.[32,33] Svirko and Mellanby[34] focused on perceived 'information load' rather than workload in two cohorts of medical students and arrived at similar results. It makes intuitive sense that students who feel they are struggling under a mountain of work will look for short-cuts and sacrifice deep integration of information for recite-and-regurgitate approaches.

Regardless of the type of assessment used, perceptions of the assessment mode impact on the use of deep or surface strategies. If students believe that an assessment measures higher levels of cognitive reasoning and demands deep-level engagement they are more likely to use that approach, while those who perceive the assessments as knowledge-based, and rewarding rote recall, use surface strategies.[35] Thus, case-based studies and problem-based learning may be no more likely to foster deep learning than just working out of a textbook, if students fail to perceive the extra dimension of engagement and thought they aim to elicit. Interestingly, perceptions of how appropriate the assessment is are also important – assessments thought to authentically reflect future professional practice encourage deeper learning.[36]

Of course, there are also certain characteristics of students that have been linked to the adoption of a deep approach. Mature students are more likely to deep learn,[31,37] perhaps because they have chosen to return to education to study something they find particularly interesting and/or because they have a clear idea of its usefulness in their professional career plans. Studies of personality types (the 'Big Five' personality traits[38]) suggest that those students who are more conscientious, agreeable, open to experience and emotionally stable are more likely to use the deep approach.[39,40] Unpacking some of the relationships between individual and course-related characteristics is the next step for this research in figuring out how we can teach our students to learn.

Metacognition, Self-Regulation and Learning

As discussed at the beginning of this chapter, around the same time as the paradigm of deep and surface approaches to learning began to emerge, cognitive and educational psychologists began to focus on higher-order thinking skills and the concept of metacognition. Flavell[2] defined metacognition as 'knowledge and cognition about cognitive phenomena'. Later work expanded that definition to go beyond purely cognitive activities; many suggest that being able to think and reflect on our performance, or our motivational or emotional processes, should also come under that umbrella term of metacognition.

Various theorists have refined their views on the construct since the 1970s and several points of agreement emerge. Metacognition is usually described as having two separate but related components, *metacognitive knowledge* and *self-regulation*. Metacognitive knowledge is the stable body of information that we know about ourselves and other people as thinkers. It typically concerns tasks and strategies and is generally something that we are able to report aloud. Examples of metacognitive knowledge might include knowing that you find algebra (task information) more difficult than your sister does (person information) but that you could improve with practice (strategy information). Self-regulation, by contrast, comprises a set of on-task behaviours that keep an individual focused and oriented in the task at hand. Self-regulation includes planning what to do next and what strategies to use, monitoring progress on a task and ensuring that planned goals are met, and evaluating outcomes, both during the task and at the end, to see if improvements could be made in future. These phases of self-regulation are cyclical, with information and experience from one phase shaping what the learner does next in subsequent steps.[41]

Developmentally, it seems that metacognitive knowledge emerges first, as children learn to distinguish between different cognitive activities and begin to amass an understanding of strategies, tasks and individual limitations, usually before school age.[42] Schwanenflugel et al.,[43] for example, showed that by age 6–7 children demonstrated understanding of the factors that affect attention and memory (specifically the notion of interference in short-term memory), how context helps us to remember, and how visual or auditory distractions can make it hard to concentrate. Self-regulation is later developing and more difficult to achieve: young children can be taught to use new strategies for learning or problem solving but have difficulty generalizing them to new situations without prompting, and despite improvements with age, performance doesn't reach optimal levels even by the end of childhood. Markman[44,45] asked children to read paragraphs containing blatant inconsistencies or missing information. Six-year-olds showed virtually no evidence of self-regulation of their comprehension and the oldest participants, aged 12, still showed noticeable weaknesses. Children with high IQs can generally report larger amounts of metacognitive knowledge than average-ability peers, and the strategies and insight they show are often more sophisticated. When it comes to self-regulation skill, however, there is very little difference between children with high and average IQs until late childhood, further supporting the idea that self-regulation is later emerging.[46]

These two components of metacognition are undoubtedly interlinked and influence each other in a cyclical way. It is likely that development of metacognitive knowledge about ourselves as learners supports the emergence of self-regulation. Similarly, successes and failures of self-regulation are assimilated into, and modify, the personal bank of metacognitive knowledge.

Studies of self-regulated learning and metacognitive skills

Self-regulated learners sound like ideal students. Confident operators in the classroom, they show a resourcefulness when it comes to tasks that more passive students lack. They are aware when a piece of information or skill is missing from their repertoire and will work to ensure they acquire it, adapting their behaviour to overcome obstacles such as unsuitable study conditions, confusing instructions or difficult texts. These pupils view learning as a process that is within their control, leading to an understanding of the role that their hard work has played in the success that they have achieved.

The question we ask in the title of this chapter is 'Can we teach people how to learn?' Research on implementing metacognitive interventions in the classroom sets out to answer this in a very practical way. Generally these studies attempt to teach students to regulate their own behaviour on-task in order to plan, monitor and evaluate their progress, making corrections each time to ensure that they stay on track and stay focused. They also attempt to build learners' repertoires of strategies so that they acquire new ways to work around problems as they arise, rather than passively waiting to be told what to do next. We will consider interventions in a number of subjects and with a range of ages and explore the efficacy of these attempts to create better learners.

Reading comprehension

Reading underpins every aspect of the school curriculum. Interaction with written texts is critical in every school subject, and even mathematics depends on secure reading and comprehension skills in order to conceptualize questions and tackle them appropriately.[47,48] The reading difficulties that learners can face are described in Chapter 4. Readers who struggle to comprehend what they read can benefit from instruction detailing self-regulatory strategies such as re-reading, paraphrasing and activating prior knowledge. Struggling readers can be reluctant to do this as there is a preconception (particularly amongst primary-schoolers) that a good reader is one who can read quickly without making mistakes, and who only needs to read things once.[49-51]

One of the best-known research interventions on reading was undertaken by the educator Anne Brown and her PhD student Rosemary Palincsar[52] exploring the impact of a technique called 'reciprocal teaching' on poor comprehenders. In this approach an adult model serves as a guide to help students work through four activities designed to foster

---

Box 7.3   Four steps of reciprocal teaching

1. Summarizing directs students' attention to key points in the text and requires them to check for understanding.
2. Formulating questions based on the text requires attention to, and comprehension of, the main ideas.
3. Critical evaluation is needed in order to clarify what has been read.
4. Predicting what will happen next in the text encourages inferential thinking and hypothesizing.

All of the strategies also depend on the student activating prior knowledge about the subject.

---

self-regulation, specifically for comprehension fostering and comprehension monitoring. The focus was on encouraging children to summarize, question, clarify and predict (Box 7.3).

The technique is a form of cognitive apprenticeship – at first the adult guide does much of the work in modelling the self-regulatory strategies, but the child gradually takes over with the adult acting as a critic who monitors the quality of the output and checks that the self-regulatory processes are being used. Eventually, even this critical role should be adopted by the child as they gain practice with regulating their on-task comprehension.

In Palincsar and Brown's study, seventh-grade pupils (who were adequate decoders but poor comprehenders) were assigned to one of four groups: the reciprocal teaching group, a group who received instruction on locating information within texts, a group who completed the daily assessment tasks that the intervention groups were set, and an untreated control group, who took a pre- and post-test only.

Figure 7.2 shows the results from this study. The reciprocal teaching group made significant gains in their reading comprehension, ultimately doing almost as well as the average readers (normally achieving seventh-grade readers) in their peer group, while none of the other groups made significant improvements over the course of the intervention.

Palincsar and Brown's study spawned a substantial number of follow-up investigations with different settings and populations[53–56] that suggest a short intervention of this nature for 1–2 months can lead to a measurable

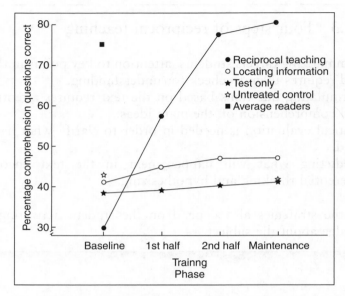

Figure 7.2   Graph of results from Palincsar and Brown's[52] study showing gains made by students on reciprocal teaching intervention. Palinscar and Brown, 1984. Reproduced with permission from Taylor & Francis.

improvement in strategy use and gains in reading comprehension. A meta-analysis of 16 studies using reciprocal teaching showed mean effect sizes of 0.32 for standardized reading tests and 0.88 for experimenter-developed tasks in favour of pupils participating in reciprocal teaching over control groups.[54]

Finding the best way to introduce our students to metacognitive techniques is tricky and it is not entirely clear which methods are most effective. Is it better to have the teacher structure and direct the process, taking the lead in listing lesson objectives, providing detailed guidance and practice, and giving explicit feedback while monitoring student progress? Or would an approach such as reciprocal instruction, where the teacher acts as facilitator and as a model of expert techniques in a shared problem-solving context, be best?

De Corte et al.[57] followed four teachers who implemented a reading strategy programme of activating prior knowledge, clarifying difficult words, creating schematic representations of text and regulating reading over four months with 10–11-year-olds. The children showed good immediate uptake of these strategies and maintained them over two months, even using them in other lessons. However, attitudes towards reading did not change over time, nor did age-standardized comprehension scores,

---

Box 7.4 Metacognitive skills and mathematics

Without metacognitive skills, maths risks becoming divorced from the real world. Alan Schoenfeld (1987) gives a sample question from the US National Assessment of Educational Progress, taken by 45,000 students: *An army bus holds 36 soldiers. If 1128 soldiers are being bussed to their training site, how many buses will be needed?*
  Try the computation yourself before you look at the answer.
  Twenty-nine per cent of the students said that the answer was '31 remainder 12'. Eighteen per cent said that 31 buses were needed. Only 23% of the students correctly answered that 32 buses were required to carry all the soldiers. Schoenfeld wryly observed that a group of students deciding how many cars were needed to go someplace after class would never make those sorts of miscalculations. *What's all the fuss about metacognition?*[58]

---

perhaps because it is difficult to apply reciprocal teaching techniques in whole-class situations: helping students to develop the required strategies is pedagogically challenging and labour intensive. In the case of struggling readers, it may be more important initially to try to increase the fluency of reading, in order to reduce working memory-load – something that is discussed more fully in Chapter 2.

Mathematics

Traditional mathematics teaching focused on memorizing abstract rules and formulae and recognizing where they should be applied, rather than on conceptual understanding. For that reason, maths probably causes anxiety for more students than any other subject. On the other hand, research shows that teaching maths in a way that emphasizes metacognitive strategies, and getting to grips with the conceptual structure of maths problems, not only reduces maths anxiety but can raise attainment too (Box 7.4).[58,59]

  Metacognitive knowledge and skills are important in mathematical performance in both primary and secondary school children.[60–64] Data from the PISA 2003 studies in Germany estimate that metacognitive knowledge accounts for roughly 18% in the variance of maths performance – a finding of practical relevance since metacognitive knowledge is

Box 7.5   The IMPROVE metacognitive training system (Mevarech and Kramarski 2003)

Introducing new concepts
Metacognitive questioning
- comprehension: check for understanding
- connection: activate prior knowledge
- strategy: choose appropriate way to approach problem
- reflection: check reasoning, evaluate progress, debug problems

Practising
Reviewing
Obtaining mastery on lower and higher cognitive processes
Verification
Enrichment

malleable and its growth is likely to result in improved maths performance. With that in mind, we turn to some classroom interventions devised to improve mathematics learning using metacognitive techniques to increase pupils' repertoire of mathematical strategies and to promote self-regulatory behaviour. A better sense of the relationships that underpin various topics in mathematics and an increased sense of self-efficacy in maths learning are frequent by-products of such interventions.

Since the mid-1980s Zemera Mevarech, Bracha Kramarski and colleagues in Israel have been tweaking and exploring the application of a metacognitive training system in mathematics that they call IMPROVE. In a number of studies, Mevarech and colleagues have demonstrated that pupils taught to use the IMPROVE system make larger gains in their mathematics attainment and maintain these over time compared with control groups who are taught using more traditional methods for maths instruction (Box 7.5).

Kramarski and colleagues[65] found that third-grade students using the IMPROVE method showed significant increases in positive feelings towards maths, and decreases in negative sentiments, anxiety and maths avoidance, compared to a control group. Pennequin et al.[66] found that five strategy-training sessions over seven weeks, comprising direct instruction, expert pupil modelling and reflection, improved children's capacity to predict their performance on maths problems, increased metacognitive knowledge in low-attaining children and led to higher scores on a post-test for pupils of all achievement levels compared to the control group. The effect sizes in this study were medium to large, suggesting that the training did have a measurable impact on the children's performance.

Some researchers argue, however, that specifically learning from worked examples should be more beneficial to learners than either traditional teaching or instruction focused on building metacognitive skill. Sweller's[67] cognitive load theory describes how working memory is easily overloaded for novice learners and that while performing new tasks students are most likely working with small pieces of information that have not yet been 'chunked'. This means that they do not have the processing capacity to deal with extra metacognitive strategies for monitoring and evaluating progress.[68] Mevarech and Kramarski[69] compared the effects of the IMPROVE programme versus worked examples in 122 14-year-olds in mixed ability classrooms who studied in cooperative learning groups. The students spent four weeks learning about time, speed and distance in a variety of representations, including symbolic (formulae), verbal (stories about moving objects) and graphs. All of the students studied from the same textbook and worked cooperatively in groups to attempt the same problems; in addition, the teachers standardized their introductions and reviews so that all students were exposed to the same questions. Those students in the worked-example condition were given one example that specified each step with written explanations, and four problems of the same type to practise. In the IMPROVE group, students were expected to generate metacognitive questions according to the IMPROVE framework to guide their progress. Again, each new problem was followed by four practice questions which students would take in turns to read aloud to their small group and attempt to solve using the metacognitive questioning technique.

The groups did not differ significantly in performance on a pre-test, and when split according to high or low achievement in maths no group differences were evident. After the intervention, a test on the topics studied showed that those students in the IMPROVE group scored significantly higher than those who studied worked examples, and the effect sizes for improvement were much greater for lower achievers using the IMPROVE method compared to high achievers (effect sizes of 0.51 and 0.14 respectively). In addition, both low and high achievers who used the IMPROVE method significantly outperformed their counterparts in the worked examples group on the quality of their verbal explanations of mathematical reasoning and on their ability to express problems and solve them using algebra. Interestingly, when tested again one year later those same

Box 7.6   Strategies for translation of modern foreign language

Dependent: e.g. wait for the teacher to explain the text.
Word: look up words in the dictionary.
Avoid: e.g. guess from the pictures.
Metacognitive: e.g. go back and double-check for sense.

group differences were evident. Evidence from video recordings of the small groups of students in each condition showed that those using worked examples did indeed conceptualize the problems in a more instrumental way, as described by Skemp,[59,70] and were fixed on following the rules of sample questions. The IMPROVE group, on the other hand, through the monitoring and evaluation of strategies and the verification of solutions, built a more complete model of the question and actively debugged certain difficulties, including identifying where common keywords did not function in the usual way (e.g. signifying subtraction instead of addition).

Modern foreign languages

Since the UK government removed the requirement for students to take a modern foreign language at GCSE, there has been a slump in numbers choosing to study languages at school, with research indicating a decrease in student enjoyment and motivation over time.[71] Any interventions that can counter this trend are therefore of great interest. Concerning classroom practice, Macaro and Erler[72] introduced metacognitive strategies for helping translation from French to English to 11-year-old English schoolchildren. They firstly administered a questionnaire to determine what strategies for translation the children were currently using. This involved four sorts of strategies (Box 7.6).

The programme for teaching metacognitive strategies continued over two school years (15 months in total). The children were taught to use techniques such as guessing from words around a problem word or activating prior knowledge by thinking about similar words in either language. There was a lot of scaffolded practice of these metacognitive techniques. At the end, the pupils' scores on a translation test were compared with those of pupils in a control class who had not been exposed to the metacognitive training (Figure 7.3). The pupils who received

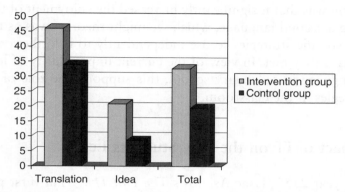

Figure 7.3 Effect of teaching metacognitve strategies on translation scores. Translation scores are correct words; Idea is a score based on comprehension of the ideas in the passage to be translated. *Source*: Drawn from data in Macaro and Erler.[72]

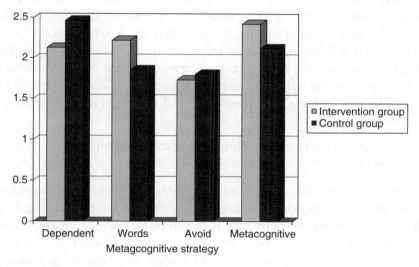

Figure 7.4 Effect of metacognitive intervention on strategies used by students (see Box 7.6 for explanation). *Source*: Drawn from data in Macaro and Erler.[72]

metacognitive training scored higher than the matched controls. However, the authors were at pains to point out that while this was a promising result it was not a fully controlled study as different teachers were involved in the intervention and control classes. Re-administration of the questionnaire at the end of the training period showed small decreases in dependent strategies and small increases in metacognitive and 'word' strategies (Figure 7.4). Probably the most important effect of the intervention was that it significantly increased the enjoyment of the pupils in learning a second language, which we might theorize was as the result of having specific strategies to use independently to help them overcome the problems they met. In view of the current unpopularity of learning a second language in secondary school, this supports the role of teaching such strategies in the classroom.

The Impact of IT on the Way Students Learn

Set in the year 2157, Isaac Asimov's *The Fun They Had* (first published in 1951) told the story of Tommy and Margie's amazement at finding 'a real book' which described life at school in the days when *a man* was in charge of a whole class full of children instead of each individual child being tutored at home by a robotic teacher with a vast mechanical memory store. Sixty years after it was published, Asimov may have missed the mark with some of the smaller details of the future of school (such as homework being written in punch code), but the broader picture of the central role of ICT in education is taking shape. Chapter 13 in this book more fully discusses the role of technology in modern education systems, but in this section we will focus in particular on how technology can both help and hinder learners' metacognitive and self-regulation processes.

Studies of metacognition in computer-based learning environments

Roger Azevedo and his colleagues have done extensive work looking at the role of metacognition in online and computer-based learning hyper-media environments. Hypermedia is a computer format where students can access text, graphics, audio and video clips that are linked together and can be read, stored, searched and edited. It is the basic format of many web pages on the Internet.

One example of such hypermedia is Microsoft's Encarta encyclopaedia. Azevedo and Cromley[73] tested whether teaching students metacognitive skills could help them acquire knowledge more effectively from Encarta. They asked 131 non-biology undergraduates to learn as much as they could about the circulatory system in 40 minutes. Half of the group received a 30-minute training session beforehand explaining the purpose of self-regulation when studying and describing strategies to help regulation of cognition, motivation and behaviour. The undergraduates who received the self-regulation training did significantly better in the post-tests of labelling diagrams, constructing a flow diagram and writing a short essay. These students more frequently showed evidence of activation of prior knowledge, planning, feeling of knowing and judgement of learning, self-questioning, summarizing and inferential reasoning.

If learners benefit from receiving training in metacognitive skills, the next obvious question is whether a computer program can be used to deliver this training as well. Kramarski and Gutman[74] investigated this by taking elements of the successful IMPROVE programme for training metacognition in mathematics described earlier and working it into a series of e-learning maths exercises for 14–15-year-olds. All students practised 10 interactive problem-solving tasks based on linear functions, receiving feedback on their results from the computer. Half of the students also received interactive messages designed to prompt aspects of self-regulation – metacognitive questions were posed to be answered by typing the answers into a box on-screen, explanations sought, and metacognitive feedback delivered. While there were no differences in procedural problem-solving between the groups at the outset, by the end of the study period those students who received the metacognitive support performed significantly better than their peers on a post-test of the topic and on a transfer task of more complex problems. These required higher-order thinking skills such as finding connections, drawing conclusions and making generalizations based on available information. Importantly, many of these behaviours chime with the descriptions of what students taking deep approaches to learning do as they engage with study material.

So does this mean that teachers will soon be unnecessary? Probably not, because at the moment research still indicates that a human can do a better job than a computer can alone. Azevedo and colleagues[75] explored whether having a human tutor on hand helped students self-regulate their learning on a novel computer-based learning task. One hundred and twenty-eight adolescents in middle and high school (11–19 years) were tested on their level of knowledge of the circulatory system using three tasks: matching relevant vocabulary to diagrams, describing the system in a short essay, and completing a blood-flow diagram. The latter two tasks in particular were designed to explore the sophistication of the students' mental models of the working of the circulatory system (i.e. from a very basic understanding that blood circulates and transports oxygen, to detailed descriptions that circulation is a double-loop system detailing the roles of heart, lungs, vessels, and the functions of the system).

The students were then instructed to spend 40 minutes using Encarta to learn as much as they could about the circulatory system. Half of the group were accompanied by a tutor whose job it was to help them with

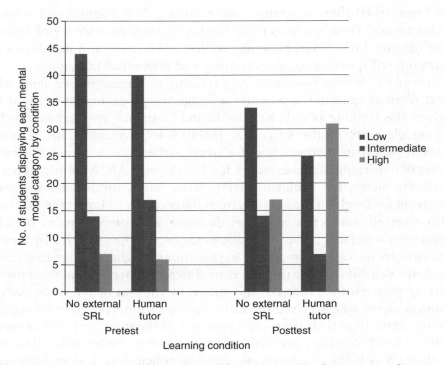

Figure 7.5   Comparison of mental model sophistication (low, intermediate, high) developed in students with no external self-regulation support and those who had help from a human tutor. *Source:* Drawn from data in Azevedo et al.[75]

self-regulated learning (SRL) by scaffolding, including prompting them to use certain strategies at the appropriate time. When re-tested, both groups improved on vocabulary matching, suggesting that the computer-based learning had increased some basic knowledge for each group. However, compared to those who worked alone, the students who experienced the help from a tutor were able to produce a much more accurate blood-flow diagram and almost twice as many students had made a shift from a simple to a sophisticated mental model of the circulatory system as in the control group (Figure 7.5).

The improved results on the test for the group who experienced working with a tutor were not the only evidence of the tutor's positive influence. The students were asked to think aloud as they worked and their verbalizations were recorded (this type of data is known as a 'continuous verbal protocol' in psychological research). The tutor group made almost 10 times the number of statements aimed at activating their prior knowledge of the subject. They were far more likely to use judgements of learning and 'feelings of knowing' to assess their progress and twice as likely actively to monitor their own progress towards goals. These students showed four times as many instances of generating inferential arguments and coordinating disparate information sources, and they were more likely to draw and summarize information. Students who were left to their own devices were not so proactive in trying to integrate new information with what they already knew, and seemed more passive in their task engagement; they were more likely to evaluate the content of the material to see if it was suitable, re-read text, search for new information (sometimes without a specific goal in mind) and attempt to memorize.

It is easy to see how getting a good grasp of the workings of complex systems of the sort presented by Azevedo et al., where it's necessary to integrate information from a variety of sources to understand relations between physiological, cellular, organ and system-level functions, would be most effective with a deep learning approach. Self-regulation skills can help learners to stay on track as they navigate information that is multi-layered and non-linear, coordinating multiple representations, in order to support this deep learning.

The evidence suggests that time spent 'learning' on computers is not sufficient to support deepening understanding of key concepts without some form of support for self-regulation. Azevedo and colleagues[75-76] have started to develop a system called 'MetaTutor' to bring together the best-practice features of incorporating self-regulated learning support into computer-based learning. The system first of all employs a training phase to model good self-regulatory behaviours and then requires students to discriminate between poor and useful regulation behaviours in certain contexts, and to detect instances of good SRL from videos of other people learning. Then the learning environment itself presents a goal for the session, after which learners must list a set of sub-goals to be achieved. An interesting feature is a list of SRL processes that is presented in a menu on-screen alongside the hypermedia learning environment. Users are encouraged to select a particular process by clicking on it before they engage in it as a way of consciously reminding the learner of the SRL processes they are using.

Overall Impact of Self-Regulated Learning Interventions

The research literature on intervention studies is broadly consistent, showing that good self-regulation skills have a positive impact on academic attainment and learning motivation.[77] Dignath and Buettner[78] carried out a meta-analysis of 49 studies at primary school level and 35 at secondary school that aimed to teach pupils skills in regulating their cognitive, metacognitive or motivational strategies. While the overall mean effect size for the interventions was 0.69 – quite large for educational research – interesting differences between primary and secondary schools could be teased apart that reflect the developmental trajectory of metacognitive skills discussed earlier. In primary schools, cognitive apprenticeship-type interventions, with an emphasis on modelling techniques and strategies such as reciprocal teaching, tended to be most effective. At secondary school, metacognitive reflection training was most useful. As metacognitive skills and experience increase with age, post-primary-aged pupils will already have a range of strategies and declarative metacognitive knowledge at their disposal and so instruction on the reflective aspects of self-regulation is most appropriate to help them capitalize on what they already know. Primary pupils, on the other hand, may not yet be able to cope with the cognitive load incurred by monitoring and reflection and so their academic performance can best be improved in the first instance by increasing their metacognitive strategy repertoire.

Interventions in mathematics had most impact at primary school, whereas those on reading and writing had most effect on older children. Alexander et al.[79] found that reading and writing exert large cognitive demands in younger children, leaving little room for metacognitive processes; older children by contrast have largely automated these skills. The decline in usefulness of mathematics interventions is most likely linked to negative student achievement beliefs regarding maths increasing with age.[80]

Perhaps the most concerning finding in Dignath and Buettner's analysis was that in both primary and secondary schools effect sizes were significantly higher if interventions were carried out by researchers rather than teachers. Exploratory qualitative studies have shown that many teachers' knowledge of metacognition and self-regulation is unsatisfactorily low if they are to promote higher-order thinking in the classroom.[81,82] If educational research on self-regulation is to embed into classroom practice it is vital that teachers are equipped and confident to implement the strategies and interventions to improve student achievement.

Summary

- Two different, but related, research traditions explore whether it is possible to teach people how to learn. Very few attempts have been made to link and integrate these research paradigms to date.

- The first tradition is frequently termed 'student approaches to learning' (SAL) and is rooted in qualitative research that focuses on students' experiences of learning and the impact of their motivations and perceptions of their learning environment on the way they study. It focuses on the distinction between deep approaches and surface approaches to learning. The deep approach involves striving to extract meaning, relating information to previous knowledge and to other topic areas. A surface approach means that learners are more inclined to skim over topics and to rote-memorize, focusing on facts.

- The second research tradition is based on the concept of self-regulated learning (SRL). Based on models and principles from cognitive psychology, it explores students' ability to learn in a more quantitative way, investigating their on-task behaviour as they engage with learning while managing their cognitive resources.

- Education at all levels, but particularly higher education, should strive to create learners who are reflective and critical, and who are confident problem-solvers. Teaching people how to learn is based on the ideal that education should involve more than just accumulating facts.

- Deep and surface approaches to learning are not stable personality traits. A complex set of factors and contexts underpins the decision to adopt a certain approach. Student perceptions of high workload, unsupportive teaching, inappropriate modes of assessment and lack of engagement with the topic can lead to surface approaches. Deep learning is thought to be fostered by perceptions that the form of an assessment requires integration of knowledge, of perceived usefulness of material to later career, and of teaching styles that facilitate discovery and conceptual change.

- Metacognitive interventions tend to focus on self-regulation of learning, which in turn increases metacognitive knowledge of strategies and personal strengths and weaknesses. Both reciprocal teaching and direct teacher-led instruction interventions have had positive effects on learning outcomes and attainment in reading, mathematics, modern foreign languages and in computer-based learning scenarios.

- The type of metacognitive intervention employed should reflect the age and development of the intended learners. Primary school children benefit from strategy instruction that increases metacognitive knowledge, whereas secondary school and older learners see most effect from self-regulation training.

Educational implications

- Attempts to induce deep learning experimentally have occasionally backfired and encouraged a more surface approach. Teachers, textbook authors and learning technologists creating online learning content must carefully consider the structure of the materials they create, and whether they may unintentionally influence students to interact with the material in a more surface way. The structure of assessments is important to ensure that students engage with the material in an appropriate way – those that appear to reward straightforward regurgitation will not encourage learners to engage with material in a deep way.
- More time could be devoted in teacher training and professional development to increase teacher knowledge and comfort with the philosophy, vocabulary and research associated with metacognition and metacognitive interventions. It appears that many teachers shy away from this aspect of instruction as they don't feel they know enough to implement these ideas in their own teaching.
- Unfocused time spent online and in other computer-based learning environments probably doesn't aid student learning beyond the accumulation of facts. Online learning activities must be carefully structured, where possible with a tutor or guide to keep students on track.
- The language that we use in describing ability and attainment, and the goals of learning tasks, affect pupils' motivation and engagement with learning. Educators and parents should be cautious of describing ability as being fixed, and praising only outcomes rather than the process and effort involved. Students of all ages may need guidance in understanding that knowledge is complicated and that different topics interlink and relate rather than existing as individual 'modules'.
- Modelling metacognitive and self-regulation strategies explicitly for our pupils is likely to be beneficial. It chimes with the idea expressed above of demonstrating to students the *process* of reaching a decision, or completing a step in a task, rather than just the polished, finished outcome.

References

1   Biggs J, Kember D, Leung DYP. The revised two-factor Study Process Questionnaire: R-SPQ-2F. *British Journal of Educational Psychology.* 2001;71: 133–149.

2   Flavell JH. Metacognition and cognitive monitoring: A new area of cognitive-developmental inquiry. *American Psychologist*. 1979;34:906–911.

3   Palfreyman D. Higher education, liberal education, critical-thinking, academic discourse, and the Oxford tutorial as sacred cow or pedagogical gem. In: Palfreyman, D, ed. *The Oxford Tutorial: Thanks, You Taught Me How to Think*. 2nd ed. Oxford: Oxford Centre for Higher Education Policy Studies; 2008.

4   Marton F, Säljö R. 'Approaches to Learning'. In: Marton, F, Hounsell, D, and Entwistle, N, eds. *The Experience of Learning: Implications for teaching and studying in higher education*. 3rd ed. Edinburgh: University of Edinburgh, Centre for Teaching, Learning and Assessment; 2005:43.

5   Biggs JB. Individual and group differences in study processes. *British Journal of Educational Psychology*. 1978;48:266–279.

6   Biggs JB. Individual differences in the study process and the quality of learning outcomes. *Higher Education*. 1979;8:381–394.

7   Entwistle NJ, Hanley M, Hounsell D. Identifying distinctive approaches to studying. *Higher Education*. 1979;8(4):365–380.

8   Pask G. Styles and strategies of learning. *British Journal of Educational Psychology*. 1976;46(2):128–148.

9   Entwistle NJ, Wilson JD. *Degrees of Excellence: The Academic Achievement Game*. London: Hodder and Stoughton; 1977.

10 Festinger L, Carlsmith JM. Cognitive consequences of forced compliance. *Journal of Abnormal and Social Psychology*. 1959;58:203–210.

11 De Clercq M, Galand B, Frenay M. Chicken or the egg: Longitudinal analysis of the causal dilemma between goal orientation, self-regulation and cognitive processing strategies in higher education. *Studies in Educational Evaluation*. 2013;39(1):4–13.

12 McManus IC, Richards P, Winder BC, Sproston KA. Clinical experience, performance in final examinations, and learning style in medical students: A prospective study. *British Medical Journal*. 1998;316:345–350.

13 Reid W, Duvall E, Evans P. Relationship between assessment results and approaches to learning and studying in Year Two medical students. *Medical Education*. 2007;41(8):754–762.

14 McManus IC, Keeling A, Paice E. Stress, burnout and doctors' attitudes to work are determined by personality and learning style: A twelve year longitudinal study of UK medical graduates. *BMC Medicine*. 2004;2:29.

15 Marton F. On non-verbatim learning: II. The erosion of a task-induced learning algorithm. *Scandinavian Journal of Psychology*. 1976;17:41–48.

16 Säljö R. *Qualitative Differences in Learning as a Function of the Learner's Conception of the Task*. Gothenburg: Acta Universitatis Gothenburgensis; 1975.

17 Crawford K, Gordon S, Nicholas J, Prosser M. Conceptions of mathematics and how it is learned: The perspectives of students entering university. *Learning and Instruction*. 1994;4:331–345.

18   Eley MG. Differential adoption of study approaches within individual students. *Higher Education.* 1992;23(3):231–254.

19   Trigwell K, Prosser M. Improving the quality of student learning: The influence of learning context and student approaches to learning on learning outcomes. *Higher Education.* 1991;22:251–266.

20   Ramsden P. *Learning to Teach in Higher Education.* London: Routledge; 1992.

21   Trigwell K, Prosser M. Changing approaches to teaching: A relational perspective. *Studies in Higher education.* 1996;21:275–284.

22   Trigwell K, Prosser M, Waterhouse F. Relations between teachers' approaches to teaching and students' approaches to learning. *Higher Education.* 1999;37:57–70.

23   Prosser M, Trigwell K. *Teaching for Learning in Higher Education.* Buckingham: Open University Press; 1998.

24   Kember D, Gow L. Orientations to teaching and their effect on the quality of student learning. *Journal of Higher Education.* 1994;65(1):59–74.

25   Groves M. Problem-based learning and learning approach: Is there a relationship? *Advances in Health Sciences Education.* 2005;10(4): 315–326.

26   Biggs J. Approaches to learning in secondary and tertiary students in Hong Kong: Some comparative studies. *Educational Research Journal.* 1991;6: 27–39.

27   Blumber P. Evaluating the evidence that problem-based learners are self-directed learners: A review of the literature. In: Evensen D, Hmelo, C, eds. *Problem-based Learning: A Research Perspective on Learning Interactions.* London: Lawrence Erlbaum; 2000:199–226.

28   Greening T. Scaffolding for success in problem-based learning. *Medical Education Online.* 1998;3(4). Available at; www.med-ed-online.org. Accessed 2 December 2013.

29   Gow L, Kember D. Does higher education promote independent learning? *Higher Education.* 1990;19:307–322.

30   Ramsden P, Entwistle NJ. Effects of academic departments on students' approaches to studying. *British Journal of Educational Psychology.* 1981;51:368–383.

31   Baeten M, Kyndt E, Struyven K, Dochy F. Using student-centered learning environments to stimulate deep approaches to learning: Factors encouraging or discouraging their effectiveness. *Educational Psychology Review.* 2010;5(3):243–260.

32   Diseth A. Approaches to learning, course experience and examination grade among undergraduate psychology students: Testing of mediator effects and construct validity. *Studies in Higher Education.* 2007;32(3):373–388.

33   Kember D. Interpreting student workload and the factors which shape students' perceptions of their workload. *Studies in Higher Education.* 2004; 29(2):165–184.

34 Svirko E, Mellanby J. Attitudes to e-learning, learning style and achievement in learning neuroanatomy by medical students. *Medical Teacher.* 2008; 30(9–10):e219–e227.

35 Scouller K. The influence of assessment method on students' learning approaches: Multiple choice question examination versus assignment essay. *Higher Education.* 1998;35:453–472.

36 Gulikers JTM, Kester L, Kirschner PA, Bastiaens TJ. The effect of practical experience on perceptions of assessment authenticity, study approach, and learning outcome. *Learning and Instruction.* 2008;18:172–186.

37 Chamorro-Premuzic T, Furnham A. Mainly openness: The relationship between the Big Five personality traits and learning approaches. *Learning and Individual Differences.* 2009;19:524–529.

38 Goldberg LR. An alternative 'description of personality': The Big-Five factor structure. *Journal of Personality and Social Psychology.* 1990;59(6): 1216–1229.

39 Chamorro-Premuzic T, Furnham A, Lewis M. Personality and approaches to learning predict preference for different teaching methods. *Learning and Individual Differences.* 2007;17:241–250.

40 Diseth A. Personality and approaches to learning as predictors of academic achievement. *European Journal of Personality.* 2003;17:143–155.

41 Zimmerman BJ. Academic studying and the development of personal skill: A self-regulatory perspective. *Educational Psychologist.* 1998;33(2): 73–86.

42 Pillow B. The development of children's beliefs about the mental world. *Merrill-Palmer Quarterly.* 1988;34:1–32.

43 Schwanenflugel PJ, Moore TP, Stevens P, Carr M. Metacognitive knowledge of gifted and non-gifted children in early elementary school. *Gifted Child Quarterly.* 1997;41(2):25–35.

44 Markman EM. Realizing that you don't understand: A preliminary investigation. *Child Development.* 1977;48:986–992.

45 Markman EM. Realizing that you don't understand: Elementary school children's awareness of inconsistencies. *Child Development.* 1979;50: 643–655.

46 Alexander JM, Carr M, Schwanenflugel PJ. Metacognition in gifted children: Directions for future research. *Developmental Review.* 1995;15:1–37.

47 Barton ML, Heidema C, Barton, ML, Heidema, C. *Teaching Reading in Mathematics.* 2nd ed. Aurora, CO: Mid-Continent Research for Education and Learning; 2002.

48 Martinez J, Martinez M, Martinez J, Martinez, N. *Reading and Writing to Learn Mathematics: A Guide and Resource Book.* Boston, MA: Allyn & Bacon; 2001.

49 Eme E, Puustinen M, Coutelet B. Individual and developmental differences in reading monitoring: When and how do children evaluate their comprehension. *European Journal of Psychology of Education.* 2006;21:91–115.

50   Myers M, Paris SG. Children's metacognitive knowledge about reading. *Journal of Educational Psychology.* 1978;70:680–690.

51   Paris SG. Assessment and remediation of metacognitive aspects of children's reading comprehension. *Topics in Language Disorders.* 1991;12: 32–50.

52   Palincsar A, Brown A. Reciprocal teaching of comprehension-fostering and monitoring activities. *Cognition and instruction.* 1984;2:117–175.

53   Brown A, Palinscar A. Guided, cooperative learning, and individual knowledge acquisition. In: Resnick LB, ed. *Knowing, Learning and Instruction. Essays in Honor of Robert Glaser.* Mahwah, NJ: Erlbaum; 1989: 393–451.

54   Rosenshine B, Meister C. Reciprocal teaching: A review of the research. *Review of Educational Research.* 1994;64:479–530.

55   Le Fevre DM, Moore DW, Wilkinson IAG. Tape-assisted reciprocal teaching: Cognitive bootstrapping for poor decoders. *British Journal of Educational Psychology.* 2003;73(1):37–59.

56   Sporer N, Brunstein JC, Kieschke U. Improving students' reading comprehension skills: Effects of strategy instruction and reciprocal teaching. *Learning and Instruction.* 2009;19(3):272–286.

57   De Corte E, Verschaffel L, Van De Ven A. Improving text comprehension strategies in upper primary school children: A design experiment. *British Journal of Educational Psychology.* 2001;71:531–559.

58   Schoenfeld A. What's all the fuss about metacognition? In: *Cognitive Science and Mathematics Education.* Hillsdale, NJ: Lawrence Erlbaum Associates; 1987:189–216.

59   Skemp RR. Relational understanding and instrumental understanding. *Mathematics Teaching.* 1976;77:20–26.

60   Schoenfeld AH. When good teaching leads to bad results: The disasters of 'well taught' mathematics courses. *Educational Psychologist.* 1988;23: 145–166.

61   Carr M, Alexander J, Folds-Bennett T. Metacognition and mathematics strategy use. *Applied Cognitive Psychology.* 1994;8:583–595.

62   Carr M, Jessup DL. Cognitive and metacognitive predictors of mathematics strategy use. *Learning and Individual Differences.* 1995;7:235–247.

63   Lucangeli D, Cornoldi C. Mathematics and metacognition: What is the nature of the relationship? *Mathematical Cognition.* 1997;3:121–139.

64   Veenman M. The role of intellectual and metacognitive skills in math problem solving. In: Desoete A, Veenman M, eds. *Metacognition in Mathematics Education.* New York: Nova Science; 2006:35–50.

65   Kramarski B, Weisse I, Kololshi-Minsker I. How can self-regulated learning support the problem solving of third-grade students with mathematics anxiety? *ZDM Mathematics Education.* 2010;42:179–193.

66   Pennequin V, Sorel O, Nanty I, Fontaine R. Metacognition and low achievement in mathematics: The effect of training in the use of metacognitive skills

to solve mathematical word problems. *Thinking and reasoning.* 2010; 16(3):198–220.

67 Sweller J. Cognitive load theory, learning difficulty, and instructional design. *Learning and Instruction.* 1994;4(4):295–312.

68 Crippen P, Brooks DW. Applying cognitive theory to chemistry instruction: The case for worked examples. *Chemistry Education Research and Practice.* 2009;10:35–41.

69 Mevarech ZR, Kramarski B. The effects of metacognitive training versus worked-out examples on students' mathematical reasoning. *British Journal of Educational Psychology.* 2003;73(4):449–471.

70 Skemp R. *The Psychology of Learning Mathematics.* Harmondsworth, UK: Penguin; 1986.

71 Colman J, Galaczi A, Astruc L. Motivation of UK pupils towards foreign languages: A large-scale survey at Key Stage 3. *The Language Learning Journal.* 2007;35(2):245–280.

72 Macaro E, Erler L. Raising the achievement of young-beginner readers of French through strategy instruction. *Applied Linguistics.* 2008;29(1): 90–119.

73 Azevedo R, Cromley JG. Does training on self-regulated learning facilitate students' learning with hypermedia? *Journal of Educational Psychology.* 2004;96:523–535.

74 Kramarski B, Gutman M. How can self-regulated learning be supported in mathematical e-learning environments? *Journal of Computer Assisted Learning.* 2006;22:24–33.

75 Azevedo R, Moos DC, Greene JA, Winters FI, Cromley JG. Why is externally-regulated learning more effective than self-regulated learning with hypermedia? *Educational Technology Research and Development.* 2008;56(1): 45–72.

76 Moos D, Azevedo R. Self-regulated learning with hypermedia: The role of prior domain knowledge. *Contemporary Educational Psychology.* 2008; 33(2):270–298.

77 Zimmerman B. Theories of self-regulated learning and academic achievement: An overview and analysis. In: Zimmerman BJ, Schunk DH, eds. *Self-Regulated Learning and Academic Achievement: Theoretical Perspectives.* 2nd ed. Mahwah, NJ: Erlbaum; 2001:1–37.

78 Dignath C, Buettner G. Components of fostering self-regulated learning among students: A meta-analysis on intervention studies at primary and secondary school level. *Metacognition and Learning.* 2008;3: 231–264.

79 Alexander PA, Graham S, Harris KR. A perspective on strategy research: Progress and prospects. *Educational Psychology Review.* 1998;10: 129–154.

80 Wigfield A. Expectancy-value theory of achievement motivation: A developmental perspective. *Educational Psychology Review.* 1994;6:49–78.

81   Waeytans K, Lens W, Vandenberghe R. 'Learning to learn': Teachers' conceptions of their supporting role. *Learning and Instruction*. 2002;12(3): 305–322.

82   Zohar A. Teachers' metacognitive knowledge and the instruction of higher order thinking. *Teaching and Teacher Education*. 1999;15:413–429.

Chapter 8

Academic Selection
Do We Need to Do It and Can We Make It Fair?

Thinking Skills Assessment

Developed and administered on behalf of the University of Oxford by Cambridge Assessment.
  Copyright © UCLES 2010.
  Reproduced by permission of The Admissions Testing Service.

1. Splashford Swimming Pool charges £2 per session for adults and £1 for children.

  Also available is a Family Swimcard. At a cost of £50, the Family Swimcard allows unlimited use of the pool for one year for two adults and up to three children. For larger families, every additional child must pay half the children's rate each time.
  Mr and Mrs Teal and their four children are keen swimmers. They used their Swimcard when the family went swimming 40 times last year.
  How much did the Swimcard save the Teal family last year?

(continued)

Education and Learning: An Evidence-Based Approach, First Edition. Jane Mellanby and Katy Theobald.
© 2014 John Wiley & Sons, Ltd. Published 2014 by John Wiley & Sons, Ltd.

A   £ 50
B   £ 190
C   £ 230
D   £ 250
E   £ 270

2.   Every year in this country there are over 8000 personal accidents on golf courses, yet it is estimated that as few as five per cent of all golfers take out adequate insurance against claims for injury. If more golfers could be encouraged to take out appropriate insurance policies the number of accidents could be dramatically reduced.

Which one of the following identifies the flaw in the argument above?

A   It ignores the fact that millions of golfers never have an accident.
B   It assumes that all insurance policies provide adequate insurance against claims.
C   It implies that the occurrence of golfing accidents is causally related to the lack of insurance.
D   It overlooks the possibility that some accidents would not be covered by insurance.
E   It ignores the fact that there are different kinds of insurance for different kinds of activity.

There are millions of children in the British school system and they vary greatly in their background experiences, aptitudes and rates of learning. Educators need some way to cope with this variation and in Britain one long-standing response has been selection. In the 1940s and 50s the entire secondary system was based on a process of academic selection. The 11+ examination, taken during the final year of primary school, was used to select the most academically capable children for grammar school (with the likelihood of progressing to university). Meanwhile, the majority of pupils continued into secondary moderns or, in some cases, technical colleges. This tripartite system has now been largely superseded; however, academies are still allowed to select 10% of their intake according to 'aptitude' for their specialist subject.

More subtle selection is prevalent throughout the education system. It is common for pupils to be divided into ability groups, or sets, for subjects according to test scores or teachers' judgements. In some schools, pupils also have their course choices restricted by ability: 14–16-year-olds may be directed towards academic or vocational qualifications according to their prior attainment, or may be selected for different tiers of GCSEs. It is also quite common for schools to prevent students from taking an A-level in a subject unless they attain a B grade or above at GCSE. Finally, once pupils leave compulsory education many will face tough competition and selective practices in order to gain a place on a training scheme or university course.

Although these selection practices are common, their empirical basis is not always clear. This chapter explores the evidence relating to various modes of academic selection. We start by thinking about selection in secondary schools and whether we are best off teaching pupils in mixed groups or divided by ability (Box 8.1). We then go on to look at selection for higher education, exploring the non-academic factors that influence many admissions tests. Our aim is not to give a conclusive judgement on which measure is 'best', because this depends on the purpose for which the test is being used. Rather we aim to highlight the strengths and weaknesses of different approaches, leaving you to judge their merits.

Selection in Secondary Schools

Most UK state secondary schools operate with little or no academic selection in their entrance procedures, so their intakes will include pupils with a wide range of attainment and learning needs. In order to serve such diverse intakes many schools use setting, where pupils are divided for teaching, ostensibly according to ability. In 2003–4, Ofsted reported that roughly 80% of maths classes, 60% of science classes and 50% of English classes at Key Stage 3 (KS3) were taught in set, rather than mixed, groups.[4] Setting and streaming are slightly different practices: the former involves putting pupils into different groups for specific lessons whilst the latter involves placing pupils into a certain ability group for all their lessons (or sometimes into a completely different school). Streaming is less common in the United Kingdom* but is widespread in other countries such as Germany.

As we discuss in Chapters 5 and 11, teaching pupils in ability groups reflects a specific Western conception of ability as a fixed trait. The

---

* Analysis of the Millennium Cohort Study indicates that by age 7, up to a fifth of the children in the UK may be taught in streams. In Northern Ireland, 11% of children in the sample were streamed at this age; this rose to 19.5% in Wales. See http://www.ioe.ac.uk/newsEvents/53420.html for more information.

Box 8.1 Grammar schools: providing opportunity or reinforcing inequality?

Every few years it seems the media reignites the grammar school debate: should the few grammar schools left in England and Northern Ireland be allowed to remain selective? Should the system be allowed to expand? The longstanding question is whether, as some commentators and politicians believe, grammar schools are actually better for social mobility than the comprehensive alternative.

Advocates of comprehensive education view grammar schools as socially divisive: they argue that selective schools cream off able pupils who are disproportionately of higher SES (socioeconomic status) and are rarely ethnic minorities. This, they suggest, leaves those who fail the 11+ entrance exam in poorer-quality schools (the better teachers having headed to the grammar schools) and with lower aspirations, having been labelled 'failures' at the age of 11.

It is true that selection at the age of 11 does disadvantage pupils with English as a second language; they often underachieve at primary school and then catch up in the first few years of secondary school, once their English has improved. It is equally true that grammar schools have disproportionately few pupils receiving free school meals, an indicator of socioeconomic disadvantage. However, the percentage of pupils claiming free school meals is not a particularly good indicator of a school's socioeconomic mix since eligible pupils may not claim if they think there is social stigma attached to doing so.

To focus on these biases also overlooks a bigger picture identified in a report commissioned by education charity the Sutton Trust.[1] The report shows that the most apparently socially selective state schools are not actually academically selective. This reflects the impact of choice in the education system. Where a range of non-selective schools exist, the middle classes will apply their social and economic capital to ensure their children attend the best in an area, at the expense of parents and children from less advantaged backgrounds who have fewer resources at their disposal. Middle-class parents may move house to be in a certain catchment area, or have the time to invest in pursuing appeals if their child is not accepted to their preferred school. Admittedly, the middle classes can also gain advantage in an academically selective admissions process by hiring tutors to prepare their children for entrance exams. However, in counties with grammar schools most state primary schools also prepare their pupils for the 11+, so it may actually be easier to level the playing field in an academically than an economically driven system.

It is worth noting a second finding in the report: failing the 11+ does not destine pupils to receive a poorer-quality education. The non-selective schools that such pupils attend 'are performing no differently from all other schools'. Meanwhile, those pupils who do go to grammar schools tend to do slightly better than those of equal ability who learn in a non-selective environment. At a regional level, the combination of these two factors results in areas operating a selective system having higher average value-added scores for pupils' grades.[2] Much greater than the impact on grades, however, is the effect that attending a grammar school has in terms of life outcomes. Longitudinal research tracking former grammar school pupils finds that they are advantaged in terms of educational outcomes and, for men at least, earnings. Notably, those benefiting the most from a grammar school education are the people who were comparatively disadvantaged amongst their secondary school peers.[3]

Whilst the evidence regarding grammar school effects on academic achievement is not clear-cut, one observation from the Sutton Trust report does stand out. At the moment, it is those schools that are *not* supposed to be selective in their admissions that are the most selective in social terms. This suggests that although the tripartite school system was imperfect, allowing parental choice to dominate admissions procedures may create an even greater bias against the most disadvantaged young people in our society.

assumption is that attainment predominantly reflects intelligence rather than effort and therefore it is appropriate to divide and teach pupils according to their innate capacity to learn. However, for several reasons pupils' potential to learn and their prior attainment may not match up. A pupil might be learning in their second language, they might have experienced poor teaching in the past or perhaps they do not have a quiet place to study at home.

Once a pupil has been placed in a low set it can be hard for them to move up. Higher-set pupils are likely to be taught at a faster pace and eventually there will be too much catching up to do. Since the majority of pupils are entered into examinations according to age rather than educational progress, pupils in lower sets may never have the opportunity to learn everything that has been taught to the higher sets. Instead they continue through the education system with less foundation knowledge and lower grades. The set in which a pupil is placed can therefore have significant implications for their future educational opportunities.

The first point at which this is particularly evident is when pupils take their GCSEs. To allow for variations in pupils' ability, some papers are divided into foundation and higher tiers. This means that more questions of an appropriate difficulty can be included in the papers, which facilitates differentiation between candidates. However, it also means that foundation tier candidates are limited to attaining a C grade at best. Given that GCSE grades influence post-16 choices, access to higher education and employability, it is very important that no pupil capable of attaining more than a C grade should be entered for a foundation tier paper. Yet research by Steve Strand at the University of Warwick has indicated that in certain circumstances this may be precisely what happens to some ethnic minority pupils.

Strand's research[5] made use of data from the Longitudinal Study of Young People in England (LSYPE), a survey conducted in 2004 of a representative sample of over 15,000 children aged 13–14 studying in England, along with their parents or guardians. Strand compared the proportion of students of different ethnicities in the overall sample to the proportion that were entered into foundation and higher examinations. He found that Pakistani, Bangladeshi, black African and black Caribbean pupils were all disproportionately entered into foundation tier science and mathematics papers. For some of the groups this simply reflected low prior attainment, so controlling for KS2 scores removed the difference; however, for black Caribbean pupils the gap remained. There are certainly other influences on exam entry, for example behaviour and exclusion. However, Strand found that even after controlling for all major factors measured in the dataset, black Caribbean pupils were under-entered for higher-tier GCSEs.

Strand has suggested that the implicit stereotyping of teachers might be affecting exam entries. Poor behaviour is known to sometimes distort teachers' perceptions of pupils' academic ability, and black Caribbean pupils have significantly higher rates of exclusion and behavioural, emotional and social difficulties than white pupils. The behaviour of these pupils may cause teachers to underestimate their academic ability. The end result is that some black Caribbean pupils are erroneously entered into foundation-level papers and prevented from achieving higher-grade GCSEs, even though they might be capable of doing so.

It is evidently essential to have a reliable method of setting pupils. It is also important that teachers deciding a pupil's GCSE set, and therefore the examination tier they will be entered for, should be conscious of factors that might implicitly influence their decisions. There is no single parameter by which pupils are set, so in the following sections we try to highlight the advantages, disadvantages and assumptions of some common approaches.

Placement by SAT score: Potential vs attainment

All pupils in English state schools take standardized attainment tests (SATs) at age 10–11. Until fairly recently they also took them at 14 years, and many schools now give pupils similar, internally set examinations at the end of Year 9. SAT scores are frequently used to sort pupils into teaching groups since they are readily available and provide comparable scores for pupils who have attended different primary schools. However, historically, the scores have been presented as 'Levels', with the expectation that, for example, most 11-year-olds should be attaining a Level 4. Since a child could achieve a Level 4 in mathematics by scoring a combination of Levels 3 and 5 in different papers, there was no guarantee that children awarded a certain level had actually mastered the same, minimum set of competencies. Furthermore, pupils' attainment was not evenly distributed – most children in a year would be awarded the same Level – so for researchers, they were not a very sensitive way of differentiating between pupils of different abilities. The proposed shift to scaled scoring should address some of these problems.*

Average SAT scores vary with ethnicity, SES and gender. Using LSYPE data, Steve Strand[5] looked at the factors affecting the SAT scores of pupils from different ethnic groups. Pakistani, Bangladeshi, Black African and Black Caribbean pupils all had, on average, lower scores than their white peers. This difference in scores was equivalent to a year of National Curriculum learning (see Figure 8.1).

Strand used statistical methods to control for the effect that non-academic factors, such as poverty or motivation, had on test scores. Table 8.1 shows how the average KS3 points score of an ethnic minority pupil would compare to that of a white British pupil. In the first column raw scores are compared, with a negative number indicating that a group would on average score less than white British pupils. In each column thereafter, an additional background factor is accounted for. From this we can tell, for example, that when you account for the family background of Bangladeshi pupils they actually outperform equivalent white British

---

* At the time of writing, the government consultation on the removal of curriculum levels and their replacement with an alternative scoring system is in progress.

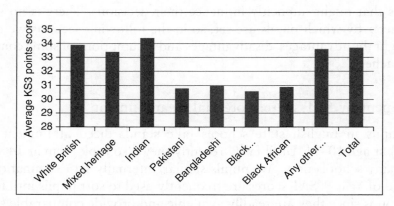

Figure 8.1   Average Key Stage 3 points score (English, maths and science) by ethnic group. *Data source*: Strand.[5]

pupils. Meanwhile, black Caribbean pupils do worse than expected compared to white British pupils, given black Caribbean parents' more positive attitudes towards education.

Whilst ethnicity significantly affected the SAT scores of pupils, Strand noted that it had only a third of the impact of low SES (measured by parental occupation and maternal education). Children of unemployed parents scored, on average, nine points lower than those of parents who were in managerial positions.

This research shows that plenty of non-academic factors influence SAT scores at 11 and 14 years. Therefore we must be careful about how these, or scores from similar internal tests, are used. SATs are a good measure of current attainment, but they are less good at identifying underlying potential. It may make sense to use the scores for setting because pupils with higher scores will tend to have a better grasp of the curriculum, so will be better placed to build on this learning. However, this may disadvantage certain pupil groups whose potential is underestimated by SAT scores. Teachers must be careful not to lower their expectations of these pupils. Ideally, they would provide additional support to boost these pupils' achievement to the levels of which they are capable.

SAT vs CAT

Not all schools use SAT scores to set pupils; a notable proportion administer the Cognitive Abilities Test (CAT) to pupils upon, or soon after, joining. This is a test of reasoning abilities, which offers a verbal, quan-

Table 8.1 The difference in Key Stage 3 scores of different ethnic groups, controlling for different background factors and individual characteristics

	Base (KS3 average points score vs white British)	*Plus family background*	*Plus parental attitudes and behaviours*	*Plus pupil attitudes, motivation and risk*	*Plus school and neighbourhood context*
Mixed heritage	−0.38	0.29	−0.25	−0.34	−0.10
Indian	−0.55*	1.39**	0.18	−0.92**	−0.49**
Pakistani	−3.09**	−0.61**	−1.34**	−2.43**	−1.49**
Bangladeshi	−2.81**	1.31**	0.30	−0.92**	0.16
Black Caribbean	−3.33**	−2.50**	−3.26**	−3.37**	−2.53**
Black African	−3.02**	−1.05**	−2.53**	−3.87**	−2.90**
Any other ethnic group	−0.27	1.58	0.66	−0.33	0.01

A negative number indicates that a group will score fewer points than a comparable white British pupil.
* indicates that the difference in scores is significant ($p < 0.05$).
** indicates that the difference in scores is highly significant ($p < 0.01$).
Source: Adapted from Strand S. The limits of social class in explaining ethnic gaps in educational attainment. *British Educational Research Journal*. 2011:37(2). Copyright © 2011, British Educational Research Journal. Reproduced with permission.

titative and non-verbal score. Box 8.2 gives examples of the type of questions one might find in a CAT paper.

The CAT and SAT actually seem to offer similar predictive power for future academic performance. Ian Deary and his colleagues undertook a study of 70,000 pupils in order to examine the predictive value of CAT scores.[6] They used factor analysis to extract a '*g*' score, or an overall measure of intelligence, from the separate CAT test results and found that 54% of variance in the top eight GCSE scores could be explained by this '*g*' factor. Meanwhile, in a large-scale study of around 2,500 pupils, MacBeath and colleagues[7] found that SAT scores accounted for 57% of variance in pupils' best five GCSE results. The CAT manual actually offers GCSE grade predictions for different CAT scores. The concerning thing

Box 8.2   Example reasoning questions

The three words written below are similar in some way. Work out how they are similar, then pick the word from the answer options that matches them:

Ruler   Scales   Tape measure _____

Pencil   Thermometer   Weights   String   Needle

Each number pair is linked in some way. Decide how each pair of numbers is linked and then pick the number that completes the third pair in the same way:

$$3 > 7 \qquad 5 > 11 \qquad 8 > \_\_$$

12   14   15   16   17

The three shapes are similar in some way. Decide how they are similar and then pick a fourth shape from the answer options that goes with them:

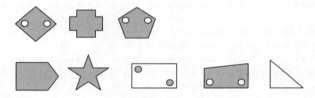

is that we know that teacher expectations can influence attainment (see Chapter 10), so these predictions may actually become self-fulfilling prophecies.

One advantage of the CAT is that the test is specifically designed not simply to assess the prior teaching of pupils. Since SATs assess progress within the National Curriculum, they are more directly dependent upon the quality of teaching received by pupils at their previous school. The 'school effect' – the impact that attending a certain school has on test scores over time – is also much smaller for CAT scores than for external test grades such as GCSEs.[8] However, CAT scores can still be biased by educational and social background. For example, roughly 30% of the variation in Year 7 verbal CAT scores can be attributed to reading ability as measured by Key Stage 2 tests.[9] Reading ability will also affect quantitative CAT scores, because the pupil must read both the questions and the answers. Some questions also require specific general knowledge in order to be answered. Pupils' scores therefore depend on taught skills as well as inherent ability.

VESPARCH: Trying to tap potential

One test that aims to overcome the biases inherent in SAT and CAT scores is the VESPARCH:[10] a verbal and spatial reasoning test for children. It was adapted from the VESPAR, which was designed as a 'culture fair' verbal reasoning test for use with physically or cognitively impaired adults who might have little or no ability to speak or write.[11] Several features of the VESPARCH mitigate the flaws inherent in other tests. Firstly, the test instructions and questions are read aloud through headphones, as well as being visible on a screen, which minimizes the impact of reading ability on test results (reading ability is known to be related to ethnicity and SES). Secondly, the verbal section of the test uses words that would be found in books suitable for children two years younger than those taking the test, so they should be familiar to all test-takers. This means that children with a larger or more advanced vocabulary (who are typically from more advantaged socioeconomic backgrounds) are not favoured unfairly. Thirdly, the test is not timed, so slow or anxious workers will not be disadvantaged. Its multiple choice format further reduces negative effects of test anxiety on performance. Finally, children are coached through five practice questions before they take each section of the test. This ensures that none are disadvantaged by lack of experience with a certain type of question or concept.

VESPARCH scores correlate highly (r = 0.6–0.7) with scores from the CAT and WISC, but the VESPARCH identifies potential in a slightly different group of pupils. Figure 8.2 shows the proportion of pupils who achieved five A*–C at GCSE and also scored in the top 20% on the VESPARCH, CAT or both (from a sample of over 1000 pupils who took the tests in Year 7). You can see that only about half of the pupils scored highly in both tests.

VESPARCH can also be used to identify underachievers, who will have a significant discrepancy between their test score and their standardized attainment scores (such as Key Stage Levels), with the standardized score

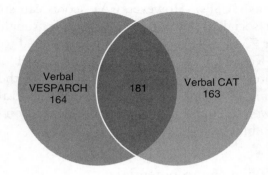

Figure 8.2   Number of students scoring in the top 20% of VESPARCH and/or VCAT and achieving five A*–C including English and Maths.

being lower. Such a discrepancy reveals relatively poor reading skills despite strong verbal reasoning and pupils who achieve this result can be given further reading and grammar tests to pinpoint areas for intervention. These interventions could address anything from attention or working-memory deficits to dyslexia, poor grammatical understanding or language comprehension. They might also involve challenging negative socio-cultural messages about the value of achievement.

Usually about 15% of a year group would be identified as underachievers, including some who would often go unnoticed because their reading age matches or exceeds their chronological age. Two forms of the test are available, one for 7–9-year-olds and another for 10–13-year-olds. If a pupil is identified for intervention in Year 7, this gives them time to improve their performance and could protect them from being placed in an inappropriate set during examination years. The VESPARCH may also be a useful tool for raising teachers' expectations of pupils who are achieving below their potential, and for ensuring that such pupils are not placed in lower sets for non-academic reasons.

The impact of setting on pupils' performance

Given the prevalence of setting in UK schools, one might assume that pupils benefit from being taught in ability groups, yet the evidence for this is equivocal. Broadly speaking, there are those who argue in favour of setting as a means to meet the specific learning needs of pupils, and those who argue against it, either as socially divisive and academically ineffective, or as detrimental to the self-concept of pupils placed in lower sets.

The evidence regarding setting can therefore be separated into two strands. Some studies examine attainment, comparing the performance of pupils placed into sets with those who have equal prior attainment but are taught in mixed ability classes. Other studies look at the attitudes to learning held by different groups, exploring the wider impact of setting on aspirations and academic self-concept.

In terms of attainment, many researchers have concluded that academic setting has minimal impact when viewed as an average score across the entire year. In other words, any reduction in the attainment of one group of pupils is made up for by an increase in the attainment of another. However, breaking down scores across sets, there is an interesting boundary effect. In general, those pupils with equal prior attainment who are placed in a higher rather than lower set will perform better in later assessments. The extent of this difference can be quite dramatic; for example, Wiliam and Bartholomew,[12] who studied 706 pupils in six London schools, found that pupils' performance could vary by as much as three GCSE grades according to their placement in a higher or lower set. So if two children with the same prior attainment were placed in different sets, by the end of their course, one could be getting an A and the other a C depending on which set they were in.

This disparity is often taken as an argument against setting: the practice may disadvantage those placed into a lower set. However, Wiliam and Bartholomew did not find this problem in every school; in schools where small-group, individualized teaching was used, being in a lower set could boost rather than reduce grades. This suggests that we must examine why those in lower sets are at risk of under performance. Ireson and her colleagues[13] interviewed over 1,500 teachers from 45 schools who taught lower-set, higher-set or mixed ability mathematics classes and found that those who taught sets often treated their students as being of much more similar, or even invariant, ability. This in itself would disadvantage pupils performing at the higher end of a low set, because they might have their potential underestimated or receive teaching at a level that did not stretch them. However, Ireson's study also highlighted a difference in the content of teaching received by pupils in different sets. Whilst those in top sets tended to benefit from challenging work and lessons that developed their knowledge of mathematical concepts, those in a low set were often subject to simplistic, repetitive teaching based on memorizing strategies, rather than building an understanding of underlying principles. Lower sets were actually receiving poorer-quality teaching that did not prepare them to understand advanced concepts. Following these observations, Ireson's team directly compared the performance of pupils in lower sets who were taught using either individualized or whole-class methods. They reported that when lower sets were taught as if they were all of the same ability, then just as described above, pupils performed below their potential. In comparison, setting had no negative impact when all sets were taught using individualized methods.

Given that setting does not always improve pupils' average attainment, one could conclude that it has no real benefits and hence the practice should be given up in favour of mixed ability classes. However, teachers often report that it is challenging to control the behaviour of a mixed ability class, and to keep all the children engaged at once. From this perspective, ability grouping may create a more effective teaching environment and facilitate the engagement of all pupils in lessons. One problem with this, however, is that the lowest set can become the group in which not just slower learners but also poorly behaved pupils are placed, so this class does not experience an environment that is conducive to learning.

It is often suggested that academic grouping is particularly damaging for pupils placed in bottom sets, as they may develop negative academic self-concept by being placed in the 'low ability' group. However, it is actually the case that neither grouped nor mixed ability teaching has purely positive or negative consequences for academic self-concept.

When people assess their ability, they do so by comparing to a frame of reference. For school children, this is typically their peers. This means that the higher the average ability in a school or class, the more likely pupils are to underestimate their ability relative to the national average, and vice versa for low average ability groups. Herbert Marsh has termed this the 'Big Fish Little Pond Effect'. He has shown, in both Australia and the United Kingdom, that when one compares across multiple schools there is a negative correlation between the average ability level of pupils in the school and their academic self-concept.[14–16]

Big Fish Little Pond Effect

I have seen this effect operate in reverse in lower-performing state schools, where pupils attaining As and Bs at GCSE believe that this is exceptional performance because they are high performers for that school: they exhibit overly positive academic self-concept.

The other consequence of the Big Fish Little Pond Effect is that when such pupils move on to college or university and are suddenly surrounded by equally high-attaining pupils, they realize that they are not such exceptional performers and their academic self-concept can dramatically decline. For high-attaining pupils, then, ability grouping can reduce the likelihood of 'coasting' and risk of harm to their academic self-concept in the future.

For lower-attaining pupils, having a narrower frame of reference for ability comparisons can also have a positive effect. Woon-Chia Liu and colleagues[17] tracked the academic self-concept of 645 children in Singapore during their first three years of secondary school. In Singapore there are four ability streams, and the sample was taken from the middle two streams into which around 75% of children are placed. Their first finding was that the academic self-concept of all the pupils declined over time. However, contrary to many reports which suggest that being placed in a lower set can have a negative impact, Liu and his colleagues found that over three years, lower-ability pupils went from having a more negative to a more positive self-concept than their peers in higher-ability groups. Over time, the pupils shifted their point of reference for social comparisons from between to within ability groups. Whilst those in higher groups recognized that others may be equally able, those in lower groups no longer saw themselves as particularly poor performers. Given these consequences of setting and streaming for academic self-concept, the real question becomes whether we want to prevent more able pupils from overestimating their abilities and whether we think it actually is a good thing for slower learners to potentially do this.

Selecting Students for University

One of the largest academic selection processes in the United Kingdom is the yearly round of university admissions. Historically, universities controlled admissions on an individual basis. However, when the expansion of higher education in the 1960s put an increasing administrative burden on institutions, the Universities Central Council on Admissions (UCCA) was established. The intention was that through this centralized agency, admissions would become more fair and objective, being based principally on academic merit as measured by A-levels. However, as ever more students achieve top A-level grades, there has been a gradual return to the use of additional entrance papers.

Universities want to select those students who are likely to be academically successful, so to evaluate the effectiveness of their admissions processes one must understand the different factors affecting students' performance. As will be discussed later, a student's success is not solely dependent upon academic ability but can depend on everything from personality to learning style. In some cases, pre-existing knowledge may be important: for example, someone studying physics may need to have advanced mathematics skills. However, for many university courses, an applicant's existing knowledge base is much less important than their ability to acquire and use new information. The key challenge for any selection procedure is therefore to identify academic potential, rather than simply assessing the effects of previous teaching.

Current assessment methods

In England, GCSE grades and predicted A-level grades are still the most commonly used selection tools for university admissions, but they are by no means perfect tools. Predicted grades are not an ideal measure for admissions because they are often inaccurate: in 2009, 42% of predictions were overestimates and 7% were underestimates, with males and entrants from higher socioeconomic groups more likely to have their results overestimated.[18] The grades are also something of a blunt instrument for the most selective universities because so many candidates achieve the highest grades: in 2012 one in eight candidates achieved three or more A or A* grades at A-level. Furthermore, as we explain in Chapter 5, attainment in these exams is strongly related to background factors such as SES and ethnicity. For example, roughly an eighth of A-level candidates come from independent schools yet in the 2011 cohort a third of the pupils who achieved top grades were from such schools (31% of those who achieved AAA or better and 36% of those who achieved A*A*A* or better).[19] Admittedly, the fact that many independent schools are selective may contribute to the disparity, but these pupils also outperformed those from grammar schools, which accept only the most able of state-school applicants. We see a similar pattern looking at deprivation: pupils from areas of high deprivation are less likely to get top A-level and GCSE grades. This tells us that using solely GCSE and A-level grades to determine university admissions is likely to result in more advantaged candidates, particularly those from independent schools, being over-represented at the most selective institutions. Indeed this is just what we see (Figure 8.3): in

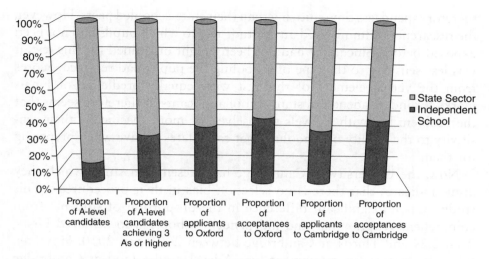

Figure 8.3 Proportion of A-level candidates and Oxbridge applicants from state and independent schools (Year 2011, home applicants only).[19–21] *Data sources*: University of Oxford; University of Cambridge; Department for Business, Innovation and Skills.

2012, two-fifths of the UK students accepted by Oxford and Cambridge were from independent schools.[20,21]

It is important to note that these universities receive a disproportionate number of applications from independent school candidates (see Figure 8.2). Furthermore, if GCSE and A-level grades reflect a candidate's knowledge and academic success, one could argue that it is not inherently unfair to select more pupils from advantaged backgrounds if they also get more of the top grades. After all, it makes sense to select the strongest candidates to be admitted. However, several papers suggest a flaw in this argument.[22,23] One study from the University of Oxford compares the performance of undergraduates who had the same GCSE grades, but who had attended either independent or state schools. Controlling for parental income and proportion of first-class degrees awarded by subject, the researchers found that for a certain GCSE score, independent school pupils were only 56% as likely as state-school pupils to achieve a first.[22]

Now, one might argue that independent school pupils are less likely to get a first-class degree for reasons other than academic potential. Maybe they have a greater sense of entitlement to an Oxford education, so feel less compulsion to excel academically in order to 'prove' themselves. Maybe these students participate in more extracurricular activities, and therefore spend less time studying than their state-schooled peers. However, the researchers administered an aptitude test to which pupils had not been exposed before. Since they had not been taught or trained for this test, it was less sensitive to the type of schooling the pupils had received. Scores from the verbal element of this test were equally predictive of Finals marks for independent and state school applicants. It therefore seems that the problem lies with A-levels themselves, or more specifically their sensitivity to the quality of schooling that candidates receive when preparing for them.

Now, the University of Cambridge has presented a study which they argue indicates that there is no selection bias in their procedures.[24] This study finds no significant difference in the proportion of students from comprehensive, grammar and independent schools who achieved Firsts, 2:1s, 2:2s and Thirds at Cambridge between 2005 and 2010. However, the only control for attainment was A-level grades (and at Cambridge almost all students have achieved three As). Without looking at GCSEs or any other aptitude measure which has more variation, one cannot rule out the possibility that independent school applicants with lower prior performance have taken the place of equally capable state-school peers.

Politicians and commentators periodically suggest that one way to address this disparity is to make the admissions criteria for less advantaged pupils more lenient. However, this really addresses a symptom rather than cause of educational inequality. Some admissions tutors also argue that this sets up such applicants for failure because they lack basic knowledge required for their course. Furthermore, if the expectations teachers hold for their pupils can affect their future performance, explicitly setting lower expectations for certain pupil groups may only fuel their underachievement. Tackling inequalities in access to selective universities will take more than a shift in admissions criteria; it needs early intervention to equalize attainment and a step change in the routes by which less advantaged young people can transition to selective universities, for example through access years or transferring from other institutions.

Ironically, both the large number of candidates achieving the highest A-level grades and the apparent bias against state-school applicants has provided good reason for universities to begin developing their own entrance tests. Since A-level grades depend on the subject-specific knowledge of candidates, some university entrance tests are specifically designed to assess more general qualities, such as a candidate's ability to reason and their potential to learn. University College London (UCL), Oxford and Cambridge have all adopted the 'Thinking Skills Assessment' (TSA) as an entrance test for a number of courses (see start of chapter). It is intended to identify problem-solving, reasoning and critical-thinking skills. Such tests do have predictive value: for example, TSA scores correlate with both first-year and Finals marks. For Cambridge students, TSA scores are reported to have a stronger correlation with university achievement than A-level grades,[25] but since almost all students there will have three A grades, it is not surprising that this test is a more effective way to differentiate between them (see Box 8.3).

This need to differentiate between straight-A candidates has also motivated the adoption of course-specific entrance tests such as the BioMedical Admissions Test (BMAT), which is currently taken by medical and veterinary sciences candidates at a number of selective UK universities. The BMAT consists of three sections: two multiple choice papers, one testing aptitude and skills, the other testing scientific knowledge and applications, and a final essay paper. Universities can decide how to weight scores for the three sections, and some will then automatically reject all candidates achieving less than a certain mark. The BMAT draws only on GCSE-level knowledge and tests problem-solving, reasoning and inference skills. It is therefore considered a more objective test of potential, being less dependent on taught knowledge than A-level grades. Yet comprehensive school candidates have significantly lower average BMAT scores than pupils from either selective state schools or independent schools,[26] which suggests that the scores are not wholly independent of background.

Whilst scores from additional entrance papers might be useful for differentiating between straight-A candidates, they are still not a completely unbiased measure of academic potential. They also still tend to focus on analytical skills rather than creativity, which as we explain in Chapter 9 is another trait we ought to value in the education system. What we really need is a test which taps potential rather than social advantage. It must be predictive over a long period of time and resist attempts by tutors and teachers to improve pupils' performance on it. Some suggest that American-style SATs could provide such a solution.

Lessons from the United States: SATs for selection

In the United States, high-school pupils take written, numerical and critical reading SAT tests which, alongside their high-school record, contribute to higher-education admissions decisions. Candidates can score between 200 and 800 on each sub-test, giving a potential maximum score of 2,400 points. These tests are not intended as direct measures of taught knowledge. Rather, they are supposed to assess general verbal and numerical abilities, and therefore aptitude for higher education.

Box 8.3   The predictive value of a test – correlation, regression and restriction of range

When researchers want to determine how useful a test is for predicting a certain outcome, they often look at the correlation between the test score and outcome, and calculate a value called r^2 which describes how closely the two variables are related. The r^2 value can range from 0 to 1, with 1 being a perfect linear relationship. For example, an r^2 value of 0.90 for height and weight tells you that these characteristics are strongly related, so a tall person in a group is very likely to be heavier than a short person.

As with all statistics, it is important to be cautious about interpreting correlations and r^2 values. This is because the strength of the correlation between two variables depends not only on how closely they are related, but also how wide the range of values is for each variable. If the range of one of the variables is particularly small, it will limit the correlation of the two variables; this is described as restriction of range.

For example, imagine everyone went to one university, so everyone wanting to study English would apply to a single course whether their A-level grades were three Es or three A*s. On each course, then, students would have a wide range of grades (see UCAS website for A-levels to UCAS score conversion) and we can guess that these would relate quite closely to their Finals marks. This would result in a high correlation between A-level grades and Finals marks, and so A-level grades would have a lot of predictive value.

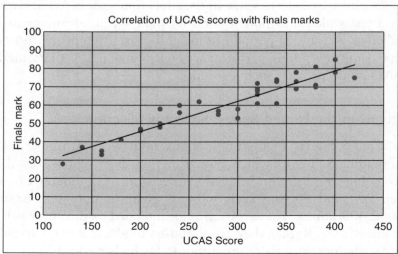

The r^2 value for this graph is 0.89.

In real life, of course, universities decide which grades an applicant needs to get onto a course. If they ask for ABB (a UCAS score of 320), then the grades of students who ultimately end up on the course might only vary from BBB to AAA – their range is restricted. The same range of Finals marks will still be awarded, but because there is much less variation in A-level grades, a student with ABB might now achieve anything from a Fail to a First. Knowing a student's A-level grades is therefore much less useful for predicting their final attainment, and the r^2 value is notably reduced.

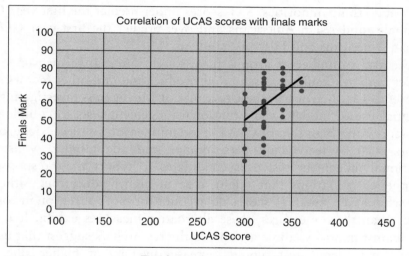

The r^2 value for this graph is 0.19.

Whilst it is true that SATs are not curriculum based, candidates' scores do not escape the effects of gender, ethnicity and SES. Average test scores increase steadily for every $20,000 increase in parental income, such that in 2012 there was a 133-point difference between the scores of pupils with the lowest parental income and those whose parents earned over $200,000 per annum. Similar trends are evident for increasing levels of parental education and school type: pupils attending independent schools have consistently higher scores than pupils from state-run institutions. Meanwhile, black, African American and Hispanic candidates have mean scores roughly 80 to 100 points below that of white Americans. Gender differences are also evident: on average, in 2012, female mathematical scores were 33 points below those of males, whilst their writing scores were 13 points higher.[27]

All of these statistics strongly suggest a bias in the design or scoring of SAT papers, but they do not inherently invalidate SATs as a predictor of higher-education aptitude. Identifying socioeconomic or gender differences does not prove they are unfounded or unfair. However, studies tracking the performance of students who have taken SATs confirm that these scores under-predict the attainment of certain groups in higher education. There is a stronger correlation between SAT scores and first-year grade-point averages (GPA) for females and white Americans than for males and ethnic minorities. SAT scores under-predict the first-year GPA of females and Asian Americans and over-predict the first-year GPA of African Americans and Hispanic students.[28]

Recently, a number of groups have sought alternative measures that predict both academic success in higher education and other factors such as absenteeism. A group at the University of Michigan is investigating the potential use of biodata and situational judgement tests to complement SAT scores and high-school GPA.[29] Biodata measures reflect background factors such as leadership, perseverance and adaptability, whilst the situational judgement test asks candidates to report their response to hypothetical situations that might arise in higher education. Although high-school GPA and SAT scores do account for more variation in college grades than these measures, these alternative measures exhibit less of a bias against minority ethnic groups, so the researchers suggest that use of these non-academic tests could increase diversity at higher-education institutions.

Considering the biases inherent in SAT scores, and the move to complement them with behavioural and motivational measures in the United States, we must question whether a shift to a system of SAT-type tests would really do much to address the current biases in the United Kingdom's university admissions system. It seems that whenever tests are designed with the aim of measuring academic aptitude, they can easily transform over time into measures of social and economic resource. SAT scores can be significantly increased with coaching, to the extent that this is the basis of many intervention programmes for underachieving groups. It is therefore unsurprising that pupils with greater financial support and better schooling should perform better on these tests.

Another option is to note that the variable predictive value of exam grades and SAT scores tells us that many other factors influence how individuals perform at university. Perhaps it would be useful to consider these in the admission process.

Intelligent personalities

Intelligence is typically identified as the main factor affecting academic achievement, yet the correlation between IQ scores and attainment declines with each level of education. In elementary school, pupil grades correlate 0.70 with IQ scores, but by university this falls to 0.40.[30] One of the suggested reasons for this is that the lower a person's academic ability, the earlier they are likely to leave the education system. As a result, at each new level of the system there is less variation in the intelligence of students than there was before. If students have very similar levels of intelligence, then other qualities that still vary between them will explain more of the variation in their attainment (see Box 8.3). One such quality is personality.

Now, just as there are many theories of intelligence (see Chapter 5), psychologists advocate a range of theories about the traits that form the basic dimensions of our personalities. However, many studies are based on use of the NEO-PI-R, an inventory developed by Paul Costa and Robert McCrae, which assesses five dimensions: neuroticism, extraversion, openness to experience, conscientiousness and agreeableness. Sabrina Trapmann and her colleagues[31] used a meta-analytic technique in order to identify common trends running across 58 such studies. When all the data was aggregated, only one personality trait consistently and significantly affected academic achievement: conscientiousness. High levels of conscientiousness were associated with achieving higher grades. However, a further trend emerged when the country in which the research was undertaken was considered: for students in East Asia, but not the West, extraversion was positively related to performance. This shows that links between personality and achievement may not be universal; some are moderated by external factors. This may explain why the relationship between personality and academic achievement appears to vary between institutions.

At UCL, Tomas Chammorro-Premuzic and Adrian Furnham[32] administered the NEO-PI-R to 247 psychology students in their first month at university. Once the students had completed their course, a retrospective comparison was made between grades and personality dimensions. Fifteen per cent of the variance in grades could be attributed to super-personality traits, with a significant positive effect of being introverted, conscientious and low in neuroticism. Meanwhile, at the University of Cambridge, Surtees and colleagues administered Eysenck's short-form scales for Intraversion–Extraversion and Neuroticism–Stability in a longitudinal study involving over 800 students.[33] In agreement with the UCL data, students who were relatively less extraverted were more likely to achieve high grades. However, whilst men who were relatively low in neuroticism were likely to do better, for women the reverse was true. The higher women scored on the neuroticism scale, the more likely they were to achieve a first-class degree.

This finding is partially replicated in work undertaken at the University of Oxford. In this case, the specific quality of trait anxiety was measured. Anxiety is one of the primary traits associated with neuroticism, and one which Chamorro-Premuzic and Furnham found to be significantly negatively associated with achievement in their sample. In contrast, at Oxford University, women, but not men, who were higher in trait anxiety had a higher likelihood of achieving a first-class degree.[34] This could reflect a state-dependent recall effect (people remember things better when in the same mood as when they learnt them, and most people are anxious in exams) and the sex difference could reflect a difference in coping mechanisms between men and women. Comparison with the UCL study demonstrates that the impact of personality on performance very much depends on context.

Given that the personality traits associated with success vary between institutions, we can conclude that personality testing will only be helpful if a clear relationship has been established between students' personality and their performance for the specific course and institution in question. For example, the implications of applicants being introverted or extraverted could vary depending on whether they want to study performing arts, mathematics or history. There is also a more basic issue, because most paper-based personality tests are quite transparent, meaning it would be easy for people to manipulate their scores. Hence a more sophisticated way of assessing personalities would be needed if this were to be considered in the admissions process (Box 8.4).

Learning styles and course requirements

Chapter 7 introduces learning styles (deep, surface or strategic approaches) and considers how metacognitive skills influence learning. In that chapter a number of studies are presented which show links between adoption of a deep learning style and higher academic performance. Does this mean that we should be testing learning styles as part of the admissions process for universities?

Actually, the study by Groves described in that chapter indicates that students' learning styles can change whilst they are on a university course. If learning styles are not stable then there is a risk in assessing them during admissions. Students who have attended very pressurized or

---

Box 8.4   Interviews and admissions

One way to assess the less quantifiable characteristics that could affect an applicant's academic performance is through interviews. Many universities in the United Kingdom interview applicants for certain disciplines, whilst Oxford and Cambridge conduct interviews for all of their courses. Some critics argue that interviews are difficult to standardize and can be intimidating to non-traditional university applicants. However, when grades correlate with SES, when personal statements can easily be written by teachers or parents and when references are no longer confidential, one can hardly argue that other assessment methods are not biased in favour of more advantaged applicants. There is real value to the flexibility and face-to-face contact inherent in the interview process. Tutors can use the interaction to gauge the applicant's motivation for studying a course. For courses such as medicine and nursing, this is also a crucial means to assess interpersonal skills that will affect occupational performance.

---

examination-oriented schools might be rejected from a course for exhibiting a preference for surface learning styles, when actually they have the potential to be deep learners in another environment.

Secondly, we know that the benefits of adopting a deep learning style may vary by course. For example, Diseth[35] identified a curvilinear relationship between the adoption of a surface approach and the academic performance of 89 psychology students. The highest achievers in this study had low or medium levels of surface learning, whilst a deep approach did not have a consistent relationship to learning outcomes. Booth and colleagues[36] found that the deep and strategic learning scores of management and accounting students were unrelated to their performance. They attributed this to the nature of the courses, which demanded memorization of specific procedures and regulations, rather than evaluation or debate of theories. Certainly if a university course requires mainly rote-learning and memorization then we may not find that students who adopt deep learning styles perform notably better. However, if a course's structure does foster a deep approach, and if the examinations assess the extent to which students have a deep understanding of their subject, then it could make sense to recruit students who exhibit a preference for deep learning.

For this reason, one of the authors recently conducted a study to see whether it would be possible to assess Oxford applicants' approaches to learning, and whether this in turn would predict their degree performance. Standard tests of approaches to learning such as the SPQ are far too transparent to use for admissions; it is too easy for participants to manipulate their scores. Hence the group developed an alternative deep learning measure: a short commentary paper, including questions that required candidates to produce persuasive arguments and to devise original methods to test theories. Responses to the commentary paper would be hard to adjust in terms of 'desirability'. Applicants were given this alongside the SPQ and, in some cases, the AH6 intelligence test.[37]

Scores on the fifth question of the commentary paper emerged as being of particular predictive value. This question required candidates to explain how they might persuade farmers to adopt organic farming practices. Candidates' scores were related to their IQ scores and to the likelihood of acceptance at interview. Crucially, scores on question 5 also predicted future academic performance: those who achieved a first in their Final examinations had significantly higher scores than those awarded a 2:1 or below. In contrast, there was no significant difference in the summed GCSE scores of these groups. The test was designed to avoid any bias towards independent school candidates; for example, candidates were asked to respond in bullet points, to avoid favouring applicants trained in essay writing. Indeed, the performance of candidates on this question, unlike in GCSEs or A-levels, was unaffected by the type of school they had attended.

Identifying new measures that are not susceptible to 'school effects' is an essential step in the process of making admissions procedures fairer. A major challenge, though, is to move from an experimental situation where it is easy to give candidates an original test, to a nationwide scenario where pupils may practise old papers and potentially 'train up' in advance. The key is to develop a test where such 'training up' has no effect on scores, so that pupils in better funded or resourced schools, or with parents who can give them extra support, cannot gain an unfair advantage. In the meantime it is up to admission tutors to judge how much they think different measures reflect an applicant's true potential.

The right measure for the job

In these sections, only a few of the many attributes that affect how a candidate will perform at university have been discussed. If the entire book were focused on this subject, we might also explore the impact of intrinsic or extrinsic motivation, of instrumentality or of mental health factors. However, examination performance, intelligence, personality and approaches to learning represent some of the more widely investigated and recognized factors affecting academic outcomes. Understanding the strengths and weaknesses of existing tests that measure these factors gives one a good reference point for critically evaluating new admissions methods that might emerge from future research.

Summary

- In many English schools, pupils are taught in ability groups, or sets, and are also selected for different examination tiers according to prior attainment. SAT and CAT scores are commonly used to do this; however, these scores are affected by the quality of prior teaching and pupils' backgrounds as well as inherent ability. The VESPARCH, which has been designed to minimize the effects of prior learning, verbal skills and practice on test scores, presents an alternative method of identifying more capable pupils and highlighting those who are at risk of underperforming.
- Setting does not have a universally positive effect on attainment. Gains in the attainment of higher-set pupils are often offset by the poor progress of lower-set pupils compared to those taught in mixed ability groups. Pupils taught in sets may experience less individualized teaching, and those in lower sets may also be taught in more simplistic, repetitive ways. In the short term, being placed in a low set may also negatively affect pupils' academic self-concept. However, in the long term the Big Fish Little Pond effect may mean that pupils taught in lower-ability groups actually have more positive perceptions of their capabilities and those in higher-ability groups are deterred from overestimating their abilities and 'coasting'.
- Universities need a reliable way to select the best applicants for their courses. They commonly use A-level and GCSE grades, but these scores correlate with ethnicity, gender and SES. Unfortunately, potential replacements such as American-style SATs and subject-specific tests like the BMAT have similar weaknesses. Universities could attempt to measure characteristics such as personality and approaches to learning in order to support the admissions process, but this would require tests that are not transparent and have been tested in context for their predictive value.

- Two aims when developing new tests should be that practice does not result in large gains in performance and that respondents cannot easily alter their responses to make them 'desirable'. This is important because tests that do not meet these criteria usually favour pupils from more advantaged backgrounds.

Educational implications

- Those who determine pupils' academic sets or streams should be aware of the extraneous factors that correlate with many standardized test scores. They should be conscious that such tests may underestimate the potential of minority ethnic and low-SES pupils, or those with poor reading skills. Teacher judgements can equally be biased by stereotypes and the impact of behaviour on perceived academic ability, therefore a range of factors should be considered when setting pupils or selecting them for exams.
- Teachers working with ability groups should be conscious of the need to account for the full range of abilities present, and should be careful not to abandon the individualized teaching practices that they might employ with a mixed ability group. It is particularly important that learners in lower sets should not receive poorer-quality teaching as a consequence of setting.
- Lower-SES pupils and those from certain ethnic minorities are more likely to be entered for lower-tier examinations and are less likely to progress to selective universities. Since much of this is explained by prior attainment it is important that schools do everything possible to identify underperformers early and intervene before they begin their GCSEs.
- Admissions tutors must be aware that using GCSE and A-level scores to determine entry to higher education can favour candidates with certain educational backgrounds, particularly those who have attended leading independent schools. It is worth considering whether this means that candidates from less advantaged backgrounds should be given lower offers, or whether this might actually fuel low aspirations and underachievement.
- If pupils with lower grades are admitted to university on the basis of their potential, consideration must be given to any additional support they might require. Such pupils may need extra lectures or seminars to bring their knowledge and skills up to the standard of their peers.
- Alternative admissions tests are not necessarily unbiased: many still favour higher-SES candidates, or those who have attended a selective

or independent school. Further efforts are needed to identify measures of academic potential that are less susceptible to the influence of background, and to develop such measures for widespread use.

• Factors other than academic achievement are predictive of attainment at university. Admissions tutors should recognize this and consider how best to apply this knowledge when admitting to specific courses.

Answers to the Thinking Skills Assessment: D and C.

References

1   Coe R, Jones K, Searle J, *et al*. Evidence on the Effects of Selective Educational Systems. Durham: CEM Centre/Sutton Trust; 2008. Available at: www.suttontrust.com/public/documents/SuttonTrustFullReportFinal1.pdf. Accessed 2 December 2013.

2   Gordon I, Monastiriotis V. Education, location, education: A spatial analysis of English secondary school public examination results. *Urban Studies*. 2007;44(7):1203–1228.

3   Dearden L, Ferri J, Meghir C. The effect of school quality on educational attainment and wages. *Review of Economics and Statistics*. 2002;84(1):1–20.

4   Kutnick P, Britain G. The Effects of Pupil Grouping: Literature Review. Brighton: DfES; 2005. Available at: http://citeseerx.ist.psu.edu/viewdoc/download?doi=10.1.1.127.9357&rep=rep1&type=pdf. Accessed 2 December 2013.

5   Strand S. Minority Ethnic Pupils in the Longitudinal Study of Young People in England (LSYPE). Nottingham: Department for Children, Schools and Families; 2007. Available at: www2.warwick.ac.uk/fac/soc/wie/research/policy/recent_projects/minority/rr_2007-002_strand.pdf. Accessed 2 December 2013.

6   Deary IJ, Strand S, Smith P, Fernandes C. Intelligence and educational achievement. *Intelligence*. 2007;35(1):13–21.

7   MacBeath JEC, Kirwan T, Myers B, *et al*. The Impact of Study Support: A Report of a Longitudinal Study into the Impact of Participation in out-of-school-hours Learning on the Academic Attainment, Attitudes and School Attendance of Secondary School Students. Strathclyde: DfES; 2001. Available at: http://dera.ioe.ac.uk/id/eprint/4624. Accessed 2 December 2013.

8   Strand S. Consistency in reasoning test scores over time. *British Journal of Educational Psychology*. 2004;74(4):617–631.

9   Strand S. Comparing the predictive validity of reasoning tests and national end of Key Stage 2 tests: Which tests are the "best"? *British Educational Research Journal*. 2006;32(2):209–225.

10 Mellanby J, McElwee S. Verbal and spatial reasoning test for children. Cambridge: Cambridge Assessment; 2010.

11 Langdon DW. *VESPAR: A Verbal and Spatial Reasoning Test.* Psychology Press; 1995. Available at: http://books.google.co.uk/books?hl=en&lr=&id =Dk_dE6HrEh8C&oi=fnd&pg=PP3&dq=vespar&ots=UCeGWK _n1t&sig=py6wXvOF_UyAcsnU_6JtQElc9HM. Accessed 2 December 2013.

12 Wiliam D, Bartholomew H. It's not which school but which set you're in that matters: The influence of ability grouping practices on student progress in mathematics. *British Educational Research Journal.* 2004;30(2):279–293.

13 Hallam S, Ireson J. Secondary school teachers' pedagogic practices when teaching mixed and structured ability classes. *Research Papers in Education.* 2005;20(1):3–24.

14 Marsh HW, Parker JW. Determinants of student self-concept: Is it better to be a relatively large fish in a small pond even if you don't learn to swim as well? *Journal of Personality and Social Psychology.* 1984;47(1):213.

15 Marsh HW, Köller O, Baumert J. Reunification of East and West German school systems: Longitudinal multilevel modeling study of the big-fish-little-pond effect on academic self-concept. *American Educational Research Journal.* 2001;38(2):321–350.

16 Marsh HW, Hau KT. Big-Fish–Little-Pond effect on academic self-concept: A cross-cultural (26-country) test of the negative effects of academically selective schools. *American Psychologist.* 2003;58(5):364.

17 Liu WC, Wang CKJ, Parkins EJ. A longitudinal study of students' academic self-concept in a streamed setting: The Singapore context. *British Journal of Educational Psychology.* 2005;75(4):567–586.

18 BIS. Investigating the Accuracy of Predicted A Level Grades as part of 2009 UCAS Admission Process. London: Department for Business, Innovation and Skills; 2011. Available at: www.bis.gov.uk/assets/BISCore/higher-education/ docs/I/11-1043-investigating-accuracy-predicted-a-level-grades.pdf.Accessed 2 December 2013.

19 Wilson F. Candidates Awarded the A* Grade at A-Level in 2011. Cambridge: Cambridge Assessment; 2012. Available at: www.cambridgeassessment. org.uk/ca/digitalAssets/204003_Stats_report_A_star_46.pdf. Accessed 2 December 2013.

20 University of Oxford. Undergraduate Admissions Statistics: School Type. Oxford: University of Oxford; 2012. Available at: www.ox.ac.uk/about_the _university/facts_and_figures/undergraduate_admissions_statistics/school _type.html. Accessed 2 December 2013.

21 University of Cambridge. Undergraduate Admissions Statistics – 2011 Cycle. Cambridge: University of Cambridge; 2012. Available at: www.study.cam.ac .uk/undergraduate/publications/docs/admissionsstatistics2011.pdf. Accessed 2 December 2013.

22 Ogg T, Zimdars A, Heath A. Schooling effects on degree performance: A comparison of the predictive validity of aptitude testing and secondary school grades at Oxford University. *British Educational Research Journal.* 2009;35(5):781–807.

23 Hoare A, Johnston R. Widening participation through admissions policy – a British case study of school and university performance. *Studies in Higher Education.* 2011;36(1):21–41.

24 Parks G. Academic Performance of Undergraduate Students at Cambridge by School/College Background. 2011. Available at: https://www.admin.cam .ac.uk/offices/admissions/research/docs/school_performance.pdf. Accessed 2 December 2013.

25 Harding R. Thinking Skills Tests for University Admission. Cambridge: Cambridge Assessment; 2004. Available at: www.cambridgeassessment.org .uk/Images/109721-thinking-skills-tests-for-university-admission.pdf. Accessed 2 December 2013.

26 Shannon M. BMAT Scores and Outcomes of Applications to the University of Cambridge for Medical and Veterinary Courses in 2003. Cambridge: Cambridge Assessment; 2004. Available at: www.cambridgeassessment.org .uk/Images/109716-bmat-scores-and-outcomes-of-applications-to-the- university-of-cambridge-for-medical-and-veterinary-courses-in-2003.pdf. Accessed 2 December 2013.

27 College Board. 2012 College-Bound Seniors: Total Group Profile Report. New York: College Board; 2012. Available at: http://media.collegeboard.com/ digitalServices/pdf/research/TotalGroup-2012.pdf. Accessed 2 December 2013.

28 Mattern KD, Patterson BF, Shaw EJ, Kobrin JL, Barbuti SM. Differential Validity and Prediction of the SAT. New York: The College Board. 2008. Available at: http://citeseerx.ist.psu.edu/viewdoc/download?doi=10.1.1.189 .1821&rep=rep1&type=pdf. Accessed 2 December 2013.

29 Schmitt N, Keeney J, Oswald FL, *et al.* Prediction of 4-year college student performance using cognitive and noncognitive predictors and the impact on demographic status of admitted students. *Journal of Applied Psychology.* 2009;94(6):1479–1497.

30 Jensen AR. Uses of sibling data in educational and psychological research. *American Educational Research Journal.* 1980;17(2):153–170.

31 Trapmann S, Hell B, Hirn JOW, Schuler H. Meta-analysis of the relationship between the Big Five and academic success at university. *Zeitschrift für Psychologie/Journal of Psychology.* 2007;215(2):132–151.

32 Chamorro-Premuzic T, Furnham A. Personality traits and academic exami- nation performance. *European Journal of Personality.* 2003;17(3):237–250.

33 Surtees PG, Wainwright NWJ, Pharoah PDP. Psychosocial factors and sex differences in high academic attainment at Cambridge University. *Oxford Review of Education.* 2002;28(1):21–38.

34   Mellanby J, Zimdars A. Trait anxiety and final degree performance at the University of Oxford. *Higher Education*. 2011;61(4):357–370.

35   Diseth A. The relationship between intelligence, approaches to learning and academic achievement. *Scandinavian Journal of Educational Research*. 2002;46(2):219–230.

36   Booth P, Luckett P, Mladenovic R. The quality of learning in accounting education: The impact of approaches to learning on academic performance. *Accounting Education*. 1999;8(4):277–300.

37   Mellanby J, Cortina-Borja M, Stein J. Deep learning questions can help selection of high ability candidates for universities. *Higher Education*. 2009;57(5):597–608.

Chapter 9
Creativity
What Is It, and How and Why Should We Nurture It?

How many uses can you think of for a doorstop?

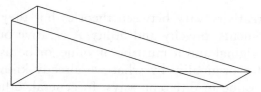

If someone talked to you about creativity, what would you think of? Maybe you would think of an artist such as Picasso, a scientific genius such as Einstein or a chef such as Heston Blumenthal? What about creativity in education: what would you think of then? Would you imagine an art class with students painting fantastic pictures, or an English lesson with students drafting poems and plays?

Creativity is a diverse and wide-ranging concept. It can refer to anything from the ground-breaking innovations of a creative genius to the simple reworking of an everyday task. It is associated with anything from entrepreneurship and wealth to mental illness. However, in all its forms, it is exceptionally relevant to education, and not just the arts. Every student has creative potential and this can manifest itself in many ways, through their learning, their behaviour and their work.

Whatever they teach, educators should be concerned about creativity, because of the benefits of nurturing it and the hazards of ignoring it. As

Education and Learning: An Evidence-Based Approach, First Edition. Jane Mellanby and Katy Theobald.
© 2014 John Wiley & Sons, Ltd. Published 2014 by John Wiley & Sons, Ltd.

this chapter explains, methods that foster creativity can promote pupil engagement and increase understanding of a subject. In contrast, overlooking the importance of creativity can result in students becoming disruptive, underachieving or even dropping out of school. By some estimates 50% of American high-school dropouts can be identified as gifted underachievers[1] – highly able and creative students who find themselves unable to function in a mainstream school environment. We ignore creativity at our own risk.

What Do We Mean by Creativity?

The most fertile combinations will often be those formed of elements drawn from domains which are far apart. . .most combinations so formed would be entirely sterile; but among them, very rare, are the most fruitful of all.

Poincaré[2]

Definitions of creativity vary between theories but they typically share two common elements: novelty and utility. A creative outcome must be innovative and original and it must be of value, or be useful. Of course, we can only judge originality by what we already know, and different people attribute value in different ways. In general, other professionals or the 'gatekeepers' to a field, such as publishers or gallery owners, dictate the value of new outputs and consequently the value of a new idea is sometimes only realized with hindsight.

Elements of creativity

Rhodes'[3] 4-P model identifies four aspects of creativity: Person, Process, Product and Press. Rhodes emphasized that creativity is dependent upon each of them. 'Person' refers to the individual factors that influence the extent of a person's creative tendencies and outputs. For example, McCrae[4] identified strong, positive correlations ($p < 0.001$) between the personality trait 'openness to experience' and scores on five tests of divergent thinking, as well as measures of artistic and investigative interest. Later in this chapter we discuss links between personality, behaviour, intellect and creativity in greater detail.

'Process' describes the stages of thinking an individual goes through to achieve a goal and can also refer to group approaches to creative problem-solving such as brainstorming. Early creativity researchers produced many stage models describing the process of creative insight, whilst more recent work focuses on specific styles of thinking (such as divergent and convergent thinking) that may underpin creativity. In this chapter we also present neuroscientific research that offers insights into the relationship between brain activity and creative thought processes.

'Product' refers to the output of the creative process; an invention, a design or a system. In some ways this is the easiest aspect of creativity to research because there is actually something concrete to study. Lastly, there is the 'Press': this is the wider environment within which a creative Product is viewed and judged. The relationship between the person, environment and situation can affect a person's creativity and determines whether we judge their outputs to have creative value. In an educational context the 'Press' can include a classroom atmosphere which is conducive to risk-taking and innovation and teachers who encourage creativity and exhibit positive attitudes towards pupils' creative outputs. We discuss creative environments near the end of the chapter.

Whilst Rhodes' model is helpful for understanding different perspectives from which one can study creativity, it is also important to consider exactly what type of creativity we are talking about. Should we be making a distinction between the creativity of a pupil in school and the creative genius of artists and composers?

Types of creativity

Kaufman and Beghetto's[5] 4-C model identifies four different types of creativity and their relevance in everyday life: Big-C, little-c, Pro-C and mini-c (Figure 9.1). Earlier versions of the model included only Big and little-c. Big-C creativity refers to creative genius, to the accomplishments

| mini-c | little-c | Pro-C | Big-C |
| (Discovering how to be creative) | (An everyday moment of creativity) | (A creative professional) | (Rare creative genius) |

Figure 9.1 From mini-c to Big-C creativity.

of people like Mozart or Marie Curie whom we recognize as having made a significant impact in their field. Conversely, little-c creativity refers to everyday occurrences of creative activity, such as the cook who mixes ingredients in a novel way when making supper. However, to account for people such as Michelin-starred chefs or famous designers who are highly creative but not eminent, Kaufman and Beghetto added Pro-C: a professional level of creativity achieved by someone at the top of their game.

Most relevant to education is mini-c; the creativity inherent in learning itself. Mini-c moments include those when a pupil completing a maths problem realizes that they could use a simpler method, or when a pupil in a design and technology class works out a new way to shape their materials. These moments of creativity may not be novel to anyone else, but they are new and valuable to the individual in question. These moments of intrapersonal insight are part of the developmental process by which someone learns *how* to be creative.

What this model offers to educators is an insight into the role schooling can play in fostering creativity. Obviously certain subjects such as music and drama are heavily focused on developing artistic creativity. People studying these subjects at degree level are probably aiming to hone their skills towards a Pro-C standard. However, mini-c creativity can be evident in every lesson. Furthermore, teachers can train pupils to either value or ignore mini-c moments depending on their response to pupils' expression of creative thinking. We discuss this in more detail later on.

Creative thinking

So what are the thought processes involved in creativity? Researchers have been proposing stage models of creative thinking for the better part of a century and Guilford[6] identified their common elements as preparation, incubation, illumination and verification. Preparation involves defining the problem at hand; this requires relevant knowledge and analytical skills. Once the problem is defined one needs some incubation time, an opportunity to step back, think about other things and stop making a conscious effort to solve it. This leads on to a moment of illumination where an idea or solution surfaces into the consciousness. Verification is then used to apply, test and evaluate this idea; it may be accepted as a solution or the individual might need to go 'back to the drawing board'.

The main criticism of stage models is their failure to explain how more or less creative outcomes are produced or which cognitive processes actually underlie each stage. Some theorists argue that it is these underlying processes that are actually important and that need to be taught.

One key process associated with creativity is divergent thinking, which was part of Guilford's Structure of Intellect theory. According to this theory, intelligence is subdivided into content, products and operations and one of the six intellectual operations is divergent production: the ability to produce lots of examples of something based on simple criteria. Guilford proposed a distinction between divergent and convergent thinking:

> In convergent thinking, there is usually one conclusion or answer that is regarded as unique, and thinking is channelled or controlled in the direction of that answer. In tests of the convergent-thinking factors, there is one keyed answer to each item . . . In divergent thinking, on the other hand, there is much searching or going off in various directions. This is most clearly seen when there is no unique conclusion.[7(p274)]

However, as psychologist Sarnoff Mednick noted, divergent thinking alone may be insufficient to produce useful creative outputs. Mednick proposed that creative thinking involves:

> the forming of associative elements into new combinations which either meet specified requirements or are in some way useful. The more mutually remote the elements of the new combination, the more creative the process or solution.[8(p221)]

This definition resonates with Poincaré's description of creativity involving 'elements drawn from domains which are far apart'. According to Mednick, creativity requires divergent thinking to generate apparently unrelated concepts but also convergent thinking to see connections between them.

Brophy[9] suggests that creative problem-solving should operate as a zigzag between these divergent and convergent processes. Divergent thinking produces possibilities, but convergent thinking helps to narrow them down to a solution. A third process is also necessary: critical thinking is required to evaluate the value or utility of the final solution.

At the end of this chapter we consider how these thinking processes can be facilitated in the classroom, but firstly we will look at how these models affect the way creativity is measured. It is important to understand this interdependency because studies and experiments are only as reliable as the measures they use.

Measuring creativity

Batey and Furnham[10] list eight different methods used to assess different aspects of creativity: divergent thinking tests, attitude and interest inventories, personality inventories, biographical inventories, peer, teacher or supervisor ratings, judgement of products, ratings of eminence and the self-reporting of creative activities.

Psychometric, or cognitive, tests of creativity look at a person's style of thinking. They treat creativity rather like intelligence in the way it can be formally measured. These measures are particularly popular with researchers as they produce standardized results which can be quantitatively analysed and replicated with different populations. However, they vary in both their reliability and predictive validity.

One very well-established set of psychometric creativity tests is the Torrance Tests of Creative Thinking (TTCT). Ellis Paul Torrance became well known in the 1960s and 70s for his seminal research into creativity. He worked in schools, looking at how creative children behaved and were treated. His aim was to identify conditions that would help to nurture and encourage creativity. For this, however, he needed a measure of creativity and so he developed the TTCT.[11,12] The tests were originally scored according to the four characteristics of divergent thinking: fluency, flexibility, originality and elaboration.[6,7] These refer, respectively, to the ability to produce many responses, many types or categories of responses, original responses and detailed responses. However, Torrance later moved away from these scoring criteria owing to the strong similarity between flexibility and fluency scores. The most recent version of the TTCT includes five verbal and three figural activities. An example of a verbal activity would be the Unusual Uses test. Like the example at the start of this chapter, a participant will be given an item and told to think of as many uses as possible for it. For the figural activities, participants are presented with pages of complete or incomplete shapes and asked to create pictures incorporating them.

The TTCT do have their flaws. Conceptions of original responses may vary across cultures[13] and, just like other cognitive tests of creativity, factors such as motivation and verbal ability may influence test scores. Notwithstanding these problems, the main strength of the TTCT is that they have existed long enough to check if they actually predict future creative achievements. Torrance and his team administered the TTCT to hundreds of school children in Minnesota in the late 1950s. They then contacted those children again throughout their lives, monitoring the quality and quantity of their creative achievements. For the 80 participants who were successfully contacted in 1998, fluency, flexibility and originality scores from the TTCT did significantly correlate with the quantity and quality of their creative achievements, and were more predictive of quality than IQ (although this also had a significant impact).[14]

One must remember that no measure of creativity is perfect. Just as IQ tests measure a narrowly defined conception of intelligence, psychometric creativity tests measure whatever the researcher defines as creativity (often no more than divergent thinking). Even measures of real-life creative achievement are subjective and depend on the quality and content of the survey to accurately capture respondents' creative output. It is therefore important to remain sceptical when reading about interventions that supposedly promote creativity, at least until you know how that creativity was measured.

Creative personalities and behaviours

As well as attempting to measure creativity directly, some researchers have sought personality traits or behaviours that differentiate creative people such as architects,[15] photographers,[16] artists and scientists[17,18] from their peers. Some of the traits they identify, such as imaginativeness, inventiveness and unconventionality, might seem rather obvious. However, other characteristics are less intuitive and are worth highlighting because they can help us identify creative pupils, and to understand the causes of behaviours which can appear disruptive or antisocial.

A clear example of this is the trait of impulsivity (others use the terms excitability or enthusiasm). Impulsivity, although closely associated with creativity, can be difficult for teachers to deal with as impulsive pupils may become easily distracted or may interrupt their peers during whole-class discussions. American psychotherapist Mahnaz Sadre has presented a number of case studies of children whose creative behaviours were misinterpreted as ADHD. For example, 10-year-old Michael was diagnosed with ADHD and placed in a special education class; however, once his creativity was recognized and nurtured he re-entered mainstream education and ultimately ended up in a 'gifted and talented' programme.[19]

Researchers in America have begun empirically investigating the links between ADHD and creativity. They have found that university students with ADHD (n = 45) score higher on tests of divergent thinking and lower on tests of convergent thinking than age-, gender- and achievement-matched controls.[20] Looking at real-life creative achievement, measured using the Creative Achievement Questionnaire, they compared 30 undergraduates with ADHD to age- and achievement-matched controls, and again found that those with ADHD reported significantly greater levels of creative achievement (p = 0.001).[21] Now, both of these studies involve university students so we can assume that all the participants were academically able. It is less clear whether ADHD confers a creative advantage across the spectrum of academic ability. What we do know, however, is that children with ADHD (n = 8, age 8–11) attain significantly lower elaboration scores on a divergent thinking tasks when they have taken Ritalin in the previous hour, compared to when they have not taken it for 12 hours. Thus the same medications that significantly reduce symptoms of ADHD may also constrain creativity.[22]

Two more creative characteristics that can be difficult to manage in the classroom are independence and unconventionality. Creative people are not necessarily pro-social; they may prefer working independently so as not to feel constrained by the norms or preferences of others. However, this can lead highly creative pupils to become isolated or even bullied for standing out from the crowd. Conversely, pupils may choose to suppress their creative tendencies in order to fit in. Torrance[23] found that between the third and fourth grade about half of elementary school children showed a significant drop in their creativity scores; a so-called fourth-grade slump. Although this was initially attributed to their educational environment, it has since been suggested that natural maturation causes children of this age to become more aware of convention and more eager to conform, and hence to be less creative.[24]

Other traits linked to creativity are not necessarily problematic in the classroom, but may need nurturing if creative children are to fulfil their potential. Joseph Renzulli, a prominent psychologist in this field, developed a 'Three Ring Model' of giftedness which identifies ability, creativity and task commitment as contributing to gifted behaviour (see Figure 9.2). Although task commitment (or determination) is a trait commonly identified in successful creative adults, it may not actually be necessary for creative thought. Instead, task commitment may specifically differentiate those people who act on their ideas to successfully produce creative outputs. Hence if we want to promote successful creative production in adulthood, we may want to intentionally incorporate challenges into pupils' school work, so they learn to persevere and overcome setbacks from an early age.

Two final traits which can be particularly hard for teachers to foster are risk-taking and tolerance of ambiguity. In an interesting comparison of entrepreneurs and business managers, Begley and Boyd[25] found that one distinguishing characteristic of entrepreneurs was their tolerance of

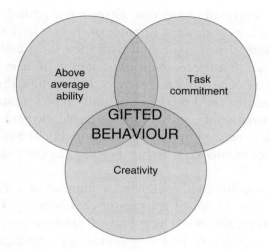

Figure 9.2 The Three Ring Model of giftedness. *Source*: Adapted from Renzulli, J. What makes giftedness? Reexamining a definition. *Phi Delta Kappan*. 1998;60(3). Copyright © Joseph Renzulli. Adapted with kind permission from Joseph Renzulli.

ambiguity: they were willing to try out an innovative business idea whilst uncertain of the outcome. Unfortunately, much modern schooling is devoid of ambiguity: the government (and exam boards) tell teachers what they should be teaching and the teacher sets this out to pupils at the start of each lesson through clearly defined learning goals. If educators and politicians are serious about promoting creativity, they may need to consider how some lessons can be structured to incorporate more ambiguity and flexible learning goals.

Teachers' responses to creativity

Teachers often report believing that creativity is important to their students' development and can enhance students' academic learning. However, psychologists frequently observe teachers discouraging creativity by dismissing unexpected comments or devaluing independent behaviours. Indeed, when teachers are presented with personality profiles of pupils with creative traits they rate these children as likely to be more disruptive than the average pupil.[26] If teachers genuinely value creativity, why does this contradiction arise?

It appears that teachers' conceptions of creativity do not always match those held by researchers. Westby and Dawson[27] demonstrated this mismatch in a study of American elementary school teachers. They presented 16 teachers with a list of more or less creative traits and asked them to indicate that they associated with their most and least favourite pupils. Those traits that the teachers associated with their favourite pupils were those least associated with creativity. Meanwhile, the teachers' conceptions of a creative child were not actually representative of all facets of the creative personality, only more desirable elements. For example, teachers did not associate impulsivity, emotionality or making up rules as you go along with creativity, whereas they did associate sincerity, reliability and logic.

Runco and his colleagues conducted a number of surveys comparing parents' and teachers' implicit theories of creativity.[28,29] These confirmed that teachers and parents do not find all aspects of creativity to be desirable. Both impulsivity and dreaminess are considered creative but undesirable, whilst caution and conformity are considered desirable but uncreative.[29] Further research has shown that teachers do not necessarily associate behaviours such as divergent thinking with creativity, whereas they do associate other qualities such as intelligence with creativity, even when there is no definitive empirical evidence to support this link.

Teachers are rarely given formal training in recognizing and nurturing creativity. Consequently, we see natural misconceptions develop, where teachers know that creativity is supposed to enhance performance at school and at work, but they may not realize that it can also be associated with some less desirable or unmanageable personality traits. It seems that when teachers talk positively about creative pupils they might actually be envisioning gifted children. Thus if we want all of our most creative pupils to be supported and encouraged, not just those who also have high attainment, teachers may need more formal support to identify them and understand their needs.

The Development of Creativity

All young people have some capacity for creativity and yet when we think about eminent creators we often perceive them as being distinctly different. It can be hard to imagine that any child could attain the same level of creative genius as Bach or Dali simply through practice. In this section we explore evidence for the roles of nature and nurture in the development of creativity.

Born creative or achieving creativeness?

Early creativity research focused primarily on identifying special characteristics that contributed to eminence. Researchers looked at the biographies of eminent individuals in an attempt to pinpoint unusual, recurrent factors that contributed to success. These included the loss of a parent in early life, birth order and social class. The findings are well summarized by Simonton[30,31] so we do not revisit them here. What must be noted, however, is a weakness in biographical studies. One can easily pick out salient life-events or personal characteristics and conclude that they contributed to eminence when they were in fact completely incidental. It is important to consider how many people had a certain experience and did not go on to greatness, and how many people who became eminent did not experience a certain influence in their youth. A good example is a study by Albert.[32] He looked at samples of British prime ministers, American presidents and eminent scientists and found that between 25 and 35% had lost a parent before they were 16 (the population average is 8%). However, he identified a comparable rate of parental loss amongst samples of prisoners and depressed patients, showing that this characteristic was not unique to eminent individuals.

Many modern creativity researchers are interested in everyday creativity rather than eminence, so they have started to look at the impact of population-wide experiences on little-c creativity. One hypothesis is that SES may correlate with creativity much as it correlates with academic achievement. Dai and colleagues[33] recently conducted a small study to investigate this, comparing the creativity scores of 126 pupils in a lower-SES urban middle school with those of 108 pupils from two higher-SES suburban middle schools. The pupils completed tests of divergent thinking and surveys of creative traits. The higher-SES pupils had a significantly higher mean creativity score. However, even suburban pupils with matched levels of parental education had higher creativity scores than those from the urban schools, suggesting that there was some interactive effect with type of environment. The combination of school location and parental education explained 20% of the variation in creativity scores, which suggests that SES does affect creativity, but that many additional factors must also be influential.

The key message from this section is that there are numerous environmental factors which may affect the development of creativity but none is guaranteed to engender eminence.

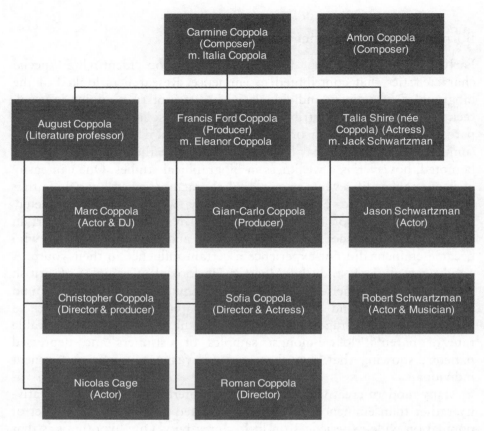

Figure 9.3   The Coppola family tree: evidence for the heritability of creativity?

Heritable factors in creativity

Certain families seem to be particularly creative and this can encourage a perception that creativity must be heritable. However, trying to determine whether such connections are due to genes rather than environment is difficult. For example, as evident from Figure 9.3, the Coppola family seems to have an overabundance of highly creative people. One might attribute this to genetics, but growing up surrounded by people who work in the film industry can also make this a much more viable career option than it is for the average young person. From an early age, members of the Coppola family will have seen that success in this industry is possible. They will have had better access to social connections and inside knowledge of the field. Hence creativity can run in families without being heritable.

In order to overcome this confounding of environment and genetics, modern researchers will typically give individuals (ideally twins) from many families some standardized tests of creativity and see whether the similarity between the scores depends on the extent to which people are related. Early twin studies produced an upper estimate of 20% heritability of creativity.[34,35] More recently, Niels Waller[36] and his colleagues looked at creative traits rather than scores on creativity tests, and found that the heritability of these traits would be calculated as greater than 100%. Since it is not actually possible for a trait to be more than 100% heritable, this suggests that creativity might be emergenic. This means that when a person possesses multiple, lower-level heritable traits, then creativity will emerge as a higher-level trait. Because the likelihood of all the traits co-occurring is so low, it will look like the heritability of creativity exceeds 100%.

About 20 years ago, Eysenck[37] suggested that the trait of psychoticism predisposed people to be creative and that this trait, amongst others, might be inherited. He further proposed that high levels of psychoticism could lead some people to develop schizophrenia. Creativity and mental illness have long been linked through romantic notions of the tortured artist expressing their inner turmoil through painting or writing. In fact, many studies do find a higher incidence of mental illness amongst creative people (both artists and scientists) than in the general population. However, this leads to a conundrum, because severe mental illness can be debilitating. People with severe depression can find themselves so despondent that they cannot get out of bed, let alone produce something creative. Similarly, whilst schizophrenia is associated with so-called 'positive' symptoms such as hallucinations, delusions and unusual thoughts, it also produces 'negative' symptoms such as withdrawal and poor everyday functioning. So how can experiencing mental illness facilitate creativity, and how does this connect to creativity in everyday life?

Everyday creativity and mental illness

There seems to be a link between occurrences of mental illness within families and creative traits or everyday creative production. In an early study, Richards et al.[38] found that the relatives of people with manic depression reported higher levels of everyday creativity than individuals with no family history of mental illness. More recently, studies have linked the occurrence of affective disorders (such as depression) and of positive schizophrenic traits with everyday, real-life creativity (see Schuldberg[39]).

Claridge and Blakey[40] conducted a study with 78 undergraduates to see whether traits linked to schizotypy (measured using the O-LIFE [The

Oxford–Liverpool Inventory of Feelings and Experiences]) or affective disorders (measured using the TEMPS-A [Temperament Evaluation of Memphis, Pisa, Paris and San Diego Autoquestionnaire]) were more closely related to creativity. They measured creativity using two divergent thinking tasks and the Creative Styles Questionnaire (CSQ-R), which assesses beliefs and strategies for creativity. In fact, they found that responses to some scales on both the O-LIFE and TEMPS-A were correlated and that scales from both these measures were significantly related to scores on the CSQ-R and divergent thinking tasks. Claridge and Blakey therefore concluded 'that both schizotypal and affective elements play a part in creativity.'[40(p823)]

The fact that traits associated with mental illness are also measurable in normal populations has led to an interesting theory. Whilst mental illness can be debilitating, it might be that possessing these traits at a subclinical level (i.e. without actually being ill) gives people a creative advantage. For example, as we have discussed, creative people are often seen to be both individualistic and impulsive and one of the diagnostic traits for schizophrenia is impulsive nonconformity. Thus having a subclinical level of impulsive nonconformity might predispose someone towards creativity. Schizophrenics have particularly low levels of latent inhibition (the ability to block out previously irrelevant inputs) and Carson and colleagues[41] have shown that undergraduates with greater degrees of creative accomplishment have significantly lower levels of latent inhibition than their less creative peers (n = 178). Along similar lines, whilst depression can remove motivation, mania can make someone excitable and enthusiastic. Hence the attributes of excitability and enthusiasm may link creativity to bipolar disorder.

Once one starts thinking about creativity in this way, it has some interesting implications. We tend to think about mental illness only in negative terms; however, it might have a crucial link to the development of civilization. After all, how would society advance if it weren't for creative thinkers?

Creativity and the brain

This chapter started with a quote by Poincaré who, just like Mednick, suggested that creativity must involve making links between distant and apparently unrelated domains. There is a specific neurological disorder which is associated with excessive activity in neuronal networks, sometimes localized and sometimes spreading across the brain: epilepsy. Interestingly, there are numerous cases where the onset of epilepsy has been associated with new creative productivity. Impey and Mellanby[42] presented the case of the artist and author Alfred Kubin, who was not particularly creative until he had a strange sensory experience during a funeral, which may have been a temporal lobe seizure. Shortly after this incident Kubin began to produce highly original drawings and then went on to author a fantastical, if rather disturbing, book – *Die Andere Seite*. It seems his drawings and book were inspired by his experiences during seizures and as his seizures became less frequent so his creativity waned. Although we are not certain that Kubin suffered from epilepsy, there are other authors like Dostoyevsky who are known to have experienced seizures. There are also many examples of artists who have produced novel works inspired by the auras and hallucinations they experienced as a result of epilepsy (see Schachter[43]). An open question, though, is whether the value of such cases is the insight their art provides about the experience of epilepsy (as neurologist Steven Schachter suggests) or, as Impey and Mellanby propose, whether they offer an insight into the neural underpinnings of creativity. During an epileptic seizure, there is an abnormal co-activation of neuronal circuits. Perhaps it is a similar co-activation of neuronal circuits (above the average level of connectivity) that elicits all creative cognition.

Jausovic[44] used EEG to look at the neural activity of 48 individuals as they solved open and closed problems (those with many solutions or only one). He sorted the participants into creative, intelligent, average and gifted groups according to whether they had high scores on creativity tests, intelligence tests, neither or both. As they solved the problems creative people showed more connectivity between distant areas of their brains. Other researchers have shown that when people complete tests of creativity whilst EEG recordings are being made, those with more creative responses also have more dispersed pattern of synchronized activity in the brain.[45,46]

Researchers in Japan have been using fMRI to look at the activity of different brain areas at rest and when people perform tasks. Over 150 university students were given divergent thinking tests before participating in brain imaging. The results showed that when the participants were resting, the more creative people had significantly higher levels of functional connectivity between two brain areas, the medial prefrontal cortex and the posterior cingulate cortex. Both of these areas are part of the 'default mode network', a group of brain areas typically involved in internally focused tasks like imagining the future.[47] When 63 of the participants completed an *n*-back working memory task (see Chapter 2 for more information), an area of the brain called the precuneus also showed

Box 9.1   Left-brain and right-brain thinking

The pop-psychology theory of left-brain and right-brain thinking is well known. It suggests that people who think with their left brains are more logical, whilst people who think with their right brains are more creative. It is true that some studies indicate that the right brain is more involved in solving creative insight problems. However, if we look across all the neuroscientific studies that relate to the many different modes of creativity, they do not support the idea that creativity only involves the right hemisphere. Instead, creative processes have been linked to activity in both hemispheres and perhaps more importantly seem to involve increased connectivity between areas throughout the brain.[49,50]

less deactivation in more creative individuals. Again, the precuneus is part of the default mode network.[48] The researchers believe this might show that creative people allocate their attention to new stimuli less efficiently. Thinking back to the idea of schizophrenics having reduced latent inhibition, this again suggests that creative people may be less likely to focus on a single input or to block out potentially irrelevant stimuli. This in turn fits with the psychological research that is starting to link ADHD and creativity. See Box 9.1.

Creativity and Intelligence

We noted earlier that some teachers associate creativity with intelligence. However, the link between the two is still unclear. Sternberg and O'Hara[51] describe a range of possible theoretical relationships between creativity and intelligence. The key questions for educators, however, are whether all children, regardless of their academic ability, have equal potential to be creative and whether creativity can confer any academic advantage of its own.

Do you need to be intelligent to be creative?

Few studies look at the relationship between real-life creative outputs and IQ scores; however, some have identified a positive relationship between them. Kéri[52] had 111 Hungarian adults complete a Creative Achievement Questionnaire and found that the scores were weakly positively correlated with IQ ($r = 0.23$, $p < 0.05$). IQ was also correlated with lifetime creative achievements in Torrance's longitudinal study.[14] However, in both cases plenty of other factors also predicted creative achievement, suggesting that intelligence might be necessary but not sufficient to be creative.

Most studies that look at the relationship between creativity and intelligence use psychometric tests of creativity. Kim[53] performed a meta-analysis of such studies and found that overall there was a weak positive correlation between intelligence and creativity, although the results of individual studies were variable and included positive and negative relationships. Kim suggested that these variations may have been due to the type of creativity test used and the way it was administered. For example, if the creativity tests were administered in a game-like situation, scores had a slightly lower correlation with IQ. This makes sense, as people's performance on IQ tests partly reflect their ability to work quickly while under pressure. If they take a creativity test in the same conditions then that ability will show up in the creativity scores too, causing a greater correlation with IQ.

Some researchers support the threshold theory of creativity, which suggests that a basic level of intelligence is required to be creative but that once this is attained other factors become more important. If the theory holds, then up to an IQ of around 120 we would expect to see a linear relationship between creativity and IQ scores (the more intelligent you are, the more creative you are) but above IQ 120 the two should no longer correlate. In fact, some researchers find exactly this pattern,[50,54] but others find no difference in correlations between IQ and creativity scores for IQs above and below 120 (e.g. Preckel et al.[55]; Sligh et al.[56]). Kim also tested the theory as part of her meta-analysis, but found that the correlation between IQ and creativity was not significantly stronger for lower IQ scores.

Although threshold theory was inspired by studies of creative individuals, tests of the theory are largely based on psychometric measures of creativity, which can correlate with IQ scores for many other reasons. Although some academics may consider it logical that IQ and creativity should go hand-in-hand, it is quite possible that the relationship between intelligence and creative production depends on the field in question; one might need a higher IQ to make innovative breakthroughs in science or mathematics than in literature or fine art, even if the level of creativity required is comparable. With no clear evidence either way, most theorists err on the side of caution and suggest that educators should expect to see creative potential in children with all levels of academic ability.

Academic performance, creativity and intelligence

The seminal study addressing the question of whether creativity can independently boost academic performance was conducted by Getzels and Jackson.[57] They administered creativity and IQ tests to 449 American high-school pupils (age 12–17) and thereby identified a high-creativity/low-IQ group (26 pupils) and a high-IQ/low-creativity group (28 pupils): pupils who scored in the top 20% on one set of tests and the bottom 20% in the other. When the school performance of both groups was analysed, they were found to be achieving above the average for all pupils. As a result, Getzels and Jackson suggested that creativity could be independently related to academic performance.

This study has received a lot of criticism and has therefore been repeated a number of times. For example, Wallach and Kogan[58] pointed out that the creativity tests were conducted under academic test conditions, which probably increased the correlation of creativity scores with academic achievement, since both relied partially on ability to perform well in tests. They conducted a replication of the experiment using game-like creativity tests and reported that their 'high-creativity/low-IQ' students were not academically successful but had a fear of evaluation, could be socially withdrawn and sometimes exhibited disruptive behaviours. In other words, when the creativity tests were less similar to academic tests, they no longer identified model, high-achieving pupils.

More recent studies suggest that although IQ might be the more significant predictor of academic performance (not unexpectedly, given that most IQ measures were developed for the purpose), creativity seems to have an independent effect. Rindermann and Neubauer[59] found that creativity was independently related to the academic performance of German Gymnasium pupils, but less strongly than intelligence. For Spanish students, achieving a high creativity score has been linked to significantly higher grades in chemistry, biology, history and languages, even when the groups did not have significantly different levels of intelligence.[60] In a group of Malaysian students, those with lower IQs did have higher grades if they were more creative, but they still did not exhibit the same level of performance as higher IQ students.[61]

It is now common practice in UK state schools to select pupils for 'gifted and talented' or 'able' programmes, which may involve additional lessons, resources or educational trips. However, the research discussed so far suggests that educators can easily underestimate the potential of highly creative pupils. Teachers might be biased against identifying creative pupils as gifted because of their tendency to focus on academic performance and to dislike some creative behaviours that cause problems in the classroom. Meanwhile, psychometric creativity tests often measure qualities that are not related purely to creativity but to what we might call 'creative intelligence' or test-taking ability. We have noted in Chapter 5 that labelling pupils as gifted and talented may not be the most effective way to help all pupils fulfil their potential. Nonetheless, if this practice is to be undertaken it is essential that gifted creative pupils be identified and supported as much as their purely academically oriented peers.

Fostering Creativity in the Education System

We hope that you are now convinced that it is worth nurturing the creativity of young people. As an EU review of creativity in education notes,[62] ultimately it is up to individual pupils and teachers whether they actually behave and work creatively. However, there are some contexts where creativity is much more likely to flourish than others and the presence of multiple 'enablers' can set the scene for creative behaviour.

Creative environments

In her 2005 publication, Anna Craft describes the experience of individuals in creative organizations. Read down this list and consider whether you see any similarities or differences with your expectations of pupils' experiences in the average school:

Feel challenged by their goals, operations and tasks
Feel able to take initiatives and to find relevant information
Feel able to interact with others
Feel that new ideas are met with support and encouragement
Feel able to put forward new ideas and views
Experience much debate within a prestige-free and open environment
Feel uncertainty is tolerated and, thus, risk-taking is encouraged[63(p48)]

Most researchers argue that there are too many differences between the ideal creative environment and that found in most schools. As one group of American academics have suggested, schools have been designed based on standardization, whereas creativity needs the opposite.[64] However, a school environment can be adapted to support creative behaviours.

Carl Rogers presented one of the earliest theories about environments conducive to creativity. He suggested that such environments should offer both psychological freedom and psychological safety.[65] This means that pupils need to feel free to express themselves and develop original ideas. They need to feel that they can offer up their own opinions, perhaps even challenge the teacher's view, and not be in danger of punishment for doing so.

Traditional teaching methods involve asking closed questions: What is $a^2 + b^2$? Who can name the capital of Iceland? However, such questions can reduce psychological safety because there is only one way to be right and many ways to be wrong. Open, divergent questioning styles are more conducive to creative responses because they create psychological safety by avoiding the idea of 'correct' answers altogether and allowing for varied opinions and beliefs. Nonetheless, closed questions are sometimes essential to test pupils' knowledge or understanding. Where these are used, pupils need to feel that it is safe to be wrong. Pupils should feel they can ask questions, take an (educated) guess at responses and discuss their problems openly without fearing punishment if they do not understand something immediately. This encourages them to try out innovative but risky problem-solving approaches, rather than just focusing on learning the accepted method to reach an answer. See Box 9.2.

Grading and evaluation

In many schools, pupils are told they should work hard in order to get good results. In Chapter 7 we discussed how such extrinsic motivation may not be conducive to deep learning, but what effect might it have on creativity?

Teresa Amabile and her colleagues advocate the view that intrinsic motivation is better for creativity. Consequently, they argue that things that reduce intrinsic motivation (such as external evaluation and using grades as extrinsic rewards) are likely to reduce creative productivity. Amabile and her colleagues have shown that college students who expect external evaluation of their work produce much less creative outputs than those who do not[67,68] and that offering a reward for task completion will sometimes reduce the creativity of both adults' and children's responses.[69]

Robert Eisenberger and his colleagues, however, suggest that reward and evaluation reduce creativity in Amabile's experiments because the participants are not instructed to be creative and do not associate creativity with good performance. They note that when participants are told in advance to be creative on a task, they will often produce more novel or creative responses[70,71] and this effect can be increased by offering them a reward.[72] Hence Eisenberger argues that when reward is linked to task

Box 9.2 Case Study: Creative ethos in secondary school

Sara Bragg and Helen Manchester have conducted a study looking at the ethos of schools and how this can support creativity. Amongst the schools they worked with was a secondary school for 11–16-year-olds which they referred to as 'Sherman School'. Here they found many aspects of the creative environment we have described:

- Safety: Teachers and pupils remarked that pupils were free to share their opinions. They knew that their comments would be respected and valued.
- Clear boundaries: Pupils at Sherman School had agreed behaviour rules with teachers. As a result, they knew when they were stepping over the line, but also felt safe to be creative when it was appropriate to the task.
- In control of learning: In one class where the teacher was absent, pupils who had finished their work were observed not to sit and chat, but to participate in peer review and learning. Pupils had a say in their learning and therefore felt responsible for it.[66]

performance and not just task completion, as it is in Amabile's studies, then it can facilitate creativity.[73]

So does this mean that reward and evaluation will reduce or increase productivity? Well, in an education system where standardized responses are typically rewarded through higher grades, Amabile's work suggests that pupils who anticipate evaluation or reward are unlikely to be creative. However, Eisenberger's research indicates that if pupils are specifically instructed to be creative and are clear that their evaluation will depend on it, then they may well produce more creative work. This fits with our description of the creative environment; if we want pupils to be creative then they need to feel it is safe and acceptable to do so.

Amabile's research also suggests that offering a reward for task completion can shift people's focus away from the task and towards the reward itself.[69] So giving pupils a grade for their work may result in more time being spent comparing grades with friends than considering how to improve their work. This is why educators throughout the United Kingdom have been encouraged to use 'Assessment for Learning':[74] focusing assessment not just on the end result but on the process pupils have worked through and providing not just a grade but also comments for improvement. Assessment for Learning also incorporates peer- and self-assessment, forms of evaluation which are conducive to creativity. Peer review facilitates creativity because it encourages pupils to debate and defend ideas, and to learn from the work of others. Meanwhile, self-assessment skills are essential when pupils work independently on original ideas, since they need to learn to recognize and generate their own learning goals and then monitor their progress towards them.

Assessment for Learning can be difficult to implement in large classes, as it is harder for the teacher to monitor pupil progress. In Chapter 13 we discuss how new technologies are facilitating this form of learning, but it is worth considering whether they are facilitating creative thinking at the same time.

Creativity and the curriculum

In England, Wales and Northern Ireland the curriculum specifies what pupils in each year should learn across a wide range of subjects. Teaching, particularly in secondary school, is typically divided by subject area. Yet one of the recurrent observations made by researchers is that creativity involves making links between apparently separate areas or ideas; this is after all the basic principle of divergent thinking. Consequently, some educational psychologists argue that in order to promote creative thinking pupils should be given interdisciplinary projects that incorporate crossover between subjects. Some state secondary schools are therefore developing cross-curricular frameworks where pupils are taught in themes rather than by subject. Accrington Academy is one such example (see Box 9.3).

In Scotland, the Curriculum for Excellence was specifically designed to facilitate a greater level of interdisciplinary study (see www.educationscotland.gov.uk/thecurriculum/). The Curriculum is based on four capacities: successful learners, confident individuals, responsible citizens, effective contributors. A successful learner is described as demonstrating 'openness to new thinking and ideas' and having the capacity to 'think creatively and independently'. The hope is that creativity (and learning in general) will improve because teachers have more freedom to choose what to teach and are being encouraged to work cooperatively to support joined-up, interdisciplinary learning. All teachers are expected to take responsibility for improving learners' mathematics and literacy skills.

Box 9.3 Case Study: Accrington Academy

Accrington Academy is a 'School of Creativity', one of 55 schools in England identified as having outstanding practice in creative teaching and learning. The school promotes creativity through events such as the Literacy Festival, where pupils participate in activities such as puppet shows narrated in modern foreign languages, and debates with the community hosted in a local park (www.creative-partnerships.com).

At Accrington Academy, however, creativity is not confined to one-off events. Years 7 and 8 follow the 'Exciting Minds' curriculum. They are taught according to a competence- rather than content-based curriculum framework. Their year is split into six units, each focusing on one of the following competencies (with the last unit combining all of them):

1. Personal qualities
2. Team working
3. Skills for thinking
4. Opportunities to develop
5. Relationships

Creativity is included within the 'Skills for Thinking' competency.

Rather than organizing teaching by subject content, it is organized around a theme such as 'Going Places' or 'Megastructures'. The content of the National Curriculum is then incorporated into the unit theme. Accrington Academy staff believe that this approach develops life-long learners by keeping the pupils inspired and engaged (www.accrington-academy.org).

Whilst thematic learning may facilitate creativity, it also faces criticisms. In Scotland, teachers have found it quite challenging to transition from a prescriptive curriculum to a situation where they have freedom and responsibility to choose what they teach. There is also considerable uncertainty about how to prepare senior pupils for exams when they might all be learning different things. Meanwhile, as we mentioned in Chapter 1, in England prominent educationalists such as Tim Oates advocate the maintenance of separate subjects on the basis that this provides a better framework for the acquisition of knowledge.

The role of knowledge in creativity

An ever-present concern when the level of prescription within a curriculum is reduced is that pupils may no longer acquire certain essential knowledge. Conversely, many researchers argue that the more that the government tries to control what pupils are taught and to monitor this through standardized testing, the less freedom there is for both teachers and pupils to be creative. Research with teachers in England shows that perceived scope for creativity declines the higher up the education system that teachers work, because pressure to help students pass examinations means an ever-greater focus on transmitting specific knowledge, and less scope for original and creative detours.[75]

It is a fundamental misconception that creative production can occur independent of knowledge, or that creative thinking can only be developed at the expense of fact-based learning. Whilst children can exhibit mini-c creativity from a young age, to be genuinely creative a person needs to understand a discipline, know how to create within it and be able to judge the originality of their outputs. One often hears about the '10-year rule' for eminent creativity – that creative individuals' most innovative or impressive achievements are produced about 10 years into their careers. At this point they are likely to have acquired enough knowledge and experience to truly understand the field, whilst still believing that accepted principles or ways of doing things can be challenged.[76-78] Teaching for creativity therefore should not and does not require teachers to sacrifice factual content; they only need to present this content in a manner that enables learners to both retain information and manipulate it creatively (see Box 9.4).

Teaching for creativity

All teachers have a role to play in promoting creativity amongst their pupils and, importantly, teaching for creativity does not demand that the individual teacher is particularly creative. Commonly observed characteristics of teachers who encourage creativity include being open, accepting and flexible.[82,83] Of course, teachers have a vital role in establishing a psychologically safe classroom environment. Those who take an authoritarian approach, demanding conformity and the right response first time, are unlikely to encourage their pupils to demonstrate creativity.[83] After all, how many pupils would dare to express alternative opinions when they know they will always be repudiated?

Box 9.4 How much knowledge do we need to be creative?

There is tension amongst researchers about the amount of knowledge needed to be creative. Some suggest an inverted-U relationship, where the optimal level of knowledge is that which is sufficient to create without getting caught up in convention.[79] Others suggest a 'foundational model' where increasing levels of knowledge act as an ever-firmer basis for creative output.[80] Either way, the level of knowledge thought by some to inhibit creativity is beyond that learnt at school.[81] Consequently, it is commonly accepted that acquiring school-level knowledge (if done in a conducive environment) will benefit creative output. Researchers who advocate models of creative learning do not suggest that pupils no longer need to memorize some information; they simply view this as a foundation for creativity rather than the end in itself.

The mode of instruction adopted by teachers is also important. It is not enough for teachers to tell pupils to be creative if they then go on to lecture the class and set a pre-structured task as work. Teaching for creativity involves allowing pupils to control their own learning and to study independently. It requires avoiding an excessively didactic approach, in favour of giving students some power and autonomy. Craft and Jeffrey[84] call this a 'learner inclusive' approach, where both parties collaborate and the teacher is also engaged in the learning. Of course, whilst this approach is desirable, it is not always practical as there might not always be scope for originality in a task. Pupils therefore need to be taught to recognize when it is time for obedience and conformity or time for free-thinking and originality.

Some critics argue that encouraging independent activity results in pupils not learning very much at all. We have already clarified that creativity depends on a solid foundation of knowledge. The art of teaching for creativity is to impart this knowledge in a relevant, interesting and flexible way. In the United States during the 1960s, Torrance[85] advocated planned learning experiences, where the teacher maps out a sequence of experiences that will lead learners to extend their knowledge. Meanwhile, in the United Kingdom, the Nuffield Foundation was beginning its long-standing involvement in the development of mathematics and science curricula, based on the principle of 'I do and I understand'. Rather than rote-learning facts, pupils were given the opportunity to conduct their own experiments. Through this 'inquiry learning' pupils were supposed to discover knowledge for themselves by formulating questions, making predictions, investigating and reflecting on their findings. Some aspects of this approach soon received criticism, particularly the notion that pupils might, during a single laboratory session, discover scientific principles that had taken eminent scientists a lifetime to discern. However, the broader principles of 'Inquiry Learning' remain popular with some educationalists. It is argued that Inquiry Learning can lead to better recall and understanding than didactic teaching, and can allow for creative exploration whilst maintaining test scores.[86] However, the teacher is still needed to guide pupils' learning and others are quick to warn that Inquiry Learning can lose its creative edge if the process involves too much direction and becomes 'recipe-book science'.[87]

Creative thinking

All the suggested changes previously discussed boil down to one thing: encouraging creative thinking. We have seen that there are many different models of creative thinking and each one leads to different recommendations for promoting such thinking in the classroom.

Stage models of creative thinking highlight the importance of 'incubation' time. If creativity does rely on preparation, incubation, illumination and verification then we need to allow time for pupils to withdraw from problems and reach moments of illumination. Long-term school-based projects might naturally incorporate incubation time by having days between lessons, but in single lessons teachers may have to consciously build in such thinking space to allow for subconscious productivity.

We already discussed how important open questions are for creating psychological freedom and safety in the classroom. Whilst closed questions favour convergent thinking and academic intelligence, open questions encourage divergent thinking because pupils are encouraged to generate plenty of ideas in response to a question or problem. Questions that focus on translation of information to new areas, interpretation, application, analysis and evaluation all encourage a more creative response.

You may hear about specific strategies for promoting creative thinking, such as brainstorming[88] (Box 9.5), Six Thinking Hats[89] or, more recently, Anna Craft's 'Possibility Thinking'[90]. The empirical basis for these strategies varies, but what is clear is that pupils can benefit from being instructed to think creatively and can be taught to do so.

Box 9.5 Does brainstorming boost creativity?

Brainstorming is a creative problem-solving technique intended to boost the creativity and productivity of groups who adhere to the following rules:

- Generate as many ideas as possible with no concern for quality.
- Say every single idea that comes to mind.
- Build on ideas that are presented by others.
- Do not judge or criticize one another's ideas (this should only be done later at the idea selection stage).[91]

Following these rules does increase the productivity of groups.[92] However, when researchers have compared the output of brainstorming groups to nominal groups (groups where each individual works on their own before their output is pooled, with replications removed), it actually turns out that nominal groups are more productive.[93–95]

Paulus and colleagues[96] have summarized various reasons why this occurs. First, people may suffer from *evaluation apprehension*. Even though brainstorming is not supposed to be a critical activity, they may still be concerned about what others will think of their ideas and therefore restrict which ones they share. Second, there may be *social loafing*, where some people contribute fewer ideas on the basis that they can rely on others to do so instead. Third is *blocking*: only one person can speak at once so others may forget their ideas or not get a chance to voice them. Fourth, people may infer the average level of contribution by *social comparison* and try to match it in order to reduce conflict and 'fit in'. Finally, individuals may not pay attention to others' ideas so may be unable to respond to them.

To overcome these issues Paulus and colleagues make the following recommendations for optimal brainstorming:

- Introduce competition.
- Set high performance standards or provide role models.
- Encourage full participation.
- Provide time for idea incubation before sharing.

(continued)

- Prevent production blocking by keeping ideas concise or exchanging ideas in writing.
- Use facilitators to keep the group focused and to limit over-elaboration or social loafing.
- Use electronic brainstorming.
- Instruct individuals to memorize others' ideas, thus forcing them to pay attention.

The Benefit of Fostering Creativity

Before summarizing, it is worth reiterating just how important it is to foster creativity. We have already discussed how highly creative pupils can be wrongly identified as disruptive or having a learning difficulty.[19] Indeed, in the United Kingdom, there are children whose behaviour in the normal school system leads to them being described as 'feral' and yet they thrive in a more inclusive, creative environment.[67]

In the United States, Kim and Hull[97] aggregated the responses to four questions from the National Educational Longitudinal Study as measures of creativity:

'It is okay to ask challenging questions.'
'It is okay to solve problems using new ideas.'
'How often do you make up methods to solve science problem?'
'How often do you conduct own experiments in science?'

Amongst the 24,599 respondents, the researchers found that a one-unit increase in the aggregate score from these four questions was associated with a 62% increase in the rate of dropout. In comparison, participation in an academic honours society was associated with a 64% decrease in the likelihood of dropout. This suggests that being creative can increase the risk of school dropout. However, there were many other factors, such as being involved in cheerleading or participating in work-based learning experiences, which were also associated with an increased likelihood of dropout. Meanwhile, exhibiting perseverance, another personality characteristic linked with creativity, could moderate this risk. Like so many other psychological traits, there is no one-to-one link between creativity and educational outcomes. However, it is evident that some pupils who flounder in traditional classroom environments would benefit from being allowed to apply and express their creative abilities.

In the modern world, creativity is an essential skill for every individual, providing a competitive advantage in many fields. Scientists need it to inspire discoveries and it is vital for the success of entrepreneurs. As we discuss in Chapter 11, a major criticism of many East Asian education systems – often lauded for their examination excellence – is that they produce individuals who are academically competent but not creative. As Joseph Renzulli puts it:

> history tells us it has been the creative and productive people of the world . . . who have become recognized as 'truly gifted' individuals. History does not remember persons who merely scored well on IQ tests or those who learnt their lessons well.[98(p49)]

Summary

- Creative products are typically defined as those which are novel and of value. The creative process is often divided into four stages: preparation; incubation; illumination; and verification, and is thought to require a combination of divergent, convergent and critical thinking.
- Neuropsychological research has linked creative production with greater connectivity between distant brain areas, higher resting-state activity of the default mode network and reduced latent inhibition. This affirms the view of creative production as making original links between apparently unrelated concepts.
- There are numerous ways to measure creativity, including psychometric tests, reports of real-life creative outputs, and personality tests. It is important to be aware that some test scores will also reflect extraneous qualities such as motivation, attention span and vocabulary.
- Creativity appears to be partially heritable and may be emergenic, so that people with a certain combination of traits are much more likely to be creative. A pupil's socioeconomic status (and hence their home environment) may affect their propensity to creativity; however, differences in the school environment can also have a significant effect.
- The relationship between creativity and intelligence remains unclear and may depend on the chosen field of creative endeavour.

Nonetheless, there is evidence that amongst pupils with comparable IQs, those who are creative may have higher attainment.

- Instances of mental illness tend to be more common in highly creative individuals than in the general population. Those traits and cognitive characteristics linked with mental illness, such as reduced latent inhibition and excitability, may also confer a creative advantage.
- Some researchers are beginning to draw links between ADHD and creativity: for example, highly able students with ADHD have higher levels of creative production than their peers. However, it is by no means clear that all cases of ADHD are linked with greater creativity and further work is needed in this area.

Educational implications

- Kaufman and Beghetto's 4-C model reminds us that mini-c creativity can be exhibited in many subjects. Educators should not solely focus on developing artistic potential but should allow scope for creativity in all subjects.
- Creativity is associated with personality traits including unconventionality, impulsivity, perseverance and independence, the expression of which can be misinterpreted as misbehaviour in the classroom. It is important for parents and teachers to recognize possible links between these characteristics and creativity and to try to channel these behaviours towards constructive outcomes.
- Schools can support creativity by establishing psychologically safe and free environments where there are clear boundaries within which pupils can experiment, take initiatives and propose new ideas. Encouraging peer- and self-assessment and the use of comments rather than grades can also facilitate creative rather than convergent working.
- Knowledge is important for creativity, but must be taught in a manner conducive to divergent thinking and novel application. Interdisciplinary projects promote divergent thinking as pupils are encouraged to transfer and apply their knowledge across diverse subject areas. Teachers can also encourage divergent, convergent and critical thinking by posing open and ambiguous questions, encouraging self- and peer-evaluation and allowing incubation time.
- We know that creative pupils are at higher risk of disengagement and school dropout. Fortunately, all teachers, whether or not they consider themselves creative, can try to adopt the behaviours and teaching methods discussed in this chapter. Such changes are essential if we want our most creative young people to flourish.

References

1   Kim KH. Underachievement and creativity: Are gifted underachievers highly creative? *Creativity Research Journal*. 2008;20(2):234–242. doi:10.1080/10400410802060232.

2   Poincaré H, Halsted GB. *The Foundations of Science: Science and Hypothesis, The Value of Science, Science and Method*. New York: Science Press; 1913.

3   Rhodes M. An analysis of creativity. *Phi Delta Kappan*. 1961;42(7): 305–310.

4   McCrae RR. Creativity, divergent thinking, and openness to experience. *Journal of Personality and Social Psychology*. 1987;52(6):1258–1265. doi:10.1037/0022-3514.52.6.1258.

5   Kaufman JC, Beghetto RA. Beyond big and little: The four C model of creativity. *Review of General Psychology*. 2009;13(1):1.

6   Guilford JP. Creativity. *American Psychologist*. 1950;5(9):444–454. doi:10.1037/h0063487.

7   Guilford JP. The structure of intellect. *Psychological Bulletin*. 1956;53(4):267–293. doi:10.1037/h0040755.

8   Mednick S. The associative basis of the creative process. *Psychological Review*. 1962;69(3):220–232. doi:10.1037/h0048850.

9   Brophy DR. Understanding, measuring, and enhancing individual creative problem-solving efforts. *Creativity Research Journal*. 1998;11(2):123–150. doi:10.1207/s15326934crj1102_4.

10   Batey M, Furnham A. Creativity, intelligence, and personality: A critical review of the scattered literature. *Genetic, Social, and General Psychology Monographs*. 2006;132(4):355–429.

11   Torrance EP. *Torrance Tests of Creative Thinking: Norms Technical Manual*. Research ed. Princeton, NJ: Personnel Press; 1966.

12   Torrance EP. *Norms-Technical Manual: Torrance Tests of Creative Thinking*. Lexington, MA: Ginn & Co; 1974.

13   Kim KH. Can we trust creativity tests? A review of the Torrance Tests of Creative Thinking (TTCT). *Creativity Research Journal*. 2006;18(1): 3–14.

14   Cramond B, Matthews-Morgan J, Bandalos D, Zuo L. A report on the 40-year follow-up of the Torrance Tests of Creative Thinking: Alive and well in the new millennium. *Gifted Child Quarterly*. 2005;49(4):283 –291. doi:10.1177/001698620504900402.

15   Mackinnon DW. Personality and the realization of creative potential. *American Psychologist*. 1965;20(4):273–281. doi:10.1037/h0022403.

16   Domino G, Giuliani I. Creativity in three samples of photographers: A validation of the Adjective Check List Creativity Scale. *Creativity Research Journal*. 1997;10(2–3):193–200.

17   Chavez-Eakle RA, Lara M del C, Cruz-Fuentes C. Personality: A possible bridge between creativity and psychopathology? *Creativity Research Journal.* 2006;18(1):27–38. doi:10.1207/s15326934crj1801_4.

18   Feist GJ. A meta-analysis of personality in scientific and artistic creativity. *Personality and Social Psychology Review.* 1998;2(4):290–309.

19   Sadre M, Brock LJ. Systems in conflict: Labeling youth creativity as mental illness. *Journal of Family Psychotherapy.* 2008;19(4):358–378.

20   White HA, Shah P. Uninhibited imaginations: Creativity in adults with attention-deficit/hyperactivity disorder. *Personality and individual differences.* 2006;40(6):1121–1131.

21   White HA, Shah P. Creative style and achievement in adults with attention-deficit/hyperactivity disorder. *Personality and Individual Differences.* 2011;50(5):673–677. doi:10.1016/j.paid.2010.12.015.

22   Swartwood MO, Swartwood JN, Farrell J. Stimulant treatment of ADHD: Effects on creativity and flexibility in problem solving. *Creativity Research Journal.* 2003;15(4):417–419.

23   Torrance EP. A longitudinal examination of the fourth grade slump in creativity. *Gifted Child Quarterly.* 1968;12(4):195.

24   Runco MA. Fourth grade slump. In: Runco MA, Pritzker SR, eds. *Encyclopedia of Creativity.* Elsevier; 1999:743–744.

25   Begley TM, Boyd DP. Psychological characteristics associated with performence in entrepreneurial firms and smaller businesses. *Journal of Business Venturing.* 1987;2(1):79–93.

26   Scott CL. Teachers' biases toward creative children. *Creativity Research Journal.* 1999;12(4):321–328. doi:10.1207/s15326934crj1204_10.

27   Westby EL, Dawson V. Creativity: Asset or burden in the classroom? *Creativity Research Journal.* 1995;8(1):1–10.

28   Runco MA, Johnson DJ, Bear PK. Parents' and teachers' implicit theories of children's creativity. *Child Study Journal.* 1993;23(2):91–113.

29   Runco MA, Johnson DJ. Parents' and teachers' implicit theories of children's creativity: A cross-cultural perspective. *Creativity Research Journal.* 2002; 14(3–4):427–438. doi:10.1207/S15326934CRJ1434_12.

30   Simonton DK. *Greatness: Who Makes History and Why.* New York: Guilford Press; 1994.

31   Simonton DK. *Origins of Genius: Darwinian Perspectives on Creativity.* Oxford: Oxford University Press; 1999.

32   Albert RS. Family positions and the attainment of eminence: A study of special family positions and special family experiences. *Gifted Child Quarterly.* 1980;24(2):87–95. doi:10.1177/001698628002400208.

33   Dai DY, Tan X, Marathe D, Valtcheva A, Pruzek RM, *et al.* Influences of social and educational environments on creativity during adolescence: Does SES matter? *Creativity Research Journal.* 2012;24(2–3):191–199. doi:10.10 80/10400419.2012.677338.

34 Canter S. Personality traits in twins. In: Claridge G, Canter S, Hume WI, eds. *Personality Differences and Biological Variations*. New York: Pergamon Press; 1973:21–51.

35 Nichols RC. Heredity and Environment: Major Findings from Twin Studies of Ability, Personality and Interests. 1976. Available at: www.eric.ed.gov/ERICWebPortal/contentdelivery/servlet/ERICServlet?accno=ED131922. Accessed 2 December 2013.

36 Waller Jr. NG, Bouchard TJ, Lykken DT, Tellegen A, Blacker DM. Creativity, heritability, familiality: Which word does not belong? *Psychological Inquiry*. 1993;4(3):235–237. doi:10.2307/1448975.

37 Eysenck HJ. Creativity and personality: Suggestions for a theory. *Psychological Inquiry*. 1993;4(3):147–178. doi:10.1207/s15327965pli0403_1.

38 Richards R, Kinney DK, Lunde I, Benet M, Merzel AP. Creativity in manic-depressives, cyclothymes, their normal relatives, and control subjects. *Journal of Abnormal Psychology*. 1988;97(3):281–288.

39 Schuldberg D. Six subclinical spectrum traits in normal creativity. *Creativity Research Journal*. 2001;13(1):5–16.

40 Claridge G, Blakey S. Schizotypy and affective temperament: Relationships with divergent thinking and creativity styles. *Personality and Individual Differences*. 2009;46(8):820–826. doi:10.1016/j.paid.2009.01.015.

41 Carson SH, Peterson JB, Higgins DM. Decreased latent inhibition is associated with increased creative achievement in high-functioning individuals. *Journal of Personality and Social Psychology*. 2003;85(3):499.

42 Impey M, Mellanby J. Epileptic phenomena as a source of creativity: The work of Alfred Kubin (1877–1959). *Journal of Moral and Social Studies*. 1994;7:153–171.

43 Schachter SC. *Visions: Artists Living with Epilepsy*. 1st ed. New York: Academic Press; 2003.

44 Jausovec N. Differences in cognitive processes between gifted, intelligent, creative, and average individuals while solving complex problems: An EEG study. *Intelligence*. 2000;28(3):213–237.

45 Fink A, Grabner RH, Benedek M, *et al*. The creative brain: Investigation of brain activity during creative problem solving by means of EEG and FMRI. *Human Brain Mapping*. 2009;30(3):734–748. doi:10.1002/hbm.20538.

46 Razoumnikova OM. Functional organization of different brain areas during convergent and divergent thinking: An EEG investigation. *Cognitive Brain Research*. 2000;10(1–2):11–18.

47 Takeuchi H, Taki Y, Hashizume H, *et al*. The association between resting functional connectivity and creativity. *Cerebral Cortex*. 2012. doi:10.1093/cercor/bhr371.

48 Takeuchi H, Taki Y, Hashizume H, *et al*. Failing to deactivate: The association between brain activity during a working memory task and creativity. *NeuroImage*. 2011;55(2):681–687.

49   Dietrich A, Kanso R. A review of EEG, ERP, and neuroimaging studies of creativity and insight. *Psychological Bulletin.* 2010;136(5):822–848. doi:10.1037/a0019749.

50   Jung RE, Segall JM, Jeremy Bockholt H, *et al.* Neuroanatomy of creativity. *Human Brain Mapping.* 2010;31(3):398–409. doi:10.1002/hbm.20874.

51   Sternberg RJ, O'Hara LA. Creativity and intelligence. In: Sternberg RJ, ed. *Handbook of Creativity.* Cambridge: Cambridge University Press; 1999:251–272.

52   Kéri S. Solitary minds and social capital: Latent inhibition, general intellectual functions and social network size predict creative achievements. *Psychology of Aesthetics, Creativity, and the Arts.* 2011;5(3):215–221. doi:10.1037/a0022000.

53   Kim KH. Can only intelligent people be creative? *Journal of Secondary Gifted Education.* 2005;XVI(2):57–66.

54   Canter S. Some aspects of cognitive function in twins. In: Claridge G, Canter S, Hume WI. eds. *Personality Differences and Biological Variations.* New York: Pergamon Press; 1973.

55   Preckel F, Holling H, Wiese M. Relationship of intelligence and creativity in gifted and non-gifted students: An investigation of threshold theory. *Personality and Individual Differences.* 2006;40(1):159–170. doi:10.1016/j.paid.2005.06.022.

56   Sligh A, Conners F, Roskos-Ewoldsen B. Relation of creativity to fluid and crystallized intelligence. *Journal of Creative Behavior.* 2005;39(2):123–136.

57   Getzels JW, Jackson PW. *Creativity and intelligence: Explorations with gifted students.* New York: John Wiley & Sons; 1962.

58   Wallach MA, Kogan N. *Modes of Thinking in Young Children: A Study of the Creativity-intelligence Distinction.* New York: Holt, Rinehart and Winston; 1965.

59   Rindermann H, Neubauer AC. Processing speed, intelligence, creativity, and school performance: Testing of causal hypotheses using structural equation models. *Intelligence.* 2004;32(6):573–589.

60   Limiñana Gras R, Bordoy M, Juste Ballesta G, Corbalán Berná J. Creativity, intellectual abilities and response styles: Implications for academic performance in the secondary school. *Anales de psicologia.* 2010;26(2):212–219.

61   Palaniappan AK. Academic Achievement of Groups Formed Based on Creativity and Intelligence. Reviewed research papers selected for publication and presentation at the 13th International Conference on Thinking, Norrkoping, Sweden. Lingkoping University; 2007.

62   Ferrari A, Cachia R, Punie Y. Innovation and Creativity in Education and Training in the EU Member States: Fostering Creative Learning and Supporting Innovative Teaching. 2009;52374. *JRC Technical Note.*

63   Craft A. *Creativity in Schools: Tensions and Dilemmas.* London: Routledge; 2005.

64 Christensen CM, Horn MB, Johnson CW. *Disrupting Class: How Disruptive Innovation Will Change the Way the World Learns*. Maidenhead: McGraw-Hill Professional; 2008.

65 Rogers C. Toward a theory of creativity. In: Parnes SJ, Harding HF, eds. *A Source Book for Creative Thinking*. New York: Scribner; 1962: 64–72.

66 Bragg S, Manchester H. *Creativity, School Ethos and the Creative Partnerships programme*. The Open University; 2011. Available at: www .creativitycultureeducation.org/creativity-school-ethos-and-the-creative -partnerships-programme. Accessed 2 December 2013.

67 Amabile TM. Effects of external evaluation on artistic creativity. *Journal of Personality and Social Psychology*. 1979;37(2):221–233. doi:10.1037/ 0022-3514.37.2.221.

68 Amabile TM, Goldfarb P, Brackfield SC. Social influences on creativity: Evaluation, coaction, and surveillance. *Creativity Research Journal*. 1990;3(1):6–21. doi:10.1080/10400419009534330.

69 Amabile TM, Hennessey BA, Grossman BS. Social influences on creativity: The effects of contracted-for reward. *Journal of Personality and Social Psychology*. 1986;50(1):14.

70 Eisenberger R, Armeli S, Pretz J. Can the promise of reward increase creativity? *Journal of Personality and Social Psychology*. 1998;74(3):704–714. doi:10.1037/0022-3514.74.3.704.

71 Eisenberger R, Shanock L. Rewards, intrinsic motivation, and creativity: A case study of conceptual and methodological isolation. *Creativity Research Journal*. 2003;15(2–3):121–130.

72 Chen C, Kasof J, Himsel A, Dmitrieva J, Dong Q, *et al.* Effects of explicit instruction to "be creative" across domains and cultures. *Journal of Creative Behavior*. 2005;39(2):89–110.

73 O'Hara LA, Sternberg RJ. It doesn't hurt to ask: Effects of instructions to be creative, practical, or analytical on essay-writing performance and their interaction with students' thinking styles. *Creativity Research Journal*. 2001;13(2):197–210. doi:10.1207/S15326934CRJ1302_7.

74 Black P, Harrison C, Lee C, Marshall B, Wiliam D. Working inside the black box: Assessment for learning in the classroom. *Phi Delta Kappan*. 2004;86(1):8–21.

75 Craft A, Cremin T, Burnard P, Chappell K. Teacher stance in creative learning: A study of progression. *Thinking Skills and Creativity*. 2007;2(2): 136–147.

76 Gardner HE. *Creating Minds: An Anatomy of Creativity Seen Through the Lives of Freud, Einstein, Picasso, Stravinsky, Eliot, Graham, and Gandhi*. New York: Basic Books; 1993.

77 Kaufman S, Kaufman JC. Ten years to expertise, many more to greatness: An investigation of modern writers. *Journal of Creative Behavior*. 2007;41(2): 114–124.

78 Simonton DK. Creative productivity: A predictive and explanatory model of career trajectories and landmarks. *Psychological Review*. 1997;104(1):66.

79 Simonton DK. Formal education, eminence and dogmatism: The curvilinear relationship. *Journal of Creative Behavior*. 1983;17(3):149–162.

80 Weisberg RW. Creativity and knowledge: A challenge to theories. In: Sternberg RJ, ed. *Handbook of Creativity*. Cambridge: Cambridge University Press; 1999:226–250.

81 Sawyer RK. *Explaining Creativity: The Science of Human Innovation*. Oxford: Oxford University Press; 2006.

82 Dacey JS. *Fundamentals of Creative Thinking*. Lexington, MA; Lexington Books; 1989.

83 Halpin G, Goldenberg R, Halpin G. Are creative teachers more humanistic in their pupil control ideologies? *Journal of Creative Behavior*. 1973;7(4):282–286. doi:10.1002/j.2162-6057.1973.tb01099.x.

84 Craft A, Jeffrey B. Creativity and performativity in teaching and learning: Tensions, dilemmas, constraints, accommodations and synthesis. *British Educational Research Journal*. 2008;34(5):577–584. doi:10.1080/01411920802223842.

85 Torrance EP. Nurture of creative talents. *Theory into Practice*. 1966;5(4):167–173.

86 Longo C. Fostering creativity or teaching to the test? Implications of state testing on the delivery of science instruction. *The Clearing House*. 2010;83(2):54–57. doi:10.1080/00098650903505399.

87 Kind PM, Kind V. Creativity in science education: Perspectives and challenges for developing school science. *Studies in Science Education*. 2007;43:1–37. doi:10.1080/03057260708560225.

88 Osborn AF. *Applied Imagination*. Oxford: Scribner's; 1953.

89 Bono ED. *Six Thinking Hats*. New York: Little, Brown; 1985.

90 Craft A. *Creativity and Early Years Education: A Lifewide Foundation*. London: Continuum International Publishing Group; 2002.

91 Osborn AF. *Applied imagination: Principles and Procedures of Creative Problem Solving*. 3rd rev. ed. New York: Charles Scribner's Sons; 1963.

92 Parnes SJ, Meadow A. Effects of "brainstorming" instructions on creative problem solving by trained and untrained subjects. *Journal of Educational Psychology*. 1959;50(4):171.

93 Taylor DW, Berry PC, Block CH. Does group participation when using brainstorming facilitate or inhibit creative thinking? *Administrative Science Quarterly*. 1958;3:23–47.

94 Diehl M, Stroebe W. Productivity loss in brainstorming groups: Toward the solution of a riddle. *Journal of Personality and Social Psychology*. 1987;53(3):497.

95 Lamm H, Trommsdorff G. Group versus individual performance on tasks requiring ideational proficiency (brainstorming): A review. *European Journal of Social Psychology*. 1973;3(4):361–388.

96 Paulus PB, Putman VL, Dugosh KL, Dzindolet MT, Coskun H. Social and cognitive influences in group brainstorming: Predicting production gains and losses. *European Review of Social Psychology.* 2002;12(1):299–325.

97 Kim KH, Hull MF. Creative personality and anticreative environment for high school dropouts. *Creativity Research Journal.* 2012;24(2–3):169–176. doi:10.1080/10400419.2012.677318.

98 Renzulli JS. Symposion.pdf. *Wege Zur Begabungsforgerung.* Vienna; 2004. Available at: www.popperschule.at/schule/symposion/Symposion.pdf#page =72. Accessed 11 January 2012.

Chapter 10

Education Policy
How Evidence Based Is It?

1. By the age of 3, a child living in poverty will be how many months behind a child from a higher-income background in the development of their vocabulary?
   a. 2 months
   b. 5 months
   c. 12 months

2. Roughly what is the percentage point difference in the proportion of British-born Chinese pupils getting five A*–C grades at GCSE, including English and maths, compared to the proportion of British-born black Caribbean pupils achieving this benchmark?
   a. 10 percentage points
   b. 20 percentage points
   c. 30 percentage points

3. How much more likely is a young person from one of the 20% most advantaged geographical areas of England to go to university than a young person from the 20% most disadvantaged areas?
   a. Twice as likely
   b. Three times as likely
   c. Four times as likely

Education and Learning: An Evidence-Based Approach, First Edition. Jane Mellanby and Katy Theobald.
© 2014 John Wiley & Sons, Ltd. Published 2014 by John Wiley & Sons, Ltd.

Ministers are constantly declaring new education policies: reforms to the examination system, changes to the curriculum, new types of school. They perceive a need for reform because every year too many young people leave education without the basic skills necessary to become productive members of society. In 2011, over 40% of 16-year-olds in England did not manage to get a C grade or above in five GCSEs including English and mathematics:[1] basic qualifications that are considered a prerequisite for entry into many post-16 courses and most jobs. Furthermore, there are large variations between pupils from different backgrounds. Whereas 74% of Indian pupils educated in Britain achieved five A*–C grades including English and mathematics, only 49% of black Caribbean pupils did so (note that whenever we discuss ethnic groups in this chapter, this refers to the ethnic origin of British pupils who live and are educated in Britain). Most concerning was that only 35% of pupils in receipt of free school meals (FSM, an indicator of low income) managed to achieve these benchmark grades. We need reform to raise and equalize the attainment of these groups.

We also need our education system to improve because, as we discuss in Chapter 11, our young people are increasingly competing in a global marketplace. Consequently, our apprentices and graduates need skills and knowledge comparable to that of students educated at the best institutions in the world.

Politicians like to describe their policies as evidence based, implying that they are supported by solid scientific evidence. In this chapter, we evaluate that claim by looking at a range of policies, including Sure Start, free schools, the discontinuation of Aimhigher and increases in university tuition fees. For each policy we present the evidence that supports or challenges educational change. We take a particular interest in the impact of educational policies on social inequality and the attainment of ethnic minority pupils; sex differences in attainment are addressed in Chapter 6.

Inequalities in the Early Years

Variations in educational outcomes do not emerge only when pupils take their GCSEs: social and ethnic differences in cognitive development are evident before children even begin school. We discuss some of these differences in Chapters 3 and 4, where we present studies highlighting early socioeconomic gaps in children's reading and language skills and ways to remediate them. Data from the Millennium Cohort Study give a broader perspective on inequalities amongst English children. This longitudinal project has tracked a group of over 15,000 children since their birth in the year 2000. At 3 years old the participants were given a test of naming vocabulary from the British Ability Scales (BAS) along with the Bracken School Readiness Composite (BSRC). The scores of children whose parents were highly educated (with a degree qualification or above) were 10 months ahead on the BAS and 12 months ahead on the BSRC compared to those whose parents had no qualifications. Meanwhile, children whose parental incomes were below the poverty line scored five months behind those not living in poverty on the BAS and 10 months behind on the BSRC. In terms of ethnicity, white children scored highest, while Bangladeshi and Pakistani children typically had more delayed development.[2] However, some ethnicity differences may arise if ethnic minority children do not have English as a first language and it is important to note that given the right educational environment, children with English as an additional language can catch up with, or even overtake, their peers. What these data show, though, is just how early some differences in cognitive development emerge.

These differences go on to affect the performance of children in school. For example, every child in England now has a Foundation Stage Profile completed by their teacher, which describes their mathematical, physical, personal, social and emotional development, their communication, language and literacy skills and their knowledge and understanding of the world. Eight thousand, six hundred and seventy-one (8,671) children from the Millennium Cohort Study were matched to their profiles, which revealed that a doubling of parental income was associated with children being a month ahead on each Foundation Stage Profile indicator. Similarly, where children's parents were educated to degree level or higher, they scored six months ahead of those whose parents did not have at least five GCSEs or equivalent. Controlling for parental income and education, children living in social housing also had lower scores.[3]

Goodman and Gregg[4] reviewed a range of older longitudinal studies with similar findings. They also examined the factors that contribute to the differing cognitive outcomes of children from high- and low-income families, and Figures 10.1 and 10.2 illustrate the results. They indicate that at age 3 most of the gap is attributable to differences in family background and home environment, but by age 5, when the child has just started school, prior ability already explains more than half the variation. This makes a strong case for early intervention, trying to address any differences in the child's environment before big gaps in cognitive development can emerge. The home learning environment (see Box 10.1) is of particular interest to researchers looking for targets for intervention,

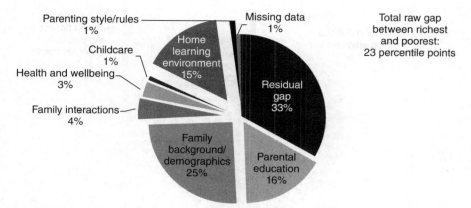

Figure 10.1   Explaining the gap between the poorest and the richest at age 3: decomposition analysis. *Source*: Poorer children's educational attainment: How important are attitudes and behaviour? Goodman A, Gregg, P, Eds. Joseph Rowntree Foundation; 2010. © Institute for Fiscal Studies 2010. Reproduced by permission of the Joseph Rowntree Foundation.

because it has a significant independent effect on cognitive development even after controlling for parental education and income.[5,6] In other words, it is one factor which explains why certain children from low-income families exhibit more advanced cognitive development than others.

Intervention in the early years

It is important to tackle disadvantage early on, because socioeconomic differences in attainment at secondary school have their roots in a much earlier phase of education: Key Stage 2 attainment (levels at the end of primary school) can predict 79% of the variation in Key Stage 3 attainment (13–14-year-olds at the end of Year 9).[7] All of the political parties recognize this, and it motivated the Labour government to set up Sure Start. The programme was established in 1998 with the service provision outlined as follows:

(1)   outreach and home visiting;
(2)   support for families and parents;
(3)   support for good quality play, learning and childcare experiences for children;

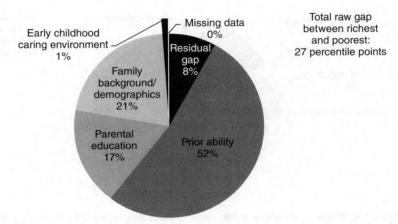

Notes: The relative contributions of each set of factors are calculated by multiplying the difference in the proportions of rich and poor with each characteristic by the coefficient estimates from a regression model of cognitive outcomes, which includes all explanatory characteristics simultaneously. For more details, see Dearden *et al.* (2010).

Figure 10.2   Explaining the gap between the poorest and richest at age 5: decomposition analysis. *Source*: Poorer children's educational attainment: How important are attitudes and behaviour? Goodman A, Gregg, P, Eds. Joseph Rowntree Foundation; 2010. © Institute for Fiscal Studies 2010. Reproduced by permission of the Joseph Rowntree Foundation.

(4)   primary and community health care and advice about child health and development and family health; and

(5)   support for people with special needs.[8]

The idea of this programme was to tackle socioeconomic attainment gaps through early intervention, but initial evaluations were not very positive. So if the evidence was there, what went wrong? Well, the service specification was kept loose to allow adaptation to local needs, but this led to inconsistency, with some very good models of provision and others that were ineffective. Furthermore, the service provision was kept open to all to avoid any stigma being associated with using it, but it was actually the more proactive (and typically more advantaged) parents who made most use of the new resources on offer. The intervention did not always reach those whom it was designed to help.[9]

Frustratingly, this early disappointment might have been avoided. The early Sure Start proposals cited evidence from successful intervention programmes in the United States, such as the Perry Pre-School Program and Early Head Start.[10] Academics had already warned that not all of the

Box 10.1   The home learning environment

The home learning environment is an important factor in explaining the cognitive development of children. The questions used in the Millennium Cohort Study to measure home learning environment were:

Age 3

- How often do you read to your child?
- How often do you take your child to the library?
- How often do you help your child to learn the ABCs or the alphabet?
- How often do you teach your child numbers or counting?
- How often do you teach your child songs, poems or nursery rhymes?
- How often does your child paint or draw at home?

Age 5

- How often do you read to your child?
- How often do you tell stories to your child not from a book?
- How often do you play music, listen to music, sing songs or nursery rhymes, dance or do other musical activities with your child?
- How often do you draw, paint or make things with your child?
- How often do you play sports or physically active games outdoors or indoors with your child?
- How often do you play with toys or indoor games with your child?
- How often do you take your child to the park or to an outdoor playground?[4(p22)]

programmes performed equally well. The Perry Pre-School Program and Chicago Child–Parent Center Program were examples of more successful interventions, producing statistically significant improvements in the rates of literacy, grade retention, high-school completion, high-school dropout, juvenile arrests and even adult earnings of the participants.[11,12] However, these programmes followed very clearly specified models of service provision. In contrast, Head Start was a more varied and rather less expensive initiative, which offered holistic services targeted at low-income families who could not afford private pre-kindergarten programmes. Just like Sure Start, Head Start centres offered early education, access to health-care and social services for children and families. The evidence for their effectiveness was also much weaker; service provision was inconsistent and the impact was variable and often short-lived.[13]

Academics in the United Kingdom were aware that US programmes differed in their design and effectiveness, but their concerns were overlooked when Sure Start was first planned. Only after early negative evaluations was the Sure Start programme revised and developed into Sure Start Children's Centres, which offered more targeted and clearly specified services. Research suggests that these centres are more effective. Melhuish and colleagues[14] identified 5883 children aged 3 in Sure Start areas and then selected a sample of data from 1879 children from the Millennium Cohort Study who lived in similarly deprived areas but had not participated in Sure Start. Controlling for background factors, they found that children who had been involved in Sure Start had better social development, exhibiting more positive social behaviour (p = 0.001), and greater independence (p < 0.001), and that this was mediated by improvements in parenting and the home learning environment. Later research following the same comparative design[15] has shown that when children are 7 years old, the mothers of those who attended Sure Start Children's Centres provide a better home learning environment (p < 0.001) and engage in less harsh discipline (p < 0.001) than if they only participated in the Millennium Cohort Study.

One disappointment is that many evaluations do not find large differences in the attainment of children who attend Sure Start versus control groups. Melhuish and colleagues suggest that one reason for the absence of a significant effect could be that all of the children would have been eligible for free part-time pre-school provision, even if they did not participate in Sure Start. Attending such pre-schools has in itself been associated with higher educational attainment. Melhuish and colleagues also suggest that there is scope for further improvements in Sure Start provision, particularly in terms of boosting children's language capabilities. It seems, then, that Sure Start Children's Centres need to continue adapting and improving if they are to have a greater impact in the future.

Unequal Outcomes in Primary Education

Early gaps in cognitive development tend to widen during primary school. Figure 10.3 shows the difference in the proportion of pupils who have

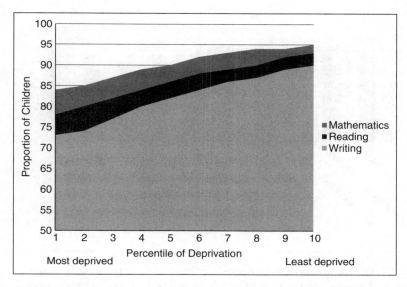

Figure 10.3 The proportion of children achieving Level 2 at Key Stage 1 according to percentile of deprivation.[16] *Data source*: National Pupil Database.

achieved Level 2 in Key Stage 1 tests according to the level of deprivation in their local area. You can see, for example, that only 73% of pupils from the most deprived 10% of areas achieved Level 2 in writing. In contrast, 90% of pupils from the least deprived areas achieved this level. Figure 10.4 illustrates similar ethnic and social inequalities in Key Stage 2 attainment.

Steve Strand[18] analysed the attainment of 5,160 primary school pupils in London in order to understand how ethnicity, gender and FSM (Free School Meals) status related to changes in educational attainment during Key Stage 1. Looking at these variables separately, the analysis showed that pupils in receipt of FSM made lower than expected progress, while those with English as an additional language made greater than expected progress during Reception, Year 1 and Year 2. However, more complicated was the interaction between different characteristics. In comparison to average white British children, Caribbean and other black boys and Caribbean pupils with high baseline attainment made lower than expected progress during Key Stage 1. English and Welsh children who were entitled to FSM also made below average progress. There was also significant variation between schools in the progress pupils made. This was one of the first studies to highlight differences between headline attainment figures and the performance of smaller groups and to signal the

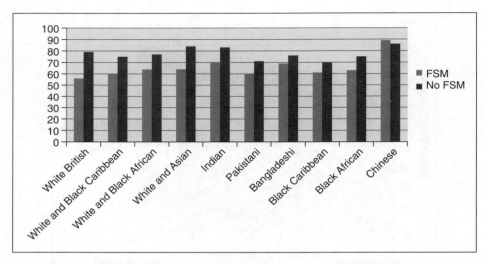

Figure 10.4 The proportion of pupils achieving Level 4 in Key Stage 2 English and maths, divided by FSM status and ethnicity.[17] *Data source*: Department for Education.

importance of analysing the attainment of pupils separately by gender, FSM status and, particularly, ethnic subgroups.

Clearly we face a problem, because if children leave primary school with disparities in their attainment then this is likely to feed through into their secondary attainment. This is one reason why the government introduced phonics testing. As we discuss in Chapter 4, early phonological awareness is a strong predictor of later reading abilities and it is particularly important if children are being taught to read using the synthetic phonics method, as the Department for Education now recommends. Early phonics testing is supposed to identify children who have poor phonological skills and who are therefore at risk of falling behind with their reading. They are then supposed to receive additional support before they fall behind and start to think they are 'bad at reading'. The tests use nonsense words to avoid overestimating the skills of children who have memorized the appearance and sound of words, rather than understanding their phonological structure. Theoretically, then, this type of early testing is to be welcomed. The concern, of course, is that the test will become just another way to label underperforming schools. We will have to see whether the government leaves national phonics screening solely as a tool for identifying pupils in need of reading support. We will also have to see whether schools and teachers use this information effectively to target interventions towards those pupils who need it.

Do smaller class sizes help raise attainment?

Practices such as phonics screening do rely on the feasibility of offering individual support to pupils. A pedagogical emphasis on personalized teaching, rather than the whole class learning at one pace, has led to a general assumption in the West that smaller classes are better. There is a notable difference in average class sizes in Scotland and England. In England, there has been a cap of 30 pupils in 4–7-year-olds' classes since 1998, but no limit beyond these early years. In Scotland, however, the average primary class size (up to 11 years) in 2011 was 23 pupils and ongoing efforts are being made to keep class sizes down. So should parents in England whose children are in classes of 30 or more be concerned about the possible impact on their offspring's attainment?

As is often the case, we do not actually have clear evidence for or against the impact of class size on educational outcomes. There are many reasons for this: firstly, to establish that class size rather than any other factor is affecting attainment, researchers have to conduct experimental or longitudinal studies, both of which are expensive and take a long time to run. These studies also need to compare teachers and classes that are as closely matched as possible, to avoid extraneous factors having an effect. Secondly, many researchers argue that one not only has to consider whether reducing class sizes can help raise attainment, but also how this compares to other potential interventions in terms of impact and cost. Schools spend about 70% of their budget on staff and an additional teacher's salary (about £24,000 a year for a newly qualified teacher) could equally be spent equipping a classroom with new technology or perhaps on employing two teaching assistants.

A major research project investigating the impact of class size and pupil:adult ratios on educational outcomes in England was conducted by academics at the Institute of Education. They followed over 10,000 pupils who started primary school in 1996 or 1997, entering classes ranging in size from under 20 pupils to over 30 pupils. The magnitude of the sample meant that the researchers could control for factors such as SES (socioeconomic status) and gender and focus on the impact of class size on educational outcomes. The researchers found that pupils in smaller Reception classes (with fewer than 20 pupils) had higher mathematics and literacy scores than those in larger classes (over 30 pupils), with the lowest-attaining pupils showing the greatest difference for literacy.

However, the benefits of such small class sizes were only retained through to Year 1 for literacy, not numeracy, and only if the pupils stayed in small classes. Differences in average attainment according to class size were no longer evident by the time pupils reached Year 3.[19]

Although the impact of class size on attainment may not be sustained beyond the early years, further data from the same project identify qualitative differences in the educational experience of pupils in large and small classes. Blatchford and colleagues[20] conducted systematic classroom observations in 27 primary schools and 22 secondary schools. They recorded rates of different types of pupil–teacher interaction, pupil–pupil interaction and independent activity. Pupils in larger classes were found to interact with the teacher less frequently and to be the focus of individual attention less frequently. Low-attaining pupils in particular exhibited more off-task behaviours in larger primary and secondary classes.

Even if these differences do not significantly affect attainment, they may affect pupils' progress in other ways. For example, if pupils in smaller classes have a more positive experience they may have better attitudes towards school and therefore stay in education for longer. There is some evidence to suggest that this occurs, but the size of the effect is small. Dustmann and colleagues[21] used data from nearly 4,000 English and Welsh participants in the longitudinal NCDS study, which began when they were born in 1958, to show that an increase in the ratio of teachers to pupils in a school very marginally increases (by about two percentage points) the likelihood of pupils staying on. Meanwhile, in a famous US study – the STAR project – researchers found that for pupils in receipt of free school lunches, there was an 18 percentage point difference in the proportion that graduated between those who had spent all their early years in a class of 13–17 pupils (88.2% graduated) and those who had spent four years in a class of 22–25 pupils (70.2% graduated); a significant difference ($p < 0.001$).[22]

A consistent positive effect of class size on attainment has not been demonstrated across multiple studies. Where a positive effect is identified, the effect size is typically small – an average of 0.13 compared to a typical effect size of about 0.40 for other potential educational interventions.[23] One reason for this may be that teachers do not adapt their teaching methods to smaller classes,[24,25] and therefore the potential benefits in terms of individualized and interactive teaching are not actually realized. Consequently, many researchers would argue that for the same investment, other interventions will offer greater academic returns. It is important to note, however, that a number of studies find a larger positive impact on pupils from lower-income or ethnic minority backgrounds, or with lower initial attainment.[19,22,26,27] Therefore, while reductions in class size may not be the most efficient way to raise average attainment in all schools, it may be worthwhile in schools where many pupils face additional challenges or disadvantage.

Attainment in Secondary School

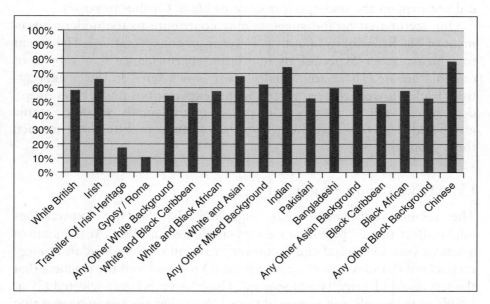

Figure 10.5 Ethnicity differences in the percentage of pupils who achieve five A*–C at GCSE including English and maths. *Data source*: Department for Education.

There are socioeconomic, ethnic and gender differences in attainment throughout secondary school and roughly half of this variation can be explained by prior attainment.[28] However, there is an interesting interaction between ethnicity and SES. While the average raw scores of white British pupils are higher than those of many ethnic minorities, once one controls for factors such as family income and education, Indian and Bangladeshi pupils actually outperform white British pupils from similar backgrounds.[7]

This raises an interesting question: which factors lead some pupils with similar background characteristics to perform better than others, or lead pupils of certain ethnicities to outperform others? Analysing data from the LSYPE (Longitudinal Study of Young People in England, see Chapter 8), Steve Strand showed that 21% of variation in attainment at the end of Year 9 was not explained by prior attainment in Year 6. Strand used the statistical technique of multiple regression to show that factors such as level of maternal education, social class, parents' educational aspirations for their children, pupils' future educational aspirations and the level of deprivation in their schools all explained some of the variation in attainment. However, accounting for a full set of background factors still did not explain the underperformance of black Caribbean pupils.[7]

One factor that Strand suggests may contribute to the underachievement of black Caribbean pupils is lower teacher expectations. The extent to which teacher expectations may affect performance is a subject of ongoing debate. There are actually many issues here: do lower expectations lead to lower achievement, do higher expectations raise achievement, do teachers vary their expectations according to pupils' social or ethnic group and could this therefore help explain attainment differences between these groups?

Expectations and performance

The seminal experiment that suggested that teacher expectations might affect pupils' performance was conducted in 1968. At the start of a school year Rosenthal and Jacobson[29] gave all the pupils in an elementary school (Grades 1 to 6) a non-verbal IQ test and told the teachers that the test could identify 'late bloomers'. They then randomly selected about a fifth of the pupils and informed the teachers that the test indicated that these children were likely to show a sudden increase in intellect over the next year. Over the year the pupils in this experimental group gained on average about 12 IQ points, which might seem to suggest that raising teacher expectations had some effect. However, as critics have noted,[30] the control group actually gained 8 IQ points, leaving only a 4-point difference. Furthermore, only first- and second-grade pupils in the experimental group made significant IQ gains compared to their peers. At best, then, the study indicated that manipulating teacher expectations could affect their interactions with pupils, and therefore pupils' intellectual development, if the pupils were in the first few years of education and if the teachers' expectations were manipulated early in the year.

Jussim and Harber[30] have reviewed many studies that have followed this seminal work and suggest that, in general, inaccurate teacher perceptions have only a small effect on pupil attainment and that the impact of positive expectancy effects are better proven than the impact of negative expectancy effects. In other words, there is more evidence of increases in performance in response to unusually high expectations than decrements in performance in response to unusually low expectations. However, it is important to note that some studies find a particularly strong impact on certain groups such as ethnic minority pupils or those who have lower attainment. Jussim and colleagues[31] used maths grades from elementary school pupils to explore whether teachers' expectations predicted future attainment. They took pupils' fifth-grade maths results as baseline and looked at how these and teachers' reported perception of performance, talent and effort predicted pupils' sixth- and seventh-grade results. Amongst a predominantly white population, teacher expectations were more predictive of African American ($n = 72$) than white pupils' ($n = 1536$) grades ($p < 0.01$). In a smaller subsample (about 1000 pupils) from the same population, they also found that teacher expectations predicted the grades of lower-SES pupils more accurately than those of middle-class pupils ($p < 0.01$). Interestingly, the greater degree to which teacher expectation predicted female pupils' grades did not quite reach significance ($p < 0.08$, $n = 1765$). In a further paper using the same data source the researchers also showed that teachers' expectations were more predictive of low- than high-achievers' grades ($p < 0.01$). Specifically, only over-estimations of performance were predictive for high achievers whereas both over- and under-estimations predicted low achievers' grades.[32]

In the United Kingdom, stereotypes are sometimes perpetuated about the performance of different groups. On average, lower-SES pupils and those from black Caribbean backgrounds perform worse on standardized tests and so may be stereotyped as 'lower ability'. Meanwhile, Indian and Chinese pupils often perform above average and may be stereotyped as 'higher ability'. Of course, based on actual attainment one can accurately expect that *on average* pupils from the former groups will have lower attainment. However, this does not mean that every pupil will perform poorly and there is concern that teachers will automatically underestimate the potential of their pupils on the basis of such ethnicity or SES, leading their pupils to underachieve.

Much research into this area focuses on low expectations for black Caribbean pupils. However, it is often based on qualitative reports, either from pupils claiming that their teachers underestimate their ability, or from teachers claiming that, for various reasons, many black Caribbean pupils will not perform well academically (e.g. Haynes et al.;[33] Tikly et al.[34]). The issue with this type of report is that it doesn't demonstrate causality. As black Caribbean pupils may start secondary school with below average attainment, their teachers may feel they are accurately anticipating these pupils' future performance, rather than perpetuating low expectations. Conversely, some pupils admit that 'Some of them [black Caribbean pupils] are saying there's no point trying because they are not going to get anywhere'[34(p59)] and in that situation a somewhat defeatist attitude from teachers may be a reaction to the same attitude amongst pupils.

There are a few studies that try to look at more measurable aspects of expectation to see whether teachers are underestimating the ability of certain groups of pupils. Burgess and Greaves[35] combined data from the National Pupil Database (NPD) and Pupil Level Annual School Census (PLASC) to compare the Key Stage 2 Levels awarded to over 2 million 11-year-old pupils by their teachers via internal assessment to those they attained in externally marked standardized tests (SATs). After controlling for SES, school characteristics and school fixed effects (unidentified variations between schools), they found that black Caribbean and black African pupils were significantly more likely to have a teacher-assessed level in English below their standardized test level, while Chinese, Indian and white Asian pupils were significantly more likely to have a teacher-assessed level that exceeded their SAT score. They found similar results for maths and science. This indicates that teachers may be influenced by stereotypes when they grade pupils; however, it is worth noting that the bias was reduced when the researchers accounted for the SAT scores attained by pupils of that ethnicity who were taught by the teacher the previous year. In other words, part of the reason for over- and underestimation was that teachers were generalizing from previous experience with pupils from the same ethnic group.

NPD and PLASC data for secondary pupils have been used to make similar comparisons between teacher scores and standardized marks for Year 9s (age 13–14). This study did not find significant differences according to ethnicity, but the researchers also used wider ethnic categories such as Asian and black. As Burgess and Greaves' research shows, such broad categories may mask within-category differences, for example between Pakistani, Bangladeshi and Indian pupils. Steve Strand employed finer-grained distinctions when he used data from the LSYPE to show that, controlling for Key Stage 2 attainment, black Caribbean pupils were only two-thirds as likely as white pupils to be entered for a higher tier in Key Stage 3 mathematics and science tests. Indian pupils, meanwhile, were 1.45 times as likely to be entered for higher-tier mathematics tests as white British pupils.[7] This would lend support to the idea that the potential of some pupils is persistently over- or under-estimated depending on their ethnicity.

Various initiatives have sought to tackle low teacher expectations. In the early years of the Labour government the Excellence in Cities programme was created to raise expectation and standards in inner city schools. Then in the year 2000 academies were introduced – schools that receive funding directly from central government and are free from local authority control. Initially, academies replaced only 'failing' schools, those where a very low proportion of pupils, perhaps 30% or less, were achieving five A*–C grades at GCSE. The idea was that in a new school, with new staff, expectations and standards could be raised. All schools are now allowed to apply to convert to academy status, although the government can still force 'failing' schools to make the change.[36]

Academies were inspired in part by the American model of charter schools. These are privately sponsored state schools, intended to provide a high-quality education in areas where existing schools are delivering poor results. More recently charter schools have returned to the spotlight with the introduction of free schools by the coalition government. Free schools and academies are actually very similar, except that free schools are new schools set up in response to parental demand whereas academies are conversions of existing schools. So what evidence is there to support this model, and is it working in England?

Charter schools, free schools and academies

The example of charter schools in New Orleans and New York – which have transformed the life chances of poorer children in those cities – have been critical in developing free-school policy.
            Secretary of State for Education, Michael Gove[37]

Charter schools are run as not-for-profit organizations; they are subject to less legislation than state schools regarding staffing, budgeting and the curriculum, but they are still closely monitored for performance and risk closure if they do not provide a sufficient quality of education. According to Michael Gove, such additional freedoms are supposed to act as 'an unstoppable driver of success'.[38]

In fact, research into the effects of attending a charter school has produced highly variable results. There are plenty of studies reporting overall positive and overall negative effects, and others that find improvements in mathematics but not reading or vice versa.[39-43] Part of the difficulty is that charter schools do not operate according to a single model and so their success varies greatly.

One recent study compared middle-school pupils who entered a lottery for charter-school places and were or were not assigned one. It is important that all of the pupils had entered the lottery, because pupils who apply to attend charter schools may well differ from the wider population. For example, their parents might be more involved in their education, which can also affect attainment. Sampling only pupils who have applied to charter schools helps control for these background factors and makes it more likely that any differences in the attainment of charter-school pupils compared to the control group can actually be attributed to their attendance at that school. The researchers looked at all the pupils' grades two years on and found that *overall* there was no statistically significant effect of attending a charter school rather than a state school. However, when they broke down the analysis to the individual school level, they found that 11 schools had a positive effect on students' reading grades (none statistically significant) and 17 a negative effect (four effects were statistically significant). For mathematics, 10 had a positive effect (three statistically significant) and 18 had no effect or a negative effect (7 statistically significant).[43] This shows that some charter schools are effective at improving achievement, just not all of them.

Investigating these differences further, Angrist and colleagues[44] evaluated urban and non-urban charter schools (17 middle and 6 high schools) against state schools in the Massachusetts area. In general, they observed that charter schools had longer school days, higher spend per pupil, were more likely to have parents and pupils sign a contract agreeing to certain behaviours and were more likely to have a formal reward system for good behaviour or work. Comparing the maths and English performance of pupils who had or had not been successful in the charter-school lottery, they found that urban pupils benefited from attending charter schools, showing significant improvements in attainment compared to applicants who ended up in a state school. However, in non-urban areas where overall attainment was higher, charter-school pupils did not show gains and sometimes had worse performance than their state-school counterparts. Broadening out the sample to investigate which qualities led some charter schools to be particularly effective, they found that oversubscribed schools running a lottery and those following a No Excuses approach were particularly successful in raising attainment, while per-pupil spend and length of school day appeared to have no significant impact. Notably, though, there was little evidence that a No Excuses approach – strict discipline, student contracts, long school days and Saturday school – was effective in non-urban areas since data were only available from one non-urban school operating this approach, and significant attainment gains were not evident. Hence the authors suggested that this model might be particularly effective for lower-attaining, non-white, low-income urban pupils. However, No Excuses schools focus on mathematics and English, which were the scores used to measure performance in this paper. More evidence is needed about the strengths or weaknesses of charter schools in other academic and non-academic areas.

In Sweden, free schools have been introduced with the intention of raising standards across the school system. Unlike American charter schools, Swedish free schools, or independent schools as they are also known, receive a certain amount of money per student and are allowed to make a profit if feasible. Unsurprisingly, this has been controversial, partly because the schools can profit from public funds but also because they do not have to offer the same facilities or range of educational programmes as municipal schools and because there have been accusations of grade inflation being undertaken by teachers in free schools.[45]

Despite these criticisms, though, there is evidence that Swedish free schools have been effective in improving overall educational standards. A number of studies have looked at how the grades of state-school students change when free schools open in an area. Even though the researchers themselves do not seem overeager to identify positive results, they repeatedly find positive correlations between the number of free schools in an area and the test scores and grades of students at state schools.[46,47] Admittedly, some of this increase could arise if free-school teachers were engaging in grade inflation (see above), but there is little evidence to indicate that introducing free schools negatively affects achievement.

One cause for concern, however, is whether the benefits from introducing free schools are evenly spread across the population. Some Swedish research indicates that lower-SES pupils benefit less from the introduction of free schools (in terms of attainment gains) than their more advantaged peers.[47,48] Concerns have also been raised that increased school choice reinforces the effects of existing geographical divisions between social and ethnic groups, an issue also highlighted by American researchers. For example, a study of charter schools in North Carolina found that they were more ethnically segregated than public (state) schools, although this was mainly attributed to location and preferences for certain educational programmes on offer.

State-school admissions in the United Kingdom depend on one's home location, so some parents will move house to get their children into specific schools. Such parental choice means that our schools are more segregated than those in most OECD countries[49] and it may constrain the extent to which academy conversions and new free schools can have a sustained impact on attainment gaps. The first academies specifically replaced 'failing' state schools, so typically served highly disadvantaged areas. However, using attainment and FSM statistics from 35 academies set up between 2002 and 2006, Steven Gorard[50] has argued that in those academies where pupils' GCSE performance increased, this was often accompanied by a decrease in the proportion of pupils at the school who received FSM. In other words, the gains in performance could have partly or wholly reflected a shift to a more advantaged pupil base.

Machin and Vernoit[51] have also investigated whether improvements in school performance following academy conversion might actually reflect a change in the pupils being admitted. They looked at the KS2 scores of pupils from the same year group who either joined schools just before they converted to academy status between 2001/02 and 2008/09 or who joined schools that converted to academies after this date. They found that the KS2 scores of incoming pupils significantly increased after schools converted to academies, indicating that they attracted a higher-attaining pupil base. Meanwhile, the average attainment of pupils joining neighbouring schools dropped significantly after the conversion. However, controlling for changes in KS2 scores, the proportion of pupils gaining five A*–C grades including English and maths still rose significantly in the academies that converted between 2001/02 and 2006/07. Furthermore, schools neighbouring the early convertors also showed an increase in KS4 results. In contrast, the academies that converted after 2006/07 did not produce a significant increase in KS4 results. This would suggest that introducing a new, competing school can drive up academic standards in some local areas, but not in every case.

Overall there is evidence to indicate that introducing more autonomous schools such as free schools or academies can help to raise educational standards in disadvantaged areas where pupils have below average attainment. However, there is less evidence to suggest that these positive outcomes transfer across contexts, for example to non-urban areas in America or to more effective schools in the United Kingdom. Given the costs involved in converting or establishing new schools, it is important that we do not assume that these approaches will be universally effective without evidence to this effect.

Post-Compulsory Education

Given that there are inequalities in educational outcomes throughout compulsory schooling, it is hardly surprising that these are sustained into

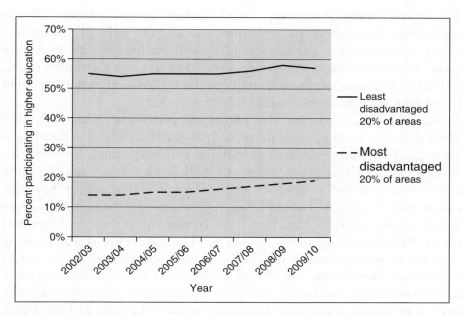

Figure 10.6 Participation rate of young people in higher education according to socioeconomic quintile.[53] *Data source*: Department for Business, Innovation and Skills.

post-16 and higher education. Data from the LSYPE has been used to map out the educational trajectories of young people from different backgrounds who finished their GCSEs in 2006. By the age of 18, those from the lowest socioeconomic backgrounds were most likely to be NEET (Not in Education, Employment or Training) or in non-university education. Young people whose parents had intermediate (typically skilled manual) jobs were most likely to have started an apprenticeship or be in work-based training. Meanwhile, young people whose parents were professionals were most likely to have stayed in full-time education and to have progressed to university.[52] In fact, young people from the top 20% most advantaged areas are more than twice as likely to participate in higher education as those who live in the 20% most disadvantaged areas (see Figure 10.6), a situation which has barely changed since 2002.

The major factor that drives differences in educational progression is prior attainment and we have already explained how this tends to vary with SES, gender and ethnicity. If pupils want to continue to A-levels and university then most will need to have achieved at least five A*–C grades at GCSE, typically including English and maths. They are also often expected to have achieved a B grade or higher at GCSE in the subjects they want to continue studying. Based on these criteria, roughly 75% of pupils from the highest socioeconomic quintile but only 21% from the lowest socioeconomic quintile would be able to continue on to A-level study.[4] However, there is also variation by ethnicity: ethnic minority pupils with a given level of attainment are typically more likely to participate in 16–19 education than their white British peers*.[54,55]

The same variation is seen for participation in higher education, with ethnic minority young people more likely to go on to university. Amongst the highest-attaining pupils these differences are minimal; however, for those who have GCSE scores below 49 (between a B and C grade), white British followed by Bangladeshi and Pakistani young people have the lowest rates of participation and Indian young people the highest.[56] More complex, however, is the variation in the type of universities these students attend. Pakistani, Bangladeshi, Indian and black students as well as those from lower socioeconomic backgrounds are concentrated in the newer universities. Meanwhile, other Asian students and white students are more likely to attend Russell Group universities (a group of 20 universities such as the University of Glasgow, University of Manchester and LSE, which are well established and typically more selective in the grades they require from applicants), as are those from private schools or those with professional parents.[57]

This is concerning, because research suggests that the income returns to a degree vary according to the type of university a person attends. We often hear the headline figure that graduates will earn £100,000 more over a lifetime. However, Chevalier and Conlon[58] examined the earnings of people who graduated in 1985, 1990 and 1995 and found significant differences depending on the university they attended. The raw difference in earnings between those who attended a Russell Group or new university was 17% for the 1985 group, 11% for the 1990 group and 6–9% for the 1995 group. However, students at different types of university are likely to have different levels of prior achievement, as measured by A-level grades, and also different background characteristics, both of which might affect earnings potential. Using a statistical model to match graduates from different types of university by these characteristics (and hence control for them), the researchers found that male graduates from Russell Group universities could on average be expected to earn between 0 and 6% more than gradu-

---

* From 2015, it will be compulsory to remain in education or training until the age of 18. However, the evidence in this chapter indicates that we may still see socioeconomic and ethnic differences in the type of education and training that young people select, e.g. apprenticeships versus full-time.

ates from new universities, while female graduates could be expected to earn about 2.5% more. In other words, someone who goes to a new university is likely to earn less over their lifetime than someone with the same A-level grades and family background who attends a Russell Group university. It is important to note, though, that with the expansion of higher education these patterns have become less stable. As increasing numbers of young people are educated to graduate level, the earnings gains from attending a selective university, and in fact any university, may fall.

A number of researchers have explored why socioeconomic and ethnic differences in rates and types of participation emerge, in particular with concern that some older universities might be discriminating against ethnic minority applicants. Connor and colleagues[59] reviewed existing literature on ethnicity differences in higher education participation and then conducted a survey in 2002 and 2003 of nearly 1,000 potential entrants to higher education (Year 13 pupils, including high numbers of lower-SES and ethnic minority pupils). Amongst this sample, ethnic minority pupils were more likely to associate attending university with improved employment and earnings prospects, more likely to believe their family wanted them to go, and to feel they had always been expected to go. This survey sample was not representative, but representative data from the LSYPE also indicate that ethnic minority pupils and their parents are more likely to aspire to participation in higher education.[7] While this helps to explain why ethnic minority pupils are more likely to go to university, it does not explain why the majority of non-white students are concentrated in newer institutions.

One contributing factor is that ethnic minority pupils are more likely to take vocational qualifications at secondary school and these are less likely to be accepted at older or Russell Group universities.[59] Similarly, the lower attainment of black Caribbean, Pakistani and Bangladeshi students can limit their university choices. Shiner and Modood[60] used UCAS data from the 1996–97 application round to investigate whether attainment (A-levels only) and socio-demographic factors could explain ethnicity differences in attendance at different types of higher education institution. Although there were large ethnicity differences in the raw proportion of candidates accepted by institutions (for example, 70% of applications from white pupils but only 57% from black African pupils received an initial offer), after the number and grade of A-levels and proportion of re-takes were accounted for, only Pakistani applicants were significantly less likely to receive an offer than white applicants. Meanwhile, Chinese applicants were significantly more likely than white applicants to receive an offer. Ethnic minority students were more likely to apply to post-1992 universities and this partially explained their over-representation at these institutions. However, the researchers also found evidence indicating that pre-1992 institutions were significantly less likely to accept applications from non-white students. These data are now quite old, but there is still a problem with under-representation of students from many ethnic minorities at selective universities, particularly Oxford and Cambridge, to which very few apply.

As well as seeking explanations for these institutional variations we need to understand why white British pupils from the most disadvantaged backgrounds are the least likely of all to attend university. Chowdry et al.[61] analysed applications to universities in 2003–05 in order to investigate this trend. Combining data from the National Pupil Database and Higher Education Statistics Agency, they used a regression analysis to identify factors linked to differences in the higher education participation rates of pupils from the highest and lowest quintiles of deprivation. The initial participation gap was 29 percentage points for males and 35 percentage points for females. Controlling for individual-level characteristics (neighbourhood deprivation quintile, neighbourhood parental education quintile, ethnicity, month of birth, English as an additional language, special educational needs) reduced this gap to 14 percentage points and 20 percentage points respectively. Accounting for prior attainment at Key Stages 2 to 5 reduced the gap to 1 percentage point for males and to 2 percentage points for females. The main reason identified for unequal participation in higher education, as identified by numerous studies, was therefore simply that these pupils did not have the grades to apply to university. If we want to equalize participation in higher education, we have to raise the academic performance of lower-SES pupils. However, Chowdry et al.'s study shows that even low-SES pupils with sufficient attainment are less likely to apply to university than wealthier peers.

Focus group research with higher-attaining 16–18-year-olds has been used to explore why this occurs. Often lower-SES young people want to start work and start earning immediately. Some may have aspirations to careers that do not require a degree. However, other potential applicants are deterred by the cost of university, the likelihood of accruing debt and uncertainty about the financial support available.[62] There is a wider issue here, around a lack of knowledge about higher education. Many lower-SES pupils come from families with no experience of higher education and therefore rely heavily on teachers to introduce the possibility of university and assist with applications. Despite the importance of school-based support for these pupils, two programmes that facilitated progression through education and into university – Connexions and Aimhigher – have recently been discontinued.

Aimhigher was set up at the turn of the millennium as a programme to encourage young people from under-represented groups to aspire to higher education. It was also intended to help raise the attainment of these young people so they had the grades to apply to university and to offer the necessary information, advice and guidance to young people and their parents. These goals were pursued through a combination of school-based interventions, in-school information, advice and guidance, mentoring, summer schools and campus trips.

Most qualitative evaluations of Aimhigher were positive, suggesting that participants were encouraged to consider higher education and motivated to achieve higher grades as a consequence.[e.g. 63–65] However, there are few robust quantitative evaluations of the impact of Aimhigher on application and entry to higher education. This is partly because many of the outcomes, such as increased motivation, were difficult to quantify, partly because it was difficult to identify good control groups and partly because little comprehensive data collection was undertaken.

Chilosi and colleagues[66] attempted to quantify the impact of Aimhigher on attainment and higher education participation by comparing whole-school statistics from a single partnership area where approximately 10,000 pupils participated in Aimhigher between 2003 and 2006. Their difference-in-differences regression (comparing years before and after the introduction of Aimhigher) indicated that participating in Aimhigher increased the likelihood of pupils attaining five A*–C grades at GCSE by 3.8 percentage points and increased the likelihood of applying to university by 4.5 percentage points and of being accepted by 4.1 percentage points. However, because they used whole-school statistics and could not control for all other influencing factors, these estimates were tentative. Emmerson and colleagues[67] compared higher education participation rates in local authorities that did or did not participate in Aimhigher: Excellence Challenge (the predecessor to Aimhigher). They found no significant overall impact on participation rates, but a significant positive effect on students from disadvantaged backgrounds. They suggested that such pupils were roughly 15 percentage points more likely to participate in higher education if they lived in an Aimhigher area.

Ireland and colleagues[68] surveyed 3,877 16–19-year-olds who had experienced Aimhigher activities and found a correlation between these experiences (such as discussing higher education with teachers, visiting a university or Aimhigher roadshow or participating in a residential trip) and positive attitudes towards higher education and intentions to attend. However, this survey could not show any causal impact of Aimhigher because one could argue that pupils would be more likely to undertake these activities if already positive about, or intending to apply to, higher education. Furthermore, intentions to apply to higher education may not translate into participation: 19% of 18–19-year-olds who had indicated an intention to apply to higher education when in Year 11 had not done so, and were not intending to go.

Multiple studies, and the author's personal experience, suggest that most young people will now consider going to university at some point during secondary school, even if they are from very disadvantaged backgrounds.[69–72] As yet, there is also little evidence to suggest that the increase in tuition fees has deterred those from lower-income backgrounds from applying to university any more than those from wealthier homes.[73] However, many factors make higher-SES young people more likely to actually reach university. They are likely to have higher attainment, fewer financial concerns, more direct and indirect experience of university (via family members who have already been) and parents who are more capable of giving them advice and guidance about their educational choices. Aimhigher compensated for some of these factors by introducing pupils with no family history of higher education to the concept at an early age and then offering a range of experiences, information and guidance to make it seem like a feasible goal. It is questionable whether schools will be able to maintain this momentum without a designated Aimhigher coordinator to make it a priority.

The Connexions service, which provided broader careers advice and guidance services to schools, was also discontinued in September 2012. Schools now have a responsibility to commission their own guidance provision, which must be independent and unbiased by their own interests (they should not, for example, discourage high-achieving students from moving to another sixth form). Although careers guidance in English schools has long been of variable quality, the benefit of Connexions was that it had ring-fenced funding and was a truly independent service. One of the authors of this book conducted research into careers guidance at three schools in the South East of England. In every school there were some disengaged Year 11 pupils who were at serious risk of leaving education and becoming unemployed at 16. In the two schools that used Connexions, however, the pupils felt they could trust their adviser to offer unbiased advice (which was not their perception of most teachers). In many cases, it was the adviser rather than parents or teachers who ensured that these vulnerable young people had a positive plan for the year ahead.

Although Connexions was not perfect, it at least guaranteed all pupils access to independent careers advice. Teachers, while knowledgeable about their subjects, may not know about other qualifications or careers. Meanwhile, school performance is still judged primarily by examination results, so there is little incentive to spend time organizing careers guidance or work experience, rather than preparing pupils for tests. The development of destination measures, which track what young people do after leaving school, may change this. However, until the measures are reliable enough to be included in performance tables, there is a risk that many schools will choose not to invest in good quality, effective careers guidance.

Summary

- In answer to the quiz at the start of this chapter:
  - By the age of 3, a child living in poverty will be 5 months behind a child from a higher-income background in the development of their vocabulary.
  - There is a 30 percentage point difference in the proportion of British-born Chinese pupils and British-born black Caribbean pupils who achieve five A*–C grades at GCSE including English and maths (see Figure 10.4).
  - A young person from one of the 20% most advantaged geographical areas of England is roughly three times as likely to go to university as a young person from the 20% of most disadvantaged areas.
- Socioeconomic and ethnic differences in cognitive development are evident before children even start school. The best predictor of future attainment is past performance, so any efforts to reduce these socioeconomic and ethnic differences in educational attainment must involve intervention at an early age, to bring the performance of less advantaged children up to the levels of their more advantaged peers.
- Sure Start centres are the main vehicle for early intervention in England and in recent years research has shown that past attendees experience improved home learning environments and exhibit more positive social behaviours. However, further improvements in the model are needed as these children still have lower attainment than their socioeconomically advantaged peers.
- Reading proficiency is essential for education and working life. The government now advocates synthetic phonics as the primary method to teach children to read and has introduced phonics screening to identify children who need additional support at an early age, before they fall too far behind. While effective for the majority of pupils, synthetic phonics does not work for everyone and there is a case for

allowing teachers more flexibility to meet different children's learning needs.

- In many Western countries there is a presumption that reducing class sizes will help raise attainment. However, the evidence for this is mixed and, if anything, suggests that benefits are restricted to certain groups such as lower-achieving pupils. Given the expense of employing more staff, there may be more cost-effective ways to raise average attainment in the education system.

- Politicians often talk about the need to raise expectations for under-performing pupils. There is mixed empirical evidence for the impact of teacher expectation on performance. However, teachers do seem to underestimate the potential of some ethnic minority groups and this must be addressed to avoid unwarranted restriction of their educational opportunities.

- Free schools and academies have been introduced to increase choice and raise standards in the education system. Evidence from the United States and Sweden suggests that autonomous state-funded schools can help raise results, particularly in mathematics and English. However, there are concerns that the benefits are not evenly distributed across society, hence these schools may not help tackle socioeconomic and ethnic inequalities in attainment as much as is hoped.

- Lower-SES young people are more likely to leave school at 16, more likely to study vocational qualifications and less likely to go to university. Aimhigher and the Connexions service helped to address this imbalance and the decision to discontinue these programmes may result in greater inequalities emerging amongst future school-leavers.

- Many ethnic minority students are overrepresented in higher education but under-represented at more selective universities. This may hinder their employment prospects and result in lower future earnings than they expect upon graduation. A preference for vocational qualifications, lower attainment, lack of knowledge and the lower likelihood that their applications will be accepted may all contribute to these patterns of participation.

Educational implications

- Teachers who are given the opportunity to work with small classes should remain conscious of the need to adapt their methods accordingly if the children are to benefit from the lower pupil:teacher ratio.
- Teachers should be aware that their past experience with pupils of different ethnicities may implicitly bias their assessment of other pupils'

potential. They should make every effort to avoid these biases influencing the way in which they assess these pupils or direct them towards different courses and examinations.

- Head teachers in secondary schools should not underestimate the importance of high-quality careers guidance for giving pupils a clear vision for their future, which can motivate them to work hard in the short term. They should ensure that as external services are cut, careers guidance still receives sufficient time and funding within their school.

References

1   DfE. GCSE and Equivalent Results in England, 2010/11: Revised. London: Department for Education; 2012. Available at: http://dera.ioe.ac.uk/13719/. Accessed 2 December 2013.

2   George A, Hansen K, Schoon I. *Cognitive Development*. London: Centre for Longitudinal Studies, Institute of Education; 2007. Available at: www .cls.ioe.ac.uk/shared/get-file.ashx?id=1400&itemtype=document. Accessed 2 December 2013.

3   Hansen K. Teacher Assessment at Age 5. London: Centre for Longitudinal Studies, Institute of Education; 2010. Available at: www.cls.ioe.ac.uk/ shared/get-file.ashx?id=1065&itemtype=document. Accessed 2 December 2013.

4   Goodman A, Gregg P. Poorer children's Educational Attainment: How Important Are Attitudes and Behaviour? York: Joseph Rowntree Foundation; 2010. Available at: www.jrf.org.uk/sites/files/jrf/poorer-children-education-full.pdf. Accessed 2 December 2013.

5   Melhuish E. Impact of the Home Learning Environment on Child Cognitive Development: Secondary Analysis of Data from "Growing Up in Scotland". Scottish Government Social Research; 2010. Available at: www.scotland.gov .uk/Resource/Doc/310722/0098010.pdf. Accessed 2 December 2013.

6   Melhuish E, Phan MB, Sylva K, Sammons P, Siraj-Blatchford I, *et al*. Effects of the home learning environment and preschool center experience upon literacy and numeracy development in early primary school. *Journal of Social Issues*. 2008;64(1):95–114. doi:10.1111/j.1540-4560.2008.00550.x.

7   Strand S. Minority Ethnic Pupils in the Longitudinal Study of Young People in England (LSYPE). Nottingham: Department for Children, Schools and Families; 2007. Available at: www2.warwick.ac.uk/fac/soc/wie/research/ policy/recent_projects/minority/rr_2007-002_strand.pdf. Accessed 2 December 2013.

8   Ellison S, Hicks L, Latham P. Cost Effectiveness in Sure Start Local Programmes: A Synthesis of Local Evaluation Findings. Birkbeck, University of London: Institute for the Study of Children, Families and Social Issues; 2005.

Available at: www.york.ac.uk/inst/spru/pubs/pdf/SureStartCostEffect.pdf. Accessed 2 December 2013.

9   Belsky J. *The National Evaluation of Sure Start: Does Area-Based Early Intervention Work?* Bristol: Policy Press; 2007.

10 Welshman J. From Head Start to Sure Start: Reflections on policy transfer. *Children & Society.* 2010;24(2):89–99. doi:10.1111/j.1099-0860.2008 .00201.x.

11 Reynolds AJ, Temple JA, Robertson DL, Mann EA. Long-term effects of an early childhood intervention on educational achievement and juvenile arrest. *JAMA.* 2001;285(18):2339.

12 Schweinhart L, Barnes H, Weikart D. *Significant Benefits: The High/Scope Perry Pre-School Study Through Age 27.* Ypsilanti, MI: High Scope Press.

13 McKey RH, Condelli L, Ganson H, Barrett BJ, McConkey C, *et al. The Impact of Head Start on Children, Families and Communities. Final Report of the Head Start Evaluation, Synthesis and Utilization Project.* Washington, DC: CSR, Inc; 1985. Available at: www.eric.ed.gov/ERICWebPortal/ detail?accno=ED263984. Accessed 2 December 2013.

14 Melhuish E, Belsky J, Leyland AH, Barnes J. Effects of fully-established Sure Start Local Programmes on 3-year-old children and their families living in England: A quasi-experimental observational study. *Lancet.* 2008;372(9650): 1641–1647. doi:10.1016/S0140-6736(08)61687-6.

15 Melhuish E, Belsky J, Leyland AH. The Impact of Sure Start Local Programmes on Seven Year Olds and Their Families. London: Department for Education; 2010. Available at: https://www.education.gov.uk/publications/ eOrderingDownload/DFE-RR220.pdf. Accessed 2 December 2013.

16 DFE. National Curriculum Assessments at Key Stage 1 in England, 2011. London: Department for Education; 2011. Available at: https://www.gov.uk/ government/publications/national-curriculum-assessments-at-key-stage-1-in-england-2011. Accessed 2 December 2013.

17 DfE. National Curriculum assessments at Key Stage 2 in England 2010/2011 (revised). *The Department for Education.* 2011. Available at: https://www.gov .uk/government/publications/revised-national-curriculum-assessments-at-key-stage-2-in-england-academic-year-2010-to-2011. Accessed 2 December 2013.

18 Strand S. Ethnic group, sex and economic disadvantage: Associations with pupils' educational progress from baseline to the end of Key Stage 1. *British Educational Research Journal.* 1999;25(2):179–202.

19 Blatchford P, Bassett P, Goldstein H, Martin C. Are class size differences related to pupils' educational progress and classroom processes? Findings from the Institute of Education class size study of children aged 5–7 years. *British Educational Research Journal.* 2003;29(5):709–730. doi:10.1080 /0141192032000133668.

20 Blatchford P, Bassett P, Brown P. Examining the effect of class size on classroom engagement and teacher–pupil interaction: Differences in relation to

pupil prior attainment and primary vs. secondary schools. *Learning and Instruction*. 2011;21(6):715–730. doi:10.1016/j.learninstruc.2011.04.001.

21 Dustmann C, Rajah N, van Soest A. Class size, education, and wages. *The Economic Journal*. 2003;113(485):F99–F120. doi:10.1111/1468-0297.00101.

22 Finn JD, Gerber SB, Boyd-Zaharias J. Small classes in the early grades, academic achievement, and graduating from high school. *Journal of Educational Psychology*. 2005;97(2):214–223.

23 Hattie J. The paradox of reducing class size and improving learning outcomes. *International Journal of Educational Research*. 2005;43(6):387–425.

24 Evertson CM, Randolph CH. Teaching practices and class size: A new look at an old issue. *Peabody Journal of Education*. 1989;67(1):85–105.

25 Hargreaves L, Galton M, Pell A. The effects of changes in class size on teacher–pupil interaction. *International Journal of Educational Research*. 1998;29(8):779–795.

26 Molnar A, Smith P, Zahorik J, Palmer A, Halbach A, *et al*. Evaluating the SAGE program: A pilot program in targeted pupil–teacher reduction in Wisconsin. *Educational Evaluation and Policy Analysis*. 1999;21(2):165–177. doi:10.3102/01623737021002165.

27 Word E, Johnston J, Bain HP, Fulton BD, Zaharies JB, *et al*. Student/Teacher Achievement Ratio (STAR), Tennessee's K-3 Class Size Study: Final Summary Report, 1985–1990. Nashville, TN: Tennessee State Department of Education; 1990.

28 DCSF. *Measuring Progress at Pupil, School and National Levels*. London: Crown Copyright; 2009. Available at: https://www.education.gov.uk/publications/eOrderingDownload/DCSF-RTP-09-02.pdf. Accessed 2 December 2013.

29 Rosenthal R, Jacobson L. Pygmalion in the classroom. *The Urban Review*. 1968;3(1):16–20.

30 Jussim L, Harber KD. Teacher expectations and self-fulfilling prophecies: Knowns and unknowns, resolved and unresolved controversies. *Personality and Social Psychology Review*. 2005;9(2):131–155.

31 Jussim L, Eccles J, Madon S. Social perception, social stereotypes, and teacher expectations: Accuracy and the quest for the powerful self-fulfilling prophecy. *Advances in Experimental Social Psychology*. 1996;28:281–388.

32 Madon S, Jussim L, Eccles J. In search of the powerful self-fulfilling prophecy. *Journal of Personality and Social Psychology*. 1997;72(4):791.

33 Haynes J, Tikly L, Caballero C. The barriers to achievement for White/Black Caribbean pupils in English schools. *British Journal of Sociology of Education*. 2006;27(5):569–583. doi:10.1080/01425690600958766.

34 Tikly L, Haynes J, Caballero C, Hill J, Gillborn D. Evaluation of Aiming High: African Caribbean Achievement Project. Bristol: Department for Education and Skills; 2006. Available at: www.academia.edu/1023867/Evaluation_of_Aiming_High_African_Caribbean_Achievement_Project. Accessed 2 December 2013.

35   Burgess S, Greaves E. Test Scores, Subjective Assessment and Stereotyping of Ethnic Minorities. Bristol: University of Bristol, CMPO; 2009. Available at: www.bris.ac.uk/cmpo/publications/papers/2009/wp221.pdf. Accessed 2 December 2013.

36   New Schools Network. Comparison of Different School Types. 2011. Available at: http://newschoolsnetwork.org/sites/default/files/files/pdf/Differences across school types.pdf. Accessed 2 December 2013.

37   Gove M. Michael Gove at the National College Annual Conference. 2012. Available at: https://www.gov.uk/government/speeches/michael-gove-at-the-national-college-annual-conference. Accessed 2 December 2013.

38   Gove M. Michael Gove Speaks to the Schools Network. 2011. Available at: https://www.gov.uk/government/speeches/michael-gove-speaks-to-the-schools-network. Accessed 2 December 2013.

39   Barnett WD. A Comparative Analysis of the Academic Outcomes of Ohio Public K-8 Charter Schools and Their Comparison Districts. DPhil Dissertation, University of Toledo, OH; 2008.

40   Berends M, Watral C, Teasley B, Nicotera A. Charter school effects on achievement: Where we are and where we're going. Paper presented at the National Center on School Choice Conference. Nashville, TN: Vanderbilt University; 2006.

41   Bifulco R, Ladd HF. School choice, racial segregation and test-score gaps: Evidence from North Carolina's Charter School Program. *Journal of Policy Analysis and Management.* 2007;26(1):31–56.

42   Finnigan K, Adelman N, Anderson L, Cotton L, Donnelly MB, *et al.* Evaluation of the Public Charter Schools Program. Washington, DC: Department of Education; 2004.

43   Gleason P, Clark M, Clark Tuttle C, Dwoyer E, Silverberg M. *The Evaluation of Charter School Impacts.* Alexandria, VA: National Center for Education Evaluation and Regional Assistance, Institute of Education Sciences, US Department of Education; 2010.

44   Angrist JD, Pathak PA, Walters CR. Explaining Charter School Effectiveness. National Bureau of Economic Research; 2011. Available at: www.nber.org/papers/w17332. Accessed 2 December 2013.

45   Arreman IE, Holm A. Privatisation of public education? The emergence of independent upper secondary schools in Sweden. *Journal of Education Policy.* 2011;26(2):225–243. doi:10.1080/02680939.2010.502701.

46   Ahlin Å. Does School Competition Matter? Effects of a Large-Scale School Choice Reform on Student Performance. Uppsala, Sweden: Uppsala University, Department of Economics; 2003. Available at: http://ideas.repec.org/p/hhs/uunewp/2003_002.html. Accessed 2 December 2013.

47   Sandstrom FM, Bergstrom F. School vouchers in practice: Competition will not hurt you. *Journal of Public Economics.* 2005;89(2–3):351–380.

48   Bohlmark A, Lindahl M. The Impact of School Choice on Pupil Achievement, Segregation and Costs: Swedish Evidence. 2007. Available at:

http://papers.ssrn.com/Sol3/papers.cfm?abstract_id=987491. Accessed 2 December 2013.

49   OECD. Education at a Glance 2012 – Country Note – United Kingdom; 2012. Available at: www.oecd.org/edu/EAG2012%20-%20Country%20 note%20-%20United%20Kingdom.pdf. 2 December 2013

50   Gorard S. What are Academies the answer to? *Journal of Education Policy*. 2009;24(1):101–113. doi:10.1080/02680930802660903.

51   Machin S, Vernoit J. Changing School Autonomy: Academy Schools and their Introduction to England's Education. London: London School of Economics; 2011. Available at: http://cee.lse.ac.uk/ceedps/ceedp123.pdf. Accessed 2 December 2013.

52   Crawford C, Duckworth K, Vignoles A, Wyness G. Young People's Education and Labour Market Choices Aged 16/17 to 18/19. London: Department for Education/Centre for Analysis of Youth Transitions; 2011. Available at: https://www.education.gov.uk/publications/eOrderingDownload/DFE-RR182.pdf. Accessed 2 December 2013.

53   BIS. Widening Participation in Higher Education 2012; 2012. Available at: https://www.gov.uk/government/publications/widening-participation-in-higher-education-2012. Accessed 2 December 2013.

54   Payne J. Patterns of Participation in Full-Time Education after 16: An Analysis of the England and Wales Youth Cohort Study. Norwich: Department for Education and Skills; 2001. Available at: http://dera.ioe.ac.uk/4577/1/RR307.pdf. Accessed 2 December 2013.

55   Payne J. Choice at the End of Compulsory Schooling: A Research Review. London: DfES; 2003.

56   Hills J, Brewer M, Jenkins S, *et al*. An Anatomy of Economic Inequality in the UK: Report of the National Equality Panel. London: Government Equalities Office; 2010.

57   Machin S, Murphy R, Soobedar Z. Differences in Labour Market Gains from Higher Education Participation. London: London School of Economics/National Equality Panel; 2009. Available at: http://sta.geo.useconnect.co.uk/staimm6geo/pdf/Variation%20in%20gains%20from%20university%20education.pdf. Accessed 2 December 2013.

58   Chevalier A, Conlon G. Does It Pay to Attend a Prestigious University? Dublin: Centre for Economic Research; 2003.

59   Connor H, Tyers C, Modood T, Hillage J. Why the Difference? A Closer Look at Higher Education Minority Ethnic Students and Graduates. London: Department for Education and Skills; 2004.

60   Shiner M, Modood T. Help or hindrance? Higher education and the route to ethnic equality. *British Journal of Sociology of Education*. 2002;23(2): 209–232.

61   Chowdry H, Crawford C, Dearden L, Goodman A, Vignoles A. Widening Participation in Higher Education: Analysis Using Linked Administrative Data. London: Institute of Education; 2010.

62   Connor H, Dewson S, Tyers C, Eccles J, Regan J, *et al.* Social Class and Higher Education: Issues Affecting Decisions on Participation by Lower Social Class Groups. Norwich: Department for Education and Employment; 2001. Available at: https://www.education.gov.uk/publications/standard/publicationDetail/Page1/RR267. Accessed 2 December 2013.

63   Church E, Kerrigan M. "We Thought It [University] Was a Different World" – A Longitudinal Study of Aimhigher Northamptonshire learners. Loughborough: Aimhigher Northamptonshire; 2011.

64   Hatt S, Baxter A, Tate J. "It was definitely a turning point!" A review of Aimhigher summer schools in the south west of England. *Journal of Further and Higher Education.* 2009;33:333–346. doi:10.1080/03098770903266034.

65   Passy R, Morris M. Evaluation of Aimhigher: Learner Attainment and Progression. Slough: National Foundation for Educational Research; 2010.

66   Chilosi D, Noble M, Broadhead P, Wilkinson M. Measuring the effect of Aimhigher on schooling attainment and higher education applications and entries. *Journal of Further and Higher Education.* 2010;34(1):1–10. doi:10.1080/03098770903477052.

67   Emmerson C, Frayne C, McNally S, Silva O. Aimhigher: Excellence Challenge: A Policy Evaluation Using the Labour Force Survey. London: Department for Education and Skills; 2006. Available at: https://www.education.gov.uk/publications/eOrderingDownload/RR813.pdf. Accessed 2 December 2013.

68   Ireland E, Golden S, Morris M. Evaluation of Integrated Aimhigher: Tracking Surveys of Young People. Nottingham: Department for Education and Skills; 2006.

69   Atherton G, Cymbir E, Roberts K, Page L, Remedios R. How Young People Formulate their Views about the Future. Department for Children, Schools and Families; 2009. Available at: https://www.education.gov.uk/publications/eOrderingDownload/DCSF-RR152.pdf. Accessed 2 December 2013.

70   Ipsos MORI. Youth Aspirations in London. 2010a. Available at: www.ipsos-mori.com/DownloadPublication/1374_sri-third-sector-youth-aspirations-in-london-march-2010.pdf. Accessed 2 December 2013.

71   Ipsos MORI. Young People Omnibus 2010: A Research Study Among 11–16 year olds on Behalf of the Sutton Trust. London: Ipsos MORI; 2010b.

72   Kintrea K, St Clair R, Houston M. The Influence of Parents, Places and Poverty on Educational Attitudes and Aspirations. York: Joseph Rowntree Foundation; 2011. Available at: www.jrf.org.uk/sites/files/jrf/young-people-education-attitudes-full.pdf. Accessed 2 December 2013.

73   UCAS. How Have Applications for Full-Time Undergraduate Higher Education in the UK Changed in 2012? UCAS; 2012. Available at: www.ucas.com/news-events/news/2013/how-have-applications-full-time-undergraduate-higher-education-uk-changed-2012. Accessed 2 December 2013.

Chapter 11

Comparative Education
What Lessons Can We Learn from Other Countries?

This graph shows how the speed of a racing car varies along a flat 3 kilometre track during its second lap.

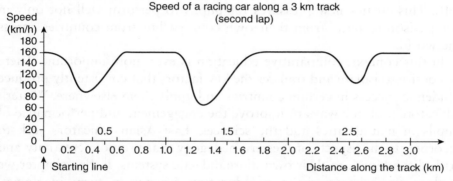

Note: In memory of Claude Janvier, who died in June 1998. Modified task after his ideas in Janvier, C. (1978): *The interpretation of complex graphs – studies and teaching experiments*. Accompanying brochure to the Dissertation. University of Nottingham, Shell Centre for Mathematical Education, Item C-2. The pictures of the tracks are taken from Fischer, R. & Malle, G. (1985): *Mensch und Mathematik*. Bibliographisches Institut Mannheim-Wien-Zurich, 234-238.

QUESTION 7.1
What is the approximate distance from the starting line to the beginning of the longest straight section of the track?
A. 0.5 km
B. 1.5 km
C. 2.3 km
D. 2.6 km

Figure 11.1   Question given to school pupils all over the world as part of the OECD Programme for International Student Assessment (PISA). *Source*: OECD. Take the Test: Sample Questions from OECD's PISA Assessments. PISA, OECD Publishing; 2009. http://dx.doi.org/10.1787/9789264050815-en. Copyright © 2009, OECD Publishing. Reproduced with permission of OECD Publishing.

Education and Learning: An Evidence-Based Approach, First Edition. Jane Mellanby and Katy Theobald.
© 2014 John Wiley & Sons, Ltd. Published 2014 by John Wiley & Sons, Ltd.

In 2006, the question shown in Figure 11.1 was given to school pupils all over the world as part of the OECD Programme for International Student Assessment (PISA). Can you answer it?

As modern technology shrinks the world, education is becoming an increasingly international affair. Pupils across the globe can use the same materials and take the same examinations at the end of their secondary education. International measures of pupil performance such as PISA and TIMSS (Trends in International Mathematics and Science Study) allow educators in one country to compare the performance of their education system with others across the world. Higher education institutions and employers are increasingly operating in a global marketplace, with individuals from many nations applying for the same courses and the same jobs. This creates new pressures for pupils to perform well not only in comparison to peers from their own country, but from countries across the world.

In this context, comparative education is ever more important. There is a desire to isolate and transfer the key factors that consistently produce academic success in certain countries and apply them elsewhere. Western educators look for ways to improve the engagement and performance of pupils in mathematics and the sciences. East Asian educators seek to incorporate the aspects of Western pedagogy that promote creativity and critical thinking into their own more didactic systems. In this chapter we explore four characteristics of education systems in turn: ideologies, pedagogies, structures and curricula. We focus particularly on education systems that perform well in international comparisons or in preparing their students for the world of work.

International Comparisons

One of the primary reasons that educators or politicians take an interest in a country is the performance of its pupils according to international measures. Two major programmes offer comparative data about the performance of pupils from multiple countries: PISA and TIMSS.*

For PISA, the literacy, mathematics and science performance of 15-year-olds is measured using tests which are, as much as possible, similar across

---

* Since the time of writing, PISA 2012 data have been released. Notably, Finnish students no longer rank in the top 10 for mathematics performance.

Table 11.1   Top ranking countries in PISA 2009 (including non-OECD)

Rank	Mathematics	Mark	Science	Mark	Reading	Mark
1	Shanghai-China	600	Shanghai-China	575	Shanghai-China	556
2	Singapore	562	Finland	554	Korea	539
3	Hong Kong-China	555	Hong Kong-China	549	Finland	536
4	Korea	546	Singapore	542	Hong Kong-China	533
5	Chinese Taipei	543	Japan	539	Singapore	526
6	Finland	541	Korea	538	Canada	524
7	Liechtenstein	536	New Zealand	532	New Zealand	521
8	Switzerland	534	Canada	529	Japan	520
9	Japan	529	Estonia	528	Australia	515
10	Canada	527	Australia	527	Netherlands	508
Average	*Mathematics*	496	*Science*	501	*Reading*	493
UK score	*Mathematics*	492	*Science*	514	*Reading*	494

Data source: What students know and can do: Student performance in reading, mathematics and science. OECD Publishing, 2010. Copyright © OECD.

all the countries. It therefore assesses pupils' capacity to apply existing knowledge to new types of problem. Sixty-five countries participated in PISA 2009 and the top-ranking countries are listed in Table 11.1.

TIMSS is conducted by the International Association for the Evaluation of Educational Achievement and measures the performance of pupils on tests that are directly related to the curriculum in their own country. In order to produce a test that is relevant to so many curricula, representatives from many of the countries (from 40 in 2011) collaboratively develop new items. A panel also rates how many of the final items are relevant to their own countries' curriculum, allowing the test administrators to check

Table 11.2   Top ranking countries in TIMSS Mathematics 2011[1]

	Mathematics Grade 4 (age 10)		Mathematics Grade 8 (age 14)	
1	Singapore	606	Republic of Korea	613
2	Republic of Korea	605	Singapore	611
3	China – Hong Kong	602	China – Taipei	609
4	China – Taipei	591	China – Hong Kong	586
5	Japan	585	Japan	570
6	GB – Northern Ireland	562	Russian Federation	539
7	Belgium (Flemish)	549	Israel	516
8	Finland	545	Finland	514
9	GB – England	542	United States	509
10	Russian Federation	542	GB – England	507

Data source: TIMSS 2011 Assessment. Copyright © 2012 International Association for the Evaluation of Educational Achievement (IEA). Publisher: TIMSS & PIRLS International Study Center, Lynch School of Education, Boston College, Chestnut Hill, MA and International Association for the Evaluation of Educational Achievement (IEA), IEA Secretariat, Amsterdam, the Netherlands.

that there are no major discrepancies between pupils' performance on these items and the remainder. More than 60 countries participated in the 2011 survey and the top-ranking countries are listed in Tables 11.2 and 11.3.

It is evident that East Asian countries dominate the top rankings of PISA, in particular Singapore, Korea, the Chinese regions and Japan. Meanwhile, the only European country whose pupils perform consistently well in the survey is Finland. The results for TIMSS are slightly different, most likely reflecting the difference in the content of the tests. The comparatively higher ranking of England and the United States in TIMSS would suggest that teachers in these countries are relatively good at delivering the content of the curriculum, but that perhaps either the content or its delivery does not always prepare pupils to apply their knowledge in new contexts.

As we noted in the introduction, one purpose of education can be to prepare young people for the world of work. Hence a second reason to be interested in a country's education system may be if it exhibits strong economic performance and, in particular, low rates of youth unemployment. Singapore, for example, has few natural resources from which to derive economic growth, so it relies predominantly on the strength of the country's human capital to maintain productivity. Historically, the country

Table 11.3 Top ranking countries in TIMSS Science 2011[2]

	Science Grade 4 (Age 10)		*Science Grade 8 (Age 14)*	
1	Republic of Korea	587	Singapore	590
2	Singapore	583	China – Taipei	564
3	Finland	570	Republic of Korea	560
4	Japan	559	Japan	558
5	Russian Federation	552	Finland	552
6	China – Taipei	552	Slovenia	543
7	United States	544	Russian Federation	542
8	Czech Republic	536	China – Hong Kong	535
9	China – Hong Kong	535	GB – England	533
10	Hungary	534	United States	525

Data source: TIMSS 2011 Assessment. Copyright © 2012 International Association for the Evaluation of Educational Achievement (IEA). Publisher: TIMSS & PIRLS International Study Center, Lynch School of Education, Boston College, Chestnut Hill, MA and International Association for the Evaluation of Educational Achievement (IEA), IEA Secretariat, Amsterdam, the Netherlands.

has exhibited strong economic growth and, notably, Singaporean pupils also rank highly in PISA and TIMSS. Later in the chapter we discuss how the effective vocational training systems in countries such as Singapore may help to keep youth unemployment rates low (see Table 11.5).

A final reason to take an interest in another country's education system is to investigate how a specific characteristic of that system affects academic performance. Trying out every possible structural and pedagogical approach within one country is impractical and would be disruptive. Researchers therefore look to other countries' education systems in order to evaluate whether a certain structure or teaching method could be worth adopting. This chapter presents comparative research that relates to topics introduced elsewhere in this book, such as school starting age, class sizes, setting by ability and the structure of the education system itself.

Values and Ideologies

Looking at the data in the previous section, it becomes clear that there is something of an East–West divide in levels of academic performance: the top-performing countries are disproportionately East Asian. It is important to point out early on that this does not mean pupils in East Asia get an all-round better education, because that depends entirely on what society values as educational outputs, be it cooperativeness, creativity or competence. However, it does indicate that when tested on mathematics, science and reading, core subjects at the heart of most education systems, East Asian pupils tend to perform best. The next question that comes to most researchers' minds, and probably yours as well, is why? The first step to finding the answer to this question is to understand the ideologies intrinsic to an East Asian education.

For over 2,000 years, Confucianism has been one of the strongest influences within East Asian culture and, therefore, its education systems. A civil servant by occupation, K'ung-fu-tzu (latinized to Confucius by Jesuits) developed a set of philosophical teachings regarding the ideal state of the human mind and behaviour, both individual and collective. Whilst these teachings were adapted with the rise of the Han Dynasty, Buddhism and, most recently, in response to Western cultural influences, the core values of Confucianism are still evident in many modern East Asian cultures.

Two of the central teachings of Confucianism are the Five Constant Virtues and the Three Cardinal Guides:

The Five Constant Virtues
Ren/Jen (仁, Humanity/Benevolence)
Yi (義, Righteousness)
Li (禮, Propriety/Ritual)
Zhi (智, Knowledge/Wisdom)
Xin (信, Integrity/Sincerity)

The Three Cardinal Guides
Ruler guides subject
Father guides son
Husband guides wife
(Adapted from Zhou[3])

As you can see, knowledge is one of the Five Constant Virtues and is therefore at the heart of Confucian values, although, as we explain below, the other virtues have their own influence over the way in which pupils behave and learn. The Three Cardinal Guides are a reminder of how important it is, according to Confucianism, to respect authority and elders. In an educational context, this means respecting parents by working hard to honour them, and respecting teachers by not questioning their knowledge or teaching.[4,5]

Attainment and ability

The attitude that Confucius perpetuated towards ability was quite the opposite to that of many Western educators. One quotation that can be applied to many contexts, including education, is: 'By nature people are similar; they diverge as the result of practice'.[6(pp200, 17:2)] As we have touched on in Chapter 5, the Confucian view is that everyone is educable and hence it is effort rather than ability that determines the amount that a person is able to learn. The emphasis is on working hard to achieve educational and occupational success: for example, students are encouraged to be 'Arduous in Action'.[7]

Stevenson and colleagues[8] demonstrated this difference as part of a longitudinal study of school pupils in Minnesota, Sendai (Japan) and Taipei. They conducted a survey of 212 American, 93 Japanese and 169 Chinese 11th-grade pupils (age 16–17), asking them which factors contributed to their performance in mathematics. The majority of Asian pupils (72% from Sendai and 59% from Taipei) said that studying hard was important, compared to only 27% of American pupils. Meanwhile, more than half the American pupils said that a good teacher was important compared to 18% of the Chinese and 14% of the Japanese respondents. American teachers were also more likely to select 'innate intelligence' (41%) rather than 'studying hard' (26%) as the cause of academic success, whilst Japanese teachers took the reverse view (7 vs 93%). Other studies also show that when explaining poor academic performance, Western children and parents give more weight to lack of ability and less weight to lack of effort than their counterparts in Japan or China.[9,10]

One can argue that attributing performance primarily to effort rather than ability makes long-run improvement more likely. The basic premise behind attribution theory[11] is that attributions can have different characteristics: internal–external, controllable–uncontrollable, stable–unstable. Ability is a stable, internal and (at least according to Western beliefs) uncontrollable factor. Therefore attributing one's performance to ability implies that there is little one can do to change it. In contrast, effort is an unstable, internal and controllable factor. Attributing performance to effort therefore implies that the outcome could be changed if more or less effort were applied. In Confucian-influenced cultures, teachers will commonly tell pupils who are not performing at the expected level that they are 'not trying hard enough'.[12] If pupils do not grasp a new skill, it will be demonstrated repeatedly by both teacher and peers, and the pupils will be instructed to keep trying until they succeed.[13] This belief that effort drives success extends beyond the classroom and helps to explain why East Asian pupils are known for their intensive timetables of study, both in extra lessons and at home.

The ethos of hard work that is so commonly observed among East Asian pupils is one aspect of much broader cultural differences that are often used to explain the success of these pupils in international assessments. However, it is worth noting that in Finland, where pupils also score highly on PISA and TIMSS, the common Western attribution pattern prevails. Young Finns and their parents are most likely to attribute good performance primariy to ability, but failure to lack of effort.[14] Therefore an over-riding emphasis on the importance of hard work may not be essential for educational success.

Pedagogical Approaches and Learning Styles

On the face of it, Eastern and Western educational principles are quite distinct. Dominant Western pedagogies are based on the learner-centred, constructivist approach. Teachers have been encouraged to move away from 'chalk and talk' to help pupils to construct their own learning experience. Instead of passing on knowledge, the teacher is framed as a guide, facilitating knowledge acquisition. Good teachers are supposed to account for the fact that every pupil will learn at a different pace, in a different way. These methods are encouraged for a number of reasons. Allowing pupils to direct their own studies is supposed to prepare them to become independent, life-long learners. Meanwhile, capitalizing on pupils' interests, avoiding rote-learning and focusing on understanding rather than memorizing is supposed to foster intrinsic motivation and keep less academically oriented pupils engaged.

In contrast to this model, many East Asian classrooms are still very much teacher centred. Confucian cultures, as we have already discussed, place great emphasis on the teacher as the source of knowledge and a figure of authority. Pupils are expected to listen carefully and absorb what they are told. Contrary to some assertions, the learning process is not supposed to be wholly passive and one-sided. However, whilst independent thought is encouraged, the expression of opinions or unplanned questioning is not, because this could be seen as questioning the teacher's knowledge and thereby disrupting harmony. It could also be thought quite egotistical to express a personal opinion in class, as this wastes time and implies that your own view is more important than that of the teacher or classmates.[13,15]

Responding to individual abilities

It is common practice in most East Asian elementary and middle schools to have mixed ability classes, which contrasts with the prevalence of setting and streaming in Western schools (see Chapters 5, 8 and below). Many British and American educators endorse the view that pupils should learn at their own pace, on the basis that both highly able and slower learners will become frustrated and disengaged if they are forced to follow the average speed of the class. In contrast, in both Korea and Japan it is common for pupils of varying abilities to work together so that group members can assist one another with problems. The long-standing attitude in Japanese state schools has been that the class should proceed together. This is reinforced by the centralized prescription of curriculum, which sets out clearly what pupils in a certain grade should know. If pupils finish a task ahead of time, they may circulate alongside the teacher and assist those who need help.

The interesting thing is that, far from disengaging slower learners, there is evidence that this whole-class approach encourages them. The class only moves ahead once everyone has grasped a concept, so slower learners are not left behind. Instead, they see that they can become as competent in a given topic as their peers. Combined with the cultural emphasis on effort over ability, this negates the idea of being 'bad' at a subject and the associated loss of motivation that can be seen in some faster-paced mixed ability classes. Meanwhile, faster-learning pupils experience the reward of assisting others and therefore helping the class to progress.

There is, however, highly competitive academic selection in the later stages of these education systems. This explains a second feature of the Japanese, Chinese and Korean systems, which cannot be overlooked. As described in Box 11.1, attendance at extra lessons is commonplace. At Juku, Hagwon and cram schools, slower learners can receive extra help whilst faster learners can be pushed in preparation for competitive examinations. Attending Juku certainly helps weaker pupils to stay on pace in their state-school classes. However, faster learners can become bored and disruptive in state-school classes as they repeat content that they have already learnt.

Rote-memorization and learning styles

The interaction of Confucian values with a highly competitive examination system means that lecture-style teaching, drilling and rote-learning are prevalent in many secondary schools. This is the only way that teachers can transmit and pupils can learn all the information they need to know for their exams. As we explain in Chapter 7, traditional Western educational theory links repetitive, rote-learning with a surface approach, where the learner attempts to memorize key pieces of information rather than understanding its meaning. Hence there is a stereotype of East Asian learners as being very good at memorizing information, but not very good at acquiring deep understanding, transferring their knowledge or branching out beyond the facts. However, more recently, questions have been raised about this assumption. After all, if these pupils only rote-learn methods and facts, how could they do quite so well in international tests that require them to apply their knowledge in novel contexts?

It turns out that beliefs about the relationship between memorization and understanding are not the same in the East and West. In many East Asian cultures, rote-learning and repetitive learning are differentiated. The latter is thought to aid understanding, on the basis that each time one re-reads or hears something again, one can gain new insights and understand the meaning more completely. In Confucius' *The Mean*, the learning process is described as 'studying extensively, enquiring carefully, pondering thoroughly, sifting clearly, and practising earnestly' (cited in Lee[18(p35)]).

Dahlin and Watkins[19] highlighted this difference through interviews with 18 German and 48 Hong Kong Chinese learners, aged 15 to 20 years, all of whom lived and studied in Hong Kong. All of the learners were asked about their views on the use of recitation and repetition for memorizing and understanding. Three key differences in their responses were: the greater extent to which the Chinese learners expressed a belief that

---

Box 11.1 Cram schools

Hagwon and Juku are the Korean and Japanese names for schools providing extra lessons, which are central to the education of many East Asian pupils. In China, they are simply referred to as 'cram schools'. Depending on age, and how much parents are willing to spend, pupils can spend one night to five nights a week attending these schools, possibly even weekends too.

The main purpose of cram schools is to help pupils prepare for the ruthless examinations that determine access to the next level of education and, ultimately, a respected university. In China, the crucial examination point is the crossover between junior middle school and high school (age 15–17). Certain high schools are known as 'key schools' and have better teachers and resources than other schools in an area. It is considered essential to attend one of these schools if a pupil wants to get a good grade in the National Higher Education Entrance Exam and get into university. Similarly, in Japan, the upper secondary school that a pupil attends is a major determinant of their admission to a well-respected university. Hence roughly half of all Japanese parents pay for their children to attend Juku while in middle school.[16]

The South Korean government has tried to reduce selection and examination pressure in the school system. However, there are still some selective high schools, and, ultimately, to get into university a pupil must do well on the Korean Scholastic Aptitude Test. Therefore the pressure is on from a young age to perform well academically. The Korean government has tried everything, from limiting teaching hours to limiting tuition fees to discourage the use of Hagwon, and yet in 2010 a reported 73% of middle-school pupils attended them.[17]

---

things they recited as young children could be useful in later life (33 Chinese vs 4 German learners); the greater extent to which the Chinese learners agreed that repetition plus 'attentive effort' could result in new meaning (30 Chinese vs 6 German learners); and the fact that five German but no Chinese learners presented repetition as a way to check (rather than attain) understanding. Thus the Chinese learners in this group more clearly differentiated repetition and memorization, viewing the former as a way to concentrate on content and to think about it in different ways.

Of course, the examination system in China does put pressure on learners to retain facts, and Chinese educators recognize that the sheer volume of information to be remembered can force learners to adopt a surface approach. However, the impact that course design can have on learning styles is just as evident in the United Kingdom. As I was just starting this book I was also helping a Chinese friend with PhD applications. Her degree was partly taught in China and then at a partner university in London. In the application she described how friends on her course would just look at past exam papers, identify trends in the questions and memorize model answers in order to do well. She wrote how she preferred to make extensive notes and really understand the topic, as well as passing the exam. I commented that I had read about the exam pressure in China, the tendency to memorize facts and repeat them in the exam. I explained that in contrast, higher education in the United Kingdom is designed to develop understanding. At this point she stopped me: 'Oh no, in China we must understand things, I am writing about my course in London!'

Motivation

In Western educational theory, a preference for memorization and a surface approach to learning are thought to reflect extrinsic motivation. In fact, several additional features of the typical East Asian education have fuelled a stereotype of East Asian learners as more extrinsically motivated than their Western peers. For one thing, a teacher-centred, didactic pedagogy does not offer much scope for pupils to pursue their own interests during lessons (something associated with intrinsic motivation). Also, pupils appear to be motivated by pressure from both teachers and parents to perform well in key examinations and thereby gain a place at a good university; they work hard to honour their parents and to avoid 'losing face' in class.[20] Again, though, if East Asian learners are extrinsically motivated then it is difficult for Western educational theory to explain why they seem able to retain, understand and apply so much information, or why they should express a genuine interest in what they learn.

In fact, an oppositional theory of intrinsic and extrinsic motivation does not seem to transfer well across cultures. Lin et al.[21] gave 72 Korean psychology students questions from the Motivated Strategies for Learning Questionnaire and found that the highest-attaining students had high intrinsic motivation coupled with moderate, rather than low, extrinsic motivation. This effect was more pronounced for Korean students than any samples of American students who were given the same questionnaire. Kember, Wong and Leung[22] asked 55 Chinese students at Hong Kong Polytechnic about the content of their courses and what made the course good and bad. Without being asked about motivation directly, 40% of students mentioned a combination of intrinsic and extrinsic factors motivating their interest in the course. For example, one student pointed out that a joint honours course was good because it improved students' career prospects by giving them a broad knowledge base, and yet also complained that it restricted the opportunity to learn about each topic in great depth. This student balanced the typically extrinsic motivation of improving career prospects with an apparently intrinsic motivation to learn about a subject.

It seems that this motivational theory does not transfer well because pressures that are indisputably linked with extrinsic motivation in a Western context may actually become internalized for an East Asian pupil. Students in Confucian heritage cultures are exposed to signals that identify education as having value not only to the individual but also to the family and society. Parents may remind their children that good academic performance is vital to having a good career and salary, but they do so in a context of closely knit families, where parents will make considerable sacrifices in order to give their children the best education, and will in turn expect their children to support them in old age. Therefore a well-paid career benefits the family as much as the individual. Similarly, teachers can form strong pastoral bonds with pupils. In Japan, for example, the homeroom teacher stays with a class throughout their time at a school, so they build up a meaningful relationship with individual pupils.[23] Therefore pupils who perform poorly may experience genuine guilt at letting their teacher down.

Iyengar and Lepper[24] demonstrated how East Asian pupils internalize apparently extrinsic motivators through work with fifth-grade children from East Asian and American backgrounds. The relationship they explored was that between choice and intrinsic motivation: when given a choice, people are expected to pursue what interests them and therefore to be more intrinsically motivated to persist with the task. Iyengar and Lepper compared a situation where pupils were either allowed to choose an anagram task to solve, were told which one to solve or, importantly, were told that their mothers had selected the task. Whilst Western pupils conformed to expectations and showed the strongest performance and greatest intrinsic motivation on the task where they had personal choice, East Asian pupils did not. They performed best and exhibited most intrinsic motivation when they were told that their mothers had taken the choice. Later, East Asian pupils were shown to be similarly motivated when their classmates, but not unknown pupils, had apparently made choices on their behalf. It seems that whilst the intrinsic motivation of

Western pupils is centred within themselves, for East Asian pupils the locus of such motivation extends to family and friends.

Western researchers have started to acknowledge that it is overly simplistic to identify intrinsic motivation as good and extrinsic motivation as bad. Based on their more recent research with American pupils and students, Ryan and Deci[25] have now proposed a spectrum of extrinsic motivation. Toshihiko Hayamizu[26] explored whether such a spectrum could also apply to Japanese learners. He administered the Stepping Motivation Scale to 483 junior high-school pupils and identified four types of motivation: 'external', 'introjected', 'identified' and 'intrinsic'. Examples of each type of motivation are given below:

- External: I study because my parents jump on me if I don't study.
- Introjected: I study because I want teachers to regard me as a good pupil.
- Identified: I study because studying science will be useful for me in the future.
- Intrinsic: I study because it is interesting for me to solve the problems.

One-fifth of the Japanese pupils in this sample were intrinsically motivated, whilst 40% were somewhere between the two motivational extremes. This agrees with wider research which challenges a simplistic view of East Asian pupils as more extrinsically motivated than their Western peers.

Systems across the World

In contrast to the diverse ideologies underpinning education across the world, the structures and curricula of education systems can seem relatively homogeneous. In Table 11.4 the structure of some of the top-performing systems is outlined, along with that of England and the United States. It is worth noting that this diagram only captures the routes of the majority of pupils in each country (for example, it does not include middle schools in England, or any forms of special education).

Looking at Table 11.4, certain differences stand out immediately. Firstly, the age at which children start school is notably earlier in England than in many of the top-performing countries, particularly Finland. Second, there is a clear distinction in most of these systems between vocational and academic routes, typically occurring when pupils are 16 years of age.

Table 11.4 The structure of different education systems

England	Japan	China	Korea	Singapore	Finland	USA
Nursery (3–4 years)	Kindergarten (3–6 years)	Kindergarten (3–6 years)	Kindergarten (3–7 years)	Kindergarten (3–6 years)		Nursery (3–4 years)
						Kindergarten (4–5 years)
Primary School (4/5–11 years)	Elementary School (6–12 years)	Elementary School (6–12 years)	Elementary School (6/7–12/13 years)	Primary School (6–12 years)	Pre-primary (6 years)	Elementary School (5/6/7–10/11/12 years)
					Comprehensive School (7–16 years)	
Secondary School (11–16 years)	Junior High School (12–15 years)	Junior Middle School (12–15 years)	Middle School (12/13–15/16 years)	Secondary School (12–16/17 years)		Middle School (10/11/12–12/13/14 years)
						Junior High School (12/13/14–14/15/16 years)
University Technical College (14–19 years)	Senior High School (15–18 years)	Senior Middle School (15–18 years)	High School (15/16–17/18 years)	Junior College (16/17–17/18 years)	General Upper Secondary School (16–19 years)	Senior High School (14/15/16–18 years)
School Sixth Form (17–18 years) / Sixth Form or FE College (17–19 years)	Technical College (15–20 years)	Vocational School (15–18 years)	Vocational School (15/16–17/18 years)	Centralised Institute (16/17–18/19 years)	Vocational Upper Secondary School (16–19 years)	
Further or Higher Education: Junior College	University	University	University	University	University	University
University	Junior College	Vocational College	Junior College / Polytechnic	Polytechnic	Polytechnic	Community College

Both of these distinctions undoubtedly affect both the pupil experience and the individuals these education systems shape.

The early years

There is great variation in the age at which children start kindergarten and school. Children in the United Kingdom must start formal education by the time they are 5, much younger than in most of the PISA countries. The average school starting age in the table is 6 years, whilst Finnish children do not even begin pre-school until then, and start elementary school at 7 years old. So what does this tell us about the validity of the English approach? Do our children benefit from starting school so young?

Our politicians certainly seem to think children benefit from early education, because they support initiatives such as Sure Start and funding for free pre-school places (see Chapter 10). Analysis of the PISA 2009 dataset indicates that, across multiple countries, those children who attended pre-school performed better in the PISA tests than those who did not.[27] However, a positive average masks significant variation between countries. Whilst attending a pre-school boosted reading performance (after accounting for socioeconomic background) by over 60 points in Italy, Belgium and France, it made no significant difference in Finland, Korea or the United States. In the United Kingdom, out of interest, it boosted performance by over 55 points. The PISA analysis finds that the greatest positive impact is achieved when pre-school education is offered to a large proportion of the population, over a relatively long period of time, with a small pupil:teacher ratio and high investment per child.

It is important to remember that in different countries, pre-school actually entails very different things. In both Japan and Finland, the emphasis is on developing children's social skills rather than on any formal learning. In Japanese kindergartens, cooperative social skills are encouraged by placing children in work groups who will complete tasks together and who may be graded together as well. Classes are typically 30-strong and the whole class will be given a shared goal, which is often social rather than academic. The teacher will openly discuss the meaning of social activities such as smiling with the children, so they become conscious of what it means to express emotion and interact socially with others.[28] Children are encouraged to be independent and to regulate their own and one another's behaviour by keeping adult intervention to a minimum whether playing, resolving disputes or preparing for new activities.[29,30] Japanese kindergartens offer social rather than academic preparation for learning; the first grade of school is designed to accommodate children with no academic experience.[31]

In China, according to the government, the kindergarten experience is supposed to emphasize child-initiated activity and the importance of play, to focus on the process rather than the outcome of activities, to incorporate an integrated curriculum and to account for individual differences.[32] In urban model schools some aspects of this vision are evident. Children join kindergarten at age 3 and are slowly eased into formal schooling, with lessons increasing in duration from 15 minutes for younger groups to 35 minutes for the oldest (aged 6). These short periods of formal learning are more didactic than in UK kindergartens, focusing on transmission of specific knowledge rather than building on the children's curiosity or questions, but teachers do also direct the children's play to engineer learning experiences.[33] Formal teaching is interspersed with plenty of free time, sleeping and meals, all shared with the same group in a common space[12,34] (and, as noted in Chapter 2, sleep is known to help with the consolidation of memories, so it is interesting that time for rest is scheduled into the Chinese kindergarten day). Of course, whilst this is the preferred government model, there can be constant parental pressure for teachers to focus more overtly on academic content in preparation for the entrance examinations their children will face over 10 years later.[12] Meanwhile, in many rural areas of China there is neither the financial nor human resource to support child-centred practices. Children in these areas therefore experience an additional year of elementary schooling, albeit less intensive.

So what does this mean for our own education system? Does it matter what age we start teaching children if we want them to do as well as they can? We might think from the Chinese model that educational performance can be enhanced by starting formal academic schooling from a younger age. However, we can see that in both Japan and Finland, introducing academic content much later does not harm children's future performance. Aunio and colleagues[35] conducted a study of 354 children aged 4–5 in China, Finland and England, who all took comparable versions of an early numeracy test. At this age, the Chinese and Finnish children were still in pre-school whilst the English children had been in school for half a year at most. Despite this, the Chinese and Finnish children scored significantly higher than the English children in their understanding of quantities and relations, and the Chinese children also scored significantly higher in their counting skills. The authors suggested that the superior performance of Chinese children reflects the cultural value that the Chinese place on mathematical skills. This could mean that parents had practised numeracy skills with their children even though they were not yet being formally schooled in them. Other research has also suggested that the structure of the Chinese number system makes it easier to learn and manipulate numbers.[36] For example, the names of numbers follow consistent rules and correspond directly to the base-10 system (so 15 is 'ten five' and 35 is 'three ten five'). Notably, Korean, Japanese and Finnish numbers follow a similar uniform structure (in Finnish, 5 is *viisi*, 15 is *viisitoista* and 50 is *viiskyt*).

In the United Kingdom and the United States, pre-school is regarded as a means to introduce academic content earlier. Yet in Finland and Japan, where older pupils actually perform better on international academic comparisons, the emphasis during pre-school is on social development. Of course, we must account for cultural differences that give pupils from certain countries such as China a head start. However, it is worth noting that academic achievement can be supported not only by teaching more content at an early age, but by actually taking the time to prepare children to learn.

General education: Elementary and secondary

If consistent differences in early schooling cannot explain the superior academic performance of both East Asian and Finnish pupils, then one might hope that features of elementary and secondary schooling would do so. In Chapter 10 we discuss whether factors such as class size or length of the school day might influence pupils' achievement. Much research aims to find distinguishing characteristics of successful school systems so that they can be emulated elsewhere.

East Asian education systems have historically had class sizes that would shock Western teachers and parents. For example, in Chinese kindergartens there may be as many as 40 children per class, whilst in Japan small kindergarten classes are considered sub-optimal for social development.[37] Secondary classes in Japan contain, on average, over 30 pupils. However, this cannot be taken as evidence against the benefits of small classes in Western schools, because the cultural values and teaching methods applied in Japan are so different from the constructivist, learner-centred methods favoured in the West. Although classes are bigger in Japan, Figure 11.2 shows that pupil:teacher ratios are similar to those in Western systems – in other words, there are not fewer teachers per school. Rather, teachers in many East Asian countries spend proportionately less time teaching and more time outside the classroom on lesson planning and pastoral aspects of care.

So what about the time that lower-secondary school pupils spend studying? Well, there is not that much variation in the length of the main school day. In Japan this is typically six or seven hours (excluding lunch) and in

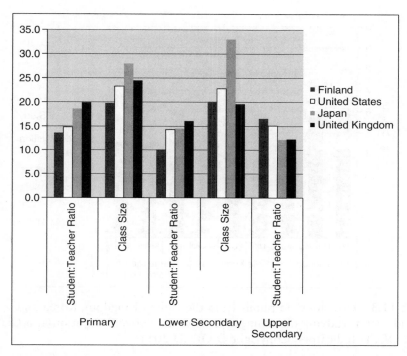

Figure 11.2 Student:teacher ratios and class sizes in Finland, Japan, the United States and the United Kingdom. *Data source*: Education at a Glance 2010. Copyright © OECD 2010.

Finland there is a cap of seven lesson hours per day for older pupils.[38] However, an obvious difference is that Japanese middle-school pupils will also spend up to three hours a day on extracurricular club participation, plus one or two hours studying at home and perhaps a further few hours at Juku. They therefore have much less unscheduled time than children in the United Kingdom. If we look at the time spent studying specific subjects (see Figure 11.3), we find that although East Asian pupils might spend longer studying their own language and mathematics than their UK counterparts, Finnish pupils do not.

If the time spent in school does not differ greatly, perhaps there are specific features of the school day that differentiate both Finnish and East Asian schools from those in the United Kingdom. Interestingly, these turn out to be largely things that go on outside lesson time. For example, in both Finland and Japan, pupils are given 10– 15-minute breaks between each lesson. We know that pupils' attention spans are shorter than most lessons, so it makes sense that they are given this time to relax, re-focus

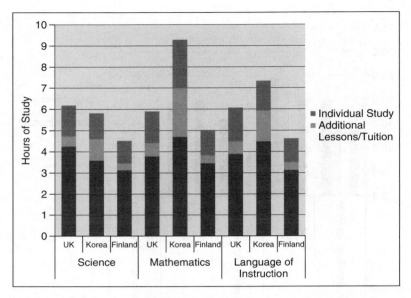

Figure 11.3 How long do pupils from the United Kingdom, Korea and Finland spend studying different subjects? *Data source*: Education at a Glance 2011: OECD Indicators. Copyright © OECD 2011.

and release pent-up energy. Yet in English state schools, particularly those with more challenging pupils, there is a tendency to minimize break times in what can only be described as an attempt at crowd control.

Another commonality between Finnish and Japanese schools is that all children eat a meal with their teachers at lunch. Indeed, in Finland there is a free hot meal for every child. In the United Kingdom, by comparison, teachers typically eat their lunch in the staffroom. Only pupils from low-income families receive free school meals and even then some teachers say that there is a stigma attached to this, which means that pupils may fail to claim them.*

A rather unusual element of the Japanese school day is cleaning. Every Japanese pupil is expected to help clean the school either after lunch or before they return home. Why? Because Japanese schooling is as much about responsibility and morality as knowledge, and communal cleaning is thought to teach these values. The pupils learn to take responsibility for their environment. Also, since they are meant to work in teams, they learn how important it is for every team member to be involved.[39]

---

* From September 2014, an entitlement to Free School Meals will be extended to all children in Reception, Class 1 and Class 2 in English schools.

In Chapter 2 we mentioned how physical exercise can have a positive effect on memory and the brain. Some studies find a positive link between physical activity and academic performance,[40] through either improved cognitive functions or improved attention spans. In the United Kingdom, on average, primary and secondary schools allocate only 7% of compulsory teaching time to physical education, which is below the OECD average of 9% for primary and 8% for secondary schools. Finland, Japan, Korea and China all allocate a greater proportion of primary teaching time to physical education,[41] which goes against the notion that spending time on exercise wastes time for learning.

Although it would be nice to find a magic number of learning hours or an ideal class size that is associated with superior academic performance, the evidence suggests that there are too many cultural factors at work to make this possible. In East Asian systems, pupils do work long hours and study much harder than many in European countries, yet evidence from Finland suggests that this is not the only way to produce strong academic performance. In fact, the main commonality between highly performing systems seems to be in the holistic approach taken to pupils' development. Attention is given to the development of physical and social as well as academic skills. Perhaps this is something from which UK educators and politicians can learn.

Vocational Education

At the start of this chapter we noted that the success of a country's education system may to some extent be reflected in its economic growth and employment rates. Although preparation for work is by no means the sole purpose of education, it is nonetheless an important outcome. This is where vocational education is particularly relevant.

In the United Kingdom, vocational education and training (VET) has returned to the spotlight now that the increase in university tuition fees is encouraging more young people to consider alternative post-18 options. Although there are some very strong apprenticeship schemes and vocational training providers in the United Kingdom, the overarching VET system has come under fire over the past decade. Employers claim that they find it hard to recruit young people with the right skills for the job, either because they have poor literacy or numeracy or have not been trained in the right occupational areas. Meanwhile, some educators and politicians have been critical of vocational qualifications that either they perceive as 'easy options' in comparison to traditional academic subjects

Table 11.5   Youth unemployment (age 15–24)

Country name	2000–06 Average (%)	2009 (%)
Switzerland	7.47	8.20
Japan	8.27	9.06
Netherlands	6.65	6.63
Hong Kong SAR, China	10.57	12.60
Australia	10.32	11.57
Singapore	9.33	12.91
Korea, Rep.	9.57	9.81
New Zealand	11.71	16.55
Canada	12.52	15.27
Estonia	15.94	27.27
United States	12.59	17.60
United Kingdom	14.58	18.86
Finland	17.73	20.47

Data source: World Bank, 2011.

or that research suggests neither prepare pupils for additional education nor boost their earnings potential. Concerns have been raised that pupils taking Level 2 vocational qualifications (which were for some time treated as equivalent to up to six GCSEs in school league tables) are often unaware that they will not be prepared to study Level 3 academic qualifications (such as A-levels) in the same area. Meanwhile, pupils have historically been able to take Level 3 vocational qualifications without even having achieved grade C in English and mathematics at GCSE. Following the Wolf Review of Vocational Education,[42] the UK VET system is in a process of change. In this section we therefore consider how these UK reforms may make the system more similar to those in two countries, Singapore and the Netherlands, that have strong reputations for VET and good records for youth employment (see Table 11.5).

The structure of the vocational system in Singapore (see Figure 11.4) overcomes two criticisms levelled at the UK system: that pupils taking vocational qualifications have been unable to move back to more academic study and that VET has been insufficiently focused on literacy and numeracy. In Singapore, in the 1990s the government took the decision that in order to become a fully developed country, specialized vocational education could only follow 10 years of general education.[43] Therefore, although pupils in mainstream education are directed into different streams – Express, Normal (Academic) and Normal (Technical) – after

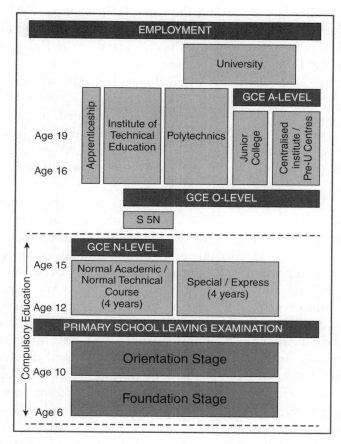

Figure 11.4 The Singaporean education system.[45] PSLE = Primary School Leaving Examinaton; GCE = General Certificate of Education. *Source*: UNESCO IBE – World Data on Education, 6th ed. UNESCO. Copyright © 2007 UNESCO. Available at: www.ibe.unesco.org/fileadmin/user_upload/ archive/Countries/WDE/2006/ASIA_and_the_PACIFIC/Singapore/Singapore .htm. Adapted with permission of UNESCO.

taking the Primary School Leaving Examination, there is flexibility to move between them.

Mathematics and English are at the core of Singapore's Technical route, with English language, 'basic mother tongue', mathematics and computer applications all compulsory subjects. In the first three years of secondary education, pupils can switch between Academic and Technical streams if both teacher and pupil consider this appropriate. Pupils in both the Normal (Technical) and Normal (Academic) streams also finish compulsory schooling by taking the same GCE exams, which makes it easy to switch streams by adding to existing qualifications and also avoids the explosion of qualifications that has occurred in the UK system. After taking final GCE 'N' exams, Technical stream pupils move to two-year courses at the ITE (Institute of Technical Education) and can then either begin work or transfer to a polytechnic, which over 50% of ITE graduates choose to do.[44] Polytechnics are designed to provide post-secondary vocational education, and produce middle managers and technologists. A further set of pupils from the GCE 'A' stream will move straight into polytechnics and can, if they choose, continue into university education.

Singapore's vocational education system is now highly effective: 85% of ITE graduates find work within three months of graduating[46] and as a trade-union representative from Singapore has stated: 'Generally, the young do not face a serious unemployment problem in Singapore'[47(p6)]. However, it is important to emphasize that this has been achieved only through sustained and targeted government efforts. Historically, vocational education was seen as a poor second to academic routes, so the government had to undertake a marketing drive to raise the esteem of VET. As the Singaporean economy changed, the government was also active in closing down redundant training courses and developing new ones. In the 1980s, for example, new qualifications such as 'Electronics' and 'Precision Engineering' were created specifically to support economic restructuring towards high-technology, value-added industries. ITE and polytechnics do not decide which courses to offer independently; they do so in conjunction with employers.[43]

The demand-led way in which Singapore's VET system works contrasts starkly with the United Kingdom, where qualifications are often said to be too 'supply led': designed to meet the needs of pupils and teachers, rather than employers, often with a reduction in the quality and difficulty of content as a result. A further criticism made by UK employers is that they face a problem with 'lack of experience' when seeking to employ young people. So which country has a good model of employer involvement in VET provision?

Figure 11.5 shows the educational transitions that Dutch pupils make before entering the workplace. As in the United Kingdom, post-secondary vocational education can be either school-based or training on the job (equivalent to an apprenticeship). Unlike the UK system, however, where a pupil can take a Level 3 qualification without ever entering the workplace, Dutch pupils in the school-based pathway spend between 20% and 60% of time on placement, for which they are paid a nominal wage.

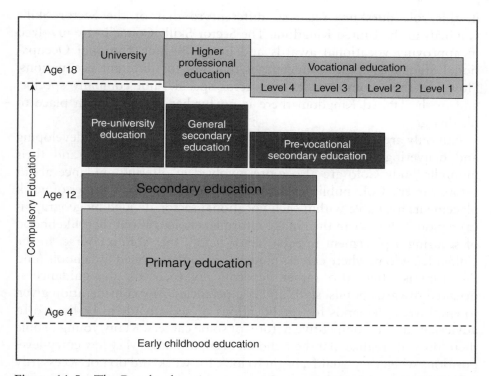

Figure 11.5 The Dutch education system. *Source*: Adapted from OCW. Key Figures 2004–2008: Education, Culture and Science; 2009.

Meanwhile, those who opt for training on the job spend four days at work, under contract and receiving a salary, and spend one day in school or college to study a theoretical component.[48] Unlike the United Kingdom, this ratio of work to study is specified by the government, which avoids the confusion that arises regarding the amount of study that apprentices should undertake, and whether this can be via workplace training or must be in a college environment.

The content of Dutch VET is linked to the labour market through a greater degree of employer involvement in formulating, delivering and advising about qualifications. There is local employer involvement in curriculum formation and the Centres of Expertise, 17 bodies that represent over 40 branches of industry, also help to develop and maintain qualifications by establishing sets of competencies that should be incorporated into different vocational qualifications. The Centres are governed by employers, unions and educators and work in partnership with social partners, schools, training institutions and ministries.[49] On the face of it, this role does not seem so different to that of the Sector Skills Councils in the United Kingdom. The Sector Skills Councils are involved in approving vocational awards and in establishing National Occupational Standards – the competencies required for different occupations. However, these competencies are sector specific, not company specific, and in the United Kingdom there is no further mechanism in place to fill this gap.

Not only are employers in the Netherlands more involved in developing and delivering qualifications, but the Centres of Expertise and their umbrella body Colo are also more involved in offering guidance about future careers. Colo publishes monthly reports listing the number of work placements available within each vocational sector, divided by geographical region.[50] Pupils can then make informed choices about their likelihood of securing a placement in each sector *before* they join a course. In the United Kingdom, where careers guidance is commissioned by schools (and therefore is often also rather academically focused), the guidance is oriented towards pupils' skills and competencies. Any consideration given to employers' demands for qualifications or skills tends to be limited to advice about the 'competitive nature' of some careers. Many young people therefore only realize that their chosen occupation has very few entry-level positions when they qualify, begin to look for work and do not necessarily find any.

Recent government reforms in England and Wales have brought the VET system closer to the Singaporean and Dutch models. The number of Level 2 vocational qualifications that are included in league tables has been greatly reduced and they are now equivalent to only one GCSE. Young people who have not achieved a grade C in maths or English at GCSE also have to keep studying them post-16 until they do so. However, there is still a lot to be learnt from other countries. For example, evidence from Singapore suggests that the status of VET is important, whilst the Dutch example indicates that close links with, and investment from, employers is essential. As always, though, one must consider the importance of context and economic background. These countries are significantly smaller in terms of population and economy (GDP) than the United Kingdom. This naturally makes it easier to forge employer links and monitor the labour market, because there are fewer links to forge and fewer vacancies and skills shortages to monitor. Nonetheless, it is hard to argue against notions such as the value of work-based experience (our own employers emphasize this) and the importance of promoting vocational education as a respectable and profitable avenue that can have parity of esteem with academic alternatives.

Learning from the Best

We have reviewed what makes different education systems unique (or similar) at the ideological, structural and pedagogical level. So, now it is time to consider just how we can learn from these examples, and how others are learning from us.

Asian reforms

Given their pupils' dominance in international comparisons, you might be forgiven for thinking that there is little need for East Asian education systems to undergo reform. However, whilst these systems might be producing very good exam takers, other aspects are causing teachers, parents and politicians concern.

There is increasing pressure to produce young people who can not only reproduce information for tests, but are also independent and creative thinkers. Many aspects of traditional Chinese and Korean educational practice are likely to dampen creativity and innovation with time: pupils' desire to avoid loss of face (which could discourage them from voicing original but controversial ideas), the fact that it is socially unacceptable to challenge one's teacher, and the focus on accurate memorization and understanding of specific concepts (i.e. convergent thinking). East Asian students studying at US or UK universities can experience quite a culture shock when required to adopt more independently directed and divergent styles of learning. However, this is not the only reason for the drive to promote creativity in East Asian schools. It also reflects a desire for economic growth, which is seen to depend partly on innovation. Indeed, Dr Yong Zhao at the University of Oregon has observed a negative correlation between PISA maths scores and scores on the Global Entrepreneurship Monitor, an index of entrepreneurial attitudes and activities which, in 2011, included 23 PISA countries[51] (see Figure 11.6). This suggests that strong test performance does not guarantee the cultivation of creative traits, which contribute to economic growth in the West. However, since Singapore, Korea and China all exhibit higher rates of GDP growth than the United States or the United Kingdom we should perhaps not assume that every education system or economy has to achieve success through the same mechanisms or by the same measures as our own.

The second motivation for reform is concern about the significant pressure that pupils experience in these exam-driven systems. In Japan, there

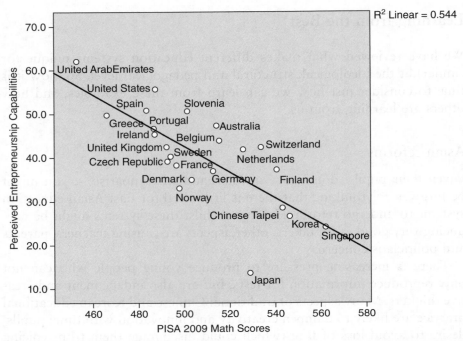

Figure 11.6   The negative correlation between entrepreneurship and PISA maths scores. *Source*: Test Scores vs. Entrepreneurship: PISA, TIMSS, and Confidence. *Education in the Age of Globalization*. Copyright © Yong Zhao, 2012. Available at: http://zhaolearning.com/2012/06/06/test-scores-vs -entrepreneurship-pisa-timss-and-confidence/. Reproduced with permission of Yong Zhao.

is an increasing trend of school refusal: not the same as truancy because it reflects a true anxiety and reluctance to attend school. In Japan, Korea, China and India there are also reports every year of young people who commit suicide owing to the pressure of their entrance examinations. In South Korea, during the 1960s and 70s, the government took action to limit competitive entry to schools for this very reason and Japan has also responded to these issues with repeated attempts at educational reform. During the early 2000s, the Japanese curriculum was reduced by 30% and Saturday school was cut. There was a shift to an 'integrated curriculum' where time was to be set aside to focus on human rights, community-based work, cross-cultural existence and international under-standing. The intention was to develop pupils' problem-solving skills and to encourage them to apply their knowledge to real-life contexts.[52,53] Although these changes were quite effectively adopted in elementary schools, lower-secondary school teachers struggled to implement them whilst retaining enough time to teach examined subjects. Some questioned the value of dedicating so much time to activities that would not contribute to examination results. Following a small drop in Japan's performance in international assessments, the curriculum was therefore extended again. However, certain Western pedagogical principles have been retained, such as an increasing emphasis on addressing the needs of individual learners and a slow reduction in class sizes.

In China there has been a similar attempt to move away from didactic teaching and rote-learning to more pupil-led, constructivist methods. The government has recognized the need for young people to become creative and innovative thinkers with the practical skills relevant to employment. To achieve this, they have tried to increase the relevance of the curriculum and have looked at creating a credit system in secondary schools where pupils take courses at a level of difficulty to suit them. They are also supporting the use of multiple textbooks as points of reference, rather than for memorization. However, this shift has faced resistance from parents and teachers. Teachers in rural areas have found it difficult to change their teaching methods so dramatically without suitable training, and have found it hard to implement constructivist methods when they are under-resourced and may have classes of close to 100 pupils. Parents are concerned that their children will no longer do well in the ever-important entrance examinations and are all too willing to step in and buy extra books or fund cram schools if they no longer think schools will do the job. Hence education leaders argue that radical reforms may be almost impossible to implement without concomitant changes in the examination system.

The real question is whether it is actually appropriate for East Asian educators to be encouraged to adopt Anglo-American pedagogical approaches when these may not align with dominant cultural values. In rural Chinese schools, which are typically underfunded, the more that the curriculum shifts to a resource-intensive Anglo-American model rather than being based on hard work and memorization, the harder it is for pupils to achieve educational success. We shouldn't forget that the original Chinese civil service exams were designed to be meritocratic and that for many Chinese young people, education and examination success is an important route out of poverty. Rather than push for wholesale reform, incremental adaptations, for example to allow for more creative thinking in certain lessons, could be more appropriate.

The Finnish approach (and UK response)

Rather unsurprisingly given its success in international assessments, plenty of researchers and policy makers have spent the past few years trying to identify why Finland has such a high-performing education system. Two of the predominant factors that they highlight are autonomy and professionalism.

Finland is notable for the extent to which its teachers and schools are given autonomy in implementing the curriculum. Whilst a national curriculum, along with assessment criteria, is determined centrally, local authorities and schools then decide how to implement it. Teachers are free to select textbooks and resources that they consider appropriate, and to adopt the methods they deem effective for teaching. Unlike the United Kingdom and United States, there is no close monitoring of performance. The only standardized assessment pupils sit is the matriculation exam at the end of nine years' compulsory schooling. There is no government inspectorate monitoring schools. It is schools themselves which are expected to devise strategies and standards for performance, and to ensure they are met. Teachers set their own tests and use continuous assessment to check the progress of their pupils. The result of this autonomy is that teachers are free to be creative and innovative with teaching methods. They can shape the curriculum to meet their pupils' interests and needs. Pupil anxiety is low because they are not constantly faced with competitive tests.

It is worth noting, however, that although teachers are at liberty to experiment with new pedagogical approaches, 'pedagogical conservatism' remains.[54] Whole-class teaching is common and some schools that have experimented with allowing pupils to select subject content and learn at their own pace have either given up or come close to closing.[55] It seems that teachers retain traditional methods as a framework within which to incorporate some novel teaching approaches and to build on pupils' interests. Given the autonomy of Finnish teachers, it is difficult to describe any 'typical' pedagogical approach that they adopt; however, teacher-centred methods certainly do not seem to be redundant in their classrooms.

The complement to teacher autonomy is the treatment of teachers as professionals. All teachers in Finnish schools have master's degrees. Furthermore, only about one-tenth of applicants to teaching courses are accepted, so the quality of trainees is high. Then, once teachers are working in schools, they are involved in continuing professional development designed to suit their own needs, not overarching government targets. The result of this approach is that a quarter of secondary graduates see teaching as the most desirable profession, even though others may be better paid[56] In the Finnish context, this approach clearly works. Parents trust teachers, and this trust is justified by pupils' academic success.

However, like all the nations we have discussed in this chapter, Finland also has cultural characteristics that support its educational success. For example, traditional Finnish values include a trust in authority and a commitment to one's social group (perhaps rather similar to some Confucian ideals?). The former value encourages parental trust in teachers even when performance indicators are not readily available. The latter supports the Finnish commitment to a fully comprehensive education system, where pupils who seem to be falling behind receive intensive additional support. Consequently, pupils are likely to receive a high-quality education regardless of which school they attend: the variation in performance between schools is one of the lowest of all countries that participate in PISA.[57]

Teachers also benefit from advantageous population characteristics. Many Americans point out the low level of immigration in Finland, which means that schools face fewer challenges in terms of overcoming language barriers of new pupils. Finland also has an unusual history of good literacy. During the seventeenth century a law was passed that no one could be confirmed in church before they could read and write. Since people could not marry unless they were confirmed, this helped to nigh-on eradicate illiteracy within a few generations. Finland remains a nation with a great number of libraries, whose citizens borrow more library books than those in any other country. This suggests that the wider societal context is supportive of intellectual improvement, particularly literacy. As noted in Chapter 3, the Finnish orthography is also more transparent than English, which makes it easier to learn to read.

The UK government has incorporated aspects of the Finnish model into recent policy reforms. Proposals have included teacher training that replicates the model in Finland, where universities training teachers are linked with special 'university schools' to offer in-classroom training opportunities. The notion of teachers as professionals has also been emphasized and the government will now only fund teacher training for graduates with at least a 2:2. Unfortunately, this is still a long way from Finland's selection of only the top tier of graduate applicants. Similarly, whilst the UK government is edging towards goals of autonomy with the increasing number of academies and the introduction of free schools, a transition to Finnish levels of autonomy seems a long way off. The English system has long operated in a fundamentally top-down manner, with Key Stage targets and league tables used to indirectly control teachers' behaviour. It does not seem that we are likely to lose league tables any time soon when they are perceived as such an important instrument for 'parent choice', and new performance measures such as the English Baccalaureate continue to be introduced.

Ultimately, although there are some aspects of the Finnish education system that the United Kingdom can readily emulate, researchers are coming to the conclusion that the performance of Finnish pupils is as much a reflection of broad cultural differences as specific features of the education system. Whilst the United Kingdom still struggles with basic literacy and focuses on competition and choice in education rather than comprehensive ideals, it is questionable whether minor structural changes will result in a replication of Finnish educational success.

Let's Not Forget . . .

In this chapter we have focused heavily on the East Asian, or Confucian heritage, education systems as well as on Finland. This reflects their standing in international assessments as well as political interest in the Finnish education system and the increasing prominence and power of East Asian economies. However, it is important to add a few caveats about the conclusions we can draw.

First of all, the main international assessments – PISA and TIMSS – evaluate only the core subjects of maths, science and the language of instruction. They test pupils only at certain ages and in certain schools. Furthermore, the structures of the tests are different, with PISA focusing more on application and problem-solving, and TIMSS looking at knowledge of curriculum content. Therefore we can't take these tests as unequivocal assessments of an education system's quality. Most obviously, we might be overlooking the strength of teaching in another area; second languages or the arts perhaps. These tests are also not measures of pupil well-being or of future employment prospects. In other words, they do what they say on the tin and nothing more: telling us which countries produce pupils who can demonstrate a good competency in maths, science and their language of instruction.

It is important to be aware that unlike most countries, which offer up a representative sample of pupils from across the nation, tests in China are conducted regionally in Hong Kong, Chinese Taipei, Macao and Shanghai. Although pupils from Shanghai topped the rankings in PISA 2009, China is a large and heterogeneous country. Generally speaking, urban schools are likely to receive more resources and better teachers than those in rural areas. Therefore, the results from Shanghai reflect the abilities of China's more advantaged pupils. We should probably not assume that every class, from every part of the country, would be so capable of excelling in the PISA tests.

Finally, despite all the interesting things we can learn from comparative studies, it is necessary to consider whether teaching methods will always transfer across the world. Just as Chinese and Japanese teachers can find it hard to adopt Western pedagogical methods, we cannot guarantee that a traditional East Asian approach would be effective in the United Kingdom. One must always consider how educational methods would interact with a country's own cultural values. Would parents in the United Kingdom really want their children studying for 12 hours each day? Would children in the United Kingdom ever spend hours reciting formulae or poems in order to understand them? Even transferring ideas from Finland, which shares many more cultural similarities, is not straightforward. The United Kingdom has a more diverse population, a less regular language and lower rates of library use, and teaching as a profession is not regarded with such high esteem. Therefore, whatever we want to transfer has to be viewed critically in a new context. On that note, though, we will review what we can learn from other education systems in contrast to our own.

Summary

- East Asian education is based on foundational principles that are very different from those of Western education, being heavily influenced by Confucian teaching. Whilst this may bring benefits by encouraging a focus on effort rather than ability, and inspiring hard work for both personal and societal benefit, it does not entirely overcome problems of disengagement and can leave children feeling pressured to perform.
- Common misconceptions about East Asian learners are that they are extrinsically motivated, tend to rote-learn content and do not engage in deep learning of material. However, there is evidence that these Western categories do not transfer smoothly to the East Asian mindset and that these pupils actually engage in deep learning during memorization. They also appear to internalize motivational factors that from a Western perspective would be considered extrinsic.
- Most children across the world do not start formal schooling as early as those in the United Kingdom and this does not seem to put them at any long-term disadvantage. In many East Asian countries, the early

years are about social development and preparing to learn. Children can be shown how to act cooperatively, how to discipline themselves and one another, and how to attend to teachers during formal periods of learning.

- There appears to be a greater emphasis on pastoral provision in the Japanese and Finnish elementary school systems than in the United Kingdom. Japanese homeroom teachers remain with the same class for many years. In both Japan and Finland, teachers eat with their pupils and Finnish pupils all receive a free hot meal every day.
- There are few obvious distinctions between the UK and Finnish education systems that can explain why Finnish pupils perform so much better in international tests. The truly comprehensive nature of the education system may be one factor, as well as the extent of teacher autonomy and the greater respect for teaching as a profession. However, cultural factors such as high literacy rates may also provide a firmer foundation for educational success.
- East Asian pupils typically work longer hours than those in the West and may attend cram schools after finishing classes at school. This reflects the extreme pressure to perform well in high-stakes examinations.
- Educators in East Asia do seem to be attempting reforms that will align their systems more closely with Anglo-American educational ideals. However, some of these reforms have met with much resistance and it is unclear whether it will be possible to adopt more individualistic, constructivist methods without sacrificing the high attainment that the existing systems are renowned for producing.
- Singapore and the Netherlands have strong VET (vocational education and training) systems that produce highly employable young people. These systems have benefited from government decisions to invest in and value VET, as well as close links with employers. It must be noted that both systems have mathematics and literacy at their core, suggesting that the UK government's focus on these basic skills is well founded.

Educational implications

- Starting formal schooling at a young age does not appear to confer a long-term academic advantage, so it may be wise to review the content of early years education in the United Kingdom and consider placing a greater emphasis on the development of children's social rather than academic skills.

- Many Confucian values, such as an emphasis on effort, hard work and cooperation, appear to contribute to the strong academic performance of East Asian pupils. It is worth exploring how these values can be promoted in UK schools.
- The Finnish and East Asian elementary school days include time for frequent breaks, sleep and a hot meal. It may be beneficial for UK educators to take a more holistic perspective on education, rather than focusing largely on the activities and outcomes that occur within lesson time.
- Strong VET systems have numeracy and literacy at their core. As the UK VET system undergoes reform, the decision to place greater emphasis on the continued teaching of mathematics and English should be welcomed, since they are essential for employability and educational success.

Answer to the PISA question at the start of the chapter: B, 1.5 km.

References

1   Mullis IVS, Martin MO, Foy P, Alka A. *TIMSS 2011 International Results in Mathematics*. Chestnut Hill, MA: TIMSS & PIRLS International Study Center, Boston College; 2012.
2   Martin MO, Mullis IVS, Foy P, Stanco GM. *TIMSS 2011 International Results in Science*. Chestnut Hill, MA: TIMSS & PIRLS International Study Center, Boston College; 2012.
3   Zhou J. *Remaking China's Public Philosophy for the Twenty-First Century*. Westport, CT: Greenwood; 2003.
4   Chan S. The Chinese learner – a question of style. *Education & Training*. 1999;41(6/7):294–304.
5   Watkins DA, Biggs JB. Teaching the Chinese Learner: Psychological and Pedagogical Perspectives. Hong Kong: Comparative Education Research Centre; 2001.
6   Confucius, Slingerland EG. *Confucius Analects: With Selections from Traditional Commentaries*. Indianapolis, IN: Hackett Publishing; 2003.
7   Sun M. Educational research in Mainland China: Current situation and developmental trends. *Comparative Education*. 2011;47(3):315–325. doi: 10.1080/03050068.2011.586764.
8   Stevenson HW, Chen C, Lee S-Y. Mathematics achievement of Chinese, Japanese, and American children: Ten years later. *Science*. 1993;259(5091): 53–58.
9   Hau K, Salili F. Achievement goals and causal attributions of Chinese students. In: Lau S, ed. *Growing Up the Chinese Way: Chinese Child and*

Adolescent Development. Hong Kong: Chinese University Press; 1996 :121–146.

10   Holloway SD, Kashiwagi K, Hess RD, Azuma H. Causal attributions by Japanese and American mothers and children about performance in mathematics. *International Journal of Psychology.* 1986;21(1–4):269–286. doi:http://dx.doi.org/10.1080/00207598608247590.

11   Weiner B. An attributional theory of achievement motivation and emotion. *Psychological Review.* 1985;92(4):548.

12   Vaughan J. Early childhood education in China. *Childhood Education.* 1993;69(4):196–200.

13   Cortazzi M. Learning from Asian lessons. *Education 3–13.* 1998;26(2):42–49. doi:10.1080/03004279885200201.

14   Natale K, Aunola K, Nurmi J-E. Children's school performance and their parents' causal attributions to ability and effort: A longitudinal study. *Journal of Applied Developmental Psychology.* 2009;30(1):14–22. doi:10.1016/j.appdev.2008.10.002.

15   Yao X. *An Introduction to Confucianism.* Cambridge: Cambridge University Press; 2000.

16   MEXT. Japan's Education at a Glance 2006. 2006. Available at: www.mext.go.jp/component/english/__icsFiles/afieldfile/2011/03/07/1303008_006.pdf. Accessed 2 December 2013.

17   Statistics Korea. The 2010 Survey of Private Education Expenditure. 2011. Available at: http://kostat.go.kr/portal/english/news/1/8/index.board?bmode=read&bSeq=&aSeq=246584&pageNo=1&rowNum=10&navCount=10&currPg=&sTarget=title&sTxt=. Accessed 2 December 2013.

18   Lee WO. The cultural context for Chinese learners: Conception of learning in Confucian tradition. In: Watkins DA, Biggs JB, eds. *The Chinese Learner: Cultural Psychological and Contextual Influences.* Hong Kong: CERC and ACERC; 1996.

19   Dahlin B, Watkins D. The role of repetition in the process of memorising and understanding: A comparison of the views of German and Chinese secondary school students in Hong Kong. *British Journal of Educational Psychology.* 2000;70:65–84.

20   Bond MH, Hwang K. The social psychology of Chinese people. In: Bond MH, ed. *The Psychology of the Chinese People.* Hong Kong: Oxford University Press; 1996:213–266.

21   Lin Y-G, McKeachie WJ, Kim YC. College student intrinsic and/or extrinsic motivation and learning. *Learning and Individual Differences.* 2001;13(3):251–258. doi:10.1016/S1041-6080(02)00092-4.

22   Kember D, Wong A, Leung DYP. Reconsidering the dimensions of approaches to learning. *British Journal of Educational Psychology.* 1999;69(3):323–343.

23   Fukuzawa RE. The path to adulthood according to Japanese middle schools. *Journal of Japanese Studies.* 1994;20(1):61–86.

24 Iyengar SS, Lepper MR. Rethinking the value of choice: A cultural perspective on intrinsic motivation. *Attitudes and Social Cognition*. 1999;76(3): 349–366.

25 Ryan RM, Deci EL. Intrinsic and extrinsic motivations: Classic definitions and new directions. *Contemporary Educational Psychology*. 2000;25(1): 54–67. doi:10.1006/ceps.1999.1020.

26 Hayamizu T. Between intrinsic and extrinsic motivation: Examination of reasons for academic study based on the theory of internalization. *Japanese Psychological Research*. 1997;39(2):98–108.

27 OECD. Does participation in pre-primary education translate into better learning outcomes at school? 2011. Available at: www.oecd-ilibrary.org/ education/does-participation-in-pre-primary-education-translate-into-better-learning-outcomes-at-school_5k9h362tpvxp-en. Accessed 2 December 2013.

28 Lewis CC. Japanese first-grade classrooms: Implications for U.S. theory and research. *Comparative Education Review*. 1988;32(2):159–172.

29 Peak L. *Learning to Go to School in Japan: The Transition from Home to Preschool Life*. Berkeley: University of California Press; 1993.

30 Wawa M. Japanese preschool: 12 things that stunned Chinese mom. China-smack. 2010. Available at: www.chinasmack.com/2010/stories/chinese-mom-japanese-preschool.html. Accessed 2 December 2013.

31 INCA. Japan. *INCA (International Review of Curriculum and Assessment) Frameworks*. 2011. Available at: www.inca.org.uk/1464.html. Accessed 2 December 2013.

32 Zhu J, Zhang J. Contemporary trends and developments in early childhood education in China. *Early Years*. 2008;28(2):173–182. doi:10 .1080/09575140802163584.

33 Rao N, Li H. "Eduplay": Beliefs and practices related to play and learning in Chinese kindergartens. In: Pramling-Samuelsson I, Fleer M, eds. *Play and Learning in Early Childhood Settings*. Vol. 1. Dordrecht: Springer Netherlands; 2008:97–116.

34 Lystad M. Children of China: A commentary. *Children Today*. 1987;16(2): 20–22.

35 Aunio P, Aubrey C, Godfrey R, Pan Y, Liu Y. Children's early numeracy in England, Finland and People's Republic of China. *International Journal of Early Years Education*. 2008;16(3):203–221. doi:10.1080/ 09669760802343881.

36 Ng SSN, Rao N. Chinese number words, culture, and mathematics learning. *Review of Educational Research*. 2010;80(2):180–206. doi:10.3102/ 0034654310364764.

37 Tobin J, Hsueh Y, Karasawa M. *Preschool in Three Cultures Revisited: China, Japan, and the United States*. Chicago: University of Chicago Press; 2009.

38 Centre for Educational Assessment. Curriculum and Distribution of Lesson Hours. The Finnish PISA 2006 Pages. 2006. Available at: www.pisa2006

.helsinki.fi/education_in_Finland/Curriculum_and_assessment/Curriculum_and_distribution_of_lesson_hours.htm. Accessed 2 December 2013.

39   Le Tendre GK. Community-building activities in Japanese schools: Alternative paradigms of the democratic school. *Comparative Education Review*. 1999;43(3):283–310.

40   Trudeau F, Shephard RJ. Relationships of physical activity to brain health and the academic performance of schoolchildren. *American Journal of Lifestyle Medicine*. 2010;4(2):138–150. doi:10.1177/1559827609351133.

41   OECD. How much time do students spend in the classroom? In: *Education at a Glance*. Paris: Organisation for Economic Cooperation and Development; 2011.

42   Wolf A. Review of Vocational Education – The Wolf Report. London: Department for Education; 2011.

43   Seng LS. Vocational Technical Education and Economic Development – The Singapore Experience. Singapore: Institute of Technical Education; 2007.

44   MoM/MoE. Educational Upgrading of Institute of Technical Education (ITE) Graduates. Singapore: Ministry of Manpower; 2008.

45   UNESCO. *UNESCO IBE – World Data on Education*, 6th edition – Singapore. UNESCO; 2007. Available at: www.ibe.unesco.org/fileadmin/user_upload/archive/Countries/WDE/2006/ASIA_and_the_PACIFIC/Singapore/Singapore.htm. Accessed 2 December 2013.

46   Sakellariou C. *Profitability of Vocational vs. Formal Education for Men and Women in Singapore Using Quantile Regressions*. Singapore: Economic Growth Centre, Nanyang Technological University; 2005.

47   Yacob H. Globalisation and Youth Employment. 2004. Available at: www.mhlw.go.jp/english/topics/globalization/dl/33.pdf. Accessed 2 December 2013.

48   Colo. Colo – Senior Secondary VET. Colo; 2011a. Available at: www.colo.nl/senior-secondary-vet.html. Accessed 16 December 2011.

49   Colo. About Colo: Colo and the Centres of Expertise on Dutch VET. Colo; 2011b. Available at: www.workplacement.nl/tl_files/bestanden/colo-folder-engels.pdf. Accessed 2 December 2013.

50   Colo. Colo – Publications. Colo. 2011c. Available at: www.colo.nl/publications.html. Accessed December 16, 2011.

51   Zhao Y. Flunking innovation and creativity. *Phi Delta Kappan*. 2012;94(1): 56–61.

52   MacDonald L. Curriculum Reform in Japan Reflections of Cultural Change via the Integrated Curriculum. Tokyo: Center for Research of Core Academic Competences, University of Tokyo; 2005.

53   MacDonald L. Curriculum Reform as a Reflection of Tradition and Change: Japanese Teachers' Approaches to Dimensions of Difference via the Integrated Curriculum. 2006. Available at: http://drum.lib.umd.edu/bitstream/1903/3447/1/umi-umd-3266.pdf. Accessed 2 December 2013.

54 Simola H. The Finnish miracle of PISA: Historical and sociological remarks on teaching and teacher education. *Comparative Education*. 2005;41(4): 455–470.

55 Carlgren I, Klette K, Myrdal S. Changes in Nordic teaching practices: From individualised teaching to the teaching of individuals. *Scandinavian Journal of Educational Research*. 2006;50(3):301–326.

56 Sahlberg P. Education policies for raising student learning: The Finnish approach. *Journal of Education Policy*. 2007;22(2):147–171. doi:10.1080/02680930601158919.

57 OECD. *Finland: Slow and Steady Reform for Consistently High Results*. Paris: OECD Publishing; 2010. Available at: www.oecd.org/pisa/pisaproducts/46581035.pdf. Accessed 2 December 2013.

Chapter 12

Life-long Learning
How Can We Teach Old Dogs New Tricks?

How is your memory doing? Test yourself on the following questions concerning lapses in everyday memory.[1] Everyday memory is what we use to carry out the actions that constitute our normal behaviour.

Use the following check list to score:

1 = Not at all in the last 6 months
2 = About once in the last 6 months
3 = More than once in the last 6 months but less than once a month
4 = About once a month
5 = More than once a month but less than once a week
6 = About once a week
7 = More than once a week but less than once a day
8 = About once a day
9 = More than once a day

Q1 Do you forget where you have put things? Lose things around the house?

Q2 Do you find television or film stories difficult to follow?

Q3 Have you forgotten a change in your daily routine such as where something is kept?

Education and Learning: An Evidence-Based Approach, First Edition. Jane Mellanby and Katy Theobald.

Q4 Have you had to go back to check whether you have done something that you meant to do?
Q5 Have you completely forgotten to take things with you, or left things behind and had to go back and fetch them?
Q6 Have you forgotten when something happened? For example, whether something happened yesterday or last week.
Q7 Have you found that a word is on the tip of your tongue? You know what it is but cannot find it?
Q8 Have you forgotten important details of what you did or what happened to you the day before?
Q9 When reading a newspaper or magazine article, have you been unable to follow the thread of the story or lost track of what it is about?
Q10 Have you got lost or taken a wrong turning on a journey, on a walk or in a building where you have *often* been before?
Q11 Have you repeated to someone what you have just told them or asked them the same question twice?
Q12 Have you got the details of what someone has told you mixed up and confused?

Add up your score. Your memory is good if your score is less than 30, average if it is between 30 and 60, and not so good if it is more than 60. Of course, if you do have a high score it may be because your life is very busy; someone leading a busy life is likely to make more of these errors – 'the greater number of situations in which lapses are possible, the greater number of lapses you will report' (Alan Baddeley).

The kind of failures of memory that the questionnaire detects become commoner as we age. In this chapter we shall consider why that should be and whether it has any bearing on the techniques that should be employed in the education of older people – life-long learning. Positive answers to many of the questions above imply increased distractability; others suggest failures of memory for space or time; some suggest failure in planning; the tip of the tongue phenomenon shows that some memories have become temporarily inaccessible.

How do these lapses map onto the divisions of memory systems that are widely accepted in cognitive psychology? (see Chapter 2). In neuro-anatomical terms the lapses map onto the activity of the hippocampus and/or the prefrontal cortex (neocortex above the eyes).

Improved health care, housing and diet have led in most of the Western world to a substantial increase over the past 100 years, but particularly over the past 60 years, in the numbers of retired elderly people depending on pensions. This has been seen as a 'drag' on the economy and the health-care system.

Box 12.1   The ageing UK population

	1985	2010
Median age of adult population:	35 yrs	40 yrs
% Over 65 yrs	15	17
Number over 65 yrs	12.7 million	14.4 million
Number over 85	0.69 million	1.4 million

Source: Office for National Statistics.

However, many of these people are able and willing to work, either physically or intellectually or both. In an increasingly technologically based environment which is rapidly changing, if such people are to continue in or to re-enter employment it is likely that they will need to acquire new skills. However, remarkably little work has been done on determining ways in which the education and training of older people may need to be tailored to the changed functioning of the brain and its behavioural output in older people. Most work has been done on determining what effect environmental factors, such as exercise and mental stimulation, have on general cognitive ability in the old.

One of the problems with studying ageing is the difficulty in obtaining reliable antecedents in very long-term longitudinal studies (e.g. more than 40 years if we want to look at the effect of learning at school or university on people over 60); after all, the researcher who obtained the original learning data concerned may have retired or even died by then. There are therefore many cross-sectional studies (that is, comparing functioning at a particular point in time between different age groups of people) and few longitudinal studies investigating such very long-term memories. A problem with cross-sectional studies is that the educational and wider environment of people brought up in (say) the 1930s was very different from that to which people growing up in the 1980s or 1990s were exposed. Thus differences between age groups may be related to this environmental difference rather than to, or as well as, age.

There has been long-standing debate as to whether the decline in fluid intelligence (see Chapter 5) and many aspects of memory in the old is the result only of the increasing prevalence of brain pathology with ageing (Alzheimer's disease, strokes, effects of diabetes etc.) or an intrinsic part of ageing. From the point of view of educating older people this distinction is important – the goals for someone with dementia will relate mainly to improving their ability to live independently; for a population that is ageing normally they will be related to continuing in work or acquiring new skills and information.

Deary and colleagues[2,3] have carried out a longitudinal study on a large group of healthy old people and have concluded that cognitive decline is indeed intrinsic to normal ageing. This population, the Healthy Old People in Edinburgh (HOPE) cohort, consisted of people aged 70 or older. They were first tested on Raven's Matrices (which is considered to be a relatively pure test of fluid intelligence) and the logical memory test from the Wechsler Adult Intelligence Scale (WAIS) (which is a test of declarative memory) and then followed up at four, seven and nine years later. Both measures declined with age; Raven's Matrices scores declined linearly, but logical memory loss actually accelerated with age. So this suggests a steady decline in fluid intelligence whilst the rate of declarative memory loss apparently increases with ageing.

In this chapter we shall first describe the acknowledged age-related changes in cognitive functions such as reasoning and memory. We shall then discuss research that has suggested that cognitive and physical (e.g. aerobic exercise) interventions may be able to improve cognitive functions. We shall propose how we might use the information concerning which memory functions are preserved and which impaired in order to tailor educational approaches for the teaching of older people. We shall also discuss the implications from very long-term studies that tell us which aspects of material taught to individuals many years ago survive best and how such long-term memories may differ from those examined soon after learning. From such work it may be possible to determine how we should be teaching younger people so that their memories may remain stable, retrievable and yet flexible into old age.

Figure 12.1 Rembrandt self-portrait when young. Reproduced with permission from the Rijksmuseum, Amsterdam.

Figure 12.2 Rembrandt self-portrait when old, dressed as St Paul. Reproduced with permission from the Rijksmuseum, Amsterdam.

What Declines with Age and What Does Not?

Professor Gillian Cohen (previously of the Open University) published a review in 1996[4] of memory and learning in older people, which provides an overview of what was known at that date and an excellent background to the present consideration of ageing.

The obvious characteristics of ageing after the age of 65 or so are:

- physical and mental slowing;
- gradual reduction in the sensory functions (including visual, auditory and 'smell' acuity);
- reduction in working-memory capacity;
- reduction in fluid intelligence (see Chapter 5) with relative sparing of 'crystallized' intelligence;
- reduction in ability to form episodic memories (autobiographical, particularly with respect to time and place), with lesser reduction in ability to form semantic memories;
- procedural/implicit memory relatively preserved (including priming and familiarity).

Much work has been done, particularly by Salthouse in the United States, on whether it is possible to explain all the deficits listed above by one overarching factor that declines with age. Salthouse[5] originally proposed that this factor was 'processing speed'. He argued that the reduction in working memory, which is likely to be an important underlying mechanism for the reduction in test scores of fluid intelligence, could be explained by the reduction in processing speed. More than 20 years ago, Salthouse carried out a cross-sectional study on working memory with adults ranging from 20 to 84 years of age. Using a statistical method (hierarchical regression), he found that most of the age effect could be explained by the reduction in processing speed. However, in later studies he showed that there was commonality (shared variance) between a wide variety of behavioural test scores, including speed of processing, and that it was probably necessary to consider some higher-order factor affecting all the processes that decline in ageing. What this might be is still very open to speculation. One attractive possibility[6] can be described as a decline in 'connectivity' between areas of the brain involved in the relevant cognitive functions: for example less effective interaction between the parieto-frontal cortices, components of Jung and Haier's P-fit model, which they have suggested underlies individual differences in intelligence (see Chapter

5). Less effective interaction could be the result of reduction in conduction velocity in the white-matter connections (through progressive loss of myelin surrounding the nerve axons), or reduced input efficacy perhaps due to loss of neurons or loss of arborization of neurons or changes in the transmission process at synapses (to make just a few suggestions).

Short-Term Working Memory/Executive-Function/Attention

Working memory involves executive function, that is, the control of attention and the integration of memories briefly stored in short-term memory with long-term memory. It is used in all kinds of decision-making. Since it is required for problem-solving and since tests of fluid intelligence are tests of problem-solving, it is unsurprising to find that working-memory scores decline with ageing.

Recent work has found that one reason for the apparent decline in working memory is the increased distractibility of older people. This can be obvious when one is talking to someone elderly. Distracting one's attention from the task in hand would be expected to reduce efficiency in problem-solving and of course this happens in both young and old people. However, older people are less good at multi-tasking, which requires rapid switching of attention between tasks. This was demonstrated by Clapp et al.[7] in a brain imaging experiment (fMRI) comparing young (mean age 24.6 years) with older participants (mean age 69.1 years). They were given a working-memory task that included interruptions, which they were instructed either to ignore or to attend to. They found that in both groups the attended interruption caused disengagement from the relevant working-memory networks and 'resources were reallocated' to the interrupting stimulus. The difference between the groups was that the older people were slow to disengage from the interrupting stimulus and re-engage with the disrupted working-memory network. Thus the difference between old and young people appears not so much to be that the older are actually any more likely to be distracted, it is that they have more difficulty in disengaging from a competing attraction and returning to the primary problem. Whilst this is a description of the nature of the problem, it does not of course actually explain why this difference occurs. Short-term memory for performance of everyday familiar tasks (such as locking the front door or turning off the gas) also appears to worsen with ageing, even though there is little change in laboratory-demonstrated short-term memory tasks such as digit span. This again is probably due to the person attending to distracting stimuli (such as thinking about what they must do next), during which time the short-term memory for a recent action decays.

Gazzeley and colleagues' earlier work[8] supported this conclusion. They conducted a different fMRI experiment on working memory and distraction. Young and old people were shown faces and scenes, and told to remember one class of stimulus and ignore the other class. Remembering scenes was accompanied by higher activity in the left parahippocampal gyrus (LPHG) than when the person was exposed to scenes or faces passively – that is, without instruction to remember. In contrast, when they were told to ignore scenes, there was suppression of activity in this area relative to when viewing was passive. This pattern was seen in both old and young but more consistently in the old. However, in a subset of the old with particularly poor working memory there was no suppression of activity in the LPHG. Gazzeley and colleagues suggested that this suppression was the neural expression of ignoring the distracting stimulus – and that some older people's difficulty in suppressing the distraction was directly related to the impairment of working memory.

A recent study by Clapp and Gazzeley[9] has again compared young and old people and has looked at the electroencephalographic (EEG) correlates of distraction or interruption. There were 24 older people, aged 61–82 (mean 69.4 years), and 21 younger people, aged 18–30 (mean 23.3). The test was similar to that in the studies quoted above and involved face recognition – a face (in this case just face without hair or background) was shown for one second, then there was a six-second delay, then another face was shown and the participant had to respond as to whether it was the same or a different face. During the six-second delay, either there was a blank screen (passive condition) or there was another face presented. In the Distractor condition the person was told to ignore this face; in the Interruption condition they had to decide whether or not it was the face of a man aged under 40. The accuracy of the same/different response was greatest in the passive condition for both groups, less in the Distractor condition and worst in the Interruption condition. In all three conditions, the older people responded more slowly and less accurately than the younger people, the difference in accuracy being greatest for the Interruption condition. Longer-term memory for the to-be-remembered faces (cue) was similar in the two groups. Interestingly, and in support of the previous work, the older participants remembered the distracting and interrupting stimuli better than the younger people; indeed they remembered them as well as they remembered the 'cue' stimuli, whilst the younger people had forgotten them. ERP measures (electroencephalographically recorded from the scalp; see Chapter 4) taken during the testing also showed the slowing of responses in the older people and that whilst the responses in the young people were larger to the cues than to the distractors and interruptors, the responses to all three were similar in the old. This suggests that the older participants engaged in a similar level of processing of the different stimuli, whereas the younger ones processed cues more. Neural suppression of response to the distractors and interrupters was associated with better working memory. This study shows that whilst distraction and interruption impair working memory in the old more than in the young, it is the effect of interruption that is particularly pronounced in the old. The increased effect of distraction and interruption on working memory is an important factor that will have to be taken into account in any programme of education for older people.

Declarative Memory: Where Did I Get That Hat?

Episodic memory

There is a large literature showing that the ability to form new explicit episodic memories declines with ageing. The learning of new concepts, ideas and facts is also weaker in older people and they take longer to acquire new skills. With autobiographical memory, what is missing is information about context, that is, when and where the memory was formed. When memories are tested in the laboratory (e.g. with word lists) some time after learning, it is found that the older people will recognize that they have encountered the stimulus before (recognition) but they are much less likely than younger people to remember the occasion of acquiring the information (knowing). In the next section we discuss that this suggests that the information, whose original context is no longer retrievable, has become implicit.

   Prospective memory, that is, remembering to do something in the future, is less good in older people but can be improved by linking the prospective action to another fairly constant future action. An example, which is very relevant for many elderly people, is remembering to take medication: 'do it at 8am' is difficult to remember whilst 'do it at breakfast time' is much more reliable.

Semantic memory

Semantic memory is considerably less vulnerable to ageing than episodic memory. This is the type of memory that education mainly involves. This relative preservation is also seen in people with amnesia caused by accidental damage, or Korsakoff's syndrome (chronic alcoholism), or neurodegenerative disease. Information acquired in childhood and young adulthood, including that acquired at school and university, can be relatively stable. Bahrick[10] showed many years ago that there is decay of the memory for Spanish learnt at high school, but not used since, in the first six years after learning. The memory then enters what he called a 'permastore' in which there is almost no decay for as long as 35 years. The memory then declined again as the person entered old age. Cohen and her associates confirmed this stability of information acquired in earlier life when tested in older individuals. A particularly relevant study[4] looked at the retention of a cognitive psychology course taught at the Open University. These part-time courses are highly structured with very detailed course material. The students are all 'mature' – that is, at least over 21 and in many cases much older. The study had a cross-sectional design and involved five different tests of retention: recognition of proper names and concepts; fact verification of specific and general facts; cued recall of proper names and concepts; concept groupings (sorting 24 concepts into 6 groups); and a recognition test for memory of research methods. Recognition of both names and concepts decayed within the first three years after learning, but concepts were better retained than names. After that, both then remained constant at around 65% correct over the next nine years. Cued recall testing involved true statements from which a particular name or concept had been deleted, leaving just the initial letter. Fact verification showed that there was a more rapid decline in memory for general than for specific facts but that after two years both remained fairly stable at around 65% correct. Overall, the results show that concepts are retained better than isolated facts such as names – something with which most of us are probably familiar in everyday life. Understanding concepts and memorizing them requires more complex processing than the acquisition of names. Particularly interesting is that the memory for the research methods part of the course (as tested by fact verification) remained stable at a high level throughout the retention period – about 75% correct. It is suggested that at least some of this knowledge may have entered procedural memory (which, as discussed above, is relatively preserved in ageing) because it was applied by the students in their experimental projects and hence would have been frequently rehearsed.

At the Open University (see Cohen 1996), there was no difference in the attainment of young and elderly students.[11] Thus in the Finals assessment their overall marks, a combination of marks on a final examination and on coursework, giving equal weight to each, were similar. Actually, the older students did slightly less well in examinations, which depend, of course, on long-term memory for information, but then they did slightly better in coursework. The success of elderly people on Open University courses is probably related to their necessarily high motivation and to the fact that they do most of their work at home where they can pace themselves and reduce distractions as appropriate.

Obviously the major problem when we consider the education and training of older people is reduced ability to learn new information. Therefore, putting more emphasis on teaching people to put new information into already established frameworks (even more so than when teaching the young) should be a major part of the teaching strategy. Also, we need to look for ways of improving the sorts of memory that are impaired (see later). Furthermore, ways of capitalizing on the relatively intact implicit memory system needs to be explored.

Implicit/Procedural Memory: One Doesn't Forget How to Drive a Car

As mentioned above, implicit and procedural learning and memory remain relatively intact in old people. Parkin and Walter,[12] in a seminal study, investigated this in small groups of young and old people. Their groups were matched for education and/or intelligence by use of the NART (New Adult Reading Test). This purports to be a measure of intelligence. It actually involves measuring the ability to read aloud correctly a series of rare words. We would argue that it is more a measure of educational level – but that is, of course, related to intelligence and is anyway a reasonable measure on which to match groups. In this experiment, they demonstrated the fragility of contextual (episodic) memory with the relatively unimpaired 'recognition' memory, which is a kind of implicit memory (see Chapter 2). Parkin and Walter tested their participants on three tests of executive function, which are considered to relate to frontal lobe function (WCST – Wisconsin card sorting test, verbal fluency and embedded figures – choosing which of four line diagrams contain a specific shape). Old participants were, as expected, worse on all these tests. They were also tested on their memory for 36 words, which had been presented on individual cards for 10 seconds each. Ten minutes later their recall of these words was tested. Seventy-two words were presented on one sheet of paper, 36 of which were those previously presented on the cards. Participants were asked to mark each word they thought they had seen before as R or K. R meant that the recollection 'involved a particular association or image at the time of learning' (i.e. they remembered the words – episodic memory); K meant 'recognized but had not evoked any specific recollection' (i.e. they had a feeling of knowing the words – implicit memory). There was a big difference between old and young on these measures: The proportion of R responses was higher in the young whilst the proportion of K responses was higher in the old. So younger people drew on episodic memory more, and older people on implicit memory.

Interestingly, further evidence for the preservation of implicit memory in older people comes from studies of the effect of distractions. The experiments described in the previous section with respect to working memory showed that older people process irrelevant information more than younger people do. Healey and colleagues[13] carried out a range of tests comparing the effect of distractions on memory in young and old people. They proposed that whilst this interferes with working memory and will therefore reduce the current task efficacy, it can sometimes actually be an advantage since there may well be occasions on which the irrelevant information becomes relevant. The old people would then have an advantage over the younger. This property could perhaps be exploited in educating the old.

People with dementia have impaired explicit memory but relatively intact implicit memory. When trying to train people with dementia, an errorless learning technique, which is believed to tap into implicit memory, has been found to be useful. This programme involves providing instruction along with only the correct answer, rather than allowing trial and error learning which relies on having explicit memory of successful and unsuccessful responses. There is, however, some evidence that errorless learning may actually involve residual explicit memory as well as implicit memory. Some studies suggest that this approach is successful in teaching simple tasks required for everyday living and for teaching recognition of faces of carers and family.[14]

Neuroanatomical and Functional Basis of Behavioural Changes in Ageing

There is ample evidence that ageing is associated with shrinkage and nerve cell loss in the brain areas which are involved in functions that decline in the elderly. Thus there is loss of volume in prefrontal cortex, hippocampus and entorhinal cortex with ageing. These changes are most marked in people with dementia and studies of these brain regions in healthy old people do not necessarily show similar changes in volume over time. And when they do, they do not always correlate with reduction in relevant function. For example, Rodrigue and Raz[15] studied healthy participants (n = 42) aged between 26 years and 82 years over a five-year period. Of the three brain regions mentioned above, only the entorhinal cortex showed age-related shrinkage that also correlated with memory loss over this period. However, a recent study by McDonald et al.[16] has shown many correlations between the rate of loss of volume in discrete brain areas and specific behavioural functions. They looked at the brains of older people with mild cognitive impairment, defined as a self-reported impairment of memory not detectable with the usual tests for memory function in the old (MMSI; mini mental state inventory). They had a longitudinal design over a period of two years so that they could measure the rate of reduction in volume of different brain areas during this period. They found that left temporal lobe atrophy was associated with the well-known problem that older people can have with retrieving names, whilst a wider area of loss was associated with the reduction in the ability to generate the names of members of a specific category (e.g. animals or vegetables) – an ability designated verbal fluency. Left entorhinal cortex decline was related to memory loss, confirming the above observation of Rodrigue and Raz; and as would be expected, loss of executive function was associated with loss of prefrontal cortex.

Changes in white matter – the myelinated nerve tracts that connect one part of the brain to another – also occur with age. We would expect that these connections need to be intact in order to sustain complex cognitive processing. Such changes do not necessarily show up in MRI scans, but a method that can detect deterioration in white matter is diffusion tensor imaging (DTI). Recently, Voineskos and colleagues[17] have used this technique in a cross-sectional study, scanning the whole of the brain of 48 individuals aged from 18 to 85 years. They administered a large battery of cognitive tests, including tests of different sorts of immediate and delayed memory, working memory, executive function, language and flexibility, and then looked for relationships between the scores on these tests and deterioration of tracts. All of the tracts between different areas of the cerebral cortex were found to have degenerated with age, including the corpus callosum, which connects the two hemispheres. Using statistical analysis (structural equation modelling) of their findings, Voineskos et al. found that there was a relation between specific pathways that were degenerated and performance on tests of fast visual processing, memory and complex visuospatial construction (recalling complex drawings).

One thing we still do not know is the proximal cause of such anatomical losses. We know that extensive use of particular brain structures can increase their volume (e.g. representation of the fingers of violinists in the cortex; posterior hippocampus in London taxi drivers), and people frequently invoke the inverse idea of 'use it or lose it' with respect to brain function, though there is sparse direct evidence for this. It is possible that reduced use of mental functions in older people might be the cause of the loss of tissue. As people get older they retire from jobs, lose their spouses, their children leave home and they may be less independently mobile. The associated reduction in social and other kinds of interaction could be the primary cause of shrinkage of relevant brain areas. But this still does not tell us *how* this leads to brain shrinkage. It just moves the question on one stage.

It has been known for many years from work on rodents that stress causes cell death in the hippocampus. Levels of cortisol production rise with age and whether this is due to stress or some alternative factor, it could lead to neuronal death in the hippocampus. Furthermore, the high levels of cortisol will reduce the production (neurogenesis) or survival of new neurons in the hippocampus. Since these have been proposed to be particularly suited to the formation of new episodic memories, which depend on the hippocampus, this might contribute to the failing of episodic memory.

The levels of sex hormones – oestrogen and progesterone in women and testosterone in men – are lower in old people: there is a rather abrupt reduction at the menopause in women whilst the levels fall gradually in men from middle age. There are many receptors for oestradiol (the compound to which both oestrogen and testosterone are metabolized in the brain) in the hippocampus and therefore we might predict some relation between sex hormone levels and memory. Whilst there have been many studies on the relation between levels of sex hormones and cognitive function, the evidence as to whether these reductions are relevant to structural changes and to declines in cognitive function is mixed and at present the jury is still out as to their importance in structural and cognitive ageing.[18]

The prefrontal cortex is involved in working memory and attentional control. Prakash and colleagues[19] have shown a relationship between loss of attentional control in ageing and decreased flexibility of the activity of areas of prefrontal cortex. Their study involved the use of Stroop tests. These are very simple tests where sensory inputs can be either congruent or in conflict; for example, a person is asked to read aloud a word for a colour which is written in ink of either the same or a different colour. The response time is measured and it is normally found that in the conflict situation (where the colour of the ink and the word for the colour are different) the response is slower than in the congruent situation. It is argued that more attentional control is needed in the non-congruent condition because the person has to inhibit the irrelevant information (in the above case, the colour of the word).

The authors measured activation of the prefrontal cortex when their participants were performing this task. In the conflict condition, there was increased activity in this area in young adults (18–35 years), but there was no difference in the activation in older adults (58–75 years). In the congruent (non-conflict) condition, the older people actually showed more activation than the younger people. The authors interpreted this as showing that older people expended greater effort on the simple task of reading the stimulus, leaving less resource available for dealing with a more difficult conflict task.

Overall, there is plenty of evidence for anatomical and functional changes in the brain during ageing but the relationship between them is far from clear.

Individual Differences

There is wide individual variability in the reduction in cognitive functions that occurs with ageing. Some of this, of course, relates to the increased prevalence of neurological degenerative disease (such as Alzheimer's) and age-related insults to the brain caused, for example, by strokes and reduction in general vascular function. However, early experience and individual differences in cognitive ability may also relate to some of the variability. In studies of healthy old people it is found that those originally of higher intelligence and who had experienced longer formal education (and of course these are related) retain memory functions for longer. In the Healthy Old People in Edinburgh cohort,[2] it has been shown that the rate of cognitive decline is not affected by early education or cognitive ability, but of course even if the rate is similar, the actual levels will remain higher for longer in those who started with higher levels of cognitive function.

A related concept is that of 'cognitive reserve'. For many years there has been an anecdotally based perception that more highly educated people recover more fully from brain injury such as stroke and seem more resistant to brain degenerative disease such as Alzheimer's. This apparent resilience has been defined as 'the ability to function normally in the face of brain insults that would cause deterioration' in less resilient individuals. That some people's cognitive function is more resistant to deficit for a given level of neuroanatomical damage is illustrated by findings from post-mortems where as many as 25% of the brains of a large sample of elderly people fulfilled histological criteria for Alzheimer's and yet they came from people who had not shown cognitive symptoms.[20,21] Similarly, the brains of many stroke patients had lesions that would be expected to cause serious cognitive impairment and yet the people were behaviourally normal.

Only fairly recently have possible antecedents of cognitive reserve been systematically investigated. In 2003, a whole issue of the *Journal of Clinical and Experimental Neuropsychology* was devoted to the subject. Scarmeas and Stern[22] reviewed studies of the relation between lifestyle and cognitive reserve. They had obtained information concerning intellectual ability, educational level (which will be related to the former) and leisure activities, including intellectual, physical and social activities, of 1772 people over 65 years of age and then followed them up over a period of up to seven years for occurrence of dementia. All of these factors appeared to be related to resilience to dementia and the most important were ability and educational level. This finding has been further supported by work reported by Brayne[21] on a large sample of demented and non-demented old people's brains at post-mortem.

If we can show for certain that it is early levels of education, rather than any intrinsic higher resilience in those of higher natural ability, which increases this cognitive reserve, this would be a strong argument in favour of increasing the educational level of everyone in early life. An important question is whether education undertaken later in life will also increase this cognitive reserve. If this is the case then we have a particularly strong argument for supporting the 'universities of the third age'.

Can We Improve Cognitive Functions?

Cognitive interventions

In Chapter 2 we discussed some methods that have been used to try to improve cognitive functioning in children and in adults. In all cases, specific training was found to produce the expected practice effects – that is, improvement in performance of the task used for training and in some cases in similar tasks. However, it is more difficult to show improvement in performance on tasks that are not closely related to those used for the training. One example of a more generalized effect was with Klingberg's[23] working-memory training, which did have a beneficial effect on hyperactivity and attention in children with ADHD. There are also a few reports of very extensive training on working memory increasing scores on measures of fluid intelligence.[24] It would be advantageous if methods of training could be found that improved the cognitive functions that fail in the elderly. So far, the effectiveness of such interventions has been rather disappointing. A recent study by Schmiedek et al.[25] in Germany compared the effectiveness of 100 hours (100 days of one hour) of training in young adults (aged 20–31 years) and older adults (aged 65–80 years), with over 100 participants in each group. They used training tasks involving verbal and spatial working memory, episodic memory and perceptual speed and then compared trained individuals with non-trained controls on performance in tests of episodic memory and fluid intelligence. There was a significant advantage in the young adults on all the tests employed to measure transfer; for the older adults, there was some enhancement of fluid intelligence as measured with Raven's Matrices and in word-pairs learning for episodic memory. Otherwise the transfer effects of training were not seen in the older adults, even though their improvement on the training tasks was similar to that seen in the younger group. However, it should be noted that there is one possibly confounding factor in this study: the older participants had spent on average 2.5 fewer years in education than the younger participants. It is conceivable from our earlier consideration of the effects of years of education on cognitive reserve that years in education may actually affect cognitive plasticity. It is possible that had the groups been matched for years in education, the older group might have shown larger transfer-task gains in response to training.

Another interesting study was carried out by Dahlin and colleagues[26] in which they compared the effect on executive function in young (average 24 years) and old (average 68 years) people of a computer-based training task involving updating in working memory. For both young and old groups they had controls matched on baseline performance on the updating task. The training was fairly intensive – 15 sessions of 45 minutes spread over five weeks (three per week), though not as intensive as Klingberg's regime for children with ADHD. In both young and old there were immediate gains in performance compared with controls and, encouragingly, this advantage was maintained at re-test 18 months after the training. This therefore showed that the brains of the older participants were still capable of plasticity with respect to executive function. However, there was virtually no transfer of the training effect to other tasks including episodic memory or verbal fluency or to speed of responding.

The experiment by Chein and Morrison on young adults, described in Chapter 2, in which extensive training in spatial and verbal working memory transferred to an improvement in reading comprehension, has recently been extended.[27] These authors looked at the effect of the same WM training on older adults (mean age 66 years; 19 controls and 21 'experimentals'). They improved the experiment by including a comparison group who were 'active controls' who were involved in a trivia program on their computers. The groups were matched for age, MMSE (Mini Mental State Examination – a test for detecting dementia; it involves simple questions such as what is the date, where are we, counting backwards in 7s from 100) and length of education (mean 17 years). The training increased the working-memory span for the trained task to a level similar to that seen for young adults in the previous experiment. They found, as in the previous experiment, that there was no change in fluid intelligence (Raven's matrices) or in forwards or backwards digit span. There was, however, an increase with training in reading span (another measure of verbal working memory) and some improvement in aspects of the California Verbal Learning Test (CVLT) – a test of episodic memory. Thus, they demonstrated that working memory itself was as malleable in old as in young adults and that some transfer effect was detectable, although they did not find improvement in fluid intelligence.

Some people believe that playing online video games can improve their cognitive function. A recent small study[28] of the effect of 30 minutes per day for seven weeks of online video-game training in elderly people (aged 60–77) produced improvement in cognitive control and reasoning ability. This effect was in comparison with an 'active' control group who answered questions about documentary films they had watched.

It has been shown by Davachi et al.[29] that the level of activation of specific brain areas by rote rehearsal of information predicts how well the information will be remembered later ('when keeping in mind supports later bringing to mind'). Such rote rehearsal, or phonological maintenance, supports encoding for subsequent remembering. Roche et al.[30] have investigated whether extended rote-learning can have a beneficial effect on tests of other kinds of memory in older adults (mean age 60.1 years, range 55 to 70). Two groups of 12 participants were matched for sex and age and on the NART (adult reading test) and the CPQ test for absent-mindedness. Both carried out a battery of memory tests at baseline. Half of the group then spent the next six weeks doing extensive rote-learning of verbal material – 500 words each week. The other half did not do any rote-learning. Both groups were then re-tested on the memory tests. In the following six weeks the other half of the group carried out the rote-learning and then both groups' memories were tested again. They found that the first group, whose compliance was much higher than that of the second group, showed significant gains in verbal/episodic memory tested six weeks after completion of the rote-learning. The second group did not show such gains, presumably because of their poor engagement in the learning programme. Imaging of the brains of the participants (H-MRS; proton magnetic resonance spectroscopy) showed that memory facilitation was accompanied by a metabolic change in the left posterior hippocampus, suggesting that this might be a correlate of the effect of the rote-learning. This experiment suggests that in these older participants it was possible to produce an improvement in verbal episodic memory that was probably associated with the activation of left posterior hippocampus. It would be interesting to see whether this effect lasted longer than the six-week period at which it was tested. Importantly, this suggests a relatively easy way of improving memory in older adults and also raises some interesting questions, such as whether this effect would pertain in younger people, including children, and whether early exposure to rote-learning (at school) would maybe lead to better memories in adulthood. This might be of especial importance in Britain where the use of rote-learning for children was much used in the past but is rather frowned upon in schools today.

Exercise

We have already mentioned in Chapter 2 that higher physical fitness appears to be associated with higher levels of a variety of cognitive functions and with greater hippocampal volume. Most of this work has been done on elderly people and rodents. Well-controlled studies in elderly people have matched experimentals and controls on relevant factors such as educational level and socioeconomic status. Colcombe and Kramer[31] carried out a meta-analysis of 18 studies on the relation between physical fitness and cognitive function in older adults (three groups: young-old, 55–65; medium-old, 66–70, old-old, >70). They found that fitness training increased performance on cognitive control tasks (executive function/working memory) by 0.5 of a standard deviation on average – a quite substantial effect. This effect was moderated by the type of training, the period over which the exercise was undertaken, the length of the sessions and the age and sex of the participants.

Higher levels of cognitive function in those with better physical fitness could be a direct result of the fitness or could be related to the increased environmental stimulation that is likely to be associated with higher levels of physical fitness – more likely to walk to the shops, more walks around town, more walking the dog etc., all of which are likely to lead to more social interaction, for example. It is therefore important to try to isolate the effect of exercise itself.

Recently, Erickson and colleagues[32,33] have looked for a relationship between exercise-induced increase in hippocampal volume and memory function in older adults (55–80 years). One hundred and twenty participants carried out a moderate exercise programme for one year under supervision from a trained exercise leader. For the experimental group this involved walking (at about 60–75% of maximum heart rate reserve), starting at 10 minutes per day and working up to 40 minutes per day over a period of seven weeks. The control group undertook stretching and toning exercises instead of the aerobic walking. There was a 1–2% increase in anterior hippocampal volume in the compliant aerobic exercise group. In the control (toning and stretching group) there was a small decrease in hippocampal volume. Memory was tested at baseline, after six months of training and at the end of training. The task was a computerized short-term spatial memory test. A card with three black dots on it was presented for half a second and the participant was asked to remember the position of the dots. After a three-second delay, another card which had one red dot on it was presented. The task was to say whether the red dot was or was not in the same position as any of the previous black dots. At each time point, 40 such trials were presented – 20 which matched, 20 which did not. The expected practice effect was seen in both groups (the memory score improved). In the aerobic exercise group the improvement in memory score was associated significantly with the increase in anterior (left and right) hippocampal volume. This study is important because it suggests that a relatively easy-to-implement exercise programme, brisk walking for 40 minutes a day, can prevent the reduction in hippocampal volume that occurs in normal ageing and at the same time improve short-term spatial memory. Obviously more studies using this exercise programme and measuring other sorts of memory are needed.

Effects of diet

Omega-3 fatty acids. As discussed in Chapter 2, there is some evidence that dietary omega-3 fatty acids have a positive effect on cognitive function. This effect might be produced via an effect on production of new neurons (neurogenesis) or their survival. Since these new neurons are thought to be likely to have a role in learning and memory, and we know that the rate of neurogenesis declines with age, it can be suggested that omega-3 fatty acids in the diet would help to preserve learning and memory functions in the elderly. Many elderly people in Britain on low incomes eat a rather restricted diet, often consisting of cheap foods that contain high levels of the omega-6 fatty acids that interfere with the production of DHA, which is the important fatty acid for the effects of omega-3s. Thus, supplementation of the diet of elderly people with cod liver oil, the best source of omega-3s, should be investigated as a way of preserving cognitive function.

Choline. Choline is a precursor of the neurotransmitter acetylcholine which is one transmitter that is known to decline in neurodegenerative diseases of ageing. The amount of acetylcholine that is synthesized in the brain depends on the local concentration of choline and this in turn is determined by the amount entering the brain from the blood, which itself depends on the concentration of choline in the blood. Hence raising the concentration of choline in the blood by increasing the levels of choline in the diet would be expected to raise the amount of acetylcholine in the brain. A study by Poly and colleagues[34] looked at the previous and concurrent dietary content of choline in a large (1,391) community-based sample of non-demented people ranging in age from 36 to 86 years. They gave them a food intake questionnaire over the period 1991–95 and again in 1998–2001 to assess their choline intake (choline is present in a wide variety of foods.) They measured verbal and visuospatial short-term memory and executive function and also did a type of structural imaging that shows up damage to white matter (myelinated nerve tracts). They found that with higher choline intake during the earlier period, there was less pathology in the white matter; but there was no difference with respect to recent choline intake. Interestingly, whilst previous intake was not related to current cognitive function, higher current intake was related to better cognitive function. This study therefore supports the idea that higher choline intake has a long-term effect in preserving white-matter integrity and that current intake preserves cognitive function. Whether this relationship has any relation to acetycholine synthesis in humans has not been ascertained.

Flavonoids. These polyphenols, which are present in teas, cocoa, grapes and particularly in berries, have been promoted as valuable diet constituents because of their antioxidant properties, which offset damaging free radicals, which are known to accumulate in ageing. However, at much lower concentrations than those required for the antioxidant effect they have been shown to facilitate cognitive function in the elderly. They appear to have a wide range of effects at these low concentrations that are likely to be relevant: they increase the levels of BDNF (brain-derived neurotrophic factor) and other neurotrophins which play a role in maintaining synaptic plasticity and maintaining neurogenesis, as well as protecting vulnerable neurons from ageing-related death, and they also increase blood flow to the brain. A large study (1640 participants), carried out over a 10-year period in people over 65 years old, showed a marked relation between cognitive function and flavonoid intake which was maintained even when age, sex and educational level had been taken into account.[35]

Glucose. A short-term way of enhancing memory in old people has involved the effect of the ingestion of glucose. Administration of 25 g glucose dissolved in water (compared with giving a sweetness-matched solution of saccharin) has been shown to improve episodic memory (but not semantic memory, working memory or speed of processing) measured immediately after learning and 20 minutes later, in adults aged 60–80 years old. The glucose load led to an increase in blood sugar from the fasting level of 5 mM to around 8 mM but it is far from self-evident as to why this should specifically improve episodic memory. If this can be replicated, it might support the idea of elderly people having a high-sugar drink or food before undertaking a task requiring recollection.[36]

Summary

- The increasing number of people aged over 65 in the population of Britain, the raising of the retirement age and the rapid advance of technology mean that there is a need to continue education into old age. But there is urgent need for research into ways in which educational strategies suitable for the young need to be adapted for the old.
- Working memory, in which we hold information briefly and manipulate it, as in problem-solving, declines with ageing. Part of this decline is related to the greater effect of distractions as people age. The problem is not so much that older people are more distractible but that they have more difficulty in disengaging from a distraction.
- The ability to form long-term declarative memories declines. Thus there is loss of context-dependent memory – where and when a memory was formed – but also some reduction in semantic-memory formation (memory for facts).
- Semantic memories can last for many decades. They decline fastest in the first few years after learning and then enter a 'permastore' until they begin to decline in old age.

- The ability to form implicit (non-declarative, unconscious) memories is much less susceptible to ageing. This is particularly obvious where 'just knowing' that something has been seen before (implicit) and recollecting the occasion of seeing it (explicit 'remembering') are compared.
- There is reduction with ageing in the volume and/or activity of those parts of the brain that are known to be involved in memory: the hippocampus, entorhinal cortex and prefrontal cortex, but also general reduction in the white-matter tracts that interconnect different brain areas.
- Ageing is associated with a reduced rate of formation (neurogenesis) and/or increased rate of death of new neurons. This could contribute to the decline in the ability to form memories since the new neurons are particularly well suited to undergoing long-term potentiation (LTP), which may be the mechanism of memory formation.
- Neurogenesis is also reduced by lack of exercise and lack of sleep, both of which are often associated with ageing.
- Memory in the aged can be improved by regular exercise (as little as 40 minutes per day of brisk walking). It is also expected that improved diet, particularly increasing its content of omega-3 fatty acids, flavonoids and choline, may help preserve memory function.
- Working memory can be improved by intensive training. It can also be improved by an intensive regimen of rote-learning – which appears to impact on hippocampal function.
- There are big differences in the susceptibility of individuals to failing cognitive function in the face of reduction in volume of relevant brain areas and damage from neurodegenerative disease or insult such as stroke. This varying 'cognitive reserve' is in part related to the level of education that a person reached earlier in life. We do not know whether cognitive reserve can also be increased at a later age, and more research is needed in this area.

Implications for the education of elderly people

- The reduction in working-memory capacity needs to be taken into account by encouraging note-taking and introducing adequate gaps between presentation of new pieces of knowledge so that they can be integrated.
- The difficulty in withdrawing attention from distractions means that it is useful to keep a plan of a lesson in a prominent position, visible at all times, throughout a learning period. Obviously, learning needs to take place in as distraction-free an environment as possible.

It is likely that the restricted working-memory capacity will make multi-tasking particularly difficult for the elderly and therefore teachers should concentrate on one aspect of a subject at a time.
- Older learners are likely to have entrenched schemata for subjects that they learnt when younger. Rather than demolishing these if they are out of date, it would be better to use them as a background for inserting new knowledge and correcting the old.
- The use of teaching methods that can direct information into implicit memory may be useful. These include rote-learning and errorless learning.
- Older people should be encouraged to practise rote-learning, take regular moderate exercise, eat foods rich in omega 3 fatty acids and flavonoids and maybe get access to recently developed working-memory training programmes (e.g. *Cogmed*).

References

1 Sunderland A, Harris JE, Baddeley AD. Do laboratory tests predict everyday memory? *Journal of Verbal Learning and Verbal Behavior*. 1983;22(3): 341–357.
2 Deary I, Skarr JM, MacLennan WJ. Is age kinder to the initially more able? Differential aging of a verbal ability in the Healthy Old People in Edinburgh study. *Intelligence*. 1998;26(4):357–375.
3 Der G, Allerhand M, Starr J, Hofer S, Deary I. Age-related changes in memory and fluid reasoning in a sample of healthy old people. *Aging, Neuropsychology and Cognition*. 2010;17(1):55–70.
4 Cohen GM. Memory and learning in normal ageing. In: Woods RT, ed. *Handbook of the Clinical Psychology of Aging*. Chichester: John Wiley & Sons; 1996; ch. 3:43–58.
5 Salthouse TA. The processing-speed theory of adult age differences in cognition. *Psychological Review*. 1996;103(3):403–428.
6 O'Sullivan M, Jones DK, Summers PE, Morris RG, Williams SCR, *et al.* Evidence for cortical "disconnection" as a mechanism of age-related cognitive decline. *Neurology*. 2001;57:632–638.
7 Clapp WC, Rubens MT, Sabharwal J, Gazzaley A. Deficit in switching between functional brain networks underlies the impact of multitasking on working memory in older adults. *Proceedings of the National Academy of Sciences*. 2011;108(17):7212–7217. doi:10.1073/pnas.1015297108.
8 Gazzaley A, Cooney J, Rissman J, D'Esposito M. Top-down suppression deficit underlies working memory impairment in normal aging. *Nature Neuroscience*. 2005;8(10):1298–1300.

9   Clapp WC, Gazzaley A. Distinct mechanisms for the impact of distraction and interruption on working memory in aging. *Neurobiology of Aging.* 2012;33(1):134–148.

10 Bahrick HP. Semantic memory content in permastore: Fifty years of memory for Spanish learned at school. *Journal of Experimental Psychology: General.* 1984;113:1–29.

11 Cohen GM, Stanhope NM, Conway MA. Age differences in the retention of knowledge in young and elderly students. *British Journal of Developmental Psychology.* 1992;10:153–164.

12 Parkin AJ, Walter BM. Recollective experience, normal aging and frontal dysfunction. *Psychology and Aging.* 1992;7:290–298.

13 Healey MK, Campbell KL, Hasher L. Cognitive aging and increased distractibility: Costs and potential benefits. In Sossin WS, *et al.*, eds. *The Essence of Memory. Progress in Brain Research.* 2008;169:353–363.

14 Clare L, Jones RSP. Errorless learning in the rehabilitation of memory impairment: A critical review. *Neuropsychology Review.* 2008;18:1–23.

15 Rodrigue KM, Raz N. Shrinkage of the entorhinal cortex over five years predicts memory performance in healthy adults. *Journal of Neuroscience.* 2004;24:956–963.

16 McDonald CR, Gharapetian L, McEvoy LK, *et al.* Relationship between regional atrophy rates and cognitive decline in mild cognitive impairment. *Neurobiology of Aging.* 2012;33:242–253.

17 Voineskos AN, Rajji TK, Lobaugh NJ, *et al.* Age-related decline in white-matter tract integrity and cognitive performance: A DTI tractography and structural equation modelling study. *Neurbiology of Aging.* 2012;33:21–34.

18 Sherwin BB. The critical period hypothesis: Can it explain discrepancies in oestrogen-cognition literature? *Journal of Neuroendocrinology.* 2006;19: 77–81.

19 Prakash R, Erickson K, Colcombe SJ, Kim JS, Voss M, *et al.* Age-related differences in the involvement of the prefrontal cortex in attentional control. *Brain and Cognition.* 2009;71(3):328–335.

20 Esiri M, *et al.* Pathological correlates of late-onset dementia in a multi-centre community-based population in England and Wales. *Lancet.* 2001;357: 169–175.

21 Brayne C, Ince PG, Keage HA, *et al.* Education, the brain and dementia. *Brain.* 2010;133(8):2210–2216.

22 Scarmeas N, Stern Y. Cognitive reserve and lifestyle. *Journal of Clinical and Experimental Neuropsychology.* 2003;25(5):625–633. doi:10.1076/jcen.25.5.625.14576.

23 Klingberg T. Training and plasticity of working memory. *Trends in Cognitive Sciences.* 2010;14:317–324.

24 Jaeggi SM, Buschkuehl M, Jonides J, Perrig WJ. Improving fluid intelligence with training on working memory. *Proceedings of the National Academy of Sciences.* 2008;105(19):6829–6833.

25 Schmiedek F, Lovden M, Lindenberger U. Hundred days of cognitive training enhance broad cognitive abilities in adulthood: Findings from the COGITO study. *Frontiers in Aging Neuroscience*. 2010;2:1–10.

26 Dahlin E, Nyberg L, Backman L, Stigsdotter A. Plasticity of executive functioning in young and older adults: Immediate training gains, transfer and long-term maintenance. *Psychology and Aging*. 2008;23(4):720–730.

27 Richmond LL, Morrison AB, Chein JM, Olson IR. Working memory training and transfer in older adults. *Psychology and Aging*. 2011;26(4):813–822.

28 Van Muijden J, Band GPH, Hommel B. Online games training and aging brains: Limited transfer to cognitive control functions. *Frontiers in Human Neuroscience*. 2012;6:221–234.

29 Davachi LA, Maril A, Wagner, AD. When keeping in mind supports later bringing to mind: Neural markers of phonological rehearsal predict subsequent remembering. *Journal of Cognitive Neuroscience*. 2001;13: 1059–1070.

30 Roche AP, Mullally SL, O'Mara SM, *et al*. Prolonged rote learning produces delayed memory facilitation and metabolic changes in the hippocampus of the ageing human brain. *BMC Neuroscience*. 2009;10:136–157.

31 Colcombe S, Kramer A. Fitness effects on the cognitive function of older adults. *Psychological Science*. 2003;14(2):125–130.

32 Erickson K, Prakash R, Voss M, *et al*. Aerobic fitness is associated with hippocampal volume in elderly humans. *Hippocampus*. 2009;19(10): 1030–1039.

33 Chaddock L, Erickson KI, Prakash R, *et al*. A neuroimaging investigation of the association between aerobic fitness, hippocampal volume, and memory performance in preadolescent children. *Brain Research*. 2010;1358: 172–183.

34 Poly C, Massaro, JM, Seshadri S, *et al*. The relation of dietary choline to cognitive performance and white matter hyper intensity in the Framingham offspring cohort study. *American Journal of Clinical Nutrition*. 2011;94(6): 1584–1591.

35 Spencer JPE. Food for thought: The role of dietary flavonoids in enhancing human memory, learning and neuro-cognitive performance. *Proceedings of the Nutrition Society*. 2008;67(02):238–252. doi:10.1017/S0029665108007088.

36 Riby LM, Meikle A, Glover C. The effects of age, glucose ingestion and gluco-regulatory control on episodic memory. *Age and Ageing*. 2004; 33:483–487.

Chapter 13

Technology

How Is It Shaping a Modern Education and Is It Also Shaping Young Minds?

We know that brains change in response to what we do (as shown by musicians, London taxi drivers, jugglers etc.). Children today are growing up immersed in a completely new environment, an environment where smart phones, e-readers and laptops provide continuous access to information on the Internet and to opinion and debate via social networks. Therefore we might well expect the brains of young people and the way that they think to be developing differently. If the environment at home, in the streets and in workplaces is changing, then so too must the environment in schools and universities. This requires a serious and radical re-think about what a modern education should provide.

In this chapter we consider this issue. In a world where information is available at a click or touch, what knowledge do young people actually need to internalize? Which skills are technology making redundant and which are becoming more essential than ever before? We also think about the impact technology is having on the way we teach, the new tools that are available to teachers and whether they are actually increasing the quality or quantity of what our young people learn. Finally, we think about those people who might be excluded from these advances: the impact on older people who may not feel comfortable with technology, and the individuals who cannot afford the latest phones or computers or even to connect to the Internet. We know that differences and difficulties

Education and Learning: An Evidence-Based Approach, First Edition. Jane Mellanby and Katy Theobald.
© 2014 John Wiley & Sons, Ltd. Published 2014 by John Wiley & Sons, Ltd.

are evident when pupils learn in a paper-based classroom, but how might their distribution change in digital schools?

Digital Natives and Net Generations: Is Technology Changing How We Think?

Many educators and psychologists, particularly those engaged with the popular press, like to talk about 'digital natives'. Just over 10 years ago, Marc Prensky popularized this concept when he presented a theory that the younger generations, having grown up surrounded by technology, treated it fundamentally differently from the older generation of 'digital immigrants'.[1] Like an adult who learns a new language, he argued, 'digital immigrants' would always have an accent when they used technology. For example, a 'digital immigrant' might print an email to read it whereas a 'digital native' would read it on-screen. A 'digital native' might look up a shop's opening times online whereas a 'digital immigrant' would call up the store.

The implications of this theory are twofold. Firstly, 'digital natives' are expected to integrate technology into all aspects of their lives. Consequently, it is argued that educators need to adjust their teaching methods to encompass modern technology in all its guises. Reading lists might include websites as well as books, and students might engage in debates via chat rooms or instant messaging as well as face-to-face. The second implication is that 'digital natives' might actually think differently, their brains having developed to function in this new technological world. They would be better at multi-tasking and dividing their attention between stimuli but less inclined to focus on uninteresting inputs. The suggestion is then that teachers might have to change their teaching styles to engage the multi-modal learner, constantly capturing their attention with fast-changing, interactive and multi-sensory inputs.

Although this theory may present an enticing perspective on the modern generation, a good deal of critical research calls into question the reality of the native–immigrant divide. On the one hand, we know that the adoption of technology is not solely a generational matter. There are some older adults who are particularly inclined to engage with new technologies and some young people who wholeheartedly avoid them. Furthermore, not all young people are confident about utilizing technology. A group of researchers from the Open University surveyed 596 students from five UK universities about their use of technology.[2] Younger students (under-25s) did consider the Internet to be more important for accessing course information and materials and were significantly more confident in using technology for a range of tasks (such as spreadsheets and presentations). However, younger students did not necessarily rate themselves as highly confident in their use of technology; for example, their average confidence rating for using virtual learning environments was 2.92 out of 5.

Researchers have also found it difficult to identify cognitive characteristics that uniformly distinguish 'digital natives' from the 'digital immigrant' generation. Garcia and colleagues[3] investigated whether technology use has influenced the cognition of 12- and 13- year-olds in Chile. After engaging with a large number of schools they selected 60 pupils who did not use ICT (which in itself challenges the idea that all young people are 'natives') and 203 who were divided into groups according to the frequency with which they used four functions: offline computing, gaming, online chat and the Internet. The participants were given two tests of working memory: a backwards and forwards digit span test (for verbal working memory) and the Group Embedded Figures Test (for visual working memory). Two groups – PC and console gamers and also children who used all four computer functions – had combined backwards and forwards digit span scores that were significantly higher than those of the control group of non-users, but this was the only significant group difference. The results are therefore ambiguous in their implications. They could show that extensive ICT use results in gains in working memory, but it could also be that children with good working memory find ICT easier or more enjoyable to use and therefore use it more extensively.

Another behavioural characteristic that is apparently expected of 'digital natives' is media multi-tasking: for example, surfing the Internet whilst also listening to music and messaging friends. Intuitively, one might think that such media multi-tasking requires good attention skills, an ability to attend to relevant stimuli whilst filtering out distractions. However, Ophir and colleagues[4] have conducted a study that contradicts this view. They gave 262 university students a survey asking them how many hours they spent using 12 different technologies (such as instant messaging and online videos) and also how frequently they engaged in these activities concurrently. From this they calculated a multi-tasking score and identified high (scores >1 standard deviation above average) and low (scores >1 SD below average) media multi-taskers. These students completed four visual tests which involved attending to target stimuli whilst filtering them out from an array of distracters (see Figure 13.1); remembering target items and identifying them whilst ignoring distracters; response control; and switching between different tasks. Surprisingly, the high media multi-taskers were actually significantly worse at filtering distracters out from

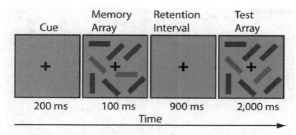

Figure 13.1 Participants had to remember the orientation of the red bar and indicate if this was different in the test array. *Source*: Ophir E, Nass C, Wagner AD. Cognitive control in media multitaskers. *PNAS*. 2009;106:37. Copyright © 2009, PNAS. Reproduced with permission of PNAS.

target stimuli, worse at ignoring them during the memory task and worse at task-switching. This could mean that students who multi-task more are actually those who find it more difficult to filter out the distractions that multimedia provides, or alternatively that media multi-tasking actually has a negative effect on attention skills over time.

Whilst this conclusion might seem worrying, Lui and Wong[5] have suggested that greater sensitivity to distracters might be advantageous in modern life. They used the same method as Ophir and colleagues to obtain a media multi-tasking score for 63 participants aged 19–28. The participants completed a pip–pop task, where they were required to identify a target bar which changed colour amongst 48 distracters (see Figure 13.2). They had to click one button if it was horizontal, another if it was vertical. In some trials a pip sound played, which participants were told was irrelevant and should be ignored. However, the sound was actually helpful as it coincided with the target bar changing colour. The high media multi-taskers actually performed worse than low media multi-taskers on trials without the pip ($p < 0.01$) (supporting the idea that they found it difficult to block out irrelevant stimuli). However, there was a weak correlation between participants' media multi-tasking scores and the extent to which their response accuracy increased with the introduction of the tone ($r(57) = 0.292$, $p < 0.05$). This could show that people who engage in more multi-tasking are better at attending to stimuli that are outside the focus of their attention but that could nonetheless be relevant, such as an instant messaging alert or an Internet browser tab that flashes when it finishes loading. Modern technology is commonly designed to draw upon precisely this sort of skill.

Although it is exciting to theorize about the way that technology could be fundamentally changing the human brain, research so far is presenting

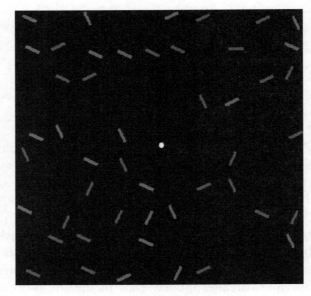

Figure 13.2   Visual stimulus: participants had to pick out a target bar from this array of distracters. *Source*: Lui KFH. Does media multitasking always hurt? A positive correlation between multitasking and multisensory integration. *Psychonomic Bulletin and Review*. 2012;19(4): Figure 1. © Springer, 2012. With kind permission from Springer Science and Business Media.

a more subtle picture. Like most things in life, it seems that use of technology, as well as being subject to inter-generational variations, also differs with personal preference and according to individual differences. In fact, now that computers and mobiles are so widespread, Prensky[6] has shifted away from differentiating 'natives' and 'immigrants' and prefers to talk about 'digital wisdom': the ability to use technology effectively to enhance our own cognitive processes and capacities. Educators may need 'digital wisdom' if they are to utilize technology effectively to enhance the learning experience, but they may also need to learn to develop the 'digital wisdom' of the next generation if they are to thrive in the modern, technological world.

Lessons for the Younger Generation

Given the ease with which young people seem to adapt to new phones or learn to play new video games, one could easily think that these young people have nothing to learn from adults about using technology. Certainly one might question what the older generations could teach these 'digital natives' about computers or the Internet. However, there is a big difference between using technology for social purposes and using it for learning or work.

Research tells us that young people, whilst confident with many of the social functions of the Internet, may not be so good at using it to access reliable knowledge. The EU Kids Online survey was conducted in 2010, and included 1,032 9–16-year-olds from the United Kingdom.[7,8] These children were very likely to use the Internet for school work, with 92% reportedly doing so. However, the survey showed that fewer than two-thirds of the children knew how to compare websites to determine whether information on them was true. Another survey of 2,131 children age 5–15, conducted by Ofcom in 2009,[9] also indicated that children may not be sufficiently critical of content they read online. A third of these children reported believing that all of the information they read on websites that they used for homework was true, whilst a quarter believed that all of the information on websites providing news and information about the world was true.

One cannot assume that older learners are any more astute. A recent study of 210 American college students investigated their use of the online encyclopaedia Wikipedia. Some college students were unaware the site could be edited by anyone, whilst a larger proportion seemed unaware that pages about sensitive topics, such as those related to racism, might be more susceptible to biased contributions than those about obscure or less controversial subjects.[10]

A major difference between online resources and books or licensed computer programs is that anyone can post information on the Internet. If pupils are going to use the Internet for education then they need the ability to critically assess the quality of the information they access, yet contemporary research suggests this is something that a large proportion cannot, or do not, do.

Hypermedia and the role of knowledge in the Internet age

It is not only the quality and reliability of online content that can pose a challenge to learners; research also suggests that pupils need help to organize this information in their minds. We discussed the structuring of knowledge in the mind in Chapter 2. Traditional textbooks are organized for the learner into a linear structure, with each section building upon previously presented content. In contrast, as explained in Chapter 7, digital hypermedia ranges from being linearly structured to offering the reader considerable flexibility in directing their reading depending on what captures their attention at the time.

When hypertexts were first developed in the 1980s, connectionism was also popular. Connectionist theory suggests that the human brain stores information not only as individual nodes, or chunks of information, but also through the strength of connection between these nodes. Information in hypertexts can be connected in multiple, non-linear ways, so they seemed to offer a means to present information in a format similar to the way it was structured in the brain. Psychologists at this time were also showing that novices and experts organize their knowledge in fundamentally different ways. For example, Chi and colleagues[11] asked eight PhD students and eight undergraduates to categorize physics problems. They found that the undergraduates (novices) sorted the problems according to surface features such as the apparatus involved, whereas the PhD students (experts) sorted them according to the physics principle required to solve the problem, a deep feature. On the basis of such experiments, psychologists began to postulate that organizing information in an 'expert' structure might speed up knowledge acquisition. The expectation, therefore, was that 'expert-organized' hypertexts might facilitate more efficient and flexible learning.[12] Unfortunately, empirical studies did not indicate that organizing hypertexts to reflect the knowledge structures of experts actually facilitated learning of factual knowledge, even when the links between pieces of information were explicitly highlighted.[13,14] It seems that the development from novice to expert understanding and structuring of information is an unavoidable aspect of the learning process.

In fact, the flexible structure of hypertexts may actually make it harder rather than easier for learners, particularly younger children, to acquire knowledge. For example, Shin and colleagues[15] designed a hypertext for 7-year-olds on the topic of food groups and varied the extent to which the pupils' navigation around the hypertext was restricted. In the restricted navigation condition pupils could access only information about foods related to the current food group, whereas in the unrestricted condition they could jump to any piece of information, including the final summary page. The team compared 110 pupils' comprehension and memory for the content in the restricted or unrestricted conditions and also considered two additional variables: their prior knowledge and whether they received advice on how to navigate the program whilst completing it. Learner knowledge increased in all conditions, but whilst learners with high prior knowledge performed similarly in both the restricted and unrestricted conditions, learners with low prior knowledge performed better in the restricted condition. In an attitude survey, pupils were also more positive about the condition where they received advice on how to navigate the program.

This resonates with the evidence presented in Chapter 7, which suggests that pupils learn more from hypertexts when they are assisted by a human tutor than when they work through them alone. Learners need good metacognitive skills to learn effectively from hypertexts, because they need to regulate and direct their learning to navigate the mass of unstructured information. Although some computerized tutoring systems such as 'MetaTutor' are being developed to help learners self-regulate and improve their learning behaviours, teachers still play an essential role in guiding the use of hypertexts as learning tools.

Some people talk about the Internet eliminating the need for pupils to learn factual information at school. After all, it contains vast swathes of information and is now so accessible that one could argue there is no need to remember anything anymore. However, the evidence presented in this section and in Chapter 2 suggests that this view is misguided. The pre-structuring of information actually helps us learn it: to construct an internal representation of the information and its connections. When we read books, the authors have provided some of this structure and context, but when we find information on the Internet it is often presented in relative isolation. We might reach it by clicking through consecutive links, but this can place such a burden on working memory that learners do not actually remember the path they took to reach information or, therefore, the context for it.[16] Even adolescents can be challenged by hypertexts, with studies involving this age group suggesting that when they are left to find information unaided in random, non-linear environments (such as search engines), this tends to result in inferior, or even negligible, shifts in conceptual understanding (see Chapter 7).

Letting students loose online to research a topic may help them to accumulate facts, but will not necessarily support their integration of those facts into a meaningful conceptual whole. That in turn means that they are less likely to be remembered. We know that the act of learning and remembering results in a transition in the way we structure our knowledge (from novice to expert). Whilst the Internet can substitute for our memories, we must remember that it cannot substitute for our thinking processes, or the creative connections we can make between apparently unrelated information. These creative connections are what contribute to the development of new scientific principles and new technologies. Hence we need to keep learning and retaining knowledge if humanity is to continue to progress.

Computer-Aided Learning

Although unstructured hypertexts present many challenges to learners, there are now many computer programs containing thoughtfully structured information, designed to facilitate and test learning. Computer-aided learning (CAL) is often regarded as a helpful way to supplement lectures in universities, particularly for courses such as medicine, dentistry and pharmacy where students ultimately need to memorize a lot of information as accurately as possible.

One of the authors of this book carried out a study with Oxford University Medical students who use a CAL course for neuroanatomy.[17] The computer program presents information in an interactive way: for example listing names of brain areas beside a diagram of the brain onto which the student drags the relevant labels. This aspect is also integrated with videos demonstrating patients' symptoms and questions relating to the diagnosis of conditions such as Parkinson's disease. In principle, the interactive nature of the CAL and the way facts are linked to the clinical context are intended to elicit a deep learning approach, rather than a surface, rote-learning approach. Each year, students rated the approach to learning they adopted for the CAL course (using the Study Process Questionnaire[18]) and, separately, for the rest of the course (lectures, tutorials, 'hands-on' practicals, essay writing). Six consecutive cohorts of students indicated that they adopted a more surface approach to learning for the CAL neuroanatomy element than for the rest of the course. Hence further research is needed to understand how CAL can be used to encourage a deep learning approach, at least with very academically able students.

Wider research on CAL for anatomy results in similarly underwhelming conclusions. Tam and colleagues[19] reviewed eight studies of CAL anatomy courses and concluded that: 'There is insufficient evidence to show that these resources have a true place for replacing traditional methods in teaching anatomy.' Mounsey and Reid,[20] meanwhile, have suggested that inclusion of case-based scenarios in CAL teaching actually reduces 'learning efficiency' – that is, the amount learnt in a given time. However, in other areas CAL may be surpassing traditional learning methods. A recent study in Norway showed that for students of middle-range ability (though not for those at the top or the bottom), immunology could be more effectively taught virtually.[21] CAL is also emerging as a particularly useful way to teach practical techniques since there is more opportunity for practice and it also reduces teaching time for clinicians. Chenkin and colleagues[22] reported that teaching the difficult technique of how to put a cannula into a blood vessel using ultrasound image guidance could be done as well by using a web-based tutorial as by attending a lecture on the procedure. It would seem, then, that the effectiveness of CAL varies according to the course, content and students involved. Given that it is less expensive to run a CAL course than employ a human teacher (although we should not underestimate the cost of developing them), it will undoubtedly have a growing place in many university and school courses. The important thing, therefore, is that each new CAL program should be carefully evaluated to ensure that it produces better learning results than any face-to-face teaching it might replace.

Using CAL to tackle social inequities

Whilst computerized tutors are not as effective as human teachers in their capacity to aid learners, or for that matter to empathize with them and offer emotional support, they are certainly better than no teacher at all. We discussed in Chapter 3 how early reading skills have a strong impact on later educational attainment. Meanwhile, in Chapter 10 we noted how the home learning environment, which includes factors such as parents reading to their children, is a good predictor of early cognitive development. Although initiatives such as Sure Start are intended to enrich the early environment of less advantaged children, there simply isn't the money to provide every at-risk child with one-to-one attention, and their parents often lack the literacy skills or confidence to provide appropriate support.

Technology may soon provide an answer with the use of e-readers. Although some e-books are essentially identical to the print version of a book, researchers in Israel have been testing out e-books with three additional functionalities. The most basic 'read only' mode incorporates sound and animations throughout the book. However, a 'dictionary' mode offers definitions of a limited number of difficult words, whilst a 'read and play' mode extends the story, for example by adding additional character dialogue or by breaking up key words into syllables to enhance phonological awareness.

The researchers have been exploring whether these books can boost the linguistic or mathematical skills of kindergartners (age 4–7) who are at risk of learning difficulties or are from lower-SES homes. So far results are promising. In a study of 79 lower-SES and 70 middle-SES children the researchers compared children using one of the reading modes to a control scenario where children participated in normal kindergarten activities. Word meaning, word recognition and sub-syllabic awareness were tested before and after e-book use, and the greatest improvements in word meaning and word recognition were found for children using the dictionary mode. Furthermore, the lower-SES children showed a greater improvement than the middle-SES children in their aggregated literacy scores.[23] More recently, the researchers worked with 110 children at risk of learning difficulties and showed that improvements in vocabulary knowledge and concepts about print (understanding the rules governing printed texts) following six sessions of e-book use (two in each mode) were comparable to improvements following six sessions where an adult read out the book to a control group. Improvements in phonological awareness were significantly greater after e-book use; however, this might simply be because the e-book incorporated a function where words were broken down into syllables and sub-syllables, whereas the adult reader did not undertake a similar activity with the control group.[24]

These studies do not indicate that e-books should replace pupil–teacher interactions. The researchers are careful to note that there are additional benefits to these interactions and that certainly in the latter study, reading the e-book does not uniformly produce better outcomes than group reading with a teacher. However, the research indicates that carefully designed interactive e-books offer exciting potential to boost the learning of at-risk children, either in school contexts where staff are under pressure or at home where parents are not able to provide the same level of input themselves.

Interactive Technologies in Schools

So far we have focused largely on everyday technologies such as e-readers and computers, which children experience at home as well as at school. However, there is another group of technologies that are designed specifically to enhance the school learning environment. If you have a child in school, or have worked in one recently yourself, you have no doubt seen interactive whiteboards in classrooms. Such technologies are not cheap to purchase, so it is important to know whether they are actually having a significant impact on pupils' learning, beyond that which a teacher can achieve alone.

Interactive whiteboards

Interactive whiteboards (IWBs) allow teachers to integrate multimedia into their lessons, save previous annotations for revision and easily distribute on-board notes and resources to both pupils and colleagues. The manufacturers of IWBs claim that they can increase motivation, engagement, understanding, collaboration and attainment. So have these whiteboards fulfilled expectations?

Prior to national uptake of IWBs in primary and secondary schools, pilot studies were conducted to evaluate pupil and teacher responses to the new technology and the impact on attainment.[25,26] The primary school studies were conducted in the Year 5 and 6 classes of about 70 English schools. Close to 100 teachers completed online diaries tracking their use of IWBs in English and maths lessons, and lesson observations were then conducted with a random sample of 30 teachers. Sixty-eight teacher interviews and 12 pupil-group interviews were used to explore subjective experiences and views on IWBs. Responses to the introduction of the IWBs from both primary pupils and teachers were largely positive. Pupils believed they paid more attention in lessons when IWBs were used and were excited about the potential for use of multimedia in their lessons. Teachers also thought that use of IWBs increased student motivation and 85% expected to see increases in attainment following their uptake. Lesson observations did indicate that IWB lessons were faster paced and that teachers used more open questions and probes, gave more evaluative responses, and more often focused their uptake or follow-up questions towards the whole class rather than falling into discussion with single pupils. In other words, they made greater use of certain techniques associated with effective teaching. However, a comparison between Key Stage 2 maths and English scores in the pilot schools and those in matched comparison schools indicated that after small but significant initial gains in mathematics ($d = 0.10$) and science ($d = 0.11$) in 2003, there was no significant difference in attainment in the IWB schools in 2004.[27] One can interpret this finding in two ways. If the main aim of introducing IWBs was to raise attainment, one could argue that considerable investment was wasted, since no sustained improvement was evident (although it must be noted that these pilot schools were already high performers). However, if one focuses on the subjective pupil and teacher attitudes to lessons with IWBs, there is evidence that this technology boosts engagement, motivation and positive attitudes to learning. Achieving these changes with no detriment to attainment could be regarded as a worthwhile and valuable outcome in itself.

The evaluation of early IWB pilots in London secondary schools[26] again showed no significant positive impact on attainment, but the schools had been using the technology for such a short time that this was expected. However, unlike the primary school pupils, secondary pupils were less positive about the impact of the IWBs on their engagement and behaviour. Some felt that their introduction had increased motivation for a short time but that this was short-lived. The most notable conclusion from this review was that the installation of IWBs did not guarantee any change in teaching methods, and could actually reinforce existing pedagogical approaches whether or not they were effective. For example, where teachers were already promoting interactivity in the classroom, or where the subject was suited to fast-paced working, use of the IWB could facilitate this. However, some teachers exploited the potential of IWBs only at a surface level, so 'interactivity' entailed pupils interacting with the board rather than interacting at a deep, intellectual level with the concepts being taught. Although the authors suggested that the technology could lead to pedagogical changes over time as teachers became confident with using IWBs, the clear message, and one echoed repeatedly in other research, was the notion that 'Technology on its own does not change pedagogy'.[27(p98)].

Researchers have learnt from this experience with IWBs and are drawing on it as they develop the next generation of interactive classroom technologies. A group at the University of Durham is currently involved in the SynergyNet project. The project uses multi-touch tables, which have a screen similar to iPads or touch-screen phones except that multiple users can manipulate the images on the table at the same time. The tables are networked with both an IWB and a portable tablet used by the teacher. This means that groups can work independently, can send information to groups at other tables and can send and receive information from the teacher. It is worth looking on http://tel.dur.ac.uk/synergynet/ to see the multi-touch tables in action.

The team has been developing software for classrooms that can act as a framework for different lessons and capitalizes on the specific qualities of multi-touch table technology, ensuring that the learning process actually changes when they are used. In one small-scale controlled test of the technology, 32 Year 6 pupils were trained to use the multi-touch tables. They were then divided into groups and completed comparable tasks where half the group worked with paper and the other half worked with the multi-touch tables. For the history task, pupils were given clues about an accident at a mine shaft and were asked to determine what happened (the task was open, with no single correct answer). The pupils were given the clues either on squares of paper or as text boxes on-screen. Use of the multi-touch tables was found to promote interactivity within the groups because, unlike the paper clues, pupils could not pick up the on-screen clues. Therefore, whilst the children using paper clues tended

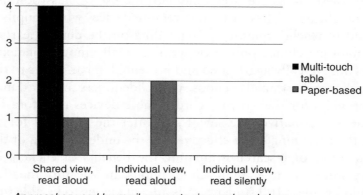

Approaches used by pupil groups to view and read clues

Figure 13.3   Pupils' initial strategies. *Source*: Higgins S, Mercier E, Burd L, Joyce-Gibbons A. Multi-touch tables and collaborative learning. *British Journal of Educational Technology*. 2011;43(6). Copyright © 2011 The Authors. Copyright British Journal of Educational Technology © 2011 BERA. Reproduced with permission.

to hold them and read them individually, all four of the multi-touch groups used a strategy where clues were viewed and read aloud together. Only one of the paper groups took this approach (see Figure 13.3). Multi-touch groups also engaged in more negotiating and collaborative talk, and finished the task faster (although this difference was not statistically significant).[28]

Classroom response systems

Introducing technology into the classroom can support independent as well as collaborative working. In Chapter 9 we discussed how individual-ized teaching and Assessment for Learning can both promote creativity in the classroom and enhance learning in general. One challenge, however, is the limited capacity of a teacher to monitor the individual progress of 30 pupils and adapt their teaching accordingly. Often techniques such as 'thumbs up/thumbs down' or individual miniature whiteboards can be used to encourage every pupil to gauge or demonstrate their level of understanding. However, some pupils may not be comfortable about indicating a lack of understanding so overtly, and pupils can also become distracted when using miniature whiteboards so that they become a form of entertainment rather than a learning tool.

Both of these issues are overcome with the use of classroom response systems, or 'clickers'. These are small remote devices which pupils can use to respond to teacher questions. Depending on the device, learners may select a multiple choice option or write a small amount of text. These responses are typically aggregated and presented in bar charts to the class, although the teacher can also choose to use identifiers to record individual pupils' progress for their own records. These devices therefore facilitate instantaneous formative assessment and offer the potential for teachers to adapt their teaching more effectively to the understanding of the class.

The majority of research evaluating the benefits of clickers involves university students rather than school pupils. In a lecture theatre where there could be 80 or 100 students, it is advantageous to be able to sustain attention and motivation, and multiple studies indicate that students find clicker sessions more interactive, engaging and enjoyable.[29,30] The clickers can also be used to encourage attendance at lectures by linking student grades to participation, and in the university context, clicker use has been linked with higher attainment.[30] For example, Preszler and colleagues[31] monitored student attitudes and attainment across six biology courses at the University of New Mexico. The students purchased and registered clickers, and in each lecture between 0 and 6 multiple choice questions were presented, with responses immediately charted on the lecturers' slides. Students could discuss their responses and therefore explore the correct answer, and the lecturers also adjusted their teaching if it appeared that many students had not grasped a concept. Between 60% and 80% of students on each course responded to evaluative surveys about clicker use, giving a sample of over 500 responses. Attitudes were largely positive, with 81% believing that using clickers increased their interest in the course and 70% believing that it improved their understanding. Students felt that using the clickers encouraged them to attend, and rather interestingly this effect was greater for lower-attaining students. Most notably, there was a significant linear relationship between the number of clicker questions used in lectures and the attainment of students on related questions in their final examinations. This indicates that using clickers (and the associated discussions and lecture adaptations) did boost student performance.

Classroom response systems are not just useful for whole-class teaching. A research team at the University of York has been piloting the use of electronic handsets for independent learning in primary classrooms. In one recent trial,[32] 42 Year 5 primary classes were paired according to demographic profiles and then allocated to either an intervention or control group. All of the classes took a pre-test and the intervention classes were then given electronic handsets to use as part of their literacy classes, with a focus on the learning of grammar. Over 12 weeks the classes were expected to complete 3–4 sessions per week with the handsets, where pupils responded to multiple choice and short-answer grammar questions and the teacher received instantaneous feedback on their progress. At the end of the intervention, the intervention group's overall performance was significantly better than that of the control group, but the effect size was small (ES = 0.16). However, the researchers found a greater effect when they compared only classes that used the handsets three or more times a week as instructed (ES = 0.27) and when they compared only the bottom third (ES = 0.26) or middle third (ES = 0.30) of achievers. Teacher feedback also suggested that the handsets were most effective for pupils who were reluctant to write, were lower achieving or were boys who found it difficult to behave and remain attentive in class. The researchers suggested that allowing these pupils to work at their own pace may have boosted their self-confidence or self-efficacy and hence their attainment. At a more basic level, 74% of pupils enjoyed using the technology and the impact on poorly behaved pupils might also be attributable to the feeling that 'Before it was boring doing grammar, now it's fun'.[32(p29)]

One can easily argue that evaluations of clicker technologies do not compare like with like. Introducing the clickers to a classroom facilitates a new form of interactive and self-paced learning which is often absent in the control classes where teaching methods go unchanged. However, looking at it from another perspective, it is clear that these relatively simple technologies have the potential to be transformative. Clickers can facilitate the implementation of existing methods such as peer instruction but they can also inspire the development of new pedagogical approaches. Throughout this book (and indeed in this chapter in the case of IWBs) we have highlighted how classroom innovations can fall flat if teachers do not adapt their teaching methods accordingly. In the case of clickers, it seems that the introduction of the technology is itself sufficient to elicit a shift in the entire approach to teaching.

Of course, a major constraint in adopting clicker technology is the cost involved. Indeed, in Preszler and colleagues' study a third of the students said they did not think that the clickers were worth the cost of purchase. However, the success of these interactive technologies is encouraging some teachers and lecturers to innovate and capitalize on the devices that learners already own, rather than requiring them to purchase new tools. For example, one can replicate basic clicker functionalities by using a form created in Google Docs and distributing it as a link to an iPod touch (or similar devices).[33]

Box 13.1   Using mobile phones as a tool for learning

Some schools and colleges in the United Kingdom are making increasing use of mobile phones as tools to enhance rather than impede the educational experience.

At Sunderland College, dyslexic students are encouraged to use their mobile phones to overcome some of their learning difficulties. Strategies include taking photographs of notes on whiteboards to improve speed and accuracy of note-taking, combining WordWeb and SpeakIt to find out definitions and pronunciations of words and reading e-books on small phone screens in order to limit the number of words that can be viewed at a given moment.

At South Nottingham College, apprenticeship students used to have to produce large folders of documentation as evidence of their learning. Often, employers were not good at providing the necessary documentation. Recently, learners have been using their mobile phones to provide evidence of their skill acquisition. Apprentices can video themselves applying their skills in the workplace and can record supplementary audio files to explain what they are doing. This is particularly beneficial since many of the apprentices have chosen the course because they are better suited to practical learning and do not feel confident writing large amounts about their experience.
Source: www.excellencegateway.org.uk/casestudies

There is something of a digital divide emerging in the attitudes that teachers are taking to the use of personal devices such as mobile phones in school. Whilst in some schools technology is being embraced wholeheartedly, in others mobile phones are still banned entirely. Personal use of mobile phones in class can undoubtedly be highly disruptive; however, mobile phones are also a fundamental aspect of most adults' lives, so exploiting their functions in the classroom can arguably be seen as a natural development. Recognizing their pervasiveness and using them as interactive learning tools converts these technologies from a problem to a solution for learning.

Learning from Paper and Screen

In many university lecture theatres it is more common to see students make notes on their laptops rather than by hand, yet in schools handwritten work is still much more common. It is therefore important that we know whether there are differences in the amount we can learn or understand when working on-screen or on paper.

Do we remember more if we hand-write notes?

Mangen and Velay[34] argue that writing by hand requires a distinctive combination of visual, motor and kinaesthetic feedback. Hand-writing a character requires a unique combination of motor movements, whereas typing a character involves a coordinate-based motor movement, which varies depending on the relative position of the keyboard and hand. Furthermore, whilst hand-writing involves a single focus of attention where pen meets page, typing divides one's attention between the screen and keyboard. Longcamp and colleagues have compared recognition for letters learnt by copying them by hand or by keyboard. In one study they gave 76 pre-literate 3–5-year-olds three training sessions over three weeks where they copied out words containing 12 key letters. At the end of the training the only group that exhibited significantly better recognition of the letters was the older children who had copied them by hand.[35] In a further study, 12 adults were taught to produce 10 novel characters (based on Bengali and Guajarati) by hand or by keyboard. They practised them 20 times per session for three weekly sessions. Straight after training, their recognition of the characters (as opposed to their mirror images) was not significantly different depending on whether they typed or wrote them. However, people who learnt the characters by typing showed a greater decline in recognition over time and were significantly worse at one, two and five weeks after training. A comparison of neural activation during recall using fMRI indicated that each mode of learning was associated with activation in distinct neural areas, and that learning by hand-writing was particularly associated with activation in areas linked to motor functions.[36]

Of course, in day-to-day life we are more likely to need to remember words than characters. Smoker and colleagues[37] conducted a very simple study where 61 participants either had to hand-copy a list of words which were written on a piece of paper or had to type the same list of words presented on-screen. Following a distraction task, the participants were asked to recall as many of the words as possible and then to recognize them within a list of 36 words. The participants were aged 18–24 and were all computer-literate, estimating that they used computers for between 2 and 15 hours a day. All of the words were selected from a sixth-grade vocabulary list, so they would have been known by the average

11–12-year-old. Nonetheless, recognition memory was significantly better (p = 0.036) when the words had been copied by hand, whilst the difference in recall approached significance (p = 0.065). The typing group also made significantly more recall errors (p = 0.032), where they recalled a word that was not on the list (see also p.32).

Although it seems logical that learning to type and write characters should use different brain areas, it is still not completely clear what implications this difference has for the development of literacy and for the application of writing or typing in education. Research reviews in this area indicate that the existing literature is equivocal, although where general conclusions can be drawn they rarely suggest that the use of technology is detrimental to literacy development.[38,39] At this stage, careful randomized studies that compare learning and recall following hand-writing or typing are required. It may be that the unique combination of motor movements required for writing does genuinely enhance our memory for handwritten notes. Equally, however, it may be that we tend to pay less attention to things we type than to things we write, in which case in the right conditions (where we do pay close attention) we might expect typing to be an equally effective mode of learning and note-taking.

Do we learn more when reading from paper?

So what about text that is already written on-screen? The Internet and e-books are gaining an ever-greater presence in educational settings, so it is important to know whether our comprehension is comparable when reading from these media and from traditional printed texts. Early studies conducted mainly in the 1980s suggested that reading from a computer screen could adversely affect reading speed, accuracy and comprehension as well as causing higher levels of fatigue and producing more negative subjective evaluations of the reading experience (see Dillon[40] for review). However, it is difficult to generalize from these studies to the modern day because so many aspects of technology have advanced. Furthermore, the researchers often attempted to control for as many variables as possible (such as distance from the reading material or task), so they ended up testing participants in highly artificial situations that did not reflect their use of computers in everyday life.

O'Hara and Sellen[41] (1997) took the opposite approach by selecting a naturalistic task where 10 volunteers were videotaped while they read and summarized an article, either on a computer or using paper and pen. Their observations indicated that note-taking was much easier in the paper condition. People felt comfortable writing on the printed article, whereas participants did not like modifying the digital document as they felt this would be altering the original. Navigation backwards and forwards through the paper document was found to be easier and more automatic, whilst scrolling through the digital document often led people to lose their place. The spatial layout of the paper document was more salient and easier to manipulate: people could easily track their reading progress and line up different papers to view them side by side, which was not feasible on the computer. This study indicated that the functionality of paper far exceeded that of a computer for a task typical of one regularly undertaken by students. Again, though, technology has improved since 1997. The introduction of touch-screen technology and tablets means that, ergonomically, computers are becoming ever more comparable with paper. Therefore, even though recent studies still suggest that university students find it easier to navigate, annotate and view multiple pages at once on paper than on-screen,[42,43] it is probably only a matter of time until computers catch up.

Despite differences in people's subjective preference for paper and screen, research does indicate that individuals can achieve comparable rates of comprehension and recall from both modalities. They can even achieve comparable accuracy in a shorter time span when editing an article on-screen rather than on paper.[44] This raises an interesting question of why people continue to prefer printed texts when they could learn equally well from computers. Ackerman and Goldsmith[45] investigated whether this could be related to learners' metacognitive skills. They conducted two experiments where participants (70 in the first, 74 in the second) were given six texts to read on computers or in print. The computer users could use Microsoft Word to highlight or annotate the texts, whilst the paper users were given a pen and highlighter. In the first experiment, all the participants had seven minutes to review each text before they completed a multiple choice questionnaire about its content. In the second experiment, participants could take as long as they liked to review each text before answering the questions. All the participants also predicted their performance before they completed the questions.

Following the first experiment, there was no significant difference between the test scores of paper and on-screen learners, showing that in time-limited conditions people can achieve similar learning in either modality. However, the on-screen learners over-predicted their performance to a significantly greater degree than those working from paper, suggesting that their metacognitive skills (their ability to gauge and regulate their learning) were hampered by working on-screen. Following the second experiment, paper learners had significantly higher test scores whereas participants' predictions of performance did not differ significantly between the paper and on-screen conditions. This suggests that people are less capable of accurately judging their level of learning when they read on a computer and may therefore stop studying prematurely, which would explain why the on-screen learners performed worse when they were controlling their own study time.

Do we perform differently on computerized tests?

One situation where metacognitive skills are particularly important is during tests, where one has to carefully regulate the time taken to plan and respond to questions. Now that students type most of their essays on computers, many universities are exploring whether students should take their examinations on computers as well.

There are already some law and business courses in America where students type all of their examinations; however, in the United Kingdom the use of computers is still largely restricted to students with special educational needs. A team at the University of Edinburgh has investigated the impact of allowing students to type their examinations. For one element of the study they offered a class of Divinity students the choice of taking a mock examination part-way through term. Thirty-seven students accepted, of whom 24 chose to type and 13 chose to hand-write their answer. The typed scripts were significantly longer (p = 0.041) although interestingly the length of the scripts was unrelated to students' previous estimates of whether they typed faster than they wrote. Typed scripts also received slightly higher average grades, but overall there was no significant difference in mark according to script format (and they included a check where all of the scripts were transcribed and marked in the alternative format).[46] Additional investigations suggested that allowing students to type examinations may not harm their performance, but that it may lead them to approach the examination in quite a different way. For example, they may plan their essays less comprehensively because it is easier to go back and restructure a word-processed essay than a handwritten text. Some students also use the volume of written pages to gauge their progress and would have to devise new metacognitive strategies to monitor their progress if typing their work.[47]

Comparisons of performance when using computers compared to paper suggest that reading on-screen or typing responses need not have a detrimental effect. However, some people may do worse because they lack experience with this medium and may have weaker metacognitive skills when reading or writing on-screen. However, most existing studies have been conducted with individuals who have grown up using books more than computers. It is possible that children who grow up using computers from an early age will be more competent at gauging their learning from this medium, so we may soon have generations whose metacognitive skills are equally strong whether learning on-screen or from printed text.

Inequalities in the Digital Age

Whilst technology offers many opportunities for improvements to learning and education, we also need to be aware of the new inequalities it might create. For example, a third of disabled people and two-thirds of over-75s have never used the Internet.[48] For older people, before we can even consider what they might learn *from* computers we have to ask how they can best learn to *use* computers. Thinking back to Chapter 12, we must remember that older people have reduced sensory functions and a poorer ability to disengage from distracters. It will therefore actually be harder for them to use computers, and particularly the Internet, because of the small size of icons and the frequent distraction from emails or advertisements popping up. Spatial abilities also decline with age, which can make it harder to navigate the hierarchical structures of computer programs intuitively. Therefore, whilst we can expect older people to learn to use computers effectively, they will not necessarily figure out programs intuitively in the same way as children and young adults. Rather, older adults will need to have the logic of the program explained and will need very clear and explicit instructions for undertaking different tasks. Furthermore, since working-memory capacity reduces with age, plenty of time must be allowed to practise each step along the way.

Another major issue in the last decade was unequal access to computers and the Internet for different socioeconomic groups. However, the results of the EU Kids Online survey suggest that the vast majority of children in the United Kingdom now have access to the Internet and that there is minimal variation between those from lower-, middle- and upper-SES households (92, 97 and 95% respectively having access to the Internet at home) (Livingstone et al. 2011. At least in developed countries, the new 'digital divide' seems to be in use of, rather than access to, the Internet. For example, the Ofcom survey described earlier indicated that children from lower-SES homes may be less digitally literate: 12–15-year-olds from these homes were less likely to think that search engines return a mixture of truthful and untruthful websites than their higher-SES peers. They were more likely to think that all the websites would be reliable, or not to consider the truthfulness of the content at all. There may also be socioeconomic differences in children's utilization of the Internet, with higher-SES children being more interested in expressing social or political views online. However, amongst the Ofcom respondents there was no difference in the proportion of children from higher- and lower-SES homes who had actually done this.[9]

Research conducted in the United States as part of the 2008–2009 American National Election Studies Panel Study did identify socioeconomic divisions in the extent to which citizens are able to make use of the Internet for learning and engaging in society. The survey gathered information on respondents' SES (measured by level of education), use of the Internet, television and newspapers to access news and, at a later date, their political knowledge. There was a significant interaction ($p < 0.05$) between SES and the political knowledge of Internet users. The political knowledge of low-frequency Internet users did not vary significantly with SES. However, amongst people who frequently used the Internet to access the news, higher-SES individuals had significantly better political knowledge than lower-SES respondents.[49] This suggests that higher-SES people were more likely to use the Internet to expand their knowledge. Therefore in the future, if we want education to be a means of reducing social inequalities, teachers may need to focus on ensuring that less advantaged pupils are equally capable of using the Internet both as a tool for education and for societal engagement.

Another area that has caused educational psychologists concern is that of possible sex differences in the use of computers. Certainly there are still large sex differences in the proportion of students who choose to study computer science in the United Kingdom: in 2012, 86% of individuals who accepted a place to study computer science at university were male.[50] This is concerning because technology is playing an increasingly central role in the workplace and is a key area for entrepreneurship and economic growth. As one case in point, we know that the vast majority of app developers (apps are simple programs one can download to a mobile phone or tablet) are male, and this rapidly growing international market is worth billions of pounds.

Interestingly, whereas studies conducted in the late 1990s and early 2000s suggested that girls were less interested in computers and might be less engaged in online learning, recent work is indicating that girls now spend just as much time online and can learn just as much from e-learning as boys. However, there are differences in the way that children spend their time online, with boys engaging in a wider range of activities and playing more games with peers online, while girls are more likely to share photos and videos with others.[7] Reassuringly, there are also many studies that find no sex, ethnic or social differences in the performance of pupils when given computerized examinations, in comparison to their performance in handwritten tests. Meanwhile, when researchers find significant differences in the extent to which boys and girls enjoy or learn from e-learning tools, it can often be linked back to surface-level characteristics of the program, such as the theme of the content or the sex of the main character. In some ways this is encouraging as it suggests that girls and boys can benefit equally from e-learning tools if they are carefully designed to be gender neutral. The worrying thing is that if the vast majority of the next generation of computer programmers is male, this gender neutrality might not be so easy to achieve.

Summary

- The notion of 'digital natives' – a generation that thinks differently because they have grown up with computers – is popular with the media. However, where cognitive differences related to computer use can be identified, they tend to be subtle, and in some cases may be a cause of, rather than consequence of, frequent computer use.
- The Internet is one example of hypermedia: information that is connected by multiple links and is rarely linearly structured. It can be harder to learn from hypermedia because it places additional demands on working memory and information may be accessed or presented with minimal context.
- Computer-aided learning can be a cost-effective method of teaching, but some courses are much more effective than others and it is important to evaluate each one on its own merits.
- Interactive whiteboards, multi-touch tables and classroom response systems can encourage collaboration and improve learning. However, it is important that teachers adapt their teaching methods if learners are to benefit from these technologies.
- Hand-writing notes uses a unique combination of visual and motor inputs which may result in better recall compared to typing; however, more research is needed in this area. Learners can achieve comparable comprehension and examination performance when using computers as opposed to pen and paper, but they often have weaker metacognitive skills for assessing their progress when using this medium.

- The new 'digital divide' may be in use of, rather than access to, technology. Older people may need explicit training if they are to benefit from the educational opportunities that computers offer. Meanwhile, there is some indication of socioeconomic divisions emerging in the way that individuals use the Internet to learn and engage in society.

Educational implications

- Although young people make frequent use of computers and the Internet, they are often not adept at assessing whether information they find online is reliable. Learners therefore need to be taught to critically assess information sources for their reliability.
- The Internet contains vast amounts of information, but teachers have an essential role in helping learners to structure and regulate their learning. Different metacognitive skills are required when using computers as opposed to pen and paper. It is therefore important that educators create opportunities for such skills to be developed.
- Given the prevalence of technology in everyday life, it may be sensible for educators to integrate the use of devices such as mobile phones into lessons rather than trying to ban them entirely.
- Girls and boys can be equally engaged by computers, so it is important that educational programs be designed in a gender-neutral manner so that neither sex is discouraged from using them or learning from them.

References

1   Prensky M. Digital natives, digital immigrants. *On the Horizon.* 2001;9(5).
2   Jones C, Ramanau R, Cross S, Healing G. Net generation or digital natives: Is there a distinct new generation entering university? *Computers & Education.* 2010;54(3):722–732. doi:10.1016/j.compedu.2009.09.022.
3   Garcia L, Nussbaum M, Preiss DD. Is the use of information and communication technology related to performance in working memory tasks? Evidence from seventh-grade students. *Computers & Education.* 2011;57(3): 2068–2076. doi:10.1016/j.compedu.2011.05.009.
4   Ophir E, Nass C, Wagner AD. Cognitive control in media multitaskers. *PNAS.* 2009;106(37):15583–15587. doi:10.1073/pnas.0903620106.
5   Lui KFH, Wong AC-N. Does media multitasking always hurt? A positive correlation between multitasking and multisensory integration. *Psychonomic Bulletin & Review.* 2012;19(4):647–653. doi:10.3758/s13423-012-0245-7.
6   Prensky MH. Sapiens digital: From digital immigrants and digital natives to digital wisdom. *Journal of Online Education.* 2009;5(3):1–9.

7   Livingstone S, Haddon L, Gorzig A, Olafsson K. Risks and Safety for Children on the Internet: The UK Report. London: London School of Economics; 2010. Available at: www2.lse.ac.uk/media@lse/research/EUKidsOnline/EU%20Kids%20II%20(2009-11)/National%20reports/UKReport.pdf. Accessed 2 December 2013.

8   Livingstone S, Haddon L, Gorzig A, Olafsson K. EU Kids Online – Final Report. London: London School of Economics; 2011. Available at: www.lse.ac.uk/media@lse/research/EUKidsOnline/EU%20Kids%20II%20%282009-11%29/National%20reports/UKReport.pdf. Accessed 2 December 2013.

9   Ofcom. UK Children's Media Literacy. Ofcom; 2010. Available at: http://stakeholders.ofcom.org.uk/binaries/research/media-literacy/ukchildrensml1.pdf. Accessed 2 December 2013.

10 Menchen-Trevino E, Hargittai E. Young Adults' Credibility Assessment of Wikipedia. *Information, Communication & Society*. 2011;14(1):24–51. doi:10.1080/13691181003695173.

11 Chi MTH, Feltovich PJ, Glaser R. Categorization and representation of physics problems by experts and novices. *Cognitive Science*. 1981;5(2):121–152.

12 Gall JE, Hannafin MJ. A framework for the study of hypertext. *Instructional Science*. 1994;22(3):207–232.

13 Dillon A, Gabbard R. Hypermedia as an educational technology: A review of the quantitative research literature on learner comprehension, control, and style. *Review of Educational Research*. 1998;68(3):322–349. doi:10.3102/00346543068003322.

14 Shapiro A, Niederhauser D. Learning from hypertext: Research issues and findings. *Handbook of Research on Educational Communications and Technology*. 2004;2:605–620.

15 Shin EC, Schallert DL, Savenye WC. Effects of learner control, advisement, and prior knowledge on young students' learning in a hypertext environment. *Educational Technology Research and Development*. 1994;42(1):33–46.

16 DeStefano D, LeFevre J-A. Cognitive load in hypertext reading: A review. *Computers in Human Behavior*. 2007;23(3):1616–1641. doi:10.1016/j.chb.2005.08.012.

17 Svirko E, Mellanby J. Attitudes to e-learning, learning style and achievement in learning neuroanatomy by medical students. *Medical Teacher*. 2008;30(9–10):e219–227. doi:10.1080/01421590802334275.

18 Biggs J, Kember D, Leung DYP. The revised two-factor study process questionnaire: R-SPQ-2F. *British Journal of Educational Psychology*. 2001;71(1):133–149.

19 Tam MDBS, Hart AR, Williams S, Heylings D, Leinster S. Is learning anatomy facilitated by computer-aided learning? A review of the literature. *Medical Teacher*. 2009;31(9):e393–396.

20   Mounsey A, Reid A. A randomized controlled trial of two different types of web-based instructional methods: One with case-based scenarios and one without. *Medical Teacher*. 2012;34(9):e654–658. doi:10.3109/0142159X .2012.689442.

21   Boye S, Moen T, Vik T. An e-learning course in medical immunology: Does it improve learning outcome? *Medical Teacher*. 2012;34(9):e649–e653. doi: 10.3109/0142159X.2012.675456.

22   Chenkin J, Lee S, Huynh T, Bandiera G. Procedures can be learned on the Web: A randomized study of ultrasound-guided vascular access training. *Academic Emergency Medicine*. 2008;15(10):949–954. doi:10.1111/ j.1553-2712.2008.00231.x.

23   Korat O, Shamir A. The educational electronic book as a tool for supporting children's emergent literacy in low versus middle SES groups. *Computers & Education*. 2008;50(1):110–124. doi:10.1016/j.compedu.2006.04.002.

24   Shamir A, Korat O, Fellah R. Promoting vocabulary, phonological awareness and concept about print among children at risk for learning disability: Can e-books help? *Reading and Writing: An Interdisciplinary Journal*. 2012; 25(1):45–69.

25   Higgins S, Falzon C, Hall I. Embedding ICT in the Literacy and Numeracy Strategies: Final Report. Newcastle upon Tyne: Newcastle University; 2005.

26   Moss G, Jewitt C, Levaaic R, Armstrong V, Cardini A, *et al*. The Interactive Whiteboards, Pedagogy and Pupil Performance Evaluation: An Evaluation of the Schools Whiteboard Expansion (SWE) Project: London Challenge. London: DfES; 2007.

27   Higgins S. The impact of interactive whiteboards on classroom interaction and learning in primary schools in the UK. In: Thomas M, Schmid EC, eds. *Interactive Whiteboards for Education: Theory, Research and Practice*. Hershey, PA: IGI Global; 2010:86–101. Available at: http://services.igi-global.com/resolvedoi/resolve.aspx?doi=10.4018/978-1-61520-715-2. Accessed 2 December 2013.

28   Higgins S, Mercier E, Burd L, Joyce-Gibbons A. Multi-touch tables and collaborative learning. *British Journal of Educational Technology*. 2011; 43(6):1041–1054. doi:10.1111/j.1467-8535.2011.01259.x.

29   Fies C, Marshall J. Classroom response systems: A review of the literature. *Journal of Science Education and Technology*. 2006;15(1):101–109.

30   Kay RH, LeSage A. Examining the benefits and challenges of using audience response systems: A review of the literature. *Computers & Education*. 2009;53(3):819–827. doi:10.1016/j.compedu.2009.05.001.

31   Preszler RW, Dawe A, Shuster CB, Shuster M. Assessment of the effects of student response systems on student learning and attitudes over a broad range of biology courses. *CBE–Life Sciences Education*. 2007;6(1):29–41. doi:10.1187/cbe.06-09-0190.

32   Sheard M, Chambers B, Elliott L. *Effects of Technology-Enhanced Formative Assessment on Achievement in Primary Grammar*. York: Institute for

Effective Education, University of York; 2012. Available at: www.york.ac.uk/iee/assets/QfLGrammarReport_Sept2012.pdf. Accessed 2 December 2013.

33   iPod Touch: Classroom Response System. North Canton, Ohio; 2010. Available at: www.youtube.com/watch?v=6VJ1qFcayS8&feature=youtube _gdata_player. Accessed October 6, 2012.

34   Mangen A, Velay J-L. Digitizing literacy: Reflections on the haptics of writing. In: Hosseini M, ed. *Advances in Haptics*. Winchester: InTech; 2010. Available at: www.intechopen.com/books/advances-in-haptics/digitizing-literacy-reflections-on-the-haptics-of-writing. Accessed 2 December 2013.

35   Longcamp M, Zerbato-Poudou M-T, Velay J-L. The influence of writing practice on letter recognition in preschool children: A comparison between handwriting and typing. *Acta Psychologica*. 2005;119(1):67–79. doi:10.1016/j.actpsy.2004.10.019.

36   Longcamp M, Boucard C, Gilhodes JC, *et al*. Learning through hand- or typewriting influences visual recognition of new graphic shapes: Behavioral and functional imaging evidence. *Journal of Cognitive Neuroscience*. 2008 ;20(5):802–815.

37   Smoker TJ, Murphy CE, Rockwell AK. Comparing memory for handwriting versus typing. *Proceedings of the Human Factors and Ergonomics Society Annual Meeting*. 2009;53(22):1744–1747. doi:10.1177/154193120 905302218.

38   Andrews R, Freeman A, Hou D, McGuinn N, Robinson A, *et al*. The effectiveness of information and communication technology on the learning of written English for 5- to 16-year-olds. *British Journal of Educational Technology*. 2007;38(2):325–336. doi:10.1111/j.1467-8535.2006.00628.x.

39   Zhu D, Torgerson C. A systematic review and meta-analysis of the effectiveness of ICT on literacy learning in English, 5–16. In: *Research Evidence in Education Library*. London: EPPI-Centre, Social Science Research Unit, Institute of Education, University of London; 2003.

40   Dillon A. Reading from paper versus screens: A critical review of the empirical literature. *Ergonomics*. 1992;35(10):1297–1326.

41   O'Hara K, Sellen A. A comparison of reading paper and on-line documents. In: *Proceedings of the SIGCHI Conference on Human Factors in Computing Systems. Atlanta*; 1997:335–342. Available at: http://dl.acm.org/citation .cfm?id=258787. Accessed 2 December 2013.

42   Rose E. The phenomenology of on-screen reading: University students' lived experience of digitised text. *British Journal of Educational Technology*. 2011;42(3):515–526. doi:10.1111/j.1467-8535.2009.01043.x.

43   Spencer C. Research on learners' preferences for reading from a printed text or from a computer screen. *The Journal of Distance Education/Revue de l'Éducation à Distance*. 2006;21(1):33–50.

44   Eden S, Eshet-Alkalai Y. The effect of format on performance: Editing text in print versus digital formats. *British Journal of Educational Technology*. 2012;44(5:675–880. doi:10.1111/j.1467-8535.2012.01332.x.

45   Ackerman R, Goldsmith M. Metacognitive regulation of text learning: On screen versus on paper. *Journal of Experimental Psychology: Applied.* 2011;17(1):18–32. doi:10.1037/a0022086.

46   Mogey N, Paterson J, Burk J, Purcell M. Typing compared with handwriting for essay examinations at university: Letting the students choose. *ALT-J, Research in Learning Technology.* 2010;18(1):29–47. doi:10.1080/09687761003657580.

47   Purcell M, Paterson J, Mogey MN. E-Check – "Exams-Comparing Handwritten Essays with those Composed on Keyboards" – Final Report. Edinburgh, Scotland: University of Edinburgh; 2012. Available at: www.docs.hss.ed.ac.uk/divinity/About%20the%20school/Elearning/HEA2012-Final%20Report.pdf. Accessed 2 December 2013.

48   ONS. Internet Access Quarterly Update, Q3 2012. London: Office for National Statistics; 2012. Available at: www.ons.gov.uk/ons/dcp171778_286665.pdf. Accessed 2 December 2013.

49   Wei L, Hindman DB. Does the digital divide matter more? Comparing the effects of new media and old media use on the education-based knowledge gap. *Mass Communication and Society.* 2011;14(2):216–235. doi:10.1080/15205431003642707.

50   UCAS. Data tables. UCAS; 2012. Available at: www.ucas.ac.uk/about_us/stat_services/stats_online/data_tables/. Accessed 2 December 2013.

Chapter 14

Conclusions
What Does the Future Hold for Education?

An evidence-based approach to teaching and learning. This is surely a worthy aspiration for teachers, politicians and parents. However, you will have realized whilst reading this book that most research raises many more questions for the modern educator than it answers. Yes, there are some things that we now know with relative certainty. We are quite sure, for example, that the early development of language is an essential foundation for reading, mathematics and complex problem-solving. We are also clear that early cognitive development is a good predictor of later educational attainment. However, we still have many questions about the best ways to nurture the developing mind. We do not know the extent to which environmental factors can outweigh the influence of genetics, nor have we established the most effective way to tackle the early socioeconomic and ethnic inequalities in cognitive development that we see amongst children.

Children are designed to absorb and learn from sensory inputs from the moment they are born. We know that young children are good at acquiring implicit memories; they can do so unconsciously, as in the acquisition of grammar, but also with conscious awareness, for example when rote-learning rhymes and multiplication tables. They also develop strategies for learning – their metacognitive skills – from an early age. Although some methods of teaching, including rote-learning, have fallen out of fashion in Britain, there is actually no evidence identifying a single,

Education and Learning: An Evidence-Based Approach, First Edition. Jane Mellanby and Katy Theobald.
© 2014 John Wiley & Sons, Ltd. Published 2014 by John Wiley & Sons, Ltd.

effective method of teaching anything. Some educational theories are interpreted as suggesting that it is somehow unnecessary or undesirable to make children learn facts. What is clear, however, is that the internalization of knowledge is an essential process. We know that the retention and mental structuring of knowledge is incredibly important. Furthermore, the way we perceive and categorize problems changes as we develop expertise. We need a basic framework of knowledge to understand more complex material. We also need information to be stored in our heads if we are to make the connections between distant facts and concepts that result in creative innovation and thought.

One of the key questions facing educators is how to respond to the large variations in children's level of cognitive development at any particular age, whether they are related to gender, ethnicity or socioeconomic status. Regarding gender, we know that some differences in the performance of boys and girls can actually be attributed to cultural rather than genetic factors. For example, simply knowing the stereotype that girls are not as good at maths or that boys are poor readers can contribute to girls and boys performing worse in these respective areas. The same can be said for some ethnic minorities: they may do worse on tests simply because they know they are expected to perform poorly.

The influence of genetics and environment on cognitive development, and the extent of their interaction, is an area where one could safely say that the more we discover, the more we realize how little we know. Whilst the gross anatomical structure of the brain is the same for all humans, the number and perhaps the efficiency of connections between neurons differ between individuals. We still do not know how much this depends on genetics or on personal experience. We used to think of genes as tapes that played out in predetermined ways during our lives. Yet now we realize that our genes can influence the environment that we seek out and that this in turn can affect how our genes are expressed and even which genes are expressed. Furthermore, our environment affects us before we are even born through the foods that our mothers eat and the stressors they experience. The power of environmental factors to influence cognitive development is clear from studies suggesting that the large differences in attainment according to socioeconomic status are, in the United Kingdom, largely attributable to environment rather than genes. However, the leap from understanding this to effectively doing anything about it is vast.

We like to think that education holds the answers to many of society's ills. We see it as a source of social mobility, a way to prevent unemployment and a way to communicate cultural values. It is tempting to try to find some magic formula for education, particularly now that we can compare the performance of learners from all around the globe. Yet digging deeper into comparative studies shows us that each education system is inextricably linked to the culture of a country. The emphasis placed on effort over innate ability, the value placed on equality and comprehensive ideals, the levels of literacy in the adult population, the very structure of a language that affects the ease with which children learn to read or count: all of these cultural factors affect children's attainment and do not transfer readily across borders. Although teachers are placed in a position of great responsibility and trust, we are yet to find evidence that the process of schooling can completely outweigh the pervasive influence of culture or family on children's cognitive development. It is still true to say that education begins at home.

There are some fundamental debates about the purposes of that education that every generation ought to have. Do we think that the priority should be to teach 5-year-olds to read, write and do arithmetic as quickly as possible, or should we look to other cultures and think about children's social development as a foundation for future learning? Which core skills do we value sufficiently to allocate more time towards developing them in our young people: creativity, second languages, spatial abilities, self-regulation of learning? If we can clearly specify precisely what our children ought to know, and at what age they are best suited to learning it, then are we willing to give teachers the autonomy to decide quite how they can best teach it? These are the types of fundamental question that need answering if we are to achieve change in our education system. These answers can then direct future research into effective ways to learn and teach.

Index

Education and Learning: An Evidence-Based Approach, First Edition. Jane Mellanby and Katy Theobald.
© 2014 John Wiley & Sons, Ltd. Published 2014 by John Wiley & Sons, Ltd.